LIBRARY OF HEBREW BIBLE/OLD TESTAMENT STUDIES

392

formerly the Journal for the Study of the Old Testament Supplement series

Editors
Claudia V. Camp, Texas Christian University
Andrew Mein, Westcott House, Cambridge

Founding Editors
David J. A. Clines, Philip R. Davies and David M. Gunn

Editorial Board
Richard J. Coggins, Alan Cooper, John Goldingay, Robert P. Gordon,
Norman K. Gottwald, Gina Hens-Piazza, John Jarick, Andrew D.H. Mayes,
Carol Meyers, Patrick D. Miller, Yvonne Sherwood

THE ARTIFICE OF LOVE

Grotesque Bodies in the Song of Songs

FIONA C. BLACK

t&t clark

Published by T&T Clark
A Continuum imprint
The Tower Building, 11 York Road, London SE1 7NX
80 Maiden Lane, Suite 704, New York, NY 10038

www.continuumbooks.com

Bakhtin, Mikhail., *Rabelais and His World*, 2261 word excerpt © 1968
Massachusetts Institute of Technology, used by permission of the MIT
Press.

British Library Cataloguing-in-Publication Data
A catalogue record for this book is available from the British Library

ISBN 978-0-8264-6985-4 (hardback)

Typeset by Data Standards Ltd, Frome, Somerset, UK
Printed on acid-free paper by the MPG Books Group in the UK

To

Rose F. M. Osgood
(1914–1996)

Your Humour, Love and Generosity
Continue to Inspire Me.

CONTENTS

List of Figures

ACKNOWLEDGEMENTS

This book is a revision of my doctoral thesis. It has been a long time since those days of writing and study, but despite the gap, this book couldn't exist without the input, influence and support of a number of people. From my days at the University of Sheffield, I thank Cheryl Exum, my supervisor, for sharing her perceptive understanding of the Song of Songs and for her guidance and mentorship. I also thank Philip Davies, Barry Matlock and Stephen Moore for their wisdom and friendship. Many tasks could not have been accomplished without the assistance of Alison Bygrave, Gill Fogg and Judith Watson.

From outside of the University of Sheffield, but no less important, I appreciate the input of Athalya Brenner and the late Robert Carroll, who were my examiners and who offered suggestions for modifications. Francis Landy has, more latterly, been a wonderfully generous colleague, and I am fortunate indeed to benefit from his unique insights into the Song of Songs. Finally, I thank Claudia Camp, the LHBOTS and GCT series editor, who has been an attentive and insightful reader of the manuscript and Haaris Naqvi, the Theology and Biblical Studies editor at Continuum, who has been generous with his time and energy.

With gratitude, I acknowledge the following organizations for awards and fellowships granted during my PhD programme: Fonds pour la Formation du Chercheurs et l'Aide à la Recherche (Québec, Canada); Social Sciences and Humanities Research Council of Canada (SSHRC); Overseas Research Scholarship Scheme (CVCP, UK). I also thank Mount Allison University for accommodations that allowed me to spend time on revisions and for funding that enabled me to present some of this material at various colloquia and conferences.

Permission from SBL Press to incorporate material from my article 'What is my Beloved? On Erotic Reading and the Song of Songs', in Fiona C. Black, Roland Boer and Erin Runions (eds), *The Labour of Reading: Desire, Alienation and Biblical Interpretation* (Atlanta, GA: SBL Press, 1999) is gratefully acknowledged.

Many thanks to my family for their generosity, love and support, manifested in various ways over the years: Christine, Donald,

Christopher, Wendy, Emily, Sarah, Suzanne, Lois, Michael, Nicola. As family does, you encouraged, cajoled, put me up, fed me meals, helped pay bills. Dev, Caryl, Joan, and Erin: thank you for being such wonderful sisters. And Tom and Corrie, your wonderful patio (my makeshift office) and gracious hospitality made the revisions most pleasant.

Finally, but never lastly, I am grateful for the friendship of many colleagues whom I have met along the way during this project. Some provided encouragement; others gin; some gave advice; some read my work at various stages and contributed greatly to it; and, probably most importantly of all, some kept me laughing: Mark Blackwell, Roland Boer, Barbra Clayton, Robert Culley, Suzie Currie, Heidi Epstein, James Harding, Janine Rogers, Erin Runions (Doyenne of the Group of Seven), Leslie Shumka, Jamie Smith, Claire Thomson, Deborah Wills.

Most especially, I thank Andrew Wilson for his love and support. You have been colleague, conversation partner, editor, friend, taskmaster, meal-maker, and many other things. Five years ago I said you had the patience of a saint; today you would make even the saints blush at their impetuosity! And now there is Liam, who teaches us that life is so much more important than work.

ABBREVIATIONS

AB	Anchor Bible
ANET	Ancient Near Eastern Texts Relating to the Old Testament
AsiaJT	*Asia Journal of Theology*
BDB	Brown, Driver, Briggs (Hebrew Lexicon)
BibInt	*Biblical Interpretation*
BibOr	Biblica et Orientalia
BKAT	Biblische Kommentar: Altes Testament
BN	*Biblische Notizen*
BTB	*Biblical Theology Bulletin*
BZ	*Biblische Zeitschrift*
CBQ	*Catholic Biblical Quarterly*
DCH	*Dictionary of Classical Hebrew*
ETL	*Ephemerides theologicae lovanienses*
FOTL	Forms of the Old Testament Literature
GCT	Gender, Culture, Theory
GKC	Gesenius, Kautzsch, Cowley (Hebrew Grammar)
HALOT	*Hebrew and Aramaic Lexicon of the Old Testament* (Koehler, Baumgartner, Stamm 1944–99)
HAT	Handbuch zum Alten Testament
HS	*Hebrew Studies*
Int	*Interpretation*
JAAR	*Journal of the American Academy of Religion*
JBL	*Journal of Biblical Literature*
JETS	*Journal of the Evangelical Theological Society*
JSOT	*Journal for the Study of the Old Testament*
JSOTSup	*Journal for the Study of the Old Testament* Supplement Series
JSS	*Journal of Semitic Studies*
KB	Koehler Baumgartner (Hebrew Lexicon)
NEchB	Neue Echter Bibel
NICOT	New International Commentary on the Old Testament
OBO	Orbis Biblicus et Orientalis

OBT	Overtures in Biblical Theology
OTG	Old Testament Guides
OTL	Old Testament Library
PMLA	*Periodical of the Modern Languages Association*
RB	*Revue biblique*
RevistB	*Revista Biblica*
RevQ	*Revue de Qumran*
SBLDS	Society of Biblical Literature Dissertation Series
SBS	Stuttgarter Bibelstudien
SEÅ	*Svensk Exegetisk Årsbok*
SJOT	*Scandinavian Journal of the Old Testament*
SR	*Studies in Religion/Sciences religieuses*
StudBib	*Studia Biblica*
TBü	Theologische Bücherei
TQ	*Theologische Quartalschrift*
TynBul	*Tyndale Bulletin*
VT	*Vetus Testamentum*
WThJ	*Westminster Theological Journal*
ZAW	*Zeitschrift für die alttestamentliche Wissenschaft*

INTRODUCTION

Around the beginning of the Common Era, Ovid penned the *Ars Amatoria*, conventionally referred to as the *Art of Love* in English translations. Posing as a 'how-to' manual, the collection is a tongue-in-cheek series of reflections on the correct conduct for men and women around courtship, marriage and lovemaking. Some years earlier,[1] a Hebrew poet penned his[2] own lengthy reflections on love and sexual relationships. Unlike Ovid's contribution, his text does not purport to be a manual on love, but is compiled as a private dialogue between two lovers. Yet it does teach some important lessons, among them, what is involved in the craft and the performance of love. It also instructs readers in their own sensibilities and amatory configurations. It is, in short, an *artificia amatoria*: it is concerned with amatory artifice, or the artifice of love.[3]

In the Song of Songs there is much to reflect – and instruct – the behaviour of lovers. There is also plenty about the Song that affects readers. The book is comprised of the encounters (or encounters sought) of two lovers,[4] their sighs and longing expressed alluringly through vivid and lyrical language. Threaded throughout, there is vibrant, perplexing

---

1   I make the occasional comment on the dating of the book in my study, but largely leave this debate to others for whose work its resolution is more relevant.

2   Though I will have a chance to speculate otherwise in my final chapter, I think it most likely that the author of this text was male. As I hope to show, though, it might not be of much consequence in the end.

3   As will become clear throughout the book, 'artifice' invokes not just the conventional meaning of trickery and cunning, but also the more traditional meanings of skill and ingenuity.

4   It is conventional to interpret the lovers in the Song as two characters, but it should be noted that earlier work on the Song, particularly dramatic readings, has posited the presence of a third character, a rustic, shepherd lover whom the woman eventually chooses over Solomon. In the end, love wins out over the attractions of money and power (see Renan 1995; also the discussion in Pope 1977: 35, who cites eighteenth- and nineteenth-century commentators Jacobi, Löwisohn, Ewald and Hazan as belonging to this tradition. Pope links the three-character plot originally to Ibn Ezra; 1977: 35). It might also be possible to suggest that the Song refers to a number of lovers, following the suggestion by some commentators

imagery, some of which features the body in provocative ways. The Song's body imagery and its propensity to confound and tease the reader is the subject of this book.

The two lovers refer to each other's bodies frequently throughout the Song. There are, however, four concentrated descriptions of the body in texts or poems[5] that are referred to in the scholarly literature as *wasfs* (4.1-5 [// 6.4-7]; 5.10-16; 7.1-10). At least one extended metaphor also functions in a similar way, 4.9-16. In these descriptions, odd combinations of natural and urban elements are imposed upon the body, rendering it a site of confusion, and perhaps unease, for the Song's lovers and its readers. At their best, the images are playful, maybe comic or the subject of teasing. At worst, they take on an unsettling quality, making the body ridiculous, conflicted, even alienating.

Biblical critics are frequently troubled by the meaning of the images and they sometimes go to great lengths to interpret them so that they fit with their ideals about the Song as love poetry. Like fly-on-the-wall documenters, readers habitually burst in on the lovers' foreplay, interjecting explanations that are based on 'common sense' or on reconstructions of the Song's sociohistorical context (some of them elaborate). Michael Fox's discussion of one of the images is a case in point:

> For the most part the images in Canticles are delightfully incongruous. 'Your neck is like the tower of David' (4:4) starts from the common denominator of length, for a long neck was considered graceful. Still, the bold juxtaposition of neck and tower is incongruous enough to forcefully convey unexpected attitudes and overtones. The incongruity is so great that there is, to be sure, the risk of losing many readers, who may find the image so abrasive, they never get around to sensing how the tower fits harmoniously into the atmosphere the image creates. But the risk was necessary in order to convey a radically different vision of love. (Fox 1983: 226–7)

It is indeed rare to find any reader of the Song who is willing to risk stopping awhile at what Fox suggests is entry-level reading. Den Hart's literalistic visual interpretation of the female body (Figure 1) illustrates

---

that it consists of a series of unrelated poems (e.g. Falk 1982; Gerleman 1965; Gordis 1974; Pope 1977). My reading of the Song posits just two main players, a man and a woman, and furthermore, it resists the urge to identify or name them.

5   Throughout this book, the term 'poem' is used to refer to a collection of images, usually the *wasfs*. 'Poem' is meant as a general description, is used interchangeably with 'text', and is not the result of a technical analysis of poetic structure in terms of form, metre or the like, in the tradition of formal analysis that once characterized Song criticism. My decision as to where the boundaries of each description or poem lie is based on attention to theme and mood. See further discussion below.

the extent of what might result from this kind of approach. Typically, the opportunity to be troubled by the images is anticipated and precluded by criticisms in mainstream commentary such as Fox's. Readers who might want to stop awhile and ponder the images' incongruity are evaluated as probably missing the point or unable to appreciate the Song's poetic complexity. Hart's comic is amusing, but should biblical scholarship take such an experiment seriously? How could readers entertain the possibility of such an oddly configured body? Should they?

This book takes up the body descriptions in the Song as troubled texts. It works on the supposition that the images are difficult to explain and often conflict with scholarly expectations about how the Song should be interpreted. Moreover, they force a readerly encounter with the body, itemized for erotic consumption. Rather than insisting on the kind of reading that Fox advocates, which is one that serves to smooth over the problem and integrate the Song's potential rough spots, this book pursues a reading that emphasizes difference, and that furthermore does not always find the incongruity to which readers such as Fox refer delightful. And if, as Fox suggests, the Song is trying to convey a radical view of love, it remains to explore what this might be, in light of the lovers' portrayals of each other's bodies in ways that seem unsettling, and perhaps unadoring.

Perhaps by no accident, some have called the Song's imagery grotesque, so far to little tangible effect on Song criticism (e.g. Boer 1999; Murphy 1990; Rudolph 1962; Soulen 1993; Waterman 1948). Taking a lead from this admission, I ask: What might happen if one intentionally unleashes the grotesque into this confused space? The grotesque plays devilishly with the textual bone-and-tissue remains of readers' encounters. Inviting it into the fray, however, is not mere whimsy, nor is it a sadistic diversion. The grotesque usefully describes some of the peculiar images that confront readers. In addition, it gives some insight into the duplicitous nature of the text – itself a signifier of desire – and the ambivalence of readerly reactions to it. This also raises some potent questions for the implications of gendered readings of the Song of Songs.

The grotesque is somewhat slippery and it resists rigid definition. The word was coined in the Renaissance to refer to a style of art that playfully incorporated animal and human bodies into various decorative designs. Since then, it has metamorphosed into more fantastic hybrids in art, and from them has had a certain literary transformation to the carnival, as popularized by Mikhail Bakhtin. Always shifting, the grotesque even more recently has come to express the 'estranged or alienated world' and exhibits attempts to 'control or exorcise' its demonic elements (Thompson 1972: 18). In using it in connection with reading the Song's images, I do not limit the conceptualization of it to one particular type or aspect of its varied development. Rather, it is the whole picture – playful, disconcerting, unsettling, dangerous – that makes the grotesque so appealing for the Song's descriptions.

Readers of this book who might be expecting a singular interpretation of what the images mean will be disappointed. The proposed reading does not advocate recognition as the 'definitive' or 'best' way to interpret the imagery. This cannot be underscored enough. Rather, it introduces the grotesque as a heuristic, a reading aid that will facilitate the exploration of the incongruity of the images. Furthermore, my interest in the grotesque is not an end in and of itself. Viewing the bodies as grotesque has implications for issues in the Song that have heretofore been pushed to the margins. These are its attendant gender politics and its complex presentation of desire. Additionally, for readers, there is the broader, more nebulous problem of how to read the book, so that readerly ambivalence towards it may be accommodated. The latter raises the question of the affect[6] of the text.

My study is divided into four main sections. In Chapter 1, I will introduce the problem of the body in the Song of Songs. This involves, first, an introduction to the conflicts caused by representing the body in a certain way in amatory discourse. I begin not with the Song, but with the work of two modern authors, André Breton and Jeanette Winterson. Next, I present the Song's body images and then review the main trends in criticism on them in order to show that they have posed a problem for interpreters. More specifically, I identify what seems to be a common interpretive thread – a 'hermeneutic of compliment' – that runs through most scholarship on the Song's imagery. Finally, I propose that the grotesque might be a suitable and alternative way to read the descriptions.

Chapter 2 is taken up entirely with a discussion of the literary and artistic construct of the grotesque. I trace its development in a loosely historical manner, introducing its beginnings and general themes in art, but then move to concentrate on the grotesque body, as manifested in the œuvre of Rabelais and explicated by literary theorist Mikhail Bakhtin (1984b). In response to Bakhtin's work, the insights of various literary critics and gender theorists are presented. These fill out the figure of the grotesque body to include its more political and sinister aspects.

A detailed investigation of the grotesque body through the consideration of five main texts in the Song (4.1-5; 4.9-16; 5.10-16; 6.4-7; 7.1-10) follows in Chapter 3. Initially, I explore some general 'first impressions'; I then follow these with a discussion of the interrelations of the images, observing them as they metamorphose from text to text. I build on my first impressions using the work of Barthes, introduced in the previous chapter, then discuss some of the grotesque themes, identified with the

---

6   Briefly, I use the term to refer to the emotional or psychological effects of reading. This is explored fully in Ch 4.

assistance of some of the theoretical tools gathered in Chapter 2. The texts are taken as evidence of particular thematic ideas, not as exhaustive explorations of each theme as it appears in the Song. Finally, in an attempt to understand the strategies of the grotesque as they are revealed in the book, I look at a number of concepts investigated by Barthes and Michel de Certeau, such as the madness of analogy and mystical discourse. It is ultimately suggested that the grotesque evinces a type of mystical departure in the Song.

Chapter 4 concerns itself with some of the issues raised in Chapter 1 (the problem of representing the body in amatory discourse), focused largely through an exploration of the readerly implications of viewing the Song's bodies as grotesque. Here, the grotesque bodies of the Song are extended to include the Song's own grotesque body (the textual corpus), following the use of Barthes well-known metaphor of the textual body. From this, I undertake an investigation into an erotics of reading in an effort to understand readerly relationships with this text. This last chapter is an effort to explore the usefulness of the grotesque for the larger context of the Song: its presentation of desire and the affect of the text. The results of these enquiries will be drawn together in the conclusion of the chapter with the work of Julia Kristeva on love and, unexpectedly, with the story of another grotesque subject, Anna Swan.

In my exploration of the body imagery, I will not provide a detailed analysis of the ways similes and metaphors work in the Song. Some begin their studies of the Song's images in this way (Good 1970; Grober 1984; Müller 1984; Soulen 1993), but their conceptualization of metaphor is not developed in detail. This may seem a strange omission in a book devoted to investigating imagery, but as will become clear, my issue is not so much with the specifics of how these poetic techniques work as it is with the interpretive framework that governs how they are read.[7]

Because I am primarily taken up with the interpretation of the Song's imagery, I will also circumvent some of the other well-known problems that the book poses for interpreters. These are, chiefly, the dating of the Song, the question of its formal or poetical structure and the issue of how the Song as a whole is to be interpreted (the main choices have been allegory, drama, cultic rite or secular love poetry). It is by and large irrelevant to my reading how the Song is structured poetically – whether it

---

7   A detailed discussion of types of biblical metaphors can be found in Watson 1995: 263–71. Some of these include Song texts. Angénieux undertakes a structural comparison and analysis of three of the descriptions of the body (1966), though his discussion of the descriptions as figurative language is not technical in a literary-critical sense. For more technical readings, readers might turn to Grober 1984 or Good 1970, but even here, those looking for analyses of the *function* of metaphors and similes will be disappointed.

is made up of six, eight, or 22 poems.[8] Similarly, I am little concerned with
some of the older schemas posited as hermeneutical keys according to
which the book might be interpreted as a whole. Like most recent work
done on the Song, I take the book's subject to be the erotic love 'story' of
two people,[9] and my reading proceeds from that point. Finally,
speculation on the date of the Song's composition is of little interest to
my study.[10] It is true that the Song's historical context has been proposed
in the past as an interpretive tool for the imagery. The argument is a
logical one: it runs that the reason the Song's descriptions are perplexing
to us is because we are ignorant of the sociohistorical context in which
they were written; exploration of this context could therefore facilitate our
understanding. Though ancient Near Eastern parallels might provide
some clues, however, in my view it is essentially impossible to know for
certain what meaning an image was meant to convey. More to the point,
even if readers could know, their own reactions or interpretations might
not necessarily gibe with these hypothesized intentions for the texts. That
is to say, this project is not based on the insights of – or directed at –
readers of former times, but rather is oriented towards readers of the
present day. The fact that the Song's imagery is problematic now is
precisely the impetus and the point of this book: this problem creates a
dark and mysterious cavern into which the grotesque neatly slithers, and
thrives.

The work of many commentators and readers has informed the study of

---

8   Relevant literature includes, but is not limited to: Angénieux 1965, 1968; Buzy 1940;
Exum 1973; Landy 1983; Shea 1980; Webster 1982. These authors see the Song as a collection
of a variety of numbers of poems, arranged in specific orders that give clues as to the unity of
the Song. There are others, however, who view the Song as a loose collection of poems
arranged in no particular order: Falk 1982: 62–70; Gerleman 1965: 59; Gordis 1974: 16–18;
Landsberger 1954; Pope 1977: 54; Rudolph 1962: 98–100; White 1978. For the most recent
and most detailed study of the poetic unity of the Song, see Elliott 1989, who splits the book
into six sections and analyses it according to stylistic and formal features. Elliott's work
provides an excellent discussion of previous work on the unity of the Song. Exum has
recently returned to the issue in her commentary (2005a: 33–41).

9   The Song is not a story in that it has a consistent narrative, though I will comment on
its occasional narrative qualities, below. I use the word 'story', however, loosely to indicate
that the book relates the experiences and discourse of two lovers. It tells their story.

10   The ascription to Solomon in Song 1.1 has made some argue for an early date for the
book, one that is located in the Solomonic era (Segal 1962). Gerleman posits it is the result of
a Solomonic enlightenment (1965: 76–7). Waterman believes it to be a critique of Solomon
(1948). One can see evidence for both early and late dates, however, in geographical
references (e.g. Tirzah – before the first half of the ninth century [Murphy 1990: 4]; cf. Gordis
[1974: 23]) and various linguistic abnormalities such as Ugaritic literary parallels (Murphy
1990: 4), at least one possible Persian loanword (פַּרְדֵּס) and the extensive use of the proclitic
particle שׁ. Most commentaries discuss the Song's dating, as might be expected (see, among
others: Exum 2005a: 63–70; Fox 1985: 186–90; Keel 1994: 4; Murphy 1990: 3–7; Rudolph
1962: 26–9), but Pope's surpasses the others in detail and rigour on this issue (1977: 22–33).

the Song texts in this book. Readers of critical work on the Song need hardly be reminded of Marvin Pope's immense and detailed study (1977) which, it has to be noted, is probably given unfair exposure here. The reasons for this are due, quite simply, to his incomparably thorough treatment of the Song. Pope of course has his own slants on the Song, one of which is a greater openness (relative to many commentators) to its sexual content. This is something that I often mention because it is appropriate to my own reading. It should also be noted that commentary on the Song – historical and contemporary – is prolific. It would be an impossible task to read and make use of all commentative work that exists on the book. Most of my critical companions are, therefore, fairly recent, largely because older commentaries tend to be concerned with historical or formal issues, which are not so relevant here.[11] In addition, the writing of three important scholars of the Song of Songs influences and informs much of what I do here: Athalya Brenner, J. Cheryl Exum and Francis Landy. The critical responses I sometimes make to their work will be, I hope, a welcome part of the ongoing conversation in scholarship about this influential book and an indicator of the high esteem in which I hold their work.

One last word should be said about the identity of the lovers before turning to their bodies in the chapters that follow. I have already noted that I am not concerned with the historical actuality behind the Song. This extends to its players. Though it might be inconvenient for readers of the book, historical identities for the lovers will not be posited. In fact, the lovers are not even named here, although the text does suggest options – Solomon is the most obvious for the man (1.1 [5]; 3.7, 9, 11; 8.11, 12); the Shulammite also occurs for the woman (7.1, x2). The decision to leave the characters nameless is based largely on the woman's identity, which is suggested in the text only twice. It is, moreover, a noun with a definite article, which suggests not a proper name, but an impersonal description. It has been the practice of some feminist scholars to name unnamed characters in biblical texts, in an effort to grant to them some sort of identity or to establish their subjectivity.[12] It is my contention, however, that the lack of identity is important, both because it means a certain unanimity and universality for the lovers' experience and because it has

---

11 I must also add that Exum's recent and excellent commentary (2005a) makes a later appearance here, for it appeared in the process of my own revisions. As a commentary that pays rigorous attention to poetics, gender-politics, readerly responses and the Song's eroticism, it provides a much-needed voice in Song of Songs scholarship.

12 See Exum (1993: 176–7), who follows the practice of Mieke Bal (1988). Exum names the woman in the Song 'Shulamit' (1998). In a later publication (1999), however, Exum reconsiders her view, noting the poetic value of the lovers' anonymity. Commentators have, of course, named the characters, especially the woman, for other reasons in earlier times. As an example, see Delitzsch's drama-based commentary (1877).

political implications for the unnamed. To name the players would be to cloud these issues. The male lover might more convincingly be called Solomon, but it is also problematic for a gender-informed study to heighten the disparity of the lovers by insisting on an identity for one (especially when the text does not) and anonymity for the other. The two remain, therefore, 'the' (or 'his' or 'her') lover.[13] Sometimes, it has to be agreed, there is a certain awkwardness in this, but I leave it to signal the awkwardness of identity in the Song, where bodies are elaborated, itemized and displayed, and where their owners are to some degree obscured from view.

13 Some choose to refer to the woman as the beloved and the man as the lover (e.g. Landy 1983). This is problematic, however, in that the former implies passivity and objectification, while the latter works on the author's ostensible perspective of the lover as active in initiation.

Chapter I

THE PROBLEM OF THE BODY IN THE SONG OF SONGS

In a 1978 issue of the *Wittenburg Door*, a periodical that describes itself as 'the world's pretty much only religious satire magazine', Den Hart offers his 'The Song of Songs, Illustrated (for our Literalist Friends)' (Figure 1). The cartoon attempts – in an excessive manner – a pictorial rendering of the strange descriptions of the body proffered by the Song's lovers. Not to be dismissed as idle doodling, however, in its effort to actualize the poem's images, Hart's work aptly encapsulates the problem of the body in the Song. It also invites the question: what happens if we read the images with Hart's proposed hermeneutical key? The cartoon is, moreover, a construction of the body, or in other words, an attempt to fabricate a 'real body' (no matter how silly) out of numerous, ostensibly idiosyncratic murmurings between the Song's players. As such, it reminds us of the corporeal possibilities of the language of lovers. The cartoon could be left as a tribute to the magazine's tongue-in-cheek perspective on the Bible, but the challenge it poses for reading the Song of Songs is too irresistible to do that.

The subject of this chapter is the problematic nature of the body imagery in the Song of Songs. This phrase, problematic nature, refers to two interrelated issues. The first is that the images have caused difficulty for interpreters, who frequently comment on their odd nature and often go to considerable lengths to make sense of what they read. The second issue is that the body in the Song's images is itemized, objectified and oddly figured, and this in turn creates a potential conflict for readers' expectations of love poetry, the context in which the body descriptions are situated.[1] The first issue takes up the majority of space in this chapter in the form of a review of various methods of reading the images in recent

---

1   In earlier scholarship, the use of the term 'love poetry' denoted a particular interpretive stance on the Song of Songs. While some posited the work as a drama, others insisted it was an epithalamium. Still others insisted on the literal, erotic sense for the Song, as love poetry. My use of the term is not meant to resurrect that debate, but to acknowledge merely that the Song represents the romantic and emotional interests of two people who express their love for each other. This perspective is in keeping with most of the recent work on the book.

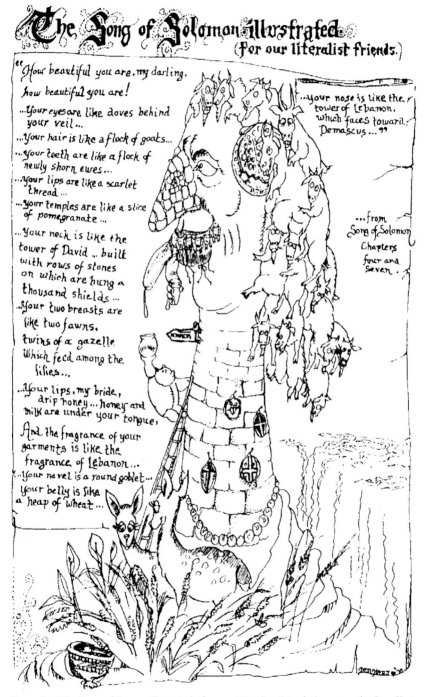

Figure 1   *'The Song of Songs, Illustrated (for our Literalist Friends)', cartoon by Den Hart*

biblical scholarship. The second issue, the problem of the body in erotic discourse, is one that I would like to introduce here and use to begin the discussion. It will reappear at the end of this study, once the implications of a grotesque reading of the Song's bodies have come to the fore.

Free Associations: Bodies in / and Erotic Discourse

Hart's cartoon is whimsy, a bit of clever and playful irreverence. It functions to overload the reader's imagination, piling all interpretive possibilities into one format, and adding a few more besides (e.g. Winnie the Pooh catching hunny dripping from the woman's mouth). The cartoon shows both what is possible and what is improbable (did the lover mean for all images to be written / drawn on the body at once?). It also presents the alluring possibility of literalistic interpretation, alluring not because it is an easy choice, but because it is what is anticipated before other interpretive avenues are explored. For instance, a nose described as a tower passes through a number of realms of possibility, including literalist ones, before a reader comes to rest on a satisfactory meaning. Is one meaning better than another? More sophisticated? More correct? The cartoon raises the question not only of the means of interpretation but also its status. That is to say, the reason interpreters have been able to insist on a particular method of reading the Song's images is in part because they have been able to discredit others, as we saw in Fox's comments above. A cartoon in a satirical magazine liberates the reader / viewer from such expectations. The question is, is this the only context that can do so?

Here we come to a matter of greater significance: Hart's cartoon leaves one important issue hanging, which is the contextualizing of the body images within the parameters of (biblical) love poetry. Nothing in Hart's piece acknowledges that context, save perhaps for two fawns looking lovingly into each other's eyes. The piece therefore prompts us to ask if Hart's ludicrous interpretive possibilities are even possible within the Song's context of love.

I make a beginning at investigating that question not with the Song itself, but with two more recent texts, a twentieth-century novel, *Written on the Body* (Winterson 1996) and a surrealist poem, 'L'Union libre' (Breton 1969: 16–17). The associations may seem strange. Nevertheless, the novel and the poem in effect crystallize the problem of the body for the language of love by raising pertinent questions about the implications of how lovers choose to represent each other.

Written on the Body tells the story of two lovers. The journey to their uniting has been difficult, not only because of the narrator's inability to find the right partner, but because both are attached in other relationships and must extricate themselves before they can be together. Then the ultimate obstacle presents itself: death by destruction of the beloved's body through illness. The narrator abandons the beloved, Louise, to Louise's estranged husband, who happens to be a specialist in his wife's disease. Trying to negotiate this loss, the narrator translates desires for a physical possession of Louise into a literary one. The narrator will study Louise's body, study her cancer, live it through writing it:

> I became obsessed with anatomy. If I could not put Louise out of my mind I would drown myself in her. Within the clinical language, through the dispassionate view of the sucking, sweating, greedy, defecating self, I found a love-poem to Louise. I would go on knowing her, more intimately than the skin, hair, and voice that I craved. I would have her plasma, her spleen, her synovial fluid. I would recognize her even when her body had long since fallen away. (Winterson 1996: 111)

The middle section of the novel is given over to a marvellous series of 'love poems' which feature Louise's body. They are a catalogue of her systems: cells, tissues, skin, skeleton, senses. The series of poems begins objectively and clinically enough, with a description of the cells in which the offending illness wages its war: 'In the secret places of her thymus gland, Louise is making too much of herself' (Winterson 1996: 115). But then the narrator moves to tissues, cavities, skin and skeleton (scapula and face), and by the time the special senses are reached, Louise's body is lost in a grotesque litany of re-membrances, desires, fears and losses.

> THE NOSE: THE SENSE OF SMELL IN HUMAN BEINGS IS GENERALLY LESS ACUTE THAN IN OTHER ANIMALS.
> The smells of my lover's body are still strong in my nostrils. The yeast smell of her sex. The rich fermenting undertow of rising bread. My lover is a kitchen cooking partridge. I shall visit her gamey low-roofed den and feed from her. Three days without washing and she is well hung and high. Her skirts reel back from her body, her scent is a hoop about her thighs. From beyond the front door my nose is twitching. I can smell her coming down the hall towards me. She is a perfumier of sandalwood and hops. I want to uncork her. I want to push my head against the open wall of her loins. She is firm and ripe, a dark compound of sweet cattle straw and Madonna of the Incense. She is frankincense and myrrh, bitter cousin smells of death and faith.
> . . .
> When she bleeds the smells I know change colour. There is iron in her soul on those days. She smells like a gun.
> . . .
> My lover is cocked and ready to fire. She has the scent of her prey on her. She consumes me when she comes in thin white smoke smelling of saltpetre. (Winterson 1996: 136)

THE SKIN IS COMPOSED OF TWO MAIN PARTS: THE DERMIS
AND THE EPIDERMIS.
Odd to think that the piece of you I know best is already dead ... Your
sepulchral body, offered to me in the past tense, protects your soft
centre from the intrusions of the outside world. I am one such intrusion,
stroking you with necrophiliac obsession, loving the shell laid out before
me ...

The dead you is constantly being rubbed away by the dead me. Your
cells fall and flake away, fodder to dust mites and bed bugs. Your
droppings support colonies of life that graze on skin and hair no longer
wanted ...

Your skin tastes salty and slightly citrus. When I run my tongue in a
long wet line across your breasts I can feel the tiny hairs, the puckering
of the aureole, the cone of your nipple. Your breasts are beehives
pouring honey. (Winterson 1996: 123)

In the book's core of love poems, we see the artful mixing of the world,
food and nature – in its cycle of growth and decay, the grim reminders of
life mixed with death – all written upon the body. This is scientifically
atomized both for the narrator's expression of grief and pleasure (and
ours?). This core of the novel is striking not only for these unexpected
mixings, but also because the minutiae of the body, its parts and its
workings, here provide the machinery for erotic language. This is no
Romantic ode to a silky breast or a sun-kissed cheek, but a piece-by-piece
dissection, a laboratory eroticization of the body for the lover. Moreover,
the metaphors that Winterson chooses (death, warfare, agriculture, food)
to express the narrator's desire for the beloved body are unexpected and
jarring as the purported language of love. As will become evident below,
these dissections, the body and its parts, and the merging with the natural
world in particular, provide the bases for grotesque figuration. The
juxtaposition, therefore, of love and the grotesque is provocative, and the
questions it engenders are critical ones, both for Winterson's book and for
the Song of Songs.

So, then, what is the place of the dissection, inversion and perversion of
the body and its boundaries in love poetry? Are the hybridizations of the
body, the fusion of parts and plants, of spices, smells and weapons,
indicative of affection? Admiration? Attraction? Desire? The beloved's
body is revered like the dead, hunted like game, consumed. It is
dismembered and fetishized. It is described in ways that do not always
appear to be complimentary or loving, at first glance. Should a reader
remark when a lover speaks of a loved one in this way? What restrictions,
if any, does the language of love place on the representation of the body?

Or, what rights should be accorded to the body when it is positioned as object by a lover?

Maybe these questions appear naïve. One could easily, for instance, object that the particularities of love and love-making do not accord a rational and reasonable recipe of dos and don'ts. Individuals behave *individually* when they are enraptured. Love-making is, after all, a private (enough) affair that renders it free from the scrutiny of others. Furthermore, who would set the rules for such exchanges anyway? And what would the implications be if Winterson were found to be acting in 'bad form'?

Winterson's poems clearly render homage to Monique Wittig's *Le Corps lesbien*, an extensive text that articulates a lover's physical and emotional relation with her lover's body. Wittig describes the work as indicative of fiction that validates (1975: 11).[2] It is an effort to generate a lesbian text in a world (1973) where little had been written or said of lesbianism (9). But it is also more than that. *Le Corps lesbien* is a bringing-into-being of the body – the lover's *and* the loved. It is 'the desire to bring the real body violently to life in the words of the book' (10). In short, it is a literary fabrication, an assemblage of the loved body through words. As such, Wittig naturally has a political aim in writing, one that extends even further than the ubiquitous desire (so Roland Barthes)[3] of a lover to actualize a loved one. Wittig wants the words of her alternative tribute to so provoke that they confront the reader into acknowledging and experiencing the different body. For what purpose? More than the narrator declaring 'this is my love! Notice it!', the tribute is a means of inviting the reader to construct the body with her, as if all of us have a role to play in creating the one who speaks, and the one of whom her words are spoken. Wittig's work is, in sum, a means of confronting the problems of language and female subjectivity as much as it is a commentary on the place of the body in erotic discourse.

It is probable that Winterson is aware of these matters when she invites Wittig into her narrative world.[4] But what of the Song of Songs? It is provocative to see *Written on the Body* – and *Le Corps lesbien* – as a modern commentary on the Song of Songs. Despite their contextual differences, the thrust of the books is the same. Love is painted as a drive experienced by

2   Wittig's comment is that lesbians and lesbian culture, heretofore unacknowledged by traditional (male) culture, are illusionary to that culture, and lesbians are forced into occupying a fictional space. As I read her, though, Wittig's point is that this fictional existence is in truth an alternate reality; *Le Corps lesbien* functions in part to actualize that reality.

3   See *A Lover's Discourse: Fragments*, in particular (1990a).

4   Winterson's later novels seem to be developing such themes (*Art & Lies*, 1994, *Gut Symmetries*, 1997, *The Powerbook*, 2000), and she confirms in a radio interview about her 2000 novel, *The Powerbook*, that *Written on the Body*, along with the later novels, is part of a project to explore female subjectivity and issues around the body (Winterson 2000).

two people to be united and it is at the same time fraught with obstacles. It is an old theme: one sees it in Sappho's poetry, in Ovid's *Amores*, in medieval courtly romance. I am, moreover, not the only one to make the comparison. The narrator in *Written on the Body* is certainly aware of the Song's powerful, universal message and its relevance is noted for the story. The loss of the lover is bitterly expressed in the Song's language:

> Your beloved has gone down into a foreign land. You call but your beloved does not hear. You call in the fields and in the valleys but your beloved does not answer. The sky is closed and silent, there is no one there. The ground is hard and dry. Your beloved will not return that way. Perhaps only a veil divides you. Your beloved is waiting on the hills. Be patient and go with nimble feet dropping your body like a scroll. (Winterson 1996: 178)

> I miss you Louise. Many waters cannot quench love, neither can floods drown it. What then kills love? Only this: Neglect. (Winterson 1996: 186)

Wittig's and Winterson's powerful recitations of the body speak to their pursuit of what is not fully attainable. In Winterson's case, absence is the culmination of loss through illness and, eventually, death. Wittig contemplates death from the very onset, but she contends on a more global level than Winterson with the absence of woman, from literature, from speech and from reality.[5] Are these themes illustrative in Hart's strange figure scribbled in the *Wittenburg Door*? Surely what is at stake there is not so grave, but yet, even the cartoon invites the matter of loss into the Song's midst. Most obviously, it appears to be poking fun at the language of lovers, not to mention at those with more literalistic tendencies in their readings of Scripture. It also, however, invites the comedic and the bathetic into the realm of love.

The questions that Winterson's and Wittig's work raise about the body in erotic discourse may well be universal. From another moment in time, the surrealist poet André Breton writes about a woman's body[6] in a manner similar to Winterson, though the images are perhaps farther fetched. The poem 'L'Union libre', whose title denotes Free Association, Free Marriage, even Free Love (Balakian 1971: 139), expresses both the speaker's estimation of a woman's body and a unique surrealist project with language that is prompted by love, idealism and the search for a new poetic vocabulary. The poem is a series of similes and metaphors, with

---

5 Winterson is interested in this problem too, however. For instance, she does not assign a gender to the narrator, thus making it difficult for the reader to interpret what goes on in the story (and/or making the reader aware of his or her heterosexist assumptions).

6 It is unclear who is the subject of this poem. It was written when Breton was between marriages, and at least one major critic believes it to represent the essential nature of woman, rather than one particular person (Balakian 1971: 139).

little or no narrative continuity. Unfortunately, it is long and there is not space to quote it in its entirety here. A shorter excerpt will suffice to give a sense of the work:

... Ma femme aux jambes de fusée[7]
Aux mouvements d'horlogerie et de désespoir
Ma femme aux mollets de moelle de sureau
Ma femme aux pieds d'initiales
Aux pieds de trousseaux de clés aux pieds de calfats qui boivent
Ma femme au cou d'orge imperlé
Ma femme à la gorge de Val d'or
De rendez-vous dans le lit même du torrent
Aux seins de nuit
Ma femme aux seins de taupinière marine
Ma femme aux seins de creuset du rubis
Aux seins de spectre de la rose sous la rosée
Ma femme au ventre de depliement d'éventail des jours
Au ventre de griffe géante
Ma femme au dos d'oiseau qui fuit vertical
Au dos de vif-argent
Au dos de lumière
A la nuque de pierre roulée et de craie mouillée
Et de chute d'un verre dans lequel on vient de boire
Ma femme aux hanches de nacelle
Aux hanches de lustre et de pennes de flèche
Et de tiges de plumes de paon blanc
De balance insensible
Ma femme aux fesses de grès et d'amiante
Ma femme aux fesses de dos de cygne
Ma femme aux fesses de printemps
Au sexe de glaïeul
Ma femme au sexe de placer et d'ornithorynque
Ma femme au sexe d'algue et de bonbons anciens
Ma femme au sexe de miroir
Ma femme aux yeux pleins de larmes
Aux yeux de panoplie violette et d'aiguille aimantée
Ma femme aux yeux de savane
Ma femme aux yeux d' eau pour boire en prison
Ma femme aux yeux de bois toujours sous la hache
Aux yeux de niveau d' eau de niveau d'air de terre et de feu.

---

7 In order to facilitate our understanding, Balakian advises that we remember that Breton replaces the usual word *comme* in his similes with *de* (1971: 141). It would not appear to be advisable, however, to use the English equivalent to *comme* ('like') in the translations, for it would make the comparisons pedantic and fail to give the impression that the French allows. An overt statement of the simile, such as might be wrought by using *comme*, would downplay the startling effect of the imagery.

[My woman[8] whose legs are spindles
Who moves like clockwork and despair
My woman whose calves are the marrow of elder trees
My woman whose feet are initials
Whose feet are bunches of keys or caulkers who drink
My woman whose neck is pearled barley
Whose throat is the Golden Valley[9]
Rendez-vous in the bed of the torrent
Whose breasts are night
My woman whose breasts are sea-knolls
My woman whose breasts are ruby crucibles
Spectre of roses under dew
My woman whose belly is the day's fan unfolding
Whose belly is a giant claw
My woman whose back is a bird in upward flight
Whose back is quicksilver
Is light
Whose nape is a rolled stone and moistened chalk
And the tumble of a glass from which one has just drunk
My woman whose hips are a small skiff
Whose hips are lustre and arrow feathers
And the stems of white-peacock feathers
Of imperceptible balance
My woman whose buttocks are sandstone and asbestos
My woman whose buttocks are a swan's back
Whose buttocks are spring
Whose sex is a gladiolus
My woman whose sex is a gold deposit and a platypus
My woman whose sex is algae and old-fashioned candy
My woman whose sex is a mirror
My woman whose eyes are filled with tears
Whose eyes are a violet panoply and magnetized needles
My woman whose eyes are a savannah
My woman whose eyes are water for drinking in prison
My woman whose eyes are wood always under the axe
Whose eyes are the level of water and air, of earth and of fire.][10]

Breton's project is perhaps more akin to play than Wittig's and Winterson's more serious undertakings. The surrealist enterprise endeavoured to push the boundaries of language, to recreate the word:

---

8   *Femme* also means 'wife', but 'woman' accords with Balakian's observations about the essentializing nature of the poem.

9   Or 'golden grape', Balakian 1971: 141.

10   Profound thanks to my colleague, Dr Monika Boehringer, for her thoughts about my translation of Breton, and for some illuminating conversation about this text and the poetic genres of the *blason* and *contreblason*.

> Along with the word play goes the play of images, the goal of both
> being to 'multiply short circuits', as Breton says in the second manifesto
> (1930), that is, to sabotage as frequently and as definitively as possible
> the usual 'realistic insanities' and to show what is on the other side of
> the accepted reality. The surrealist image is necessarily shocking – it
> destroys the conventional laws of association and logic, so that the
> objects which compose it, instead of seeming to fit side by side naturally
> and normally, 'shriek at finding themselves together'. But the same
> electrical force that splits up the habitual relationships of the ordinary
> world has the power to fuse all that has previously been separate. (Caws
> 1970: 69–70)

The images, moreover, do not intend to give a realistic vision of the world,
or even to make sense. 'Surrealist play at its best is supposed to produce in
the reader an involuntary sense of surprise which is disturbing to his
ordinary perception of the universe and to his ordinary verbal framework'
(Caws 1970: 76).[11]

The shocking combinations of images, as well as the form of the poem,
tend to remind one of the Song of Songs (Balakian 1971: 140). Moreover,
they provoke questions as to how they are to be interpreted, just as the
images in the Song do. This is especially the case here because no extended
metaphorization accompanies each image, as it does in the narrator's
tributes in *Written on the Body*. In Breton's images, how are we to
understand a neck like pearled barley, or eyes like wood under the axe, or
a belly like a giant claw? Are the bases of comparison to be shape?
Texture? Colour? Smell? Or are these the wrong questions to be asking?
Perhaps the point of images that 'shriek at finding themselves together' is
to resist questions such as these.

Breton's poem also suggests other questions, such as: do the words
reveal any particular intent on the part of the speaker towards the subject
of the poem, and if so, what? Anna Balakian finds in Breton's poetry of
this period a vision to unite his love experiences, to paint a 'universal
essence of woman over and above the miscellany' of his own relationship.[12] So it is love poetry, but after a particular fashion. The question is,
of course, how can we tell this from these words? And is there anything

---

11   One often hears the term 'automatic writing' with respect to the surrealist poets, which
is a sustained attempt to foster these chance comparisons and images in a state (roughly a
correlate to the automatic speech of mediums) that suspends the conscious production of
language. But the images that are present in 'L'Union libre' seem too contrived for that.
Breton's imagery is constructed, so Balakian observes, 'with the intricacy of a labyrinth, new
chambers are revealed with every rereading, and new difficulties of meaning. As he calls life a
cryptogram, so is his poetry. The images appear spontaneous, and yet it is clear that their
relation to each other has been lengthily considered and highly contrived' (1971: 128).

12   Balakian 1971: 138–9 (see 140–41 for a discussion of this theme with respect to
'L'Union libre'). The work becomes for Breton an intellectual project to address love in the

left of the personal (i.e. the emotive) from the speaker's abstractions and hints at essences? The narrator's feelings in *Written on the Body* are well communicated to the reader because they bring readers through the steps of the relationship; grief and a sense of loss is manifested in urgent, fearful, but affectionate means. Here, there is no narrative framework in which to insert these bizarre images (except for that provided by Balakian). And there is also no frame of reference or interpretive key (like the loss of a loved one who is dying) that is provided with the poetry. It is only a series of images, at once surprising, humorous and disturbing.

Then, we might also ask here, what of the effect of the words on the one who is being described? They are playful, surprising, but one wonders about the impression that they leave with the specific object of the speaker's affections. If there is no one specific person to whom they are addressed, then we might ask about the political effects of the poetry in terms of this idealized 'essence' of woman that is being described. Perhaps woman shrieks at finding herself displayed thus.[13]

The questions that I raised in connection with the imagery in the works of Winterson and Breton are not only restricted to their texts, nor need they be viewed only as modern concerns. One can, for example, ask the same questions of the body described in an Arabic *wasf*: 'O the breasts of my beloved are like crystal, / They yielded quinces and pomegranates' (Stephan 1922: 232); or of an Egyptian praise song: 'Her arms surpass gold, / Her fingers are like lotuses' (Fox 1985: 52).[14] And they may also be asked of the images in Song of Songs: 'Your eyes are doves behind your veil, your hair is like a flock of goats streaming down from Mount Gilead' (4.1). This biblical love poem is punctuated throughout with vibrant, perplexing figurations of the body like the ones mentioned above, which dissect and itemize the human form. Each part is blended with the world around it and presented for the lover and to the reader as if to be consumed. One might ask how this figuration finds its place in love poetry. What do the images mean? Do they lend themselves to clear

---

abstract. He says that it is 'this major operation of the mind which consists of going from the being to the essence' (Balakian 1971: 105). Part of that essence of love is the essence of woman, which Breton derives also from the particular.

13   There are, in other words – and somewhat obviously – inherent gender-critical issues in surrealist poetry (and in general, in the treatment of women by the surrealist group), which a poem like this one tends to highlight. Balakian notes that woman as she is figured in surrealist poetry of the 1920s and 30s (a pure entity) is unique in comparison to other (French) literature of the time. She observes, 'The surrealists, under the direction of Breton, restored the love theme to French poetry and gave woman the sublimated role she had not played since the salutary heroines of the Middle Ages' (1971: 111).

14   Exum's commentary provides a lucid and thoughtful discussion of the ancient Near Eastern literary context for the Song as love poetry. It is not specifically directed at the body imagery, but there is some useful discussion there (2005a: 47–63), as there is, of course, in Pope's commentary (1977: 54–89).

interpretation? Prompted, too, are questions about the politics of viewing and describing. And dare we ask, in what manner is this indeed the language of love?

Body Imagery in the Song of Songs

Background information about the authors considered above, be it biographical or supplied through critical analysis, provides a certain framework for recreating their intentions for the bodies constructed in their particular erotic texts. We do not, of course, have the same keys for the body images in the Song of Songs, in the form of an author's introduction or a narrative constructed around the descriptions. Even with Wittig's, Winterson's and Breton's texts, moreover, one cannot insist that the keys I have applied make sense as the only way of reading the textual bodies; the same conclusion would have to be made of the Song, even if we had that kind of information for it.

A conceivable framework for one who is seeking to understand the images might, of course, be the vast interpretive tradition that has grown up around the book. (Of all possible solutions, though, critics' responses are rarely Hart's literalistic, cartoonish impulses.) The scholarly legacy is worth consideration, not only because it might provide clues as to the images' meaning but also, and more importantly in this study, because it bears witness to the amount of difficulty that the images have caused readers especially over the last century. I will come to refer to this later on as a kind of interpretive anxiety, by which I mean that biblical scholars seem unable to rest comfortably with indeterminate imagery, especially when it is applied to the body, and worse, when it is determined by others to be decidedly unromantic. I do not mean to imply that biblicists are by nature uneasy nail-biters who lose sleep over the convolutions of the Song's bodies. Rather, it would seem that the volume and variety of work that has grown up around the work testifies to the enduring interpretive 'problem' of these texts, which has never really been definitively 'settled' to anyone's satisfaction.

The Descriptions

Descriptions of the lovers' bodies in the Song of Songs can be found scattered throughout the book and come in a number of formats. The most obvious would be the four main texts that stand out as attempts by both lovers to represent the bodies of each other in a systematic fashion (4.1-5//6.4-7; 5.10-16; 7.1-10).[15] These are concentrated images that

---

15 I delineate the *wasf* according to where each description seems logically to begin and end. There is a general agreement among scholars, with slight variations, on the locations of

itemize body-parts in a series, usually according to a particular order, from head to toe or from toe to head. Sometimes the texts address only a specific sphere of the body, as in 4.1-5 (and 6.4-7), where the man describes the woman from the head to the chest. Others are more complete, as in 5.10-16 and 7.1-10, where the full body (from head to toe in the first case, and toe to head in the second) appears, with many but not all parts depicted.

These representations of the body were labelled *wasfs* in the nineteenth century by scholars, and for the most part, the term is still used in biblical criticism today. The *wasfs* were originally so designated because of their structural and contextual resemblance to love poems or *wasfs* in modern (nineteenth-century) Arabic literature. In this context, the *wasf* served as part of a marriage rite where the bridegroom would sing the praises of his bride (notably of her beauty) by describing or itemizing her body-parts. The form was not, however, restricted to Arabic or biblical literature; its presence has been traced throughout the ancient Near Eastern world, in Mesopotamian, Egyptian and Ugaritic literature.[16]

In the *wasf*'s history in biblical scholarship, the work of several scholars should be mentioned briefly. Pope locates the beginnings of interest in the *wasf* with J.G. Wetzstein (1873) at the end of the last century, in his comparison of the Song to Syrian village wedding poems.[17] This interest in the form, however, was taken up and promoted by Karl Budde, who is

---

these poems. According to Horst, whose form-critical analysis of the Song was the first, the *wasf* are located in 4.1-7; 5.10-16; 6.4a, 5b-7; 7.1-6 (1961: 180). Krinetzki finds several, smaller examples to add to Horst's list: 3.6-8; 3.9-10d; 8.5a-b (1981: 21). Brenner outlines them as 4.1-5 (with a parallel at 6.4-7); 5.10-16; 7.1-10 (1993a: 236), and Murphy as 4.1-7; 5.10-16; 6.4-7; 7.1-6 (1981b: 105–24). I do not follow the usual designation, *wasf*, in my reading of these poems, below, and therefore the debate over the identification of the genre and where the boundaries of each poetic unit lies do not explicitly concern this study.

16   See Hermann (1963) for a history of the *wasf* in ancient Near Eastern texts. He traces the *wasf* through Mesopotamian, Egyptian, Ugaritic, Hebrew Bible and Qumran texts. The *wasf* has also been identified in the Genesis Apocryphon by Goshen-Gottstein (1959: 46–8), but its place in this category is questionable. Sarah's body-parts are itemized, to be sure, but the 'descriptions' merely consist of statements regarding her beauty (e.g. '[H]ow lovely are her eyes and how pleasant is her nose' (1Qap Gen 20.3; Fitzmyer 1966: 55). These are not comparisons of each part to the kinds of items that we see in the Song's *wasf* and elsewhere. See Fitzmyer 1966: 55 for text and 1966: 107–11 for commentary.

17   A brief example is provided by Keel 1994: 24–5:

> The eyebrows of my beloved / Are like the line of a stylus, drawn with ink, / And the hair of his forehead like the feathers of birds dyed with henna. / His nose is like a handle of an Indian sword glittering, / His teeth like pebbles of hail and more beautiful, / His cheeks like apples of Damascus, / His breasts beautiful pomegranates, / His neck like the neck of the antelope, / His arms staffs of pure silver, / His fingers golden pencils [*sic*].

generally credited with the popularization of the theory (Pope 1977: 56).[18] One should also mention here the lengthy compendium of modern Palestinian parallels for comparison with the Song of Songs provided by Stephen Stephan (1922). Finally, any history of the *wasf* must also include Friedrich Horst (1961), whose influential form-critical division of the Song of Songs (though not, according to Pope [1977: 66] very effective or convincing)[19] included the *Beschreibungslied*, or descriptive song (Horst 1961: 180–82). Despite any disagreements over provenance and genre, it is generally agreed by scholars that the most significant key to the identification of the *wasf* is that it must contain a description of the body-parts, usually belonging to a woman (generally a bride), in a particular order (normally head to toe).

In addition to the so-called *wasf* texts in the Song, the body figures in smaller, less detailed instances throughout the book. Sometimes these are unique – and confounding – as in the description of the woman as a 'mare among Pharaoh's chariots' (1.9). The Song provides no other frame of reference for this image and little opportunity of contextualizing it with the other descriptive language, except in very general terms (i.e. nature imagery or the like). Such incidental descriptions are, however, often repeated throughout the book in various guises, as in the case of the gazelle, used to describe both lovers (2.9; 2.17; 4.5; 7.3; 8.14) and also the terms of an oath; or the doves, which describe the eyes (1.15; 4.1; 5.12) and also signify the lovers (2.14; 5.12; 6.9).[20] These incidental descriptions do not really respect boundary lines of poems such as the *wasf*, and as a result we see them used both inside the concentrated descriptions and scattered elsewhere. Occasionally, there is, in addition, an extended metaphor of description, as in the garden imagery of 4.12-15, where the woman is described simultaneously as a closed garden and a garden spring or fountain in various forms. These two images, connected but disparate, frame further description of the woman using a list of spices and an image that perhaps pertains to a specific body-part. In this case, it is clear that the imagery is multilayered and complex. Occasionally, too, the woman will describe her own body, as in 2.1: 'I am a rose of Sharon, a lily of the valleys',[21] or 8.10: 'I am a wall, and my breasts like towers.'

---

18   The development of this idea into the theory that the Song represents a sacred marriage rite (T. Meek) should also be mentioned. See Carr (1979) for a review and discussion of the theory.

19   See, by contrast, Murphy (1973, 1981b: 105–24), who still advocates the usefulness of form criticism for studies of the Song's images.

20   It is not clear who is speaking in 2.14. Murphy believes it to be the man (1990: 141), thus it is only the woman who is referred to as 'my dove' in these three verses.

21   'Rose' and 'lily' are the more familiar and poetic translations of the flowers with which the woman compares herself. The exact flowers referred to are unknown. See Pope 1977: 367–8 and Keel 1994: 78 for discussion.

In all, it is a challenge to describe and interpret the Song's body imagery. It is complex not only because it is multilayered, but also because it features unusual combinations and permutations of the images chosen. Like Winterson's and Breton's work, we see in the Song's images the odd juxtaposition of incongruous elements and are left with pictures that seem to defy clear or coherent interpretation. What, after all, is a woman who is a mare among Pharaoh's chariots like? What is a temple like a pomegranate intended to signify? How might we read and interpret lips that drip with liquid myrrh? And when images are used and reused, repackaged in new contexts, must we resist the temptation to draw all these together, so that in our readings, hands that drip myrrh (5.2) and lips that do the same (5.13), and even body-parts that seem packed with myrrh and other spices (4.13), become compacted and conflated? When the Song's content and message is generally agreed to be erotic, how are these confusions and conflations to be understood?

One final, general comment should be made concerning the *wasf* genre. Scholarship on the Song's body imagery seems to be largely marked by a generally positive or even idyllic spirit. Much has been undertaken in the way of interpretive gymnastics in an effort to understand the images, and often with results that are idiosyncratic and might be interpreted to reveal as much about interpreters' own notions of beauty and compliment as they supply a definite meaning for the images. Readers' approaches to the Song are influenced and complicated by their expectations of the book – as love poetry. There may be many reasons behind this (and I shall address the issue more closely later in this study), but one, I suggest, could be the enduring influence of the *wasf* and the generic responsibilities that it exerts, even if it is not employed in its original, form-critical context.

Waṣf *Nest*

Few scholars still support the theory that the Song was actually used in a marriage rite, or that it even depicts a wedding,[22] but the initial suggestion seems to have served two purposes in criticism on the Song. First, it appears to have helped in the transfer – already underway – from the heavy allegorization of the book to a recognition of the more secular erotic aspects. Interpreters in the early twentieth century might not have been ready for the explicit sexual relationship of two unmarried people,[23]

---

22   Proponents of a marital or nuptial *Sitz-im-Leben* for the poems include Budde (1898), Horst (1961) and Würthwein (1969). Others agree on a marriage context for only some of the poems, e.g. Gordis (1974), Rudolph (1962). There are, however, some recent (non-formal) dramatic interpretations, such as Goulder's (1986), that involve courtship, a wedding scene, a wedding night, and so on. See also Delitzsch 1877 and Waterman 1948.

23   Murphy seems to agree (1973: 413), though he is referring to current Christian commentators.

but, through marriage, the Song could keep sex 'safe' for scholarly sensibilities.[24] And marriage proliferated a kind of sentimentality about the Song among biblical critics that had already been established through study of the book's subject matter: this was the story of two people in love, the paramour, King Solomon, and his beautiful maiden.

The study of the amatory content of the book on more literal terms, that is, as a secular love poem and not a theological or allegorical treatise, meant new challenges with respect to the descriptive language in the Song. The interpretive moves generated by efforts to see the descriptions as the *kind* of words one lover might say to another are often remarkable in their creativity. More recent work on the Song shows critics attempting to account for the imagery not by explicating cryptic metaphors, but by proposing new, less-literal ways of reading the images, for example, as evocative, rather than descriptive (e.g. Soulen 1993; Falk 1982; see below). This work also, however, maintains much of the aforementioned romanticism about the Song, viewing the relationship described in it as beautiful and idyllic. Again, I suggest that one reason for this cautiousness in biblical criticism might be the continuing influence of the *wasf*. Even though this more recent work is not interested in form-critical issues and ancient Near Eastern parallels, it still maintains the generic designation of *wasf* for these texts. Most plausibly, this is for the sake of convenience or convention. But might unwitting reliance on form-critical categories have implications where the interpretation of texts is concerned? In this case, for example, might the recognition of certain poems as *wasfs* influence interpreters to view the material positively – as the praise expressed by a bridegroom to his bride – even if they do not initially see it as flattering description?

Biblical *Scholarship and the Body Images: A Review*

It would be possible to write an entire book on the history of scholarship on the Song's figurative language. It is not that there is a proliferation of work that specifically problematizes how the descriptive language in the Song should be interpreted. Rather, one finds that there are usually identifiable aims and ideologies that govern most commentary on the Song where the imagery is concerned. So, for instance, Othmar Keel's commentary (1994) reads the imagery with the aid of Egyptian cultural artifacts and intertexts; Jill Munro (1995) attempts to recover how the images build up the book's theme of love; Carol Meyers (1993) finds in the

---

24   Gerleman suggests as much: 'Die Forderung, daß es sich bei jeder Erwähnung sinnlich erotischer Szenen um Hochzeit und Ehe handeln müßte läßt sich nur als Hineinlesen einer kirchlichen Eheethik in das Hohelied verstehen und führt wieder aufs neue zu willkürlichen Textinterpretationen' (1965: 207).

imagery a sign of female power in ancient Israelite society, and so on. Each interpreter will, in addition, have a particular take on how imagery should be interpreted (i.e. literally, evocatively, freely, or similar). Readings such as these three are also influenced by certain ideological undertakings to find in the Song's imagery descriptions of the body that are complimentary and loving. The list of commentators, and hence the variations, is long and detailed. A completely thorough examination of scholarship on the Song's imagery, therefore, would not only have to address those who specifically see the imagery as problematic and wish to suggest alternative solutions to it (Keel 1984; Soulen 1993; Falk 1982; Brenner 1993a), but also, potentially, the individual aims and suggestions of myriad commentators. Such an endeavour would be impossible in this context, not to mention tedious.

A better approach is to highlight some of the various trends of reading the imagery that have become evident in scholarship on the Song. Most of the work I consider here is quite recent (roughly 30 years old or less), though I do give a nod to allegorical interpretation because of its variety and fantastical nature of interpretations and its problematizing of the body in the Song. Readings will also, however, have particular ways of working with imagery, and in discussing each trend, it will be important to address the strategy of a particular work (if one is evident) and relate it to the others. Throughout, I will be especially concerned to point out what I perceive to be the governing hermeneutic of most if not all of these readings: for convenience, I have called this a 'hermeneutic of compliment'.[25]

Allegorical Interpretation of the Body Imagery

Allegorical readings are not generally included in reviews of scholarly literature such as these, but of course they do provide some background to modern interpretations.[26] Allegory formed the primary means of interpreting the Song of Songs up until the nineteenth century,[27] and, as a result, there is quite an extensive body of extant material. A full account

---

25   It must also be admitted that some of the readings are intentionally selected not because they represent major trends in scholarship on the imagery, but because they are pertinent to the issues involved in providing background for this work and the alternative reading of the Song's imagery that I am proposing.

26   A recent exception would be the queer reading of the Song of Songs undertaken by Stephen D. Moore (2001), which does have an extended discussion of some of the Song's allegorical history.

27   It would be incorrect to imply that allegorical interpretation of Song of Songs ceased completely after this time. For modern allegories, see, for example, Stadelman 1992 and Robert and Tournay 1963. For discussion of the return to allegory in interpretation, see Fisch 1988 and also Moye 1990, who encourages readers to resume allegorical interpretation (for the Christian community), because it allows for further depth in the interpretive process,

of it would be unnecessary here,[28] but as far as the body imagery is concerned, it is useful to show some of the ways that it has been allegorized in the Song's history of interpretation. The variety of interpretations available in this corpus of literature is repeated in secular scholarship on the Song, and is of course reflected in the Song's wild images itself.

As one might expect with such a long history, allegories differ substantially in detail, and variety is affected as much by theological (Jewish or Christian) perspective as by historical context. A quick review of some of the key 'players' in the allegories is illustrative of some of this variety. The woman might represent, among others, Solomon's Egyptian wife and / or Pharaoh's daughter, Israel, Wisdom, the passive intellect, the Church, the Soul, or (the Virgin) Mary. The male lover in the book might signify Solomon, Yahweh, the Christian God, Christ, or the active intellect. Interpreters also posited that the whole 'story' in the Song of Songs reflects the journey of Israel from the Exodus to a future messianic event, or the mystical journey of the soul in its quest to be reunited with God.

The bodies of the lovers, referred to throughout the Song, add to the interpretive possibilities for the book a hundred-fold. When the lovers' bodies are treated in allegories, it is not so that commentary may be made on the human form, in romantic, sexual, or any other kind of context. In other words, their materiality is often denied as their various parts are enlisted in the service of the theological agenda that governs the allegory. This is as one might expect. It has partly to do with the fact that many allegorical readings of the Song are homiletic, and are not, as a few like Rashi's and Nicholas of Lyra's are, verse-by-verse commentaries on the Song.[29] It has also to do with the almost universal[30] intention on the part

---

which modern emphases on literal meaning cannot give. See also Murphy's ongoing discussion concerning the transition from historical-critical to literary methods of interpret-ation. Murphy has a definite sympathy for the Song's allegorical history (1981a, 1985, 1986).

28 See Marvin Pope's thorough discussion (1977: 89–229, *passim*). For medieval (Christian) allegorical interpretation, see esp. Astell 1990, Matter 1990, Turner 1995.

29 See Schwartz and Schwartz 1983 for Rashi's text and Turner 1995: 381–409 for a (partial) reproduction of Nicholas's work. It can also be mentioned that in Christian allegorical readings, the body imagery of the Song is frequently missed, since, owing to Origen's influence which persisted despite allegations of his heresy, allegories of the Song frequently did not proceed as far into the book as the fourth chapter, where the first concentrated images, or *wasfs*, are found.

30 Theodore of Mopsuestia (fourth century) should be mentioned as an exception. Boldly, he suggested that the Song was about human love. No copies of his work are extant, and it is known only from criticism.

of allegorical interpreters to de-eroticize the Song, at least as far as the human sexual element is concerned.[31]

The repudiation of the sexual body is of interest to modern commentary on the Song, which tends instead to emphasize the subject, even though its emphasis is still subject to its own kinds of restrictions or censoring. Origen's statement about the relation between spiritual maturity, the Song and sexual content influenced much of the Christian allegorical tradition around the book. He remarked of reading it:

> [I]f those whom we have called children were to come on these passages, it may be that they would derive neither profit nor much harm, either from reading the text itself, or from going through the necessary explanations. But if any man who lives only after the flesh should approach it, to such a one the reading of this Scripture will be the occasion of no small hazard and danger. For he, not knowing how to hear love's language in purity and with chaste ears, will twist the whole manner of his hearing of it away from the inner spiritual man and on to the outward and carnal; and it will be turned away from the spirit to the flesh, and will foster carnal desires in himself, and it will seem to be the Divine Scriptures that are thus urging and egging him on to fleshly lust. For this reason, therefore, I advise and counsel everyone who is not yet rid of the vexations of flesh and blood and has not yet ceased to feel the passion of his bodily nature, to refrain completely from reading this little book and the things that will be said about it. (1957: 22–3)

Similarly, whereas attitudes about the body in the history of Jewish interpretation are reputed to be positive and affirming of human sexuality, it has been observed that they are actually quite ambivalent. It is true, notes Howard Eilberg-Schwartz, that Judaism did not lean towards the asceticism and repudiation of the body enjoyed by Christians; it still, however, manifests a particular interest in the government of the body (1992: 20).[32] And this interest leaves the body as a site of conflict in both the biblical and rabbinic records (1992: 20).

Without attempting to give a full record of each of the allegorized bodies of the Song, it is useful to consider a few very brief examples in order to show how the lovers' bodies are de-eroticized, even fully

---

31   It is generally agreed that allegorists had an interest in de-eroticization, and this should not be confused with scholarly attempts to identify erotic tendencies in the Song, or in allegories (or allegorizers) of it. For the latter, see Turner 1995, for example, and more recently, Moore 2001.

32   It is not possible to enter into this interesting area at this juncture. Eilberg-Schwartz traces the matter of the governance of the body throughout a number of biblical texts in his article (see also Biale 1997: Ch. 1). For discussion on Jewish views of sexuality in Talmudic and Rabbinic exegesis, see Biale 1997, esp. Chs 2–3, and Boyarin 1993, esp. Chs 1 and 2. Boyarin's later work on the construction of masculinity and the manipulation of the body would also be important here (1997).

removed, from the text. In Origen's analysis, the breasts[33] of the man, referred to in Song 1.2, are meritorious because they conceal treasures of wisdom and knowledge; they are compared to wine, which refers to the 'ordinances and teachings which the Bride had been wont to receive through the Law and Prophets before the Bridegroom [Jesus] came' (1957: 65). In Bernard of Clairvaux's sermons, the flock of shorn ewes (the woman's teeth; 4.2) becomes a symbol for the penitent one who has been forgiven (1971:17 [3.2]). In Rashi's commentary, the woman's thighs (7.2) signify the drainage pits of the altar (Schwartz and Schwartz 1983: 131), and the man's stomach, described in 5.14 as ivory overlaid with sapphires, represents the contents of the book of Leviticus, 'smooth like a block of ivory, but ... arranged with many details' (Schwartz and Schwartz 1983: 119). By contrast, a reader such as Nicholas of Lyra seems almost bold in his interpretations. He understands the meeting of the woman's thighs as referring to the 'coming together of Jews and Gentiles in the one Church of Christ' (Turner 1995: 405).[34] At least, we can hypothesize, Nicholas was thinking about a vaguely 'sexual union', even if he was not spelling it out.[35]

The diversity in the kinds of meanings allegorists have given to the Song's body-parts is vast and, to modern eyes, quite fanciful. Because of its spiritual content and its appearance of far-fetchedness, allegory tends to be banished from modern critical discussions on the Song. Some even insist that without its influence, the Song may be liberated (Meyers 1993; Brenner 1993b).[36] Truly, examples such as the ones given above do appear

33 Origen reads with the Vulgate, which translates דדיך in 1.2 as *ubera tua* ('your breasts').

34 It need hardly be noted that part of the Christian allegorical project involved asserting of Christianity as the one true religion, over against, naturally, the 'Law' of the Old Testament. Christian allegory is also widely noted for its anti-Semitism. Nicholas of Lyra is an interesting exception, for, though he did have a share in the anti-Semitic ideology that existed at his time of writing, he did also acknowledge his relationship to the work of Rashi. See Turner 1995: 115–16, 387, Merrill 1978 and Cohen 1986 for the exegetical relationship between the two interpreters.

35 Moore agrees, at least in general reference to the sexual content in Nicholas's work, though his take on what kind of sexuality is expressed here is of course different (2001: 21ff.).

36 Meyers uses allegorical readings of the Song as a jumping-off point for her own work. She begins her article by asserting that the 'rise of critical biblical scholarship rescued the Song from the fanciful twists and turns of spiritualized biblical interpretation' (1993: 197–8). Despite its willingness to attend to the Song's erotic content and its presentation of the body, though, Meyers finds that most modern readings are 'as unwilling to explore the use of physical imagery as ... the traditional exegetes' (1993: 199). Brenner challenges modern allegorical interpretation on the grounds that it both obscures major interpretational issues in the Song, such as its plot (or lack thereof) and gynocentrism, and that it imposes a theocentrism which is not present (1993b: 265). She states, unequivocally, that the book shows not gender mutuality, but female superiority (1993b: 273). Allegory 'perverts' and 'subverts' this situation since it 'by definition requires a presentation of the god's partner [the

to impose certain restrictions upon the Song's images, which, because they remove the body from its material and erotic sphere is problematic, especially when one is trying to investigate the body in the Song. There does, however, appear to be a certain incongruity in the work of modern biblical critics that should be identified here. In many studies, it is evident that the images can be interpreted in a manner that is just as creative or fanciful as that in allegorical readings, as we will have cause to examine below. The incongruity here is that modern scholarship claims a certain objectivity (and therefore accuracy) in interpretation because it is explicitly not allegorical.[37] There is little or no acknowledgement that the sheer variety of approaches in recent work challenges scholars' claims concerning the veracity of their interpretations.

Modern Commentary on the waṣfs *and the 'Hermeneutic of Compliment'*
In post-(non-)allegorical readings of the Song, the body images are not suppressed – at least not to the extent that they were in the book's long history as allegory. Yet when the body is allowed into the interpretive arena, and, even more to the point, when an erotic context for it is acknowledged, the Song's wild images seem to wreak havoc on it. Many have noted the difficulty that the images have caused interpreters over the years. This difficulty is frequently mentioned – almost apologetically – in most introductory material on the Song. For example, Roland Murphy in the Introduction to his commentary writes, 'Nor has any other aspect of the poetry [than the 'wealth of metaphorical imagery'] given more

---

woman] as submissive and inferior' (1993b: 274). Brenner observes the 'double change of focus' in allegory, from female to male, and from human to divine, and concludes that 'the transmutation of gynocentrism into theocentrism in allegory passes through androcentrism' (1993b: 274).

37 I do not want to accuse scholarship on the Song of misapprehension or misconception, and my observation in this instance is certainly not targeted at the work of Brenner or Meyers, which I used as examples above. My intention is simply to point out that modern or secular scholarship, as it repudiates allegory, may not be able to be as unbiased or objective as it would hope. Thus, the perception that there is a 'primary level' of meaning and by extension a (one) correct way to interpret the images should be questioned. These are old issues for allegorists. One might mention particularly the debate that ensued in the twelfth century over various levels of textual meaning in Christian allegory and, in Jewish interpretation, the interest in *peshat* and *derash* which was brought to the fore by Rashi in the eleventh century. (As Loewe cautions, the terms *peshat* and *derash* should not be made identical with 'allegorical' and 'literal', as they are employed in Christian exegesis [1966: 159–60]. See also Gelles 1981: 24, 33.) In both cases, these interpreters were pushing for the inclusion (not the exclusive use of) a more literal or basic meaning for biblical texts. Rashi's and Nicholas of Lyra's exegetical strategies (addressed at length in Gelles 1971 and Turner 1995) make for an interesting study that can be viewed against the modern debate over literal versus figurative interpretation. There is not room to develop this here, but I have made a preliminary attempt to investigate some of these issues elsewhere (Black 2000b).

enjoyment or presented greater challenges to interpreters, ancient and modern alike' (1990: 70). Munro notes in her Introduction, 'When we begin to look at the imagery of the Song, we are immediately struck by its disconcerting nature' (1995: 16). Fox observes, 'The imagery of the Praise Songs in Canticles, particularly the Description Songs, has presented a perennial problem to interpreters. These passages seem to describe the lovers, but their imagery is unexpected, sometimes even disconcerting' (1985: 272).[38]

The readings considered in this chapter address the question, either explicitly or implicitly, of how the images describe the bodies, if at all. It is not the case that all of the readings here explicitly address this problem, but nevertheless, we can see that they all underwrite it. It is even present in the allegorical readings, in a reversed fashion. There, the problem also concerned the body in an erotic setting, but the question for allegorists was (if it was at all explicit), how can the imagery *not* reflect the body? Or, better stated, how can the body be kept out of the way so that higher, theological matters can be addressed? The imagery in the Song is so fluid that it lent itself well to this enterprise, as it does to the agenda of more modern readings.

I begin with a comment from Murphy's recent commentary on the Song (1990), which seems to highlight the problem of the imagery rather well.

> In most of the Song's metaphors and similes, the basis of comparison (*tertium comparationis*) between the subject or referent and the selected image seems straightforward but not necessarily or even typically one-dimensional. Color and form are involved in many instances. For example, the man likens the woman's lips to a 'scarlet thread' and her veiled cheeks to slices of pomegranate (4.3) ... Even in essentially representational comparisons, however, a poetic playfulness is often evident, nuancing realism with suggestions of voluptuousness, unusual vitality, gracefulness, and the like. (1990: 71)

Murphy explicates his point by speculating on the meaning of a few images. For example, the comparison of the woman's hair to a flock of goats depends on colour and texture or movement; the comparison of the woman to a mare among Pharaoh's chariots is playful and captures her 'exotic, ornamented splendor'; the description of the woman as a palm tree is 'intelligible enough as a representation of the woman's full-blossomed stateliness' and it also carries an 'explicitly erotic' sense when the man declares he will climb her and enjoy her fruits (Murphy 1990: 71–

---

38   Examples abound and continue to appear in recent commentaries: Bergant 2001: xv; Longman 2001: 14; Exum 2005a: 17.

2). The imagery, however, is not always as straightforward as these few examples. Murphy continues:

> In more than a few instances, however, the *tertium comparationis* is not immediately obvious or seems to involve likenesses that strike the literal-minded modern reader as comical, even grotesque. An often noted case is the overburdened metaphor for the woman's neck in 4.4 ... Such exaggerated simile fueled allegorical interpretation in earlier times. Some recent critics have supposed that the comparison means to portray not the visual appearance of the woman's garlanded neck but her proud and pure inaccessibility; others suggest that the physical proportions of the metaphor are mythological and hence only intelligible if the female in question is a goddess.
>
> Similitudes using natural imagery are not always transparently representational in meaning. The 'garden' and 'vineyard' metaphors for the woman (e.g., 4.12-16) convey a sense of her blossoming sexuality and, at least in part, are euphemistic. Comparison of the man to a 'gazelle or a young stag' suggests his youthful beauty and swiftness but also perhaps his untamed freedom as far as the woman is concerned (2.8-9; 8.14). (1990: 72–3)

In Murphy's view, there seem to be at least two levels of figurative language: one represents images that are more logical or 'representational',[39] while the second group is believed to defy literal reading, else they might be seen to engender comical or grotesque portraits of the woman. Then, if one wishes to count the natural images as a third case (though it is difficult to sustain this split), there is yet another group where the natural images do not seem directly to represent their referents. In his division of the images, Murphy's bias in interpretation is made quite clear. It is affected by two things: realism (or logic) and his expectations that the descriptions are meant to compliment and flatter, to show evidence of the adoration of the one who is creating the description.

It is evident, however, that Murphy's system is problematic. The images that he uses as examples for each of the three groups may actually be used in any one of them, and his evaluation is really quite idiosyncratic. For instance, the comparison of the cheeks to a pomegranate requires the hermeneutic key of colour (imposed by Murphy) to make it make sense or to be 'straightforward' for the cheeks. But suppose the basis of comparison were the seeds of the pomegranate, or its smell, or its roundness, or some other feature of the fruit. Different bases of comparison would, thus, naturally affect Murphy's interpretation. Equally, the spirit behind the interpretation is important to the result.

---

39   Murphy is following Soulen's (1993; orig. 1967) division of metaphors into presentational and representational images. See below.

These are all pleasant connotations (colour, smell, shape), but one could also entertain alternative bases of comparison, such as the spoilt nature of pomegranates, already split open on the ground because they are overripe. Similarly, the second group of metaphors that Murphy believes might lead to comical or grotesque readings cannot be definitely established. These images might also belong to the first group, depending on one's basis of comparison.

Murphy's attempt to manage the Song's imagery is not unique. Others will use different overall strategies of working with the imagery (different views on how the Song's figurative language works), but in the end they too seem to be motivated by an attempt to find behind the images a realistic and attractive woman.[40] As such, one might term the organizing principle behind Murphy's and the other readings considered here a hermeneutic of compliment.[41] By this phrase, I refer to the drive evident in readings to interpret the imagery in such a way that it gives a picture of the one it describes that is realistic, but – and here is the key – only if that realism is flattering and beautiful. Sometimes, it should be said, an interpreter will implicate the poet in the process and maintain that this is what the poet intends to convey. At other times, critics hold the discussion solely on the readerly plane: they make readerly observations as to how the imagery can and should be organized and understood. Be it poet or reader (authorial intent or reader response), the 'realistic and flattering picture' that readers end up with is similar in either case. Moreover, the picture does not necessarily have to refer to the physical body; it could also refer to the character or attitude of the one being described. We will see, therefore, that the readers I consider below manifest the hermeneutic of compliment in their own particular ways.

Romancing the Text

The readers considered here, Michael Goulder and Jill Munro, take the Song's context of love or erotic poetry as the key for their interpretations of the imagery. (Roland Boer might also be treated as part of this group, but I save his work for the excesses of imagery, examined later.) This is not remarkable in and of itself: commentators such as Pope (1977) and more recently Exum (2005a) interpret the text overtly from the same perspective. The difference is that Munro and Goulder emphasize this perspective and allow it to inform certain interpretive decisions that they

---

40   The image of the man seems less important. And, as we shall see, it is often dismissed as 'different' or 'odd' in comparison to the woman's.

41   The phrase is chosen in part as a response to Soulen's 'hermeneutic of realism' (1993), which is discussed below.

make; in the process they write with what almost appears to be a romantic inclination towards the text itself.[42] Naturally, each is quite different in his or her aims and results. Goulder views the Song as a marriage drama (complete with plot) and believes that the imagery reflects the precision and artifice of the poet. Munro, meanwhile, is interested in studying the imagery in its poetic context, without benefit of plot.

Munro's study of the Song's imagery aims not to 'get behind the text in order to interpret the imagery in light of a general theory', but to 'explore the way in which the images operate throughout the poem as metaphors for love' (1995: 16). Her aim to explicate the love theme of the poetry evinces a highly romanticized and idealistic reading of the book. Her translations of the imagery, for instance, are lyrical and romantic. Where possible, odd phrases have been translated in line with her reading agenda, as in 5.4 ('My beloved thrust his hand in through the keyhole and *my heart turned over* when he spoke') or 5.6 ('*I swooned* at his flight') (1995: 28, emphases added).[43] The subsequent explication of the body imagery is then equally idyllic and romantic, as in this introduction to the natural imagery:

> The fauna of the Song, like the flora, are highly varied. There are domestic animals, sheep and goats which are associated with a pastoral way of life. They are seen moving over the hillside in search of fresh pasture land and watercourses. There are also gazelles, hinds and young stags roaming around the open countryside according to season, animals associated with the hunt and with the royal park ... Some of these animals display particular characteristics which disclose something about the lovers and their relationship. In this respect they are a rich source of imagery for the descriptive songs. More often they add movement and vitality to the natural world in which the relationship grows, mirroring the lovers' struggles and their joys. (1995: 87)

---

42   I will have cause to address this issue further in the last chapter. My point is not meant to be disparaging; rather, it indicates something of the readerly 'affair' that some have had with the Song. To this end, I would also add Walsh to the discussion here (2000). She is not interested explicitly in the imagery (though she does make some comments about it: see, e.g. 2000: 65), but she does play on the enchantment and romantic or sexual allure of the text: 'You, reader, have just been tackled from behind by an enchanting friend. I speak from experience' (2000: 45). She claims the text quickly gets personal (2000: 45). Her reading is ultimately in the service of theology, however: she points out that we have to slow down to listen to the poetic images, to love, and finally, to God (2000: 65).

43   These are perfectly acceptable translations within the range of the Hebrew. My point is merely that Munro's word choice is poetic and romantic, seemingly designed to reflect the Song's context of love poetry.

More particular analysis of images reveals better examples of the author's perspective.[44] Her study of the comparison of eyes to doves, which exists in various locations in the Song, yields the following:

> Much more clear than the objective correspondence, however, which remains ambiguous, are the qualities of gentleness (Mt. 10.16), delicacy and liveliness which are common to tenor and to vehicle. It is these same qualities of vivacity and delicate beauty that are discovered in the man's eyes later on in the Song (5.12). The simile of 5.12 far exceeds in its detail the simple metaphor of 1.15. The use of the same basic imagery, however, discloses how very deeply the two protagonists love each other; they describe each other using the same language and hence convince the reader that they are not two but one. (1995: 90)

> The initial comparison of his eyes to doves in 5.12a takes on a life of its own in subsequent colons as the poet describes how these doves sit quietly in a pool of milky foam. The image is surely of a river in spate and of doves riding the foamy current. It is an image of serene steadiness and turbulent movement, describing both the steadiness and liveliness of his gaze. (1995: 90–91)

> Apart from its beauty and vivacity, the dove is also noticeable for its shyness (Jer. 48.28). It is this quality which is emphasized in 2.14 where the woman is compared to a dove hiding in a cleft of the rock. It is also evident in 4.1 where shyness and discretion add to her beauty ... Her inaccessibility, alluded to in 2.14, adds mystery and charm to her loveliness. (1995: 91)

I have quoted Munro at length on the eyes in order to highlight certain features of her reading. First, her interpretation of the Song's natural images seems to me to be pastoral and romanticized, as in the case of the doves in the river that exhibit both steadiness and turbulent movement (Munro expresses it much more appealingly than I have). Second, her analysis of what is evidence of love is based on omnipresent and somewhat random aspects of the images – in this case that they are shared by both lovers. Third, Munro's analysis often relies on modern stereotypes about romantic relationships and might be taken to reinforce these.[45] One might mention particularly here the shyness and passivity

44   Munro does point out that nature is not idealized in the Song, and cites the references to the foxes (2.15) and the lions and leopards of 4.8 (1995: 91). I would argue, however, that it is idealized in her reading of it.

45   One might add Exum's recent commentary (2005a) to the discussion here. I think particularly of her opposition of the man's and the woman's states of being, as 'awestruck' and 'lovesick', respectively (2005a: 15–16). The text may well support this opposition, in part, but Exum exacerbates it with her insistence that the man is anxious, threatened, and quite devastated by his lover's physical presence (2005a: 17, 21, 23 and *passim*), so much so that he describes her body in a piecemeal fashion so as to diffuse the threat. With such a reading I

(and inaccessibility – is she a tease?) of the woman. My observations are intended here not to criticize what is an insightful and very competent reading, but to illustrate the directions that might be pursued by a reading that appears to be guided by the hermeneutic of compliment.

There is yet another way to explore the Song's amatory context, which is to place special emphasis on its erotic meaning. Goulder's brief commentary on the Song (1986) sets out to do just that, addressing two basic suppositions about it. The first of these is that the Song has a 'sustained sequence of plot'. The second is that the author is an accurate observer of nature and the world around him (*sic*), and that he makes precise commentary on it. In the midst of tracing his plot and explicating the imagery, Goulder also insists that a 'right' reading of the imagery (not one that sees the images as 'woolly' or merely beautiful; 1986: 4, 6) acknowledges its primarily erotic content ('The plot I have described makes sense only as a love-story, and that of an erotic rather than a romantic kind'; 1986: 7).[46]

What, then, is Goulder's interpretive strategy? Again, it seems to be something along the lines of employing common sense, combined with the added interest in positing an intention and a logic for the author, whose hand Goulder can see behind the Song. A throwaway comment at the end of his introduction is telling. In responding to criticisms of Exum's work (1973), that it employed unnecessary sexual explicitness, Goulder concedes (with John Healey) that Exum may overdo the sexual euphemisms because of certain literary decisions, but that her suggestions are 'sometimes illuminating'. For Goulder, it comes to this: 'If they seem to be right, then this is what we are after' (Goulder 1986: 8). This is alarmingly imprecise for a reader who is demanding precision of a biblical author. Goulder's measuring-stick for the images becomes his own sense of what is allowable within his construction of the Song's 'plot' and its proposed author.

But let us take a closer look at the kinds of interpretive work on the imagery that Goulder proposes. In order to establish the author's precision in his development of the imagery, Goulder looks at two examples. The first is the comparison of the eyes to doves in 5.12, and the second is the description of מֵעָיו to a pillar of ivory in 5:14. In the first, after reviewing the interpretations of a few other readers (Gerleman, Delitzsch), Goulder points out that this particular instance of the doves

---

fear that we come close to modern stereotypes about women as passive (though Exum does of course acknowledge the active role the woman plays in pursuing her man), and their bodies as a source of danger or unease.

46   Goulder insists that his project is an historical one: 'It will be disappointing if the author turns out to be a licentious or pedestrian man' (1986: 8).

finds them bathing in milk. The unique feature of doves, he observes
further, is their fan-like tail, which flutters, as would eyes. He summarizes:

> Well, we have a saying, 'Any girl has but to flutter her eyes . . .'; and it is,
> I believe, common experience that movement of the eye-lashes is
> attractive to the opposite sex ... The doves (tails) are the eye-lids, the
> milk is the iris, and the bathing is the movement which one can see as a
> bird splashes water over itself with its tail. (1986: 5)

Goulder notes that his reading 'makes the poem more interesting', but
asks, 'is it right?' In order to answer his own question, he takes on a
tougher image, that of 5.14. Here, he must first decide to what מֵעָיו refers,
and once he has (euphemistically) decided it is a euphemism for the penis
('So I ask myself, is there a part of the male body, between the hands and
the legs, which is heavily veined, and which at all resembles a column of
ivory?'; 1986: 6), he draws an astounding conclusion: '[W]hat is a column
of ivory but a tusk? And to an enthusiastic bride, such as we have
portrayed in the Song, a tusk of ivory might seem a very potent image'
(1986: 6).[47]

Goulder thus works with the imagery until it fits his hermeneutical key.
As with Murphy and Munro, the descriptions must be both flattering and
realistic. Then, for Goulder, there is also the added interest in erotic
content. He summarizes his discussion on the Song's eroticism by
acknowledging that 'two swallows do not make a summer' (1986: 6), or, in
other words, that just because he has been able to read two images as
'precise', they may not all be so. His intent is to apply his criteria for
accuracy throughout the commentary, to test his hypothesis: 'If we *can*
make sense of the poem on the hypothesis of the author's accuracy, then
we should' (1986: 6). There is little means of evaluating Goulder's
interpretations, except on the same level – do we find them precise, or
believable? The strategy is in many senses incontrovertible (though not
without controversy, and it is here that ideological criticism becomes
useful): if Goulder wants to find sensible – and complimentary – images,
he will.

Reading in Context

Other readers solve the problem of the imagery for the Song's bodies by
locating textual or artistic parallels in the literature and art of ancient

---

47 Goulder's interest as manifested in the two texts just considered (5.12) turns out to
have quite a disturbing quality as well, on two counts. In the first instance, his reading of the
dove imagery operates on the stereotypical figure of woman-as-flirt, which he then applies to
the man. The second has the woman-as-flirt much more enthusiastically looking for sex,
which might be taken as a sign of her autonomy, were it not for the arguably violent sexual
image that Goulder inadvertently conjures up.

Near Eastern cultures. A number of works could be discussed here at length: Fox 1985; Gerleman 1965; Keel 1984, 1994; Müller 1984;[48] Pope 1977; Rabin 1975;[49] White 1978.[50] It will not be possible to look at them all in detail, at this point. Thus Fox and Pope constitute my primary texts for investigation, and I will make some brief remarks about Gerleman and Keel as a way of indicating some of the general issues in this interpretive trend.

Fox's work (1985) sets out to gain a richer understanding of the 'literary treatment of love in Egypt and Israel' (1985: xx). The Egyptian texts, moreover, provide a model for reading the biblical ones, and the similarities that can be located between the two justify a theory 'of at least indirect dependence' of the Song on the Egyptian texts (1985: xxiv). Fox traces this indirect dependence in a number of areas (themes, motifs), including the individual images of the Praise Songs (*wasfs*) of the Song.[51] In his commentary (which comprises one chapter in his book), for instance, he makes occasional use of Egyptian material to elucidate the Song. For instance, in the case of Song 4.3, he observes that Egyptian women used to paint their lips to make them look more prominent (1985: 130). The intention behind such observations is not to prove that Hebrew poets relied on Egypt as a prime source for their images (1985: 274; contra Gerleman). Rather, he perceives that Egyptian texts and art might be

48   Müller's work does not exactly belong with these others mentioned, because he is not interested in ancient Near Eastern parallels to the Song, but rather, attempts to elucidate the book's even older roots in archaic magic. For Müller, the metaphorical language of the Song has an aesthetic meaning that serves to link the human condition to the natural world. Metaphorical speech and action in the Song function analagously to magic in that both depend on an extralinguistic reality. In the Song's language, Müller identifies an ambiguity or a lack of seriousness. Through its aesthetic play, though, the Song recovers true religiosity (1984: 47–8).

49   Rabin is also an odd fit in this group. He believes that the Song exhibits the influence of Tamil poetry, particularly in various themes (longing for the loved one, the woman as primary speaker, natural imagery to exhibit emotions).

50   White's work undertakes a literary analysis of Egyptian love poetry and the Song of Songs in order to show that the latter is dependent on the former. The investigation of both literatures is aimed at understanding an ancient view of love. Parallels between Egyptian literature and the Song are discussed in Ch. 4 (1978: 127–59). These include the designation of the woman as 'sister', dialogue of the lovers, expressions of mutuality and uniqueness; and various topoi such as the lovers' friends and enemies, plants and animals, lovesickness, presence and absence of the lovers and physical expressions of love (seeing, hearing, touching and smelling/tasting). The commentaries of Rudolph (1962) and Würthwein (1969) should also be mentioned for their recognition of parallels in the Song with Egyptian poetry.

51   The use of Egyptian texts in this manner is interesting, since Fox also concedes that there are only two Egyptian love songs in which the theme 'praise of the beloved' is evident (1985: 269–70). In a few others, he identifies parodies of it. Nevertheless, if Egyptian texts are going to be relied upon as a key to the interpretation of the Song's images, one might expect that descriptions of this kind were more easily located in the Egyptian corpus.

viewed as a possible source of influence, since the Song seems to reflect the same standards and ideals of beauty as the Egyptian texts.

Fox also makes comments on his strategy for reading the imagery. He cautions against literalistic interpretations of the Song's *wasfs*, saying they are 'foreign to the spirit of the poem'. He continues, 'Not only does the imagery convey little in the way of specific sensory information; it often actually frustrates transference of prominent physical attributes from image to referent' (1985: 273). If, for example, one takes the comparison of the 'girl's' nose to a tower literally, Fox notes that it is 'hyperbolic to the point of being grotesque' (1985: 273). Instead, (contra Gerleman and Soulen, whose work I consider below), he maintains that the key is in recognizing the 'sensory, objective feature' that the images have in common with their referents (1985: 275). For Fox, 'objective' refers to the possibility of verification of the feature (the basis of comparison) in image and referent by another observer (1985: 275 n. 9).[52] These are comparisons, moreover, not statements of attitude (1985: 275–6). For example, the neck is like a tower because of its length, the teeth are like sheep because of their whiteness, and so on (1985: 275).[53]

But this 'objective' resemblance is not all that one needs: Fox acknowledges that the role of the resemblance is to bridge the gap between image and referent. The rest is up to the reader, who must then supply the explanation. Moreover, the issue gets more complicated in that these are not, he thinks, *descriptive* metaphors; they do not exist to provide a literal picture of the woman (even though Fox's interpretations frequently endeavour to provide one). Instead, the objective sensory resemblance exists to make the comparison possible. Fox's explanation seems roundabout. What he seems to be saying is that the comparison relies just as much on the differences between image and referent as it does on the similarities. So the sensory resemblance (also understood as the basis of comparison, e.g. the whiteness of sheep as compared with teeth) makes a bridge between two distinct items (image and referent), showing that they are at once similar and incongruous. The maintenance of the incongruity is important because the shock 'produces psychological arousal, a necessary component of aesthetic pleasure' (1985: 276). He then recommends evaluation of metaphors (and similes) not to locate their meaning definitively, but to see how they work, and what is the 'extent of

---

52   '"Subjective" in this context means that the congruity between image and referent resides in the speaker's attitude toward both; such as qualities of gentleness, nobility, and preciousness' (Fox 1985: 275 n. 9).

53   Fox's reading does appear inconsistent at times, however, because the Song will not provide the uniformity he needs to maintain it. For example, in this introductory section, he notes, 'It is two gazelles, and not one or three, to which her breasts are compared' (1985: 275). But in commenting on 7.8-9, he is silent on the comparison of the breasts to clusters of dates and grapes. It is left to Pope to point out the woman's polymasty (Pope 1977: 634).

their representational force' (1985: 277). An example: 'The relevant similarities between the belly and a heap of wheat, for example, do not include the size of the heap, nor is the movement of the sheep meaningful in the connection between the sheep and the girl's teeth' (1985: 277).

Like Murphy and Munro, then, Fox intends to locate something in the imagery that is realistic, that might describe a real person and that seems logical and complimentary. Though his explanation may appear more involved, his strategy is essentially the same as I have explicated above. He has to admit that 'it is often difficult to determine just what does belong to the sensory nexus' (1985: 277). Here is the key:

> In principle we should beware of attributing to the image qualities not in harmony with the ideal of beauty suggested elsewhere in the Song or with the general atmosphere that the imagery creates. There is no objective way of applying this principle; only the reader's aesthetic sensitivity can decide the pertinence of this or that association (1985: 277).

Another way of accommodating the Song's odd imagery for the body is advocated by Pope in his commentary (1977). Pope never explicitly (to my knowledge) presents his preferred interpretive schema in one place in his commentary; one must instead gather clues from his discussion of the descriptions and from a few introductory remarks. Fortunately, however, he does summarize his view elsewhere (1988), and it is from this that I summarize his argument.

The key to the imagery is for Pope 'the matter of the limits of hyperbole as applied to mere mortals' (1988: 322). He observes that for ages interpreters have been able to recognize in the description of the man (5.10-16) a superhuman form, representing either the God of Israel or Christ. The figures of the woman in the Song, however, have been hidden by a rather glaring blind-spot (1988: 322). For Pope, the key signals are the neck (1977: 194, 465; 1988: 322, 326) and nose (1977: 194, 627; 1988: 322, 326). Of the latter, he says:

> The supposition that a big nose was considered beautiful can hardly be extended to include a human nose of the magnitude of Mount Hermon. Any anthropoid feature grossly out of proportion with other parts, particularly a nose, would be grotesque ... Some exaggeration is to be expected and tolerated in praise of one's ladylove, but there are limits, as Shakespeare reminded his fellow poets in Sonnet 129. It is remarkable that those who perceived that the Bridegroom of the Canticle was more than mere mortal could not perceive that the Bride is far more impressive ... If the Lady of the Canticle is the Great Goddess of Love and War, of Life and Death, equal and even superior to her divine consort, we can get over her monumental nose more easily than if she is taken to be a normal-sized human being. (1988: 322-3)

'The conclusion that [the woman] is superhuman is', as Pope says, 'as obvious as the nose on one's face' (1988: 323).

Pope intersperses his commentary with allusions to the great goddess, usually with reference to images that pertain to size. The nose is directly in proportion to the head, which is likened to Carmel (1977: 194), and in this image Pope also finds promise for his theory. The same can be said for the woman's tree-like stature in 7.8 (1977: 633).[54] Her multiple breasts (7.8) remind Pope of the polymastic goddess Artemis of Ephesus (1977: 634). Other features, such as her name, also suggest superhumanity for Pope. He finds the allusion to peace in the name 'Shulammite' apropos to the volatile nature of the 'Virgin goddess of Love and War' (Anat), notably that 'it may suggest violent modes of pacification, either marital or venereal, or both' (1977: 600). The many war images associated with the body, such as the odd phrase אימה כנדגלות (6.4, 10) and מחלת המחנים (7.1) are also suggestive for Pope (1977: 562, 606, 607).

As to the woman's identity, Pope finds that she is reminiscent of many of the great goddesses, 'Inanna, Ishtar, Anat, Athena, and the black and beautiful, tender and violent, licentious yet pure, virgin mother Kali of India' (1988: 324). Despite the fact that he is clearly most impressed by the latter, Pope seems to favour Anat as the likely candidate (1988: 324; 1977: *passim*). But Pope does not wish to limit her identity in this way. In fact, in this goddess figure in the Song, he finds fuel to feed the fires of the depatriarchalization of theology (1988: 326). The 'Lady of the Canticle' may be the 'Shekinah, Virgin Bride, Sorrowing Mother, Wisdom personified as the principle of creation, or whatever titles she may have' (1988: 326).[55]

Pope's goddess theory is not extensively developed and is, as I noted above, chiefly a response to the size-related incongruities of the female form.[56] As such, it is not satisfactory because it does not address the (potential) oddities of the other images, which seem to be interpreted by Pope as referring to a human – not divine – female. There is also another problem: in his article (1988), he bases his reasoning for the goddess theory on readings of the masculine imagery in 5.10-16, which has been interpreted by many over the years as a reference to the divine body.

---

54 Proportion is an important theme in Pope's argument. He mentions the *Shi'ur Qomah* with respect to the woman's stature (קומה) and her head and nose. In the *Shi'ur Qomah* the body of God is measured out in proportion to the human form (1977: 633; 1988: 323).

55 Pope adds that 'those who have difficulty, emotional or rational, with this eminently logical step can solve the problems with far less contortion than has accompanied efforts to identify the Bride as Israel, the church, Wisdom personified, the individual soul, or a rustic shepherd lass' (1988: 326).

56 The ancient Near Eastern parallels are explicated in a detailed manner. My comment refers to the fact that Pope does not apply the theory to the full body picture, but only to those specific images that appear (to him) to be the most difficult.

Pope's logic for the female body is thus based on allegorical readings of the male body, which would also, in my view, need to be justified before being used as a reliable basis for interpretation. His interpretation of the female form is not, moreover, allegorical (though he does suggest some theological implications for it in the conclusion of the article; 1988: 326), which means that there is a significant discrepancy in his approach for the images, and perhaps, the resulting views of each of the lovers' bodies.

The work of two other authors may be mentioned briefly here: Gerleman's commentary (1965)[57] and Keel's initial study of metaphor in the Song (1984), followed by his own commentary, which reuses much of this earlier material (1994). As has already been mentioned in discussion of Fox's work, Gerleman's commentary is noteworthy for his proposal that the body imagery in the Song is influenced by Egyptian statuary. For Gerleman, the Song is the product of a Solomonic *Aufklärung* that would have been influenced by the dissemination of art and literature from Egypt. In some of the Song's repertoire of images (e.g. the dove-like eyes; 1965: 71), in the artistic materials used such as colour (red and white; 5.10) or gold and gemstones, and in the physical structures of the images (e.g. the 'statue' in 5.10-16), Gerleman finds the influence of Egypt's well-developed artistic culture (1965: 69; see 70–71 for more examples).

Many do not find Gerleman's proposal convincing. Fox, for instance, points out that Egyptian poets did not themselves use Egyptian art to inspire their descriptions of the body (1985: 274). Moreover, those descriptions that are used in the Song do not actually appear in Egyptian statuary (except through Gerleman's questionable interpretations, e.g. almond-shaped eyes remind him of doves). Murphy questions Gerleman's reconstruction of the transmission of Egyptian culture throughout Syria–Palestine (1990: 43). Soulen points out the discrepancy between Gerleman's recognition of the evocative nature of the poetry and his insistence that it be viewed as dependent on Egyptian art for its inspiration (1993: 219). More convincing, at least to Murphy (1990: 43 n. 195), is the work of Keel, who displays the 'value of Egyptian and other ancient Near Eastern art for illustration of many of the Song's images' (Murphy 1990: 43 n. 195). Keel's first work is a study of the metaphorical technique of the Song, which consists of a discussion of the influence of various ancient Near Eastern materials on its images and a discussion in the second half of various aspects, complete with numerous pictorial examples from art.

Two issues in Keel's works should be mentioned here. One is that despite recognizing the usefulness of Egyptian materials, Keel insists that a Palestinian provenance for the Song's images can be recognized and

---

57   Before writing his commentary, Gerleman published an article on the Song's imagery (1962). This work is used and expanded on in Gerleman's commentary (1965: 65–72).

should be the first point of enquiry in investigating the imagery. He advocates a system of interpretation that looks to the Song, then the greater context of the Hebrew Bible in order to contextualize the imagery. Then, failing any insight from these sources, he suggests that the wider cultural context of the biblical material (i.e. its ancient Near Eastern influence and even beyond) be consulted. The second issue is that he argues that interpretation of imagery must emphasize not a formal or physical relationship between image and referent (e.g. necks are like towers [Song 4.4] because both are long), but must look instead to their dynamic and functional qualities (1984: 27), or their colour and values. To take again the example of the neck, Keel understands this as the pride of the woman (representing an 'old proud dynasty'; 1994: 147; see also 1984: 38) and not a physical description of her body. In sum, we can see that Keel's inclusion of bases of comparison such as values, colour and function, in addition to form, serve to broaden the interpretive possibilities for the imagery. In a like manner, the widening of the cultural contexts that may be legitimately considered to elucidate the Song's images also expands interpretive options.

'Evocative' Reading

For other readers, it is not parallel ancient Near Eastern cultural contexts or the Song's eroticism that aid in addressing the problem of the imagery in the Song. Rather, it is the manner of reading that is important. This marks an important shift from the work that has been considered so far, and it is a shift that opens up the interpretive possibilities for the images even more. Soulen, whose work has been highly influential, advocates a reading strategy that acknowledges the power of the imagery to evoke the feelings of the lover (or, at least, the poet's artful representation of these feelings), over against a desire to represent his lover's body. Marcia Falk's work is very much a critical response to Soulen's, though it does depart from it in its preference for the role of the reader (whom Soulen belatedly mentions) over the author (whom Soulen emphasizes).

Soulen's starting-point is the biblical realism or literalism of readers who insist on seeing in the Song a concrete description of the body. He engages with the work of Leroy Waterman, who, Soulen observes, employs a 'realism that contorted the object of comparison (the maiden) into grotesque and comic proportions'.[58] Soulen notes that '[f]rom the perspective of realism, Waterman was forced by his own logic to conclude

---

58   Soulen 1993: 216. Soulen's article was originally published in 1967 (*JBL* 86: 183–90), and was reprinted in 1993. I refer to the latter.

that the purpose of the Song was to humiliate Solomon as one rebuffed by a humble if not downright ugly girl from the north' (1993: 216).[59]

In response to what Soulen takes as the ridiculous readings of Waterman, he returns to the work of Gerleman and advocates a variation of his interpretive strategy, which was elaborated thus:

> Die Sehweise ist nicht konkret-anschaulich, sondern phantasievoll-anschaulich. Der Reichtum an schlagenden Bildern und Vergleichen scheint nicht in erster Linie dazu zu dienen, eine sinnliche Vorstellung zu konkretisieren, sondern will eher die Gefühls- und Stimmungswirkung steigern. Die Gegenstands-bezogenheit, die in der Körperbeschreibungen sehr marktant ist, tritt in den Landschaftsschilderungen weniger klar hervor. Im Mittelpunkt steht oft nicht ein Zustand, sondern ein Vorgang, das Aufblühen der Natur und die Freude darüber. Die Regenzeit ist vorüber, dir Blumen erscheinen, die Turteltaube singt, die Herden weiden. Von Umriß und Kontur ist hier nur wenig zu finden. Alles ist Bewegung und dynamisches Geschehen angelegt. (Gerleman 1965: 64)[60]

In line with Gerleman's reasoning (but, notably, in disagreement with his observation of Egyptian statuary parallels, which, as Soulen notes, is based on a hermeneutic of realism), Soulen advocates a more 'appropriate hermeneutical principle' (1993: 219):

> It is suggested that Gerleman is hermeneutically correct in so far as he sees the purpose of the *wasf* as presentational rather than representational. Its purpose is not to provide a parallel visual appearance, or, as we shall see, primarily to describe feminine or masculine qualities metaphorically. The *tertium comparationis* must be seen instead in the feelings and sense experiences of the poet himself who then uses vivid and familiar imagery to present to his hearers knowledge of those feelings in the form of art. (1993: 219–20)

---

59   Both Waterman and Soulen appear to be unaware of the woman's humiliation in such a scenario. Soulen's androcentric bias (and sexism) is picked up by Falk (see below).

60   Soulen has summarized Gerleman's argument as follows:

> He notes that the poems are the products of emotion, a joyous capitulation to the senses. They do not examine the beloved critically; they simply feast on what is seen. Objects are viewed fancifully, not concretely. The striking figures, he suggests, are not used to make more tangible a mental impression, but are designed to increase the Song's effect on the hearer's mind and emotions. He adds further, 'Here there is very little to do with outline and contour. Everything pertains to movements and dynamic events'. (Soulen 1993: 217–18)

He continues:

> What is suggested here then is that that interpretation is most correct
> which sees the imagery of the *wasf* as a means of arousing emotions
> consonant with those experienced by the suitor as he beholds the
> fullness of his beloved's attributes (or so the maiden as she speaks of her
> beloved in 5.10-16). Just as the sensual experiences of love, beauty, and
> joy are vivid but ineffable, so the description which centers in and seeks
> to convey these very subjective feelings must for that reason be
> unanalytical and imprecise.[61]
>
> ...
>
> The writer is not concerned that his hearers be able to retell in
> descriptive language the particular qualities or appearance of the
> woman described; he is much more interested that they share his joy,
> awe and delight.[62]

Soulen does not, unfortunately, analyse the Song's images in any detail
according to his proposed hermeneutic (see also Falk 1982: 83). He does
offer a brief whiff of what such a reading might involve, however. In the
case of 4.1, the comparison of the woman's hair to a flock of goats
descending down Mount Gilead, he notes, '[T]he point of comparison ...
has nothing to do with Egyptian sculpture, color, motion, or with the
quality of either the hair or the flock; it lies simply in the emotional
congruity existing between two beautiful yet otherwise disparate sights.'
Moreover, these kinds of images, many of which appeal to sight, fragrance
and hearing, 'titillate the sense, not the capacity to reason. Each in its own
way triggers the imagination, each is a Pavlovian bell' (1993: 223).

While there seems to be some merit in refusing to impose demands for
precision from these metaphors, Soulen's proposal does appear to suffer
from a few drawbacks. First, in insisting that images are evocative rather
than representative, Soulen denies the visual applications for the
metaphors, and in fact rejects the possibility that any visual image is
conveyed at all by the lover. As Fox notes, Soulen 'slights the
representational qualities of the metaphors', neglecting the itemization
of the body-parts and the 'sensory, objective feature' that the images have

---

61 Soulen's support for his reading is taken from P. Wheelwright's differentiation
between *epiphor* and *diaphor* (*Metaphor and Reality*, Bloomington, IN: Indiana University
Press, 1967). See Soulen 1993: 222 n. 2 for details.

62 Soulen 1993: 222–3. See also Cook 1968: 122:

> The delight the lovers take in eulogizing each other emerges in the eloquence of
> their enriched articulations. A speaker amplifies these in rapid succession,
> demonstrating the emotion behind each word through the intensity of associative-
> ness in the word chosen, in the closeness of one rich word to another. Even the far-
> fetchedness of many metaphors testifies to the speaker's leap into an expression as
> extravagant as the transport of which the words alone tell us. Sometimes the
> excitement will bring the metaphor trailing along behind in a breathless confusion.

in common with them.[63] Second, in so doing, Soulen also obfuscates the variety and the contours of the images. In the process of reading, the range of readings that the images are able to sustain – bizarre and traditional – is cut off. Third, Soulen's reading relies on a (pre-decided) understanding of what emotions the poet intends to convey in the images (i.e. loving, exuberant, joyful, sensuous, delightful, and so on).[64] He fails to notice this about his proposed hermeneutic, and also fails to observe the range of interpretation that is implicit in it – that the notion of 'emotional congruity' between images and their referents is an uncontained hermeneutical principle. He avers that this way of reading should be 'unanalytical and imprecise', yet makes demands on the images that are just as precise, just as analysed, though not according to expectations of the woman's visual appearance. Finally, then, there must also be a 'realism' inherent in Soulen's hermeneutic, only it is 'emotional' or 'evocative' rather than visual. Despite his efforts to alter the demands readers make on the images, Soulen's reading still corresponds to the hermeneutic of compliment I have been identifying so far. In this case, however, the lines are blurred a little. The 'picture' of the woman is not to be visual but emotional. It is still, nevertheless, flattering and complimentary.

Similar to Soulen's reading strategy, but also critical of it, is Falk's understanding of the Song's figurative language. Falk believes the *wasfs* to be an 'embarrassment' to the academic community (1982: 80), and argues that 'the flaw is not in our text but in the failure of scholars to appreciate the very essence of metaphor at the core of great poetry from many different eras and cultures' (1993: 227–8). This failure, she believes, is also Soulen's, though she does agree with his rejection of literalistic interpretation (where literalism 'mean[s] the need to find between tenor and vehicle

---

63   Fox explains:

> First of all, the imagery of the *wasfs* takes the *form* of an itemized physical description, with one-to-one correspondence between the images and parts of the body (your eyes are like *X*, your cheeks are like *Y*, etc.), as if the poet were seeking to be analytical and precise. The poet does not merely heap up lovely images (or images of lovely things) to overwhelm us with imagined sense-impressions, but rather seeks a particular image for each part of the body and organizes these images in an itemized list. The one-to-one correspondences between images and parts of the body make us feel that some quality peculiar to each part, and not just a general feeling of affection, calls forth these images. Second, the images have some sensory, objective feature in common with their referents, such as the length of the neck, suggested by the tower, or the whiteness of the teeth, indicated by the washed sheep. Images are selected to match the specific item on which they are predicated. (1985: 273)

64   This is clear from his repudiation of Waterman's reading, for instance. Whatever the images evoke, they do not convey the poet's ridicule or discomfort, say, in presenting a 'comical or grotesque' picture of the beloved.

a one-to-one correspondence in all details'; 1993: 228). In Falk's view, Soulen fails to address how poetry works, '*how* emotions are aroused in the reader – how ... the ineffable ideal is conveyed through words. In reducing the imagery in the *wasfs* to vague evocations of ineffable feelings, Soulen deprives the relationship between tenor and vehicle of meaning' (Falk 1982: 83). In Soulen's strategy, Falk observes that there is no way to evaluate good and bad metaphorical technique, and, moreover, that a situation exists where any metaphor could be used describe any referent (see comments by Fox, above).

Convinced that the Song is 'good poetry', and, furthermore, that the 'sophisticated' poetic sensibility of the metaphors can be 'made accessible through critical analysis', Falk instead proposes (nonliteralistic) 'inter-pretative visualization' as an exegetical strategy (1982: 83). It lies somewhere between literal interpretation, and that which merely sees the image as evocative of emotion (so Soulen). This method consists of 'taking the right focus or perspective, making explicit the implicit context, filling in the unverbalized details' (1993: 229).[65] Interestingly, however, the strategy that Falk advocates seems as imprecise as Soulen's evocative reading. The notion of filling in unverbalized details is, after all, highly subjective, and must rely on whatever a reader feels a poem is trying to convey. At this point, 'critical analysis' seems somewhat optimistic.[66]

Like Soulen, Falk does not analyse many of the images, though fortunately she does give us a few examples:

> Take the image that has so perturbed the scholars: one can easily picture hair to be like goats on a mountainside by viewing the scene from a distance. From afar, the sight of goats winding down the slopes of the Israeli countryside is striking; the dark animals weave a graceful pattern

---

65 Elliott observes that 'the problem with Falk's insistence on the concrete nature of biblical images is that in such analysis the beauty gets lost in a mire of speculation which is at best bathetic at and worst uninteresting' (1994: 143). It seems to me, however, that this is not an entirely fair evaluation: Falk's attention to detail in her translation implies that she is aware of this issue.

66 One might mention two recent commentaries at this juncture. Dianne Bergant (2001), clearly influenced by the propositions of Soulen and Falk, advocates a 'both/and' solution, observing that metaphorical language can be representational and presentational. By the latter, she refers to the creation of meaning 'by juxtaposition rather than by comparison'. She notes, '[i]n this case, the association of ideas is based on emotional response rather than physical similarity. Here the poet is more intent on reproducing the emotional reaction to the charms of the woman rather than representing her physical beauty itself' (2001: xiv). Similarly, Exum (2005a) urges that both Soulen and Falk, as well as Fox, all have considerable points to make: all are right, in some fashion. That is, there is authorial emotion conveyed in the descriptions *and* there is a one-to-one correspondence between image and referent. In all, she avers that there is not one correct way to approach the images (2005a: 19), though naturally, because of the conventions of the commentary genre, she does come to rest on a singular interpretation for most images.

against the paler background of the hills, suggesting dark waves of hair falling down a woman's back. Similarly, a herd of sheep, emerging fresh from the water, provides an ingenious metaphor when seen at a distance: the paired, white animals suggest twin rows of white teeth ... With probing, even the most abstruse images in the *wasfs* open up to visualization. Take, for example, the forehead behind the veil, which is compared to a slice of pomegranate. It is puzzling only at first; after reflecting on it with the mind's eye, we see a gleam of red seeds through a net of white membrane. Might this not be like ruddy skin glimpsed through a mesh of white veil? (1982: 84)

In these, we find the realism to which Soulen has objected, and, not surprisingly, the same hermeneutic as I have observed in other commentators above. Falk works with the images like many others ('interpretive visualization' or no), so that they may become logical and complimentary descriptions of the loved one. That is to say, how does one go about examining with the mind's eye? And what would Falk propose if one reader's mind's eye were not visually corrected by the same lenses as hers?

Another interesting feature of Falk's strategy comes out in other examples she gives, not here in her discussion of the *wasfs*, but in her own translation of the Song. Of her method in translation, she notes:

I sometimes suggested vantage points or settings so that modern English readers would see in it what the original audience might have seen ... For the same reason, I often eliminated proper place names and substituted descriptions, as here in 'the slopes' for 'Mount Gilead' ... When an image was not primarily visual, I tried to indicate its specific sensory appeal, as in 'Lips like lilies, sweet / And wet with dew'. Occasionally, to keep a metaphor from sounding hackneyed, I introduced a new detail, as in 'Hair in waves of black / Like wings of ravens' ... My goal was to let the images be vivid rather than puzzling pictures of a foreign but accessible culture, in the hopes that the imagery of the Song might eventually be demystified for both scholarly and general audiences. (1982: 84–5)

From this, it is apparent that Falk is willing to take many more liberties with the Song's text than she previously advocated. Sometimes, in fact, the MT is unrecognizable in her translation.[67] Of what value are the Song's 'sophisticated poetic sensibilities' if they are so tampered with that they cease to be themselves? Surely, at this point, we reach an impasse and must look for other strategies of reading.

---

67 Daphne Merkin, ever turning the creative phrase, agrees, noting that Falk sometimes distorts the text beyond recognition in her translations. She observes, 'there is for instance the implausible opening line of stanza 13 as Falk renders it – "At night in bed, I want him" – which suggests the zipless fuck was invented way before Erica Jong came along to coin the phrase' (1994: 241).

Soulen and Falk, it must be noted, are not actually that far apart from each other in their methods of interpretation. It would seem that both are calling the same thing (the leap between referent and image or tenor and vehicle) by different names. For, what is Falk's attempt to fill in 'unverbalized details' through looking in with the mind's eye but a nod to Soulen's 'event of language', to 'what happens to the reader' (Soulen 1993: 223)? It would appear that she is relying on what the imagery evokes, just as Soulen does, only she is concerned with the visual appearance of the body and she actually restates the comparison in some of her translations to make them clearer. Falk, in fact, might also be criticized for obscuring the jump between image and referent in her efforts to over-explain the process.

Falk is not finished with Soulen yet, however, for there is another, thornier, issue that his reading raises, which I have touched on above. Falk heavily criticizes Soulen as an example of the 'sexism' of modern literary interpretations of the *wasfs* in the Song. On the *wasf* in 5.10-16, which uniquely is spoken by the woman to describe the man, Soulen concludes that the 'poetic imagination' in this text is 'less sensuous and imaginative than in the *wasfs* of chapters 4 and 7. This is due in part to the limited subject matter and may even be due to the difference in erotic imagination between poet and poetess' (Soulen 1993: 216 n. 1). Falk disagrees:

> Soulen's evaluation ... perhaps derives from a preconception that the description of a man's body, as opposed to a woman's, is necessarily 'limited subject matter'. Indeed, such a preconception is not surprising in a culture where men are taught to believe that exaltation of male beauty is frivolous or, worse, embarrassing. (1982: 85)

Falk further exposes a double prejudice in Soulen's statement: by positing a poetess as the author of this particular *wasf*, he contradicts his assumption that the author of the Song of Songs is male. Falk calls this naïve, and accuses Soulen of dismissing the *wasf* as inferior, once its 'poetess' has been identified (1982: 85).

Falk's allegations against Soulen with reference to 5.10-16 appear to be quite justified.[68] His work is little able to answer her charges, since his treatment of this text and his discussion of the Pavlovian-bell-like nature of the images goes no further than what she has quoted. Soulen, however, is right to notice that there is something 'different' about the *wasf* in 5.10-16. Though Falk was quick to assert against Soulen that the image in 5.10-

---

68   To be fair to Soulen, one could interpret his words as a simple comparison between *this* poet and *this* poetess. However, other issues throughout the article, such as his obvious bias towards male readers, his contradiction regarding authorship (noted by Falk), and his insistence on calling the woman 'the maiden', suggest to me that he is unaware of or uninterested in gender-related issues in his interpretation.

16 was just as sensual as the others, Brenner (and others) have noted the static or artificial nature of this *wasf*: the lover is better viewed as a statue than as flesh and blood. Brenner points out that the description of the male lover in this text does more in the service of modesty and restraint that it does for actual description of the lover and sensual expression (1993a: 243). So, there is a difference here, as Soulen rightly observed (but wrongly dismissed), and it is important because its subject matter is the depiction of the male lover, and male sexuality. I shall take up these issues in my own reading of the images, below.

Body Imagery and Gender Criticism

Soulen's and Falk's disagreement over the image of the male lover in 5.10-16 raises another matter with respect to the body imagery in the Song. In the book, the female body is depicted and described much more frequently than the male body. As Soulen correctly noted, there is but one descriptive poem of the man's form, along with a few stylized, brief images scattered throughout the book (e.g. 1.13; 2.8-9). Such an imbalance should raise the interest of feminist critics of the Song. To date, however, though feminist / gender-critical interest in the Song is becoming more prominent, interest in the body images has by and large been neglected, with but a few exceptions: Brenner (1993a, 1993c) and Meyers (1993).[69]

This neglect is, moreover, more troubling than I have painted it. The omission of critical examination of the body imagery in feminist enquiry is of grave consequence to feminist readings of the Song. As it stands, feminist criticism on the book is largely positive, celebrating the autonomy (physical, sexual, verbal) that the woman in it seems to have. In fact, many perceive her to be 'more equal' than the man, in that it is her voice and her desire that predominates.[70] The thorny issue, as I see it, resides in the fact that despite eagerly observing that the woman speaks more often than her lover (and finding this to be a sign of her equality or even superiority), feminist critics have neglected to notice that in the relatively fewer instances where the man speaks, much of this space is devoted to itemizing and objectifying the female body, for his (and a presumed male audience's)[71] consumption. Furthermore, as we shall see, this objectification of the female form is potentially ridiculous and unflattering. If this is the case, then it stands to reason that the body

---

69   Meyers 1993 is a reprint of an article which appeared in 1986.

70   There is not space to give a full account of this issue here. See, for example, Brenner 1989: 90; 1993c: 28–9; Meyers 1993: 208, 211; Pardes 1992: 118–19, 128 (with some reservations); Trible 1978: 161; van Dijk-Hemmes 1993: 169–70; Weems 1992: 160.

71   It has been suggested, though, that the Song was written by women and is therefore for women. See especially Bekkenkamp and van Dijk 1993; Goitein 1993; and Brenner and van Dijk-Hemmes 1993: 71–82.

imagery might be a significant issue for the matters of gender construction
and gender equality in the Song of Songs. Brenner has already noted the
potential of the imagery for feminist enquiry:

> [T]he subject [the *wasf*] begs for feminist readings, for females are either
> objectified in the *wasfs* of the SoS (chs 4, 7), or are the speakers who
> objectify the male figure referred to (as in ch. 5). The genre thus affords
> the opportunity for discussing matters of form, author's intent, reader's
> involvement, points of view, imagery, gender differentials, authorship,
> and so forth. (1993c: 35–6)

The two feminist scholars who have written specifically on the imagery
in the Song, Brenner and Meyers, both contextualize their work within the
wasf discourse and interpret the imagery positively (ultimately). In
addition to seeing what is their specific interest in the body images, it
will also be important to look at how these readers respond to the image
of the woman they create and how or if their readings serve their feminist
aims. This subject does take us further afield from the agendum I have
been pursuing so far in this chapter, and it might even seem a little unfair
to subject Brenner's and Meyers' work to a stricter or more involved
critique. Because, however, the employment of the grotesque will take us
into gender-critical territory, it is useful to broaden the discussion and
spend some time analysing issues of gender, as well as those related strictly
to imagery, raised in these two reading strategies.

Meyers' study of the imagery in the Song begins with the observation
that recent, more 'critical' biblical scholarship – particularly that versed in
literary criticism – enables the liberation of the Song from the 'fanciful
twists and turns of spiritualized interpretation' and helps one to locate its
'primary level of meaning' (1993: 197). She also observes that recent
feminist critics are naturally drawn to the Song, a work in which 'female
behavior and status stand apart from the largely male orientation of the
rest of the biblical canon' (1993: 199). Combining both interests here, she
undertakes a gender-critical analysis of the Song's body imagery
(primarily located in, but not limited to, the *wasfs*). Her point of
departure, relative to other scholarship on the Song, is with those images
that 'startle or shock', and that 'seem inappropriate to what seems to be
the task of depicting physical attractiveness' (1993: 200). Rather than
dismissing the images, as others have done, she locates in them an unusual
source of female power and privilege, which fits into her broader project
of discovering female power in premonarchic Israel (1988). And, rather
than looking at how the images 'develop the poet's awe for the beloved',
she examines them for the 'gender associations that they hold independently of the comparative purposes to which they have been put' (1993:
201).

In order to pick up the thread I have been following so far in the discussion, it is useful to comment on Meyers' understanding of the way the imagery actually functions. Her presumption that the images have a 'primary level of meaning' (1993: 197) is noteworthy. As with Soulen and others discussed above, this presumption operates on the understanding that there is a more appropriate or correct way to interpret the images. As it happens, Meyers does not seem to be attempting that interpretation here, but looks instead to other associations that the images might have. In this way, her work fits into the more reader-oriented responses of Falk and Soulen. In the construction of her picture of premonarchic Israel through the images, however, and in her heavy reliance on what seem to be modern stereotypes about masculinity and femininity, Meyers might be said to be creating 'fanciful twists and turns' (1993: 198) of her own. Her work, then, appears to be informed by the same kind of interpretive move as that which she criticized in the beginning of her article, and which formed the point of departure for her own reading. This is an especially appropriate critique to make of Meyers' because she begins by citing Soulen (1993: 200) and, apparently (though she never foregrounds it), advocating his reading strategy: 'If the visual offerings of the biblical poet are not familiar to us, the scholar should explore them so that they become vivid and offer us the same associative potential that existed for the inhabitants of an ancient landscape for whom the images drawn from that environment were commonplace' (1993: 200).[72]

Meyers briefly outlines two types of images in the Song of Songs, faunal and military/architectural. She looks at both the actual (linguistic) and implied gender of the objects used in the comparisons, and concludes that the imagery in the book brings about an unexpected reversal of conventional stereotypes. In the Song's towers and shields (4.4; 7.4, 5; 8.10), she observes that imagery drawn from life that is 'almost exclusively associated with men' is here applied to women. A similar state of affairs occurs with the Song's faunal imagery, where three typically masculine animals, lions, leopards, and a mare – arguably female but here in a masculine setting (battle) – place the female body in typically male contexts of danger, strength, power and might (1993: 206). In cases where an animal is used to refer to both the man and the woman, however (gazelle, doves), Meyers finds opportunities for both male and female stereotypical imagery. These ultimately weaken her case. The breasts-as-gazelles image is the best example: for males, the 'grace and free movement' indicates masculinity, but for females, 'the tenderness and softness and perhaps suppleness' indicates femininity (1993: 206). The fact

---

72   This is Meyers' interpretation of Soulen's suggestion for reading. It actually seems closer to Falk's strategy than Soulen's, though, since Meyers is very much taken up with the kind of 'interpretive visualization' advocated by Falk, and seems less concerned about the attitudes of the poet.

that the imagery has a range of meaning and can be bent to fit either gender in Meyers' analysis renders suspect the rigidity of her interpretations for each wholly 'masculine' or 'feminine' image. Might these, too, therefore have a range of meaning that would mean they are appropriate for either gender?[73]

Meyers' ultimate conclusions for her findings, combined with observations about other gender peculiarities of the Song (such as the predominance of the female voice, the use of the phrase, *bet 'em*,[74] the presence of a 'folk culture' in the universality of the Song's love language) are that the book innovatively uses unusual metaphors to reveal a world that exhibits a gender-balanced expression of mutual intimacy. As she notes later in her book on Israelite women (1988): 'These associations of female with power should not be taken literally, as meaning that women were warriors or hunters. Rather, those images are metaphors for power and control, and are used in the Song to suggest female attributes' (1988: 179). The world of the Song, Meyers notes, is one of 'erotic mutuality and shared love' (1993: 211). 'The Song of Songs, set apart from the stratifying consequences of institutional and public life, reveals a balance between male and female. [N]either male nor female is set in an advantageous position with respect to the other' (1993: 211). But Meyers seems to want to have it both ways: despite its mutuality, she cannot help but notice the predominance of the female voice and the devotion of male speech to the female body. So, she concludes that the Song represents 'that aspect of life in which the female role was primary' (1993: 211–12). For Meyers, Song of Songs is not a 'chance aberration' (1988: 196), but, as a 'product of domestic life', it represents the miraculous survival of 'the cultural expression of female power in early Israel' (1988: 180).[75]

Whatever way she takes it, the 'hermeneutic of compliment' I have been discussing with respect to other interpreters in this chapter appears here

---

73   I am referring to Meyers' evaluations of implied gender for each image (e.g. danger equals masculinity) and not her observations about the linguistic gender of a noun used in an image.

74   Meyers reasons that the preference for the term *bet 'em* over the Hebrew Bible's more usual *bet 'ab* is due to the emphasis on relationships in the Song of Songs, where the 'primary orientation lies with the female of the pair' (1988: 180). She notes, 'Without the matter of lineage reckoning as part of the dynamics of the Song ... the internal functional and relational aspect of household activity, in which females played a strong, if not dominant role, is apparently expressed by "mother's house" and not "father's house"' (1988: 180). See also Meyers 1991.

75   Meyers notes that it would be a mistake to 'presume to locate' the Israelite woman in the Hebrew Bible – women we see there are 'exceptional' since they rose to prominent positions (1988: 5). Meyers is looking for 'Everywoman Eve' (1988: 4), whose identity will be found in relation to the women of the Hebrew Bible. She uses sociological and anthropological approaches and concentrates her efforts on women in the premonarchic (formative) period of Israel's history.

too, only it is modified slightly. For Meyers, the redemption of the images is to be found not in the physical beauty of the body to which they refer, but in their political power. And this is attractive indeed: 'Luckily for feminists, who often despair of discovering meaningful material in the man's world of the official canon, a single biblical book has preserved this non-public world and allows us to see the private realm that dominated the social landscape for much of ancient Israel's population' (1993: 212).

Though some of the elements of domestic life exist in the Song – food, wine, even the mother's house – the world of the Song is fundamentally unconcerned with domestic activities. It is also quite unconcerned with reproductive activities (though see Brenner on the Song's imagery and contraception, 1997a: 87–8). This does not pose a problem for Meyers' argument, since she maintains that reproduction exceeded the domestic sphere, and was primarily a public / masculine issue, governable by Israel's patriarchal system. Reproduction was a public, male-dominated issue, to be sure (see Fuchs 1985), but was the business of raising children not also intensely domestic? It seems that this is the one issue that would challenge Meyers' analysis of female power in the domestic arena; might this be a reason why it must be excluded from her analysis (see Ch. 8 in 1988)?

It would, moreover, be important to ask of Meyers to what end images from the public domain would be used to locate or identify power in the private. If a woman is described with military / architectural imagery, for example, and if we take this imagery to be 'masculine', would not the implication be that female power can also be located in a masculine world, i.e. in the public sphere, not simply a feminine one? Meyers' use of imagery that crosses over both genders seems to challenge her assertions as well, for if power can be located for women in the private sphere, then perhaps variations on this theme will also obtain. For instance, will male power be asserted in a uniquely feminine domain because of 'feminine imagery'?

One final point should be made about Meyers' work. She concludes her article by saying: 'Nor, if we listen to the words of might in the *wasfs* and other passages portraying the beloved female, was gender a constraint on power in the intimate world of a couple in love' (1993: 212). Statements such as these suggest a certain idealism in the form of expectations about love and romance, and they are not dissimilar from other work that I have considered already (e.g. Munro). From what I will show through a grotesque reading of the imagery, these notions must be called into question, for, gender and power in the Song are, it would seem, intimately acquainted.

Another provocative gender-critical reading of the Song's imagery can be found in the work of Brenner (1993a). Like Meyers, Soulen and Falk, Brenner is also keenly aware of the need to negotiate what seem to be strange and uncomplimentary descriptions of the woman in the Song of

Songs. Unlike Meyers, though, she does not set out to find empowerment for biblical women in the Song's imagery (though she does suggest this as a possible conclusion to her reading). Her concern appears to be more with the problematic nature of the imagery, and her response to it is refreshingly innovative (Whedbee agrees; 1993).

Having noticed that the *wasf* in 7.1-10 manifests some significant differences in comparison to the others in the Song, Brenner advocates reading it as a parody of the *wasf* genre. She suggests, moreover, that our failure to recognize parodies of the woman's body and the *wasf* genre may account in a large part for our confusion about these images.[76] Of all studies of the imagery considered so far, hers seems the least concerned with appealing to the 'hermeneutic of compliment' that I have been referring to in this chapter (though there are cases where it might; see below). This is because Brenner removes the assumption that the images must be flattering, and suggests instead that they should be viewed as humorous, rather than as attempts at serious description. She observes: 'By the end of the poem, we still have no idea what the loved person looks like, in the sense that no *complete* image is communicated' (1993a: 235; italics Brenner's). She believes that it is not a photographic type of image that is relayed, but, like Soulen, something which reflects the emotional state of the speaker and draws in the reader's sense and emotions (1993a: 235). The difference between Soulen and Brenner, though, is that the latter does not assume that the reader's sense and emotions necessarily have to be positive.

Brenner's interpretation of the description in Song 7.1-10 is facilitated largely through her understanding of the context in which this text is placed: the protagonist is dancing for a group of spectators and is subject to a 'running commentary', where the commentator is encouraged to be 'flippant' by other spectators, who are probably also male (1993a: 245–6). There is no 'wooing' or 'adoring' voice here, 'but a close scrutiny of a present, live woman in a public performance' (1993a: 246).

Brenner makes little comment about the first two body-parts discussed, the feet and the thighs. Then, she observes, 'your vulva' is the correct understanding of שׁרֹרֵךְ, the subject of 7.3b. Brenner also notes that אַל־יֶחְסַר הַמָּזֶג suggests not only the free flowing wine, but also the 'womb's juices' (1993a: 246).[77] The stomach and lilies are next (7.3c-d), lilies signifying the woman's pubic hair. Brenner then comments, '[i]t

---

76   Brenner asks, since love is normally a serious matter, can it be funny? More importantly, should the Scriptures laugh at love? (1993a: 237). Furthermore, should one laugh at the Scriptures? See Brenner and Radday 1990; Landy 1990.

77   This double meaning is then characteristic of a type of joke that is exclusive to those who hear it and experience its context (1993a: 247).

appears that the dancing damsel is far from slim',[78] and she later summarizes, less timidly, 'the dancer is, frankly, fat, her belly in dance motion is big and quivering, much like an unstable mound of wheat. She looks comical; her body inspires pithy comments.'[79] Brenner notes that much scholarly energy has been expended on the attempt to explain the comparison of the woman's breasts to gazelles. She reminds us of the context of this description – the woman dancing – and observes, 'The dancer is in constant motion. Together with the rest of her body, her breasts move fast, much like frolicking fawns. This is titillating, but might look ludicrous as well' (1993a: 248).

Brenner turns next to the facial features. The comparison of the woman's neck to a tower proves difficult, and Brenner eventually defers to ignorance of the context.[80] The eyes are also the subject of an equally 'opaque' image. She observes that 'the public water places outside the gates of Heshbon ... were used for drinking, watering of animals, washing bodies and clothes, and clearing debris. Their waters were probably turbid rather than serenely limpid' (1993a: 250). For the nose, Brenner relies on the assumption that its 'Lebanese proportions' were probably no more attractive then as they would be today. Finally, the woman's hair is not richly dyed as other commentators suggest, but 'wet with perspiration, much like packs of thread in the dyeing vessels' (1993a: 252). In sum, Brenner calls this woman a 'mixed bag': 'True, she dances well and suggestively (v. 2a). Her thighs are like artistic jewels (2b), her vulva guessed to be generous (3a-b) – so far on the credit side. On the other hand, her belly is fat and jumpy like her breasts (3c, 4), her neck is (disproportionately?) long, her eyes by now turbid, her nose outsize (5)' (1993: 250). She points out that there is 'no reason to assume that the picture she [the woman] now presents is aesthetically captivating' (1993a: 252).

Brenner's observations on Song 7.1-10 are unique,[81] and they are

---

78   Brenner's comment that the woman is 'far from slim' is based on the observation that the wish to see this text as complimentary might condition the interpretation of the woman's large size as the subject of an 'adoring remark' (1993a: 247).

79   Brenner 1993a: 248. Brenner points out that these are the only two features that are covered. Curiously, as Brenner observes, they are the only parts of the body that the text calls beautiful. For an insightful discussion of desire and exposure of the body in the Song of Songs, see Pardes 1992: 134-8.

80   Brenner 1993a: 249. This is surprising, since up to this point Brenner has been proposing a particular context that informs her interpretation of most of the imagery.

81   Waterman's work (1948) needs to be fitted in here. As I summarize below, a number of commentators in passing use the terms 'bizarre' or 'grotesque' of the imagery. They usually, however, make an effort to justify the imagery or interpret it in such a way that these qualities are no longer evident. Waterman's fits somewhere between the majority of readers and Brenner in that he observes the odd nature of the images and uses them in part to support his argument that the Song is a slight against King Solomon. Waterman's reading of the images in 4.1-5 is not sustained throughout the book, though, and it is difficult to see why

similar to that which I develop below – a grotesque reading of the body imagery in the Song. Two observations, however, seem necessary. First, Brenner's partial justification for her reading is that the imagery does not appear to be intended to provide a realistic or photographic image of the loved one ('no *complete* image is communicated'; 1993a: 235; original italics).[82] The same, of course, can be said for the other descriptions, perhaps more so, since they are less representative of the body. But there is still a picture presented here, and where Brenner and I will eventually disagree is over what sort of reality we posit lies behind the description. Brenner's reading depends on the presumption that behind the image is a *real* woman who has an identity and social location. She does not speculate on the identity to any great degree (to posit, for instance, that the woman is a specific biblical or historical figure), but does comment on it at the conclusion of her reading. In some sense, her reading still depends on the hermeneutic of compliment that I identified above. If the image is not complimentary – the logic of her argument would go – then it must be ridiculous (unflattering, etc.). And the recognition that it is ridiculous comes in viewing it as a parody of the other two *wasfs* (which are complimentary?), not as a strange image in its own right.

The second observation concerns the conclusion of Brenner's reading. The article is insightful in its suggestion that humour masks the unconscious. Brenner reasons that it is allowable to poke fun at an object of personal and communal desire.[83] As she says, 'humour is eminently more suitable for dealing with a flesh and blood object of desire' (1993a: 253). These observations, however, suggest something more sinister than the affectionate teasing that she has been advocating for the description throughout, such as public humiliation or the violence of pornography (see Boer's reading, below).[84] I suspect that this plagues Brenner too, for she appears to undermine her own reading in order to

---

these particular images bother him, whereas others (e.g. those in 5.10-16; 7.1-10) do not. Boer's evaluation of his work as 'staunchly realist' and as proposing a 'grotesque body' cannot really be sustained (1999: 165 n. 52). Waterman's insights are important for the threads I am tracing in this survey, though, for the admission of the imagery's odd nature and the author's comfort in allowing it to stand in his interpretation.

82   Brenner has recently reiterated the point, twice (2003: 296; 2005: 166).

83   Brenner 1993a: 250. It is especially allowed when the fun-pokers are male. Brenner does not explain this here, but she does address the subject elsewhere (1993d: 90). She speculates that perhaps, because women take love more seriously than men, they are not as easily able to make it the subject of humour or parody. This, however, might be seen to excuse men for belittling their 'objects of desire' (as if objectification is not already a problem) on the feeble (and somewhat stereotyped) grounds that they do not take love seriously.

84   Similarly, see Pardes 1992: 137 on Phyllis Trible's work on the Song: Trible fails to see the text's 'nonidyllic presentation of love, the anxiety and shame that accompany the pleasures of exposure, especially when a female body is at stake'.

account for the discomfort that a woman on display, being tormented about her body (a culturally based fear for a great proportion of womankind in the West, perhaps?) must cause. Brenner suggests that, if we 'read as women', we might see this parody as a 'protest against conventional, idolized, idealized images of love and the female love object' (1993a: 225). This would be much the same as Shakespeare's sonnet, 'My Mistress' Eyes are nothing like the Sun', only the *wasf* is women-authored.

There is, however, a significant difference between the sonnet and the *wasf*: the (assumed) gender of the authors. Shakespeare's parody works – is affectionate teasing, not humiliation – because he, the lover, still loves, despite his beloved's less-than-perfect attributes.He says as much: 'And yet, by heaven, I think my love as rare / As any she belied with false compare.' The sense of this seems to be that despite the fact that the woman does not attain (unattainable) cultural standards of beauty, the speaker still loves her. By contrast, the women, if they are the authors of this text as Brenner suggests, merely contribute to the already existing problem of objectification. Their words objectify (maybe in fun), but offer no respite from humour's humiliation, because they are not the ones who love, despite the faults.

Excess in Imagery: Psychoanalytic and Pornographic Readings
This section concludes my review of the literature and beds together two rather unlikely readings. The first, Francis Landy's reading of the Song in *Paradoxes of Paradise*, takes up the *wasf* imagery and, by tracing some of its meanderings, investigates the psychic identities and mergings of the lovers. Roland Boer's reading, a pornographic retelling of the Song, investigates other, more suspect mergings, through a liberal and extravagant use of the book's imagery. I bring these two readings together here not because they are engaged in the same enterprise, but because both read and employ the imagery to excess. That is to say, both writers are fluent and comfortable with the complexity and vibrancy of the imagery and are not at all shy about using it wherever and whenever it is appropriate (albeit in different ways). This is significant, given the existence of what I have suggested is readable as a certain discomfort about the descriptions of the body in the readings of other scholars.

Landy's detailed study of the *wasfs* comes as part of an investigation into the nature of the lovers' relationship. In reading each image, he proposes that he will 'proceed to an elaboration of its correlatives and complements, not so much for its own sake, to attempt a total elucidation, but as a gradual introduction to the descriptive techniques of the Song' (1983: 74). The 'elaboration of … correlatives and complements' translates into the elucidation of a complicated web of images in the

Song. This web reflects, as he says, the intertwining of the lovers with each other and with the world around them:

> The bodies of the lovers are disassembled and reconstructed in the Song, each constituent metaphorically combining with heterogeneous elements to give the impression of a collage, a web of intricate associations and superimposed landscapes that serves to blur the distinction between the lovers, and between them and the external world (1983: 73).

Landy's study of the web of images in the Song is directed at investigating the identities of the lovers. This is explicitly not a character study, which, Landy notes, would be unproductive as the lovers are not 'real people' (1983: 61). Rather, they are 'types of lovers, rather than single persons, a cumulative eidetic portrait': they are, in short, archetypes, with whom readers identify. The web of imagery represents the intricacy of associations between the lovers, where each sees him- or herself in the other, and where the archetypes of lover, infant and mother are made visible. For Landy, the lovers lead readers back to the poet (the lovers are images of him) (*sic*), with whom readers also identify; but this is not the end of the matter. Gradually, the poet is edged out of the picture, and the lovers create the Song with their love; it, in turn, expands to fill the space between them (1983: 62).

The subject of the Song has a universal message, as Landy goes on to explain: 'The subject of the poem is really the self as a self-contained entity that enters into relation with the world, "rounded like a stone" ... a vessel full of thoughts, feelings, activities' (1983: 64–5). It is this that is Landy's ultimate interest, and through language that reflects the imagery he studies, he traces the development of the self as revealed in the lovers.

Landy's work might remind one of Munro's at times in its romanticism, although it is much more dense theoretically in its application of literary and psychoanalytical tools to the images. One of its strengths is that, of all the work I have read on the Song, it is the most capable of capturing the convoluted and dense nature of the images. This is not so much because of what he reads into the imagery, but how he goes about discussing it. Landy's work is affective: it shows an obvious appreciation for the lyricism and intricacy of the Song's figurative language, treating an image then developing his insights by moving from image to image, building a collage. An example will help to illustrate his method.

Beginning with the comparison of the breasts to fawns in 4.5, Landy locates several keys that will be important for his development of the image-pastiche. He notes that breasts are essentially ambiguous, and that this gives them 'special status in the Song':

> They combine adult and infantile sexuality, visual and oral satisfaction, tactile and erectile qualities. They have active and passive characteristics; active in so far as they give suck, passive in that they are subject to

the baby's aggressive rage and hunger. On the adult level, they are conspicuous, attracting attention. (1983: 74)

From there, Landy follows various strands of the web: fawns, suckling, orality, the mouth, liquids, milk, foods, and so on, tracing in each the relevant images of the mother, the infant, the lover. In the Song's crossover of images, in particular, Landy is able to make his case for the 'flow of identity' between the lovers.

It could be said that Boer's reading is also concerned with the flow of identity between the lovers – in fact, between all the Song's players (real and imagined) – but it weaves quite a different kind of web with the imagery. Boer's chapter on the Song of Songs (1999) as pornography is frank – too frank for some, perhaps – but not so much from the perspective of acknowledging the Song's strangeness of image, but from its sexual potential. One needs to use a word like 'potential' here, because Boer's work is intentionally allegorical;[85] he is not arguing that the Song's actual or intended meaning is what he describes, only that it may be read this way. Boer's work is not intended to be a solution to the problematic nature of the imagery in the same way as those works I have considered above. It is worth mentioning here, however, because it is, comparatively, comfortable with, and thorough in its use of, the odd body images.[86]

Boer interweaves a pornographic reading of the Song's images with a fictional tale of a number of has-been porn stars whose final performance is a retelling of the Song of Songs.[87] Boer first provides a detailed list of the Song's images, a sort of archaeology of pornography that he believes a literal reading encourages. In the Song, he finds support for the occurrence of the sexual act in phrases such as 'lie down', 'embrace', 'hold captive', 'knock', 'open', 'ravish', 'awaken love', and so on (1999: 57). From there, he develops a catalogue of terms that refer to 'genitalia,

85   Elsewhere (2000), Boer advocates (following Moore 1998) writing a carnal allegory of the Song. He observes: '[A] carnal allegory ... would be concerned with a range of questions: the function of sexual language and poetry, narrative and sexual description, explicitness and realism, repetition, fetishism and the range of sexual practices suggested in the Song, such as sex between variously gendered partners, bestiality, inter-generational sex, group sex, water sports, menstrual sex, fisting, discipline and so on.' The work which I am presently discussing does not yet attempt this, though it does involve many of the items in his 'wish list', albeit in a fictional guise.

86   There is more to be said in response to Boer, but I reserve this for the last chapter, since it pertains more to the implications and ideology of Boer's reading than it does to my present discussion on the imagery. It is important to mention, however, a certain irony in reproducing and disseminating Boer's pornographic reading here, given its contextualization in the author's discussion on censorship.

87   The characters are named, appropriately, Sue Lammith, Isaac Moses (as Leb Bannon), Eve Adam (as Beth Rabbim), Solomon Wiseman (as Hermon Senir), Melekh Agag (as Frank Incense), Merab Saul (as Sharon Rose); even 'Murphy' makes an appearance – readers should draw their own conclusions as to his identity.

fluids, orifices, protrusions' (1999: 57). Included in the 'linguistic register'
associated with sexual acts and body-parts are various foodstuffs – myrrh,
milk, (nut) orchards, choicest fruits and many others – landforms and
miscellaneous items; even the animals may stand in for 'sexual
designators' (1999: 58).

More than being a mere linguistic register, however, Boer also points
out that the Song's sexual vocabulary implicates the reader in its sexual
strangeness, and, moreover, is fetishistic. Not only does the Song's sexual
arsenal represent items that are fetishized, Boer suggests that the words
themselves become fetishized. Moreover, in that the fetish-words are
detached from their referents, the Song is able to 'trigger imagination and
phantasy' (1999: 59), thereby walking an interesting line between fantasy
and reality. Here, Boer has occasion to write of the relation between the
Song's display of 'real' sexual acts and biblical fantasy. Comparing it to
the demands viewers make on pornography to show enough of the sexual
act and to represent orgasm convincingly so that all may be deemed
believable, Boer finds correlations in the Song's explicitness and its
tempering of sex by concealment, its repetition of sexual episodes, its
terminology and *wasfs*.

From this analysis, Boer then slips into something a little more
comfortable, namely, a pornographic retelling of the Song, which is the
point where he takes a ' "literal" reading to its logical extreme' (1999: 64).
By consequence, this is where the narrative with which he began his
chapter ('Sue's place was about an hour's walk ...'; 1999: 53), and which
has been interspersed throughout, suddenly becomes foregrounded. The
retelling, called the 'Schlong of Schlongs', is, in effect, an effort to capture
the Song's undisciplined change of scenery and scattered, wild imagery
into narrative cohesion. It makes for poor-quality narrative,[88] but, by no
coincidence, for what is fairly standard pornography. Interestingly,
though he has catalogued the Song's images previously, Boer still seems
to get stuck on some of the Song's more bizarre collection of them (the
wasfs). The reading loosely follows the text's order, making whatever use
of the Song's image-vocabulary it can:

> Repetition now sets in, with the next fuck cycle underway (2.8-17). Beth
> Rabbim and Leb Bannon make their appearance here ... It begins with
> a long tongue darting over Beth's very ample breasts, 'leaping upon the
> mountains, bounding over the hills' (2.8). As the camera pans out,
> somewhat shakily, the large pink nose and muzzle of a 'gazelle' (2.9)
> come into view. Beth has her eyes closed and groans, enjoying the rough
> tongue of the animal. But now a 'young stag' (2.9) walks over ... (1999:
> 66)

---

88   Boer admits as much in one of his asides in the chapter: 'This is not too bad, I ponder,
at least there is no plot to distract from the sex' (1999: 68).

However, by the time Boer has narrated us up to the first *wasf*, his skill as pornographer / interpreter seems to be waning:

> Without any introduction a fourth scene begins (4.1-5), focusing on the beautiful body of Beth Rabbim. Another voice over breaks into the scene, but now it is a woman, and she savours Beth's body, running her tongue over Beth's eyes, veil, hair, teeth, lips, mouth, cheeks, neck, and breasts. But the phantasies are of a grotesque body: an image grows on the screen, with doves for eyes, goats for hair, ewes for teeth, doubled over, thread for (lizard) lips, pomegranates for cheeks, a tower for a neck, and fawns and gazelles for breasts (4.1-5). The image flips over to pubic hair, labia and ass cheeks. (1999: 67)

The same thing occurs when Boer gets to 5.10-16:[89]

> A very different scene follows, in which the body of a man (Frank) is the object of the gaze, langorously perused by people whose gender is indeterminate. A queer voice runs over the body, enjoying it like a picture from a queer porn zine. The voice likes his ruddiness (5.10), head black hair, eyes, cheeks, lips, arms, body, legs, and speech. But, as with the earlier scene on the female body, this body is both fetishized and grotesque, its head becoming gold, hair as a raven, eyes doves, cheeks beds of spices, lips lilies, arms gold, body ivory and sapphires, legs alabaster columns. (1999: 69)

And again with 7.1-10:

> Finally, it is Sue's body that everybody wants to see ... This time the camera focuses not on her 'face' before fading to her ass and cunt; it begins below, with her 'rounded thighs' (7.2/1), moves up to her 'navel' and 'belly' (7.3/2) and then up to her breasts, neck, eyes, nose, head and hair (7.4-6/3-5). But this is a highly desirable body, with large thighs, rounded belly, smoky eyes and a 'Lebanese' nose; yet it is also fetishized, the scene fading into a construction of sculpture, pottery, wheat, lilies, fawns and gazelles, an ivory tower, pools, a gate and a mountain. (1999: 70)

Boer's reading endeavours to fit the body imagery into a linguistic scheme, which may be held together by a pornographic narrative. As the body images reveal, however, it would seem that the Song resists the reading in places, and this may have to do with its interplay between reality and fantasy. As a result, Boer must resort to the inclusion in the

---

89 Boer's fantasy identity as pornographer falters here, and a bit of the scholar reappears: phrases like 'langorously perused' are just not porn material. Neither are sentences like 'The image flips over to pubic hair, labia and ass cheeks' (I am convinced by the last term, but not by the first two, which suggest that Boer is being 'appropriate' here. Is it possible that the ill fit of the imagery into Boer's porn-narrative (or Boer's ill fit as porn-narrator) is manifesting itself in Boer's own voice?

'narrative' of a kind of psychedelic trip, where the odd bodies flash briefly on the screen – a sort of sexual-hallucinogenic excess. As such, Boer's reading tends to force too much out of the Song, and in the process, flattens its technique of exposing and veiling its unique vision.

A Grotesque Proposal

Recent scholarship yields a variety of responses to the Song's images. Most work acknowledges the difficult nature of these texts and attempts to create a satisfying means of working with them. As I have tried to show, almost all responses assume a certain perspective on the Song as love poetry, and try to fit the images into that context. Thus, it makes the most sense if the images are treated in a manner that maintains their status as complimentary and loving description of the loved body by the lover. The purpose of this review has not been to discredit that perspective, or to insist that it is somehow misguided, but merely to illustrate that this is an operating feature of criticism on the Song's images. Eventually, I will want to suggest that that premise be lifted in order to entertain the alternative reading that I propose.

In addition, it should be noted that there seems to be something really quite personal in readers' puzzlement over the images: it goes far beyond an attempted objective, intellectual enquiry into the meaning of cryptic imagery (despite the protestations of commentators against others' work).[90] I will be able to test this observation more fully as I turn to the notion of the affect of reading the Song in my final chapter; in the meantime, a few initial comments might suggest a rationale for the interpolation of the personal into the negotiation of the images. First, the obvious: many interpreters are visualizing a 'real' person behind the images – though not necessarily one with a particular historical identity – and they seem unable to suspend their expectations for how real bodies should be represented.[91] This seems an expected response for texts that deal with the matter of embodiment. Second, and closely connected to the first, readers visualize the Song's bodies within erotic or amatory discourse, and this means that they anticipate that the lovers' descriptions of each other's bodies will be representative of whatever ideals they (the readers) have of the language of love. Brenner is the only reader so far who seems to acknowledge that the images of 'love' discourse can create a potentially conflictual site. Third, and again related, is the fact that most

90   I am referring to something quite beyond a generally accepted view in literary criticism of the Hebrew Bible today that readers' own interests and contexts are reflected in the work that they do with these texts.

91   Pope (1977) and Gerleman (1965), as we saw, were exceptions, but Pope not consistently so.

of the Song's commentators have been men who read (again, not unexpectedly) the Song as a heterosexual love poem and who, it appears, identify with the male partner of the Song.[92] This, coupled with the fact that there are more instances where the female body is described in the book, seem to foster androcentric, heterosexual expectations of the female form in terms of ideals of beauty and sexual conduct.[93]

Yet the relationship between readers and bodies in the Song is not an easy one. It is not a matter of 'interpreting away' the odd images, so that the poem makes sense. For it seems that subsequent generations of commentators express the same fascination with the images and the same compulsion to understand them rationally. General comments about the images seem to give away a degree of readerly discomfort if they are found to be unappealing or unattractive, or the like. As we saw, Soulen referred to them (if literally read) as comical and grotesque; Waterman calls them 'bizarre if not grotesque' (1948: 63) and describes Solomon's descriptions as 'decidedly ugly or manifestly grotesque' (1925: 179); Boer sees the images as grotesque (following my reading; Boer 1999: 67, 165 n. 52); Rudolph observes that at least one image is grotesque ('Der Vergeleich der Nase mit dem Libanonturm wirkt allzu grotesk, wenn mann sich diesen als ein Bauwerk oben auf den Libanon denkt' (1962: 173); Murphy notes that some images 'strike the literal-minded, modern reader as comical, if not grotesque' (1990: 72); Segal refers to the grotesquerie of several images and calls them playful banter or gentle raillery (1962: 480); Fox retorts that playful banter has a place in the Song, but it is not everywhere ('Long series of *insults* would not be playful but merely offensive'; 1985: 273 n. 8; emphasis original); and the list goes on.

A particular word seems to appear with some regularity, and it is this

---

92   I do not intend to make comments here on the personal interests or inclinations of the Song's commentators. My observation is based on the fact that no one, to my knowledge, has yet written a queer commentary on the Song. Two partial exceptions exist in the work of Boer (1999) and Moore (2001). The former is aware of the need to include queer readings / perspectives in work on the Song, but he has not yet done so. The latter has written on 'que(e)rying' the Song, and attacks the subject primarily through allegorical readings, investigating whether allegorists were in fact seeking to relate to the male body and God, whom it represents, in a homoerotic manner.

93   Gottwald (1976: 425) provides one example:

In estimating the aesthetic impact of the imagery, we should recall that standards of taste in women have changed so radically towards slimness that we easily forget the preference for plumpness in most cultures and eras, as a sign of ability to work and of sexual fecundity. Ungenteel imagery in the Song can often be accounted for by this ancient taste.

The masculine imagery, full of 'massive and solid' items, by contrast, represents an interest in military defence and security. This brief comment on the nature of the Song's body imagery is at once stereotypical and androcentric.

word – grotesque (along with its close companions, comic, bizarre) – on which I propose rests the basis for a new reading. Suppose that one takes the admissions of grotesquerie by the above-mentioned critics at face value. What might happen to the Song's images if they were read using this hermeneutical key? The reading would use the grotesque – an artistic and literary construct that supports the comic and the repulsive, and targets both at the body – as an interpretive lens through which to view the imagery. It would not be aimed at 'proving' that the imagery was intentionally constructed by an author in this manner, nor would it be an attempt to prove that this is the 'right' or 'best' way to read the Song. Rather, it would be an experimental reading, aimed at foregrounding the discordant nature of the imagery, at that which seems comical, odd or unnatural to readers, and at that which makes them feel ill at ease with the body. Quite apart from investigating another way to read the Song's figurative language, a grotesque reading, in locating readers at the margins in this way, could situate them in an ideal position to ask challenging questions of the Song's politics of representation and gender.

To this end, much of the scholarship on the imagery that I have considered above will be useful. Most significantly, Brenner's work on Song 7.1-10 is influential for its undertaking of a more literal, comic reading. In addition, Brenner's keen awareness of the politics of love and her important questions about the role of humour and the depiction of the body in love poetry will be highly significant. Moreover, Meyers and Brenner both introduce a much needed gender-critical perspective on the Song, which must be pursued further if we are to contemplate issues such as the representation of the (female) body and the biblical relation of the sexes. In other directions, Landy's and Boer's disparate work with imagery also yields some promising resources. Landy's study captures the images' convolutions and interdependence extremely well. His comfort with non-linear or non-restrictive interpretations seems to be key to a reading that allows the Song's untamed poetic resources to come to the fore. Also, Landy's insight that the imagery is important for the constitution of the subject is something that merits exploration. Boer contributes a reading that imposes a considerable sexual excess on the imagery, which though it may be unpalatable to some, has a place in the consideration of the book's sexual politics as well as the allegorical status of interpretation. Boer also raises some useful questions, which I will take up later, about how much is too much in terms of readers' interpretations of the Song's erotic content. And yet, of course, what I propose here will cause us to depart from these several readings in particular, and go in an altogether different direction. That direction allows humour, desire, alienation, sex, and a whole other host of grotesque features and instruments to be set loose on the Song, with what I hope will be provocative results.

Chapter 2

UNCOVERING THE GROTESQUE BODY

As a literary and artistic construct, the grotesque appears to enjoy a certain dynamism – or, one might say, slipperiness. It has been identified in numerous media and across a variety of historical contexts. It is also apparent that in the course of these identifications, one person's grotesque is not necessarily another's. Moreover, just as if it is resisting being pinned down, efforts to define the grotesque precisely seem to diminish its effectiveness. Despite these difficulties, it is nevertheless important to try to gauge the grotesque in order to develop the heuristic that I am proposing for the Song of Songs. This is the project of the present chapter. In this context, an attempt at a total history of the grotesque would, needless to say, be quite impossible. Moreover, it would be quite unnecessary, since there are aspects that would be unhelpful for my proposed reading, such as the idea of the narrative grotesque, demonstrable in the work of Edgar Allan Poe, or the theological grotesque, uncovered in the writing of Flannery O'Connor.[1] As a means of narrowing the field, this chapter pursues an uncovering of the concept of the grotesque body, which will be especially pertinent to the body figurations in the Song of Songs. This uncovering will take place through interaction with critical discussion on the subject and an examination of some particular examples in art and literature.

Mikhail Bakhtin's analysis of François Rabelais' great works, *Gargantua* and *Pantagruel* is of crucial importance for a conceptualization of the grotesque body. A good part of this chapter will be concerned with Bakhtin's work and critical responses to it, along gender- and cultural-theoretical lines. The grotesque, however, might also be usefully studied in

---

1 Excellent discussions of the grotesque in narrative fiction can be found in Burwick 1987; Clark 1991; Kayser 1963 and, in a more limited capacity, Clayborough 1965: 112–52. Clark's book works through various themes in modern literature, such as 'debunking the author' or repetition and ennui, and thus addresses areas that the others do not. Barasch's discussion (1971) is also useful, but more cursory, since it is an historical overview that follows the semantic development of the word. For discussion of the theological grotesque, see especially Adams and Yates 1997.

the context of the long history of art in which it has been so prevalent, especially Renaissance art, where it was first identified by critics. Work with the artistic history of the grotesque, of course, allows me to investigate it in part as a representational device. It also allows me to show how, in just a brief period of time, the grotesque swelled to include a variety of styles and attitudes toward the body at which it is directed. Finally, the introduction of work by Roland Barthes and by Michel de Certeau, initially on several of these artworks, will further elucidate the grotesque as a visual/artistic device. It will also set the stage for my own reading in the next chapter.

In my uncovering of the grotesque body, I make much of the Renaissance, but my resulting conceptualization of this body is not intended to be historically limited to that period. Rabelais' work is viewed through twentieth-century eyes (Bakhtin's), and both authors' work is in turn critiqued through the contemporary critical perspectives of psycho-analysis and gender. In addition, the visual pieces that I initially consider are also elucidated by contemporary, post-structuralist critics. Though there is, as will become clear through Bakhtin's analysis, an arguable sociohistorical component of grotesque figuration, it is important not to see it restricted to or defined in terms of this one aspect.

Grotesque Beginnings and Developments: A Context for the Grotesque Body

The Grotesque and the Art of the Renaissance: From the Pope's Palace to the Devil's Arse

The word 'grotesque' was coined in the Renaissance to refer to a style of art that playfully incorporated animal and human bodies into various decorative designs.[2] It was applied to frescoes of fanciful combinations of human, animal and plant forms that were discovered in Nero's *Domus Aurea* at the end of the fifteenth century.[3] The frescoes were remarkable to their excavators because they were unique; in Geoffrey Galt Harpham's words, they suggested a new vocabulary for Renaissance artists.[4] For

---

2   This particular style has also been labelled the 'ornamental' grotesque by Kayser 1963, ostensibly in order to differentiate it from its more sinister cousins of the romantic period and the twentieth century. The labelling has also, I think, served inadvertently to diminish it in comparison to its later manifestations.

3   For a detailed study of the frescoes and the process of the excavation, see Dacos 1969.

4   Harpham 1982: 28. Morel provides a detailed 'vocabulary' of late Italian Renaissance grotesques, which includes animal, human and hybrid figures, zoomorphs, teratomorphs, phytomorphs, severed figures (*figures tronquées*) which support various structures, objects (masks, instruments, lamps, vases, etc.) and historical and country scenes (1997: 25). He also explicates a 'syntax' of these forms which covers methods of presentation and grouping, micro- and macro-structures, general organization of the vaults and background colour.

instance, they inspired the decorations of the Vatican loggias of the palace of Nicholas III, designed by Raphael and executed by Giovanni da Udine, which are thought to be among the most exquisite grotesques of the Renaissance.[5] As it turns out, however, the frescoes' ornamental style was only remarkable to its discoverers. In fact, its creator, reputedly called Fabullus, was criticized for his plodding, unoriginal designs (Harpham 1982: 25). Nero had apparently wanted something more 'Eastern' in flavour, befitting his newly acquired godlike persona, and the artistic record is reticent about what befell the less than fabulous Fabullus because of his failure to comply.

Renaissance excavators named the frescoes *grottesca*, not because of their formal characteristics, but because of the location in which they were found, the underground, cave-like (*grotta*) ruins of the palace.[6] The frescoes, however, show themselves to be uneasy prisoners of their last resting place, for they are light and airy and are meant to adorn soaring ceilings and vast expanses. They are playful and highly stylized, with intricate, symmetrical and brightly coloured designs. They frequently involve various mythical figures and interweave these with typical Roman decorative elements, such as vases, urns, foliage and birds. The body is represented in these early stages in the form of the occasional, detached, free-floating head that might feature in the centre of a frieze consisting of swirls and floral designs; or, it is a mild hybrid, a half-man, half-horse. These might then be flanked by griffins or cherubs or winged horses. In these designs the body is not thus a central figure, but is incorporated with many other elements for purely decorative purposes.[7]

In his decoration of the Vatican (1519), Raphael modified the *Domus Aurea*'s lexicon of designs somewhat and made more peculiar combin-

5 One should not assume that grotesque ornamentation suddenly 'appeared' as a response to the archaeological find. According to Dacos (1969: 57–61), the roots of the style can be found throughout Italy earlier in the century, though the discovery of the *Domus Aurea* was certainly influential in popularizing grotesque ornament. Clearly, medieval and Gothic style also had a part to play in the developments of quattrocento art. See Harpham 1982; Lecouteux 1993; and Morel 1997 for further study.

6 Most surveys of the grotesque begin with the Renaissance (though some acknowledge grotesque beginnings before this time), with the point at which the phrase (as *grottesca*) originated. These surveys usually work on a discussion of the word's origins (Harpham 1982; Kayser 1963; Kuryluk 1987; thus, significantly, what is considered grotesque by these surveys is frequently what has been *named* as such). My study will pay some attention to pertinent variations and applications of the word, but this is not strictly my aim here. For more on the vocabulary of the grotesque, see especially Barasch 1971.

7 Clark (1991: 18) observes that the mingling of human, animal and vegetable was done to 'eerie and nightmarish' effect, an effect that was highlighted by the cave-like context in which the forms were found. His evaluations cannot be supported, however, from the art itself or the literature about it (Dacos 1969; Harpham 1982). It took a few more years before the grotesque became what Clark suggests.

ations of human and animal forms. Here, a human head might be superimposed upon the body of a lion, or a woman's face and breasts might be joined to a winged creature (a dog or a lion) and adorned with a flowerpot.[8] The designs in the loggias were also significant for another important and strange combination, grotesque ornament and the subjects of biblical texts, which, as Harpham notes, was a daring and innovative move. The grotesque designs, however, were not imposed upon biblical subjects themselves, but decorated the borders of the spaces in which the biblical paintings were placed. Such juxtaposition raises important questions about margins and centres, to which I shall return below.

In its ornamental capacity, the new artistic vocabulary developed in Italy soon spread to neighbouring countries. Frances Barasch traces the spread of its popularity throughout France and northern Europe. Italian artists were hired, for instance, to decorate Fontainebleu. Barasch cites a number of inventories of royal and noble homes that included various grotesque forms of ornamentation (*passim*). As decorative vocabulary, the grotesque's tenure was long. It was not until the eighteenth century, when the classical form came back into vogue in painting, that the grotesque began to be repudiated (Barasch 1971: esp. Ch. 2).

At the height of its popularity, however, the grotesque was not always limited to the service of ornamentation. After Raphael's early work, it also began to creep out of the margins and become the focal point of an artistic piece. In his pictorial history, Harpham includes various ornamental engravings by Jamnitzer, Kilian, Bos and many others, where a central, grotesque figure dominates the composition. In the Jamnitzer works, for instance, monsters whose bodies are comprised of highly ornamental swirls and curls, mixed with claws, teeth and scales, strut proudly across stylized landscape. The grotesque finds itself in the spotlight for other, more significant reasons, too, such as satire and political invective. There are many such examples available, but perhaps the most noteworthy for my purposes are various political cartoons, such as those drawn by Lucas Cranach the Elder,[9] where grotesque figuration becomes the weapon of the Reformation.

In conjunction with one of his last treatises, *Against the Papacy at Rome, Founded by the Devil* (1545), Martin Luther employed Lucas Cranach the Elder to illustrate his major critique of the papacy. This piece was written chiefly as a response to two letters from the Pope. (The first letter was subsequently re-penned in a milder, second version, but both fell into Luther's hands anyway.) It questions papal authority to call

8   See the various drawings made of the designs, present in Davidson 1985; Harpham 1982; and Morel 1997.

9   There is some discussion over whether these works could be by Cranach the Elder or his son. See Dillenberger 1999: 79ff.

Figure 2   *Regnum Satanae et papae*

councils in Germany and, more significantly, whether the Pope is the true head of Christendom. The cartoons are vulgar and violent, but no more so, observes Mark Edwards, than the writing itself (1983: 189). In the three included here, a new tone and stylistic vocabulary comes on the scene. *Regnum Satanae et papae* (Figure 2) shows the Pope sitting on his throne in the mouth of a monstrous hell, where winged demons attend to his needs. *Ortus et origo papae* (Figure 3) depicts the birth of the pope and his cardinals out of the anus (?)[10] of a she-devil, and his upbringing by the three furies, Megaera, Allecto and Tisiphone. Finally, *Monstrum Romae inventum mortuum in Tiber, anno 1496* (Figure 4) shows a composite

10 The implication in the cartoon is that the Pope and his cardinals are being excreted; other scatalogical themes in some of the rest of the series not included here would certainly support this reading.

Figure 3   *Ortus et origo papae*

creature (goat, pig, donkey, chicken, fish – or sea-monster) who appears
to sport the Pope's face on its backside. Of these, the last best resembles
the compositional nature of the grotesque that I have been discussing so
far. In the other two cartoons, though, the profound interest in the
monstrous, and the preoccupation with the material body, especially in its
birthing and excreting capacities, is another hallmark of the grotesque;
these we shall see more clearly with the benefit of Bakhtin's analysis.

At some point, then, in these peregrinations from decorative margins to
satirical centre, the grotesque has the ability to move from the playful to

Figure 4   *Monstrum Romae inventum mortuum in Tiber, anno 1496*

something altogether more sinister. In all cases, however, one cannot say that once this physical shift from margins to centre is made, it is absolute. The works in Harpham's study mentioned above (Jamnitzer, etc.), for instance, are playful; in Cranach's/Luther's hands, grotesquerie has another purpose altogether (and yet another in the hands of the ecclesiastical establishment).[11] Nor can one say, therefore, that there is

11   Dillenberger includes evidence of Luther as the target of such cartoons, most usually in the persona of the Antichrist (1999: 17).

a single essence which the grotesque represents. In the examples just given, the association with the person of the Pope (the Loggia decorations and Cranach's cartoons) is a case in point. The concentration on the papacy is a coincidence of my gathering of sources, but it does conveniently illustrate the fact that the grotesque mode of figuration shifts in nuance and intent as it moves from context to context. On the one hand, it is able to support the theological agenda of one Pope, while in a different time, it is used to undermine that of another.

Renaissance Wanderings: Arcimboldo and Bosch

Grotesque figuration continued to develop in skill and sophistication over the course of the Renaissance. A closer look at some of the more visible promulgators of this mode of figuration is instructive for tracing some of these developments, as well as for investigating the mechanics and strategies of the grotesque. To this end, Giuseppe Arcimboldo and Hieronymus Bosch merit discussion here. In addition, literary critics Barthes and Certeau have explored the paintings of these artists in order to articulate something of the vision behind their work and the implications of it, in terms of meaning and interpretation. Though not explicitly theorizing the grotesque, both critics are working on wider contexts for it (the study of language and of mystics), which will be useful here and at a later stage in the next chapter. In essence, their contribution is valuable for getting at some of the broader questions involved in the study of grotesque figuration: By what means does the grotesque operate? Is there a particular spirit conveyed or effect achieved by the use of the grotesque in art? How does the grotesque manage to be effective – either as humour or as the source of unease?

Arcimboldo's myriad designs of 'heads' composed of a collage of natural or urban elements make for fanciful, largely comic grotesques. In *Wasser* (1566; Figure 5), for example, innumerable aquatic creatures (e.g. coral, crab, turtle, octopus, eel, seal, frog, various fish) are cleverly combined to create a picture of a human head. Part of the playfulness and attractiveness of the picture is its startling detail and intricacy; these draw in the viewer and make a diversion of looking. And, for those in the know, the picture also has political implications, in that the rather incongruous additions of a string of pearls and a pearl earring can be taken as homage to the Emperor Maximilian, probably the patron of the piece (Kriegeskorte 1993: 22).

Ostensibly, the picture is part of a playful series, but for Harpham, a painting such as *Wasser* indicates the grotesque because it depicts what is liminal. It is a mass of fish, but when one stands further back, it becomes a human head; somewhere in between it is both (Harpham 1982: 13–14). Harpham argues that *Wasser* has an 'impossible split reference' which

Figure 5   *Wasser*, Giuseppe Arcimboldo (1566)

makes the viewer struggle to make sense of it (1982: 13). This struggle for sense results in unease in the viewer, and this Harpham locates as the province of grotesque figuration.

What precisely, however, about the struggle for sense causes the unease? If we contrast a similar piece, *Winter* (1563; Figure 6), for instance, it is apparent that it conveys an entirely different impression –

Figure 6   *Winter*, Giuseppe Arcimboldo (1563)

and naturally I could only account for my own subjective experience here. On first examination, one can say that *Winter* has a decidedly creepy air about it, whereas *Wasser* hardly seems noteworthy in comparison. The figure is playful enough: shapes can often be made out of cracks and contours in trees, for instance. But the gnarled, aged qualities of this figure, the dead foliage, the broken, dilapidated nose and ears all speak of decay. Unlike *Wasser*, this face is not light and humorous; it is dark and ominous. It speaks of superstitions, of faces in dark trees that might come alive. *Wasser* is fanciful enough that a viewer will always know it is an artist's fabrication, an impossibility, but *Winter* seems to be more unsettling in its capture of the human condition. Therefore, *Wasser* excels the other, perhaps, in compositional cleverness, but maybe not in its ability to affect the viewer. Is the difference to be accounted for merely in personal taste? In subject matter? Because of these differences, and following Harpham, we have to ask if one requires a greater struggle for sense than the other.

Ultimately, and if we are to follow Harpham's analysis, the point is not to decide which painting is more grotesque, but to ascertain what is at work in them both as part of the mode of grotesque figuration. So far, there are at least two elements at play in the 'struggle to make sense'. In *Wasser* the struggle seems to relate to the viewer's intellectual negotiation of the semiotic components of the painting, in this case especially in terms of the mixture of genres: human, piscine and other. In *Winter*, on the other hand, the struggle seems to move beyond a recognition of signs in its simplest application, to a confrontation with the picture's contents on a more internal or emotional level. To be sure, Harpham is making an important point in his observation of the 'impossible split reference', but it appears to be a matter that requires more precision.

The problem of how viewers arrive at a meaning with respect to these works is one also taken up by Barthes in an essay-length study of Arcimboldo's famous heads (1980). Barthes believes that Arcimboldo's work is really exploiting the curiosities of language (1980: 15), and these curiosities implicate the viewer/reader in a profound way. He observes that the heads reveal a two-fold procedure. First, and quite obviously, Arcimboldo is working with analogy (an ear is [like] a clam).[12] Second, though, he pushes that analogy to the point of self-destruction: it is analogy that is radically exploited; it is analogy gone mad (1980: 16). In this case, the second part of the procedure does not replace or subvert the first, but both exist within the piece at the same time. This Barthes calls a double articulation, whereby painting becomes a genuine (written) language (1980: 24, 28). Arcimboldo's method 'violates' the pictorial system, 'improperly dividing it in two, hypertrophying its signifying, analogical potentiality, thus producing a kind of structural monster' (1980: 26). 'Double', in Barthes' hypothesized 'double articu-lation', furthermore, should not imply only two resultant meanings. Meaning emerges when meaningless elements are combined and these then form aggregates, which are not limited to one sense, but may even

12 So says Kaufmann, in an attempt to assign species to all parts of the head in *Wasser* (1987: 96).

multiply numerous times (1980: 50). So it is that Barthes is able to say that the metaphors in these works 'spatter countless meanings' (1980: 18). Above all, Barthes is careful to qualify that the heads still remain on the borders of common sense, that the resulting art is intelligible, not mad (1980: 36).

When the viewer is confronted by the new language that Arcimboldo has created (1980: 24), she experiences a 'source of a subtle (because intellectual) malaise – more penetrating than if the horror came from simple exaggeration' (1980: 26). Reading/viewing requires sophistication, especially in cases where the analogical leap is unnatural or audacious (1980: 38). Barthes explains that the malaise experienced stems from the compositional nature of the pieces: it 'comes to disturb, unsettle and disintegrate the unitary appearance of the form'. The composition incorporates, moreover, its own malaise of matter, that of the swarm. 'The jumble of living things, arranged in compact disorder, evoke a whole larval world ... lying at the edge of life, as yet unborn and already subject to putrescence' (1980: 64). This creation is monstrous – excess, metamorphosis, transmigration (1980: 66) – and it implicates those who see it. For, beyond the issues of signification and perception, there lies a world of value. The viewer, Barthes argues, moves from 'I read, I guess, I discover, I understand ...' to 'I like, I don't like. Uneasiness, fear, laughter, desire all enter into the game' (1980: 55–8). Moreover, these responses are culturally connoted; it is our context that has made these pieces affect us so significantly.

With respect to *Wasser* and *Winter*, Barthes points out that what was once a unified theme (e.g. water) comes to represent a mass of discontinuous, sharp-edged, bulging elements. Water becomes truly monstrous (1980: 62). And there is more: the notion of the swarm that these pieces evoke is effective not only because of its compositional excess but also because of its singular or elemental components. In describing *Winter*, Barthes has a specific reaction, the nature of which he unfortunately does not fully explore here:

> The effects provoked in us by Arcimboldo's art are often ones of repulsion. Look at Winter: that mushroom between the lips looks like a hypertrophied organ, cancerous and hideous; I see the face of a man who has just died, having choked on a pear sunk deep in his mouth. This same Winter, composed of pieces of dead bark, has a face covered with pustules, with scales; one would call him afflicted with a disgusting skin disease, pityriasis or psoriasis. The face of another (Autumn) is nothing but a mass of tumours; it is a turgescent face, vinous, a huge inflamed organ clogged with brownish blood.

Barthes' responses might seem extreme to another viewer (where, for instance, is there evidence of the pear?), and they are certainly conditioned by his own interpretive context. If anything, though, they do speak to the excessive nature of Arcimboldo's metaphors that Barthes is trying to illustrate, as well as to the propensity of the heads to continue signifying – indeed, the organic components to continue to metamorphose – beyond the canvas ('the floral expanse [of *Spring*] easily becomes the efflorescence of a more turbid condition of the subject; decomposition produces pulverulences'; 1980: 60).

Barthes' analysis indicates that there is much at stake in the struggle to make sense of Arcimboldo's works. That he sees the struggle as a matter of language (the double articulation, the new pictorial language) is instructive. Here, Barthes addresses not only that which he perceives is involved in the general process of signification but also the productive or generative mechanics of language. This implicates a number of issues. First, Barthes refers to the actual building of a figure through metaphor: 'One can say that in these extreme metaphors, the two terms of the metabole are not in a relation of equivalence (of being), but of actual *making*: the flesh of the little naked body *makes* (fabricates, produces) the tyrant's [Herod's] ear' (1980: 40). (And, in this case, Arcimboldo's choice of a child for Herod's body is ironic and audacious.) Second, language generates or implicates affect, as we have seen above. Barthes' response is singular and deeply felt. Third, and related to this, is the notion that Arcimboldo's works are forgeries – and here it is useful to see the word in its diversionary aspect, as well as to observe its original meaning of fabrication (1980: 32–4). Barthes compares the paintings to Rabelaisian artificial languages: they are contrived, but systematically developed. Similarly, Arcimboldo creates a state whereby a coded and an overt significance of a specific item can be determined. A viewer (and here Harpham's analysis comes quite close to Barthes') discerns one at the expense of the other, but when both are revealed, neither vanishes. It is as if a secret language is being developed.

Ultimately, however, Arcimboldo's heads are limited in terms of what they can offer my tracing of the grotesque. If we are looking to understand such issues as whether or not there is a spirit conveyed by grotesque figuration, or even what it is that creates affect in those who witness it, it would be useful to look beyond these 'drawing-room games' (Barthes 1980: 15) to a more sophisticated œuvre. The Renaissance offers up many opportunities of this nature in the works of painters such as Pieter Bruegel and Hieronymous Bosch. Both are known for their elaborations of exceptionally detailed episodes: in the case of Bruegel, of peasant life, replete with its hardships and celebrations; Bosch, by contrast, recorded a number of fantastical scenes from his imagination, often with a preoccupation for hell and the fate of the damned. One work in particular, Bosch's triptych, *The Garden of Earthly Delights*, offers up some rich rewards on closer examination.

Figure 7 *The Garden of Earthly Delights*, Hieronymous Bosch

The 'Hell' panel of Bosch's *The Garden of Earthly Delights* (Figure 7) goes some way to elaborating in the viewer the kind of unsettled response that Barthes articulated with respect to *Winter*. It is, in contrast with its companion pieces in the tryptych, dark and troubled.[13] Strange contraptions dominate the painting, and the damned are suffering various forms of torture. Peculiar monsters who are hybrids of humans and animals – and other things? – march the damned around, torture them, or eat them. Buildings explode, blood spurts from bodies; all is chaos. It is, as Gibson has described it, a nightmare (1973: 93).

Again, as with Arcimboldo, we see here the amalgamations and incongruous compositions projected onto the body. If we were to be amassing a checklist from Raphael onwards, the familiar elements of grotesque figuration are here: the hybrid bodies, the playful and the satirical, the uneasy (but expected) association of body and death, destruction and decay. Of particular interest in the painting, as far as the body goes, is the protracted and detailed use of inversion. For instance, in the bottom right-hand corner, a rabbit (once the hunted) carries off its prey (formerly, the hunter; Gibson 1973: 96). Normal items are enlarged to become instruments with which to torture the body (the harp, the lute, the horn, the lantern).[14] In addition, as with Cranach's cartoons, we see an emphasis on the anal/faecal, but the end result is less to satirize than to moralize. The central figure, who has yet to be convincingly explained in criticism, houses some of the damned in his rectum/intestine, which has been cut away.[15] In the foreground, a bird-monster (possibly a representation of Satan)[16] devours some of the unfortunate, and excretes them, whole, into a container below. And below him/it, one person excretes coins, while another vomits. Gibson observes that Bosch is at his moralizing best here (1973: 99); the seven deadly sins are all portrayed and those who have committed them are punished in appropriate ways (see Gibson 1973: 98–9 for discussion; also Baldass 1960: 229).

'Hell', though, should not really be considered without its counterparts.

---

13   There has been some discussion, in the history of criticism on this painting, over the order in which the panels are meant to be read. Different directions will affect whether the triptych is viewed as having a positive or hopeful message or a depressing one, and, accordingly, whether it is intended by the artist to be a social commentary or a theological treatise (creation, fall, redemption). See Baldass 1960: 37, 227.

14   It has been suggested that the musical instruments might be sexual symbols (Baldass 1960: 229).

15   The inside of the figure is clearly a tavern (Gibson 1973: 97). A number of options have been suggested for the figure's various parts: the disc and bagpipe allude to male and female sexual organs; the figure's headdress depicts her as a prostitute; the decaying tree-like limbs and cracked broken body signify the destruction of nature and new life.

16   See Baldass 1960: 229; cf. 90–91 for a discussion of Bosch's symbolic vocabulary and his dissatisfaction with the standard medieval depiction of the devil, which tended to be anthropomorphic.

If it represents grotesque inversions, a theological subjunctive used to represent the possibilities for the damned, does the central panel, 'Garden of Delights' maintain the indicative? To be sure, the vision in 'Garden' is as bright as 'Hell' is demonic. Bosch has dreamed up a myriad of pleasures for the eye (and the panel's bodies) to enjoy: the work is opulent, dynamic and full of energy. What cannot escape the viewer, however, is the collocation of bodies and animals, or the positioning of bodies in awkward situations, even the proliferation of forms to the point that they are evocative of Arcimboldo's swarms. Again, as with the two pieces, *Wasser* and *Winter*, considered above, we are confronted with works that seem to represent two different polarities. It is too simplistic to equate the demonic with the grotesque and the Edenic with its opposite. Rather, it is important to continue to ask about the range of signification allowed by the panels, and most importantly, what happens to the body when it is placed at the centre of such figuration. How is it that Bosch, master painter that he was, is able to convey the grotesque with such a range of visions?

Certeau, like Barthes, pursues questions of a more intricate nature with regard to how the paintings in question function in terms of viewers' responses to them. His work – again like Barthes – is part of a larger project that incorporates an involved discussion of the artistic work. Certeau is also interested in language, but explores it, via Bosch, as part of a broader study on *mystics*.[17] The painting signals an entry-point into this subject, since it is able to show visually the literary conundrum he faces with the language of mystical practice. For Certeau, mystics utilize a specialized language that both reflects and disrupts the linguistic and social conventions of their time. Certeau's project has a range of interests, including the gap between the student of *mystics* and the subject itself. It also takes on the heavily symbolic and highly specialized nature of this discourse – to the point where he suggests we encounter in it a kind of secret language.[18]

From the very beginning of his discussion, Certeau observes the unintelligibility of *The Garden of Earthly Delights*. There is no guide for the painting, nor, for the historian, is there an external discourse – a series of letters, of descriptions, of records – to map out the painting's provenance or its significance. 'I lose my way in it', he remarks (1992a:

---

17   In Certeau's work, *mystics* conveys not the plural of 'a mystic', but a correlate similar to 'metaphysics' – in this case a kind of science of mystical behaviour and discourse. *Mystics* is Michael Smith's (the translator of *The Mystic Fable*) translation of Certeau's choice of terminology, 'la mystique', which was chosen by the author in contradistinction to 'la mysticisme', or 'mysticism'. As Smith observes, the latter is 'far too generic and essentialist a term to convey the historical specificity of this object of study' (Certeau 1992: ix–x). Following Smith, when used to indicate Certeau's neologism, the word will be italicized in order to distinguish it from the plural of the noun 'mystic'.

18   I will not provide an exhaustive account of Certeau's project here. The following chapter explores his ideas further.

50). Indeed, Certeau observes that the painting 'organizes, aesthetically, a loss of meaning' (1992a: 49). It plays off the allure of looking (the viewer is drawn in by the drollerie and artifice of Bosch's figures) against a refusal of discourse (much has been written *about* it from the outside, but from the inside it refuses to speak). Three aspects engineer the painting's silence: (1) architectural features, in particular the focal point of an eye in each panel that looks out at the viewer and refuses his or her penetrating gaze; (2) enigmatic signs, in particular reading, showing and writing, all of which 'aim at meaning', but which subvert it because of the way they are represented; and (3) vocabulary. This last is a collection of items that are 'normally dispersed', but assembled here as fragments representing whole systems. They encourage the collector in us: the museum-like atmosphere of the painting hints at gaps which we desire to fill, and which prove the possibility of endless signification for the piece (1992a: 54–7).

Like alchemy, the painting's figures might be construed to represent a hidden knowledge, a 'Boschian metalanguage' (1992a: 57). Whereas the signs are complex in Bosch's painting, however, it is not a secret knowledge that Certeau finds here, but a kind of subverted alchemy. Indeed, Bosch does 'tak[e] up the signs that accommodate all the scientific curiosities of his time', but he 'makes them function differently, just as he does the various fragments that he brings together in the non-place of his painting' (1992a: 57). 'The painting modifies these signs by assigning them to the ambivalent capacity of still being understandable as fragments of meaning systems, even though they are already set within a different space, one that "converts" them into an aesthetics' (1992a: 58). In the process of this modification, Certeau reads a shift from the referential to the poetic.

As an effecter of these conversions, Certeau sees that Bosch is in essence a craftsman. As a consequence, though one may not be able to tell what something means in his work, one might analyse how it comes to be, 'how, according to what rules, it is produced' (1992a: 60). 'This sort of painting is an art of making', Certeau notes (1992a: 60). Time might be spent reconstructing some of the structures of the paintings, as Certeau does to show their geometrical balance. Or, one might analyse the shapes and classifications of the figures. All, one supposes, is in aid of illustrating the true artifice of the work, the intelligence behind the design, which speaks its own language or tells its own fable.

The bodies in these pieces are assemblages, hybrids whose creation relies primarily on the interchangeability of their parts with other elements in the picture. So, a plum stands in place of a head, etc. New combinations are made by juxtaposition or by imposition (1992a: 66). What makes them effective, Certeau thinks, is not so much the unexpected replacements, but the unanticipated shifts in proportion that accompany them (1992a: 66–7). A musical instrument is enlarged to become a weapon of torture. In turn, the bodies are part of a web of pathways and connections: *The Garden of Earthly Delights* offers endless possibilities for movement, but never goes anywhere. Like a composer, Bosch directs the stage, moving pieces here and there, seemingly on a whim, but always apparently as part of a system that has a particular logic to it. But what? Certeau points out the symmetry of certain frames or certain aspects of the panels, but at the end is still at sea in terms of what these might mean (1992a: 71).

Certeau's 'reading' of the painting is more nebulous than Barthes' of the Arcimboldo works, in that he does not exactly proceed to offer an analysis of the mechanics of figuration, even though he acknowledges that this is the way to proceed (to interrogate how, rather than what it means). His contribution is instead one that makes an observation about vision and tone. That is to say, his evaluation of the work as organizing a loss of meaning should not be taken as a failure to get anything out of it at all. On the contrary, what Certeau is in the process of showing is that certain discourses – the painting of a visionary, the ramblings of a beggarwoman in a square (the utterances of mystics) – operate differently to speech, yet are able to *speak* to us all the same. Certeau, like Barthes, writes of metamorphosis in this regard: the vocabulary of these ramblings 'changes not in content but in status. Its value of expression (relative to a referent) or of action (relative to a receiver) fades away before the "palpable" and "sensible" quality of the signifier itself' (1992a: 58). It metamorphoses into something altogether different: 'it carries the sign from one space to another, and it produces the new space' (1992a: 58).

This new space is the mystical space. It is marked by absence and difference, which refers both to the foreignness of Certeau's object of enquiry and its historical distance from him. This absence, however, is a shared absence: Certeau feels the loss of his object of enquiry and his resultant incompetence at writing about it in the same way that he believes a mystic mourns the absence of his or her object of devotion, God, and has difficulty speaking about that object (Aherne 1995: 96–7). The space is, however, not altogether unrecognizable. Glimpses penetrate ordinary life and are enough to keep mystics (poets, artists, lovers) enervated in their search for that which escapes them.

Margins and Centres

In the space of just 50 years, then, we see a significant movement in the use of the grotesque in decoration and painting. From the seemingly innocuous designs of Raphael, where the grotesque occupies the decorative borders, it shifts to become the tool of satire, and then the perpetuator of fantastical nightmare visions. The body in such figurations is modified too. Raphael's works show a playful mixing. Cranach's and Schön's reveal sinister hybridizing of the human and the monstrous. Bosch's and

Bruegel's paintings are different again: bodily boundaries are violated; humanity is melded with nature; gender becomes a site of moralizing.

The physical positioning of the grotesque in Renaissance artistic composition raises important ideological (in addition to compositional and aesthetic) questions concerning margins and centres. Harpham explains that the grotesque is 'art of the fringes', by which he simply means that it is art that is marginal or incidental to the 'art of the centre'.

> By this means two systems of art were codified: the art of the center that had a subject and signified in an intelligible and coherent way with recognizable images arranged according to traditional and conventional schemata, and an art of the fringe that, at least in terms of the center, had no subject, yielded no meaning, and represented things that were not, nor could be, nor had ever been. (1982: 32)

Harpham's phrase, art of the centre, actually refers to the physical components and contents of the artworks under consideration, but it might also be viewed as an apt phrase for the ideological and political implications of that art. Raphael's work, daring as it may have been, was completely in line with the then pope's (Leo X's) project of Christianizing the ancient past, in this case, using ancient decorative style to retell the biblical creation story. Hence, it was officially sanctioned (and, one assumes, financially supported) by the establishment. For the same reasons, the combination of the Bible and the grotesque, moreover, must still have been within the realm of what was theologically and morally acceptable, probably because the biblical material itself was not 'grotesquified', but merely enhanced by the grotesque ornament that surrounded it. Official (whether it be moral, financial or theological) sanction would make this art of the 'centre' in another sense.

This work, however, demands another, closer look, for although it may not politically or theologically challenge the status quo, it does have artistic features that are subversive after a fashion. The grotesque borders in Raphael's work, Harpham maintains, do not really achieve significant notice (in terms of the development of the grotesque), for they are incidental and intended to fill up extra space. They function as a kind of resting place for the eye: 'In them, the eye is continually soothed by the balance and proportion of the figures and continually reassured that nothing means or coheres, nothing signifies' (Harpham 1982: 30). There is, however, little soothing about the designs. In the first place, they are chaotic and always give the impression of fluidity (agreed, it is smooth or curved and not disjointed). Swirls, curves, winged creatures, human hybrids – all threaten movement and infringement upon the 'art of the centre'. More likely than being restful, they are a distraction whose lines and patterns draw the viewer in and demand involvement. Might not viewers, then, try to justify their inclusion within the entire context of the vault or pilasters on which they are painted, especially if, as Harpham observes, nothing about them coheres or signifies? Moreover, what of their juxtaposition with the biblical material? Harpham emphasizes and promotes the separation of the two types from each other, but true art of the fringes could not function in its expected manner if there were always a physical and visual separation maintained between it and the centre. For how else does it work but by continually threatening to overcome or transgress that from which it is excluded? Harpham might have done well to read the images (biblical and grotesque) against each other, and to ask not so much about artistic intent, but the impressions the juxtapositions leave upon the viewer.

Generally, what prevents such a line of enquiry is that Harpham has a rather idealized notion of grotesque art as augmentative of piety (1982: 34) and intended to channel viewers' attentions and energies into the centre – the true heart of the artistic composition – 'so that, roused, our ruffled sensibilities move on to images that are more ennobling', which would otherwise be 'too vast to comprehend' (1982: 37). In citing Bernard of Clairvaux's complaints against the twelfth-century figures, however, he does eventually acknowledge the threat that marginal art represents to the centre (1982: 35). He concedes:

> The efforts of scholars to discover the 'unrecognized underlying scheme' indicates a long-standing hunch that the ornament, especially the grotesque ornament with human elements, can be interpreted, that it can contribute to or even encroach upon the center. If this is true, and the margin and center are equally and mutually readable, and equally mysterious, then the text may become the ornament for the illuminations, the cathedral for the gargoyles. When this possibility arises, all images split, assuming incongruous double functions; and everything is thrown into doubt. These ... designs are today called grotesque not only because of certain formal characteristics, but also because they throw the reader/viewer into that intertextual 'interval'. (1982: 38)

The disarray evinced in the viewer/reader – or, one might say the ability of the grotesque to be subversive – should not merely be looked upon as a byproduct of this type of figuration, but as a prerequisite of it. It is not so much that grotesque figuration developed as a response to the centre, but that it thrived because it was in effect counter-cultural. Moreover, the mainstream always worked to regulate it, for instance by putting it in its proper place in the borders, by its use or labelling as 'ornament' if it was the focal point of the composition, or, similarly, by its employment in serious, but marginalized, ideological critique (satire). In this way, it paradoxically ensured its survival. One needs only to look at the harsh responses of art critics to illustrate this attitude towards the grotesque.

The unnatural mixing of the *Domus Aurea* frescoes, for example, was considered an outrage that compromised architectural design, the demands of verisimilitude, and indicated poor taste on the part of those who admired them. Vitruvius, writing c. 25 BCE, is worth quoting at length:

> But those subjects which were copied from actual realities are scorned in these days of bad taste. We now have fresco paintings of monstrosities, rather than truthful representations of definite things. For instance, reeds are put in the place of columns, fluted appendages with curly leaves and volutes, instead of pediments, candelabra supporting representations of shrines, and on top of their pediments numerous tender stalks and volutes growing up from the roots and having human figures senselessly seated upon them; sometimes stalks having only half-length figures, some with human heads, others with the heads of animals
> . . .
> Such things do not exist and cannot exist and never have existed. Hence, it is the new taste that has caused bad judges of poor art to prevail over true artistic excellence. For how is it possible that a reed should really support a roof, or a candelabrum a pediment with its ornaments, or that such a slender, flexible thing as a stalk should support a figure perched upon it, or that roots and stalks should produce now flowers and now half-length figures? . . . The fact is that pictures which are unlike reality ought not to be approved, and even if they are technically fine, this is no reason why they should offhand be judged to be correct, if their subject is lacking in the principles of reality carried out with no violations.[19]

John Ruskin, writing almost two thousand years later, with the retrospective of the Renaissance's wholesale adoption of grotesque ornament, was equally as resolute as Vitruvius in his criticism of the grotesque, though for different reasons. He was ultimately concerned with the waste of talent on frivolity. Whereas Vitruvius' chief objections seem to be that the work is unrealistic and decadent, Ruskin introduces a more detailed moral (and moralizing) dimension to the discussion. The grotesque is not all bad for Ruskin, however. He draws a distinction between the 'high' and the 'low' grotesque (or 'true' and 'false' or 'noble' and 'ignoble'), the former being the results of the high Gothic period, and the latter indications of the decline of the (Venetian) Renaissance. It is of the latter that he is particularly and harshly critical, and the reasons for this depravity are clear: it happened during the fall of Venice, when the unwitting Venetians slipped down the muddy slopes of morality, from

---

19 Vitruvius 1960: 210–13. It is reported that Raphael, the greatest innovator of the *Domus Aurea*'s fantastic designs, carried on his work in spite of, and even with the assistance of, Vitruvius' criticism and insights (he is said to have sponsored his own translation of Vitruvius' works). No matter, Vitruvius was long dead. The busy doodlers of the Renaissance also proceeded merrily despite (or perhaps because of?) criticism from their contemporaries.

pride to infidelity, and from infidelity to – Ruskin spits out in disapproving italics – the *pursuit of pleasure* (1904b: 135).[20]

Ruskin's criticism of the grotesque in artistic terms (sprinkled with some moralizing for good measure) has, much like Vitruvius, to do with verisimilitude:

> The cure, skill, and science, applied to the distribution of the leaves, and the drawing of figures are intense, admirable, and accurate; therefore, they ought to have produced a grand and serious work, not a tissue of nonsense. If we can draw the human head perfectly, and are masters of its expression and its beauty, we have no business to cut it off, and hang it up by the hair at the end of a garland. If we can draw the human body in the perfection of its grace and movement, we have no business to take away its limbs, and terminate it with a bunch of leaves. Or rather, our doing so will imply that there is something wrong with us; that, if we can consent to use our best powers for such base and vain trifling, there must be something wanting in the powers themselves; and that, however skilful we may be, or however learned, we are wanting both in the earnestness which can apprehend a noble truth, and in the thoughtfulness which can feel a noble fear. (1904b: 170–71)

He concludes, 'No Divine terror will ever be found in the work of the man who wastes a colossal strength in elaborating toys' (1904b: 171).

In the critiques of Ruskin and Vitruvius, then, two kinds of claims against the grotesque are evident. One is concerned with the true vocation of art. This is chiefly that it must be verisimilitudinous. Even the grotesques that Ruskin does approve of, the most elevated grotesques of the Gothic period, he avers are studies in 'real life'. But, where realism is used with good effect, as in the case of the works of Raphael, he considers it a waste of talent. The other claim is that in order to satisfy these two critics, art has to have an inherently moral and, it turns out, political dimension. Vitruvius complained of the decadence of the new style of art with which he was confronted. Ruskin insisted on beauty, in the highest and most idealized sense that the word allows. Beauty, his work makes clear, is for the educated and the affluent (i.e. those, he suggests, who do not have their wits dulled by menial labour), for these are the people who are capable of cultivating it and comprehending its intricacy and terribleness. What Ruskin cultivates is a very elitist and ostensibly decadent lifestyle. Vitruvius' preferred art is also elitist. It is for the wealthy and the learned, and has an important place in the decoration of

---

20 Ruskin's rhetoric is outrageously supercilious and moralizing to twenty-first-century readers. He gloats, 'Throughout the whole of Scripture history, nothing is more remarkable than the close connexion of punishment with the sin of vain-glory' (1904b: 146). He later notes, in referring to the inclusion of a couple of pictures of grotesque heads, 'I cannot pollute this volume by any illustration of its worst forms ... ' (1904b: 150).

their houses (decoration is part of the architectural enterprise). It is elevated into something that only the most highly skilled and educated can master, and it is to be based on the highest principles of order, symmetry, eurythmy and propriety (1960: 13–15).

Bakhtin, Rabelais and the Grotesque Body

The foregoing investigation of the grotesque in its early stages in art history and criticism has allowed for the creation of some context in which to discuss the grotesque body. In particular, the ideological and political aspects of this 'art of the fringes' should not be underestimated; nor should its ability to unhinge, unsettle and subvert. My brief interrogation of the artistic record has not yet, however, specifically examined the body. For this, the seminal (Rabelais would have appreciated the pun) work of Bakhtin (1984) on Rabelais must be considered. In Rabelais' novels, *Gargantua* and *Pantagruel*, bodies doing what bodies do naturally – copulating, giving birth, eating, excreting, dying – are described to freakish and entertaining proportions. One sees especially here that the grotesque body is the body in process, never the complete, closed and hardened body, but always the body in *the act*. It becomes dehumanized both as its detritus is emphasized and as functional integrity is denied through exaggeration.

Bakhtin's Day out at the Fair

Before any uncovering of the grotesque body is attempted, it is important to assemble some impressions of the context in which Bakhtin locates its origins.[21] From Renaissance walls and ceilings, the grotesque enjoyed a certain literary metamorphosis in the sixteenth-century writing of Rabelais (and others), which in effect moved it backwards in time to medieval carnival grounds.[22] In this setting, which is to be distinguished from the medieval feasts of the Church, Bakhtin sees the 'suspension of all rank, privileges, norms, and prohibitions. Carnival was the true feast of time, the feast of becoming, change, and renewal. It was hostile to all that was immortalized and completed' (1984b: 10). Carnival worked on the

---

21   Clark and Holquist differentiate between carnival and the grotesque as two 'subtexts' of Bakhtin's study on the 'permitted and unpermitted' discourse of the Renaissance. The first, carnival, Clark and Holquist call a 'social institution'; the second (as grotesque realism), they call a 'literary mode' (1984: 299).

22   I am dealing with artistic and literary texts in this chapter, but carnival of course had a 'real' existence in the medieval world that Rabelais attempts to capture. See Stallybrass and White 1986, especially the bibliography, for sociohistorical studies of carnival.

peculiar logic ... of the 'inside out' (*à l'envers*), of the 'turnabout', of a
continual shifting from top to bottom, from front to rear, of numerous
parodies and travesties, humiliations, profanations, comic crownings
and uncrownings. A second life, a second world of folk culture is thus
constructed; it is to a certain extent a parody of the extracarnival life, a
'world inside out'. We must stress, however, that the carnival is far
distant from the negative and formal parody of modern times. Folk
humour denies, but it revives and renews at the same time. Bare
negation is completely alien to folk culture. (Bakhtin 1984b: 11)

For Bakhtin, this strange new world is always comedic, always a source of
laughter and liberation. Moreover, it is universal, the laughter of the
people, directed to all, including those who participate and are mocked in
the festivities.

Bakhtin's understanding of carnival pivots on his conception of
laughter. In *Rabelais and his World* (1984),[23] he is especially taken up
with two important aspects of laughter, ambivalence and revolution.
Laughter is, first, festive and universal (1984b: 11), 'directed at those who
laugh' as much as at those who are the object of derision. There is,
moreover, a kind of ambivalence evident here: this laughter is 'gay,
triumphant, and at the same time mocking, deriding. It asserts and denies,
it buries and revives' (1984b: 11–12). He continues that this universal
laughter has a 'special philosophical and utopian character' and is
oriented 'toward the highest spheres' (1984b: 12). Laughter can liberate
chiefly because it overcomes fear:

> The serious aspects of class culture are official and authoritarian; they
> are combined with violence, prohibitions, limitations and always
> contain an element of fear and intimidation. These elements prevailed
> in the Middle Ages. Laughter, on the contrary, overcomes fear, for it
> knows no inhibitions, no limitations. Its idiom is never used by violence
> and authority.[24]

---

23   I write here of Bakhtin's understanding of carnival in *Rabelais and his World*. As
Morson and Emerson point out, however, there is a development in this thinking about
laughter and the carnival. In his earlier work, the more utopic and liberatory aspects are
merely visible as traces (1990: 439). Laughter in his earlier thinking (particularly in 'Forms of
Time and Chronotope in the Novel', an essay in *The Dialogic Imagination*, 1981) is part of
'"responsible carnival"', carnival still tied down to concrete personalities in a recognizably
real time and space' (1990: 436). The Chronotope essay 'holds that "humanism" and
"moderation" are Rabelais' real goals', whereas his later work emphasizes the fantastic, the
anti-historic and the de-personal (1990: 440–41).

24   Bakhtin 1984b: 90. Bakhtin was naturally criticized for his overly positive assertions
about laughter. These words are in response to Kayser's work on the grotesque, which will be
considered later as part of some criticism of Bakhtin's notions of carnival and laughter.

Uncontrolled and liberating, laughter provides the riotous, uninhibited spirit which characterizes carnival. It is the impetus which allows carnival to sustain a kind of semiotic chaos:

> In a riot of semiosis, carnival unhinges all transcendental signifiers and submits them to ridicule and relativism; by the 'radicalism of humour' (Jean Paul), power structures are estranged through grotesque parody, 'necessity' thrown into satirical question and objects displaced or negated into their opposites. A ceaseless practice of travesty and inversion (nose/phallus, face/buttocks, sacred/profane) rampages throughout social life, deconstructing images, misreading texts and collapsing binary oppositions into a mourning groundswell of ambiguity into which all articulate discourse finally stutters and slides. Birth and death, high and low, destruction and renewal are sent packing with their tails in each other's mouths. Absolutely nothing escapes this great spasm of satire: no signifier is too solemn to be blasphemously invaded, dismantled, and turned against itself. (Eagleton 1981: 145)

For Bakhtin, the 'riot of semiosis' in carnival is, moreover, creative; it engenders a new type of discourse that would have been impossible in normal, everyday life. Indeed, the Rabelaisian world, with its escape from hegemonic structures, is reflected in physical texts (*Gargantua* and *Pantagruel*) that break away from polite discourse and forge new 'discursive, not merely lexical combinations' (Clark and Holquist 1984: 297). As Clark and Holquist explain, '[T]his [carnival] led to the creation of special forms of marketplace speech and gesture, frank and free, permitting no distance between those who came in contact with each other and liberating from norms of etiquette and decency imposed at other times.' [25] Language, like the carnival in which it is newly formed, takes on a revolutionary significance, where 'unexpected juxtapositions' and new perspectives on words and concepts renew language[26] and make it liberatory (Clark and Holquist 1984: 317).[27] Thus carnival, with its heterogeneity of speech and spectacle, is more than 'merely oppositional and reactive'. Instead, it 'suggest[s] a redeployment or counterproduction

25 Bakhtin 1984b: 10. One sees here a correlation with Bakhtin's theory that problematizes the notion that a text is a 'closed, hermetic structure that is always adequate to itself' (Clark and Holquist 1984: 297).

26 In fact, Clark and Holquist point out that Rabelais is the founder of the modern French language: 'Rabelais puts these new words into contiguity with the old words that had become sclerotic through continued use by the law, the court, the church. He creates a relativity of languages' (1984: 318).

27 This subject ultimately has, of course, significance for Bakhtin's major work on the dialogical nature of speech and language and the interrelatedness of speech and subjectivity. See Clark and Holquist 1984: 317–20; Morson and Emerson 1990: 433–72; and Bakhtin 1984a: 122–37 for more on the place of carnival in the broader context of this work.

of culture, knowledge, and pleasure' (Russo 1994: 62). It is a 'site of insurgency, and not merely withdrawal' (Russo 1994: 62).

Ultimately, at the root of the always shifting, never neutral, discourse of carnival is the body:

> [C]arnival involves above all a pluralizing and cathecting of the body, dismantling its unity into freshly mobile parts and ceaselessly trans-gressing its limits. In a collectivizing movement, the individuated body is thrown wide open to its social surroundings, so that its orifices become spaces of erotic interchange with an 'outside' that is somehow always an 'inside' too. A vulgar, shameless materialism of the body – belly, buttocks, anus, genitals – rides rampant over ruling-class civilities; and the return of the discourse to this sensuous root is nowhere more evident than in laughter itself, an enunciation that springs straight from the body's libidinal depths. (Eagleton 1981: 150)

Indeed, Clark and Holquist call Bakhtin's discourse on grotesque realism a 'study of the semantics of the body, the different meanings of the body's limbs, apertures, and functions' (1984: 299).

Freaks at the Fair

The carnivalesque body works on what Bakhtin calls the material bodily principle of grotesque realism. These two terms are intertwined and require some explication. In speaking of a material bodily principle of the Renaissance, Bakhtin refers to 'the images of the human body with its food, drink, defecation, and sexual life' that are offered in 'an extremely exaggerated form' (1984b: 18). These should not be explained, as critics have done in the past, with a limited ideological view, indicated particularly by narrow-minded notions of materiality and the body. Rather, Bakhtin wants to see the body so imaged as the heritage of the culture of folk humour which has its own unique aesthetic. This aesthetic Bakhtin calls grotesque realism (1984b: 18), and he describes it as follows:

> The material bodily principle in grotesque realism is offered in its all-popular festive and utopian aspect. The cosmic, social, and bodily elements are given here as an indivisible whole. And this whole is gay and gracious ...
>
> In grotesque realism, therefore, the bodily element is deeply positive. It is presented not in a private, egotistic form, severed from the other spheres of life, but as something universal, representing all the people. As such it is opposed to severance from the material and bodily roots of the world; it makes no pretense to renunciation of the earthy, or independence of the earth and the body. We repeat: the body and bodily life have here a cosmic and at the same time an all-people's character; this is not the body and its physiology in the modern sense of these

words, because it is not individualized. The material bodily principle is contained not in the biological individual, not in the bourgeois ego, but in the people, a people who are continually growing and being renewed. This is why all that is bodily becomes grandiose, exaggerated, immeasurable. (1984b: 19)

The aesthetic of grotesque realism that engendered the grotesque body can be differentiated from what Bakhtin calls the classical canon (elsewhere, the 'literary and artistic canon of antiquity'; 1984b: 28). This canon refers primarily to a prevailing Renaissance view of the body that was informed by an 'aesthetics of the beautiful', over against which the grotesque body was deemed ugly and without form. He explains:

> [T]he body [in the classical canon] was first of all a strictly completed, finished product. Furthermore, it was isolated, alone, fenced off from all other bodies. All signs of its unfinished character, of its growth and proliferation were eliminated; its protuberances and offshoots were removed, its convexities (signs of new sprouts and buds) smoothed out, its apertures closed. The ever unfinished nature of the body was hidden, kept secret; conception, pregnancy, childbirth, death throes, were almost never shown.[28] The age represented was as far removed from the mother's womb as from the grave, the age most distant from either threshold of individual life. The accent was placed on the completed, self-sufficient individuality of the given body. Corporal acts were only shown when the borderlines dividing the body from the outside world were sharply defined. (1984b: 29)

Bakhtin sees here not a development in aesthetics, where one canon has given way to another, but rather, a coexistence of both, with the inevitable result that the grotesque became downplayed or ignored for the sake of the classical.[29] The difference is important. The grotesque thus becomes not eradicated, but marginalized, a position on which, as I noted above, it depends for its existence.

The renewing, growing body described by Bakhtin depends, he says, on a particular relation to time. This is not only its connection with the 'cycle of life', which I will address more closely below, but, he argues, a sense of

---

28   Bakhtin elsewhere notes that in this classical canon, 'sexual life, eating, drinking, defecation ... have been transferred to the private and psychological level where their connotation becomes narrow and specific' (1984b: 321). See 1984b: 320–22 for more contrasts. At this point, it is well to observe that here, as elsewhere, Bakhtin does tend to repeat himself. This is, in actuality, a certain frustration that the reader faces when ploughing through *Rabelais and his World*. It is almost as if Bakhtin intended to create his own grotesque corpus, which feeds into itself, with slight permutations and circumlocutions everywhere.

29   'But in history's living reality these canons were never fixed and immutable. Moreover, usually the two canons experience various forms of interaction: struggle, mutual influence, crossing, and fusion. This is especially true during the Renaissance' (1984b: 30).

historic time. In tracing its development, he sees that a primitive grotesque, concerned first with the 'biocosmic circle of cyclic changes' (1984b: 24–5) becomes imbued with political and historical significance:

> The sense of time and of change was broadened and deepened, drawing into its cycle social and historic phenomena. The cyclical character is superseded by the sense of historic time. The grotesque images with their relation to changing time and their ambivalence become the means for the artistic and ideological expression of a mighty awareness of history and of historic change which appeared during the Renaissance. (1984b: 25)

Although, to my knowledge, Bakhtin does not say it directly, this means in effect that the grotesque needs the classical canon against which he defines it in order to exist. It also means, however, that the notion of the grotesque that Bakhtin explicates is necessarily limited, at least on first appearance, to a particular historically defined context.

It transpires that the two manners or canons to which Bakhtin refers, the grotesque and classical, become a kind of shorthand for discussing the grotesque, especially in subsequent, post-Bakhtinian criticism. So, the grotesque is condensed to simply whatever is uncontained, unable to be completed and closed, that which resists stasis. As we saw, Raphael's decoration of the Vatican loggias with biblical stories elucidates such a contrast well. The biblical characters were painted in the typical, *realismo* classical style of the high Renaissance, and grotesqueries threatened, but never compromised them, from the borders. The binarism, grotesque/classical, however, is limited in its use, and, moreover, it does not sufficiently capture the full nature of the grotesque as Bakhtin elucidates it.

A better explanatory key is that grotesque realism works on a system of degradation, or downwards movement. Degradation involves a 'humbling, debunking, or debasing of whatever is lofty by the lowly … and the lowering of all forms of expression in language or art' (Clark and Holquist 1984: 309). In somatic terms, this means a repudiation (lowering, belittling, deriding) of the structures (manners, polite speech, and their physical correlates, etc.) that govern the body, that allow it to occupy the realm of what is considered 'proper' behaviour; hence it is a foregrounding of what Bakhtin terms the 'lower bodily stratum', that is, the reproductive, digestive and excretory elements. In short, and to put it in appropriate terms: (excessive) eating, pissing, shitting, farting, and other secretions/excretions, as well as fucking, giving birth, dying and rotting are all the stuff of the grotesque body.

The downward movement or degradation has, for Bakhtin, natural, earth(l)y, even cosmic implications:

'Upward' and 'downward' have here an absolute and strictly topographical meaning. 'Downward' is earth, 'upward' is heaven. Earth is an
element that devours, swallows up (the grave, the womb) and at the
same time an element of birth, of renascence (the maternal breasts).
Such is the meaning of 'upward' and 'downward' in their cosmic aspect,
while in their purely bodily aspect, which is not clearly distinct from the
cosmic, the upper part is the face or the head and the lower part is the
genital organs, the belly, and the buttocks ... Degradation here means
coming down to earth, the contact with earth as an element that
swallows up and gives birth at the same time. To degrade is to bury, to
sow, and to kill simultaneously, in order to bring forth something more
and better. To degrade also means to concern oneself with the lower
stratum of the body, the life of the belly and the reproductive organs; it
therefore relates to acts of defecation and copulation, conception,
pregnancy, and birth. Degradation digs a bodily grave for a new birth; it
has not only a destructive, negative aspect, but also a regenerating one.
To degrade an object does not imply merely hurling it into the void of
nonexistence, into absolute destruction, but to hurl it down to the
reproductive lower stratum, the zone in which conception and a new
birth take place. Grotesque realism knows no other lower level; it is the
fruitful earth and fertile womb. It is always conceiving. (Bakhtin 1984b:
21)

But this is not all. Most bodies defecate and copulate (and so on), but
every body is not necessarily a grotesque body. The linchpin for grotesque
realism is the *foregrounding* of the body in process, ever building and
rebuilding itself, reproducing other bodies, sliding always towards its final
end of death and decay (where, ironically, as food for worms it propels
other [wormy] bodies through the same movement). The grotesque body is
gerundive. Its key players, then, are those organs that emphasize the
body's shifting encounter with the cosmic theatre:

[T]he essential role belongs to those parts of the grotesque body in
which it outgrows its own self, transgressing its own body, in which it
conceives a new, second body: the bowels and the phallus. These two
areas play the leading role in the grotesque image, and it is precisely for
this reason that they are predominantly subject to positive exaggeration,
to hyperbolization; they can even detach themselves from the body and
lead an independent life, for they hide the rest of the body, as something
secondary. (The nose can also in a way detach itself from the body.)
Next to the bowels and the genital organs is the mouth, through which
enters the world to be swallowed up. And next is the anus. All these
convexities and orifices have a common characteristic; it is within them
that the confines between bodies and between the body and the world
are overcome: there is an interchange and an interorientation ... Thus
the artistic logic of the grotesque image ignores the closed, smooth, and
impenetrable surface of the body and retains only its excrescences

(sprouts, buds) and orifices, only that which leads beyond the body's limited space or into the body's depths. Mountains and abysses, such is the relief of the grotesque body; or speaking in architectural terms, towers and subterranean passages. (1984b: 317–18)

The focus here, then, is on permeability. The body's orifices are thus of especial interest, particularly the anus and the genitals (namely, the penis, since Bakhtin's emphasis is phallocentric and more concerned with the phallus as penetrator of orifices and victim to its own changes and disappointing permutations). In short, the grotesque body, as Bakhtin suggests, plays on the cycle of life, but it is not an elevation or a romanticizing of nature and life. It is instead a true-to-life account of process, a refusal of stasis, a denial of bodily integrity. He summarizes:

> Contrary to modern canons, the grotesque body is not separated from the rest of the world. It is not a closed, completed unit; it is unfinished, outgrows itself, transgresses its own limits. The stress is laid on those parts of the body that are open to the outside world, that is, the parts through which the world enters the body or merges from it, or through which the body itself goes out to meet the world. This means that the emphasis is on the apertures or the convexities, or on various ramifications and offshoots: the open mouth, the genital organs, the breasts, the phallus, the potbelly, the nose. The body discloses its essence as a principle of growth which exceeds its own limits only in copulation, pregnancy, childbirth, the throes of death, eating, drinking, or defecation. This is the ever unfinished, ever creating body, the link in the chain of genetic development, or more correctly speaking, two links shown at the point where they enter into each other ... The unfinished and open body (dying, bringing forth and being born) is not separated from the world by clearly defined boundaries; it is blended with the world, with animals, with objects. It is cosmic, it represents the entire material bodily world in all its elements. It is an incarnation of this world at the absolute lower stratum, as the swallowing up and generating principle, as the bodily grave and bosom, as a field which has been sown and in which new roots are preparing to sprout.[30]

30   Bakhtin 1984b: 26–7. By canon, Bakhtin says he

understand[s] the word ... not in the narrow sense of a specific group of consciously established rules, norms, and proportions in the representation of the human body. (It is still possible to speak of the classic canon in such a narrow sense at certain phases of its development.) The grotesque image never had such a canon. It is noncanonical by its very nature. We here use the word canon in the wider sense of a manner of representing the human body and bodily life. (1984b: 30)

One should not be confused by Bakhtin's alternation between the adjectives, 'modern', 'new' and 'classical' to modify canon. Bakhtin uses both the classical (i.e. Renaissance) canon and modern canons, broadly defined as above, to contrast the grotesque. All are closed, finished, hardened, in comparison to the grotesque.

Cosmic and earth(l)y, integrated with all, the grotesque body does not belong to itself; it is a universal body, in keeping with the carnival setting in which it comfortably rests.

> The bodily lower stratum of grotesque realism still fulfilled unifying, degrading, uncrowning, and simultaneously regenerating functions. However divided, atomized, individualized were the 'private' bodies, Renaissance realism did not cut off the umbilical cord which tied them to the fruitful womb of earth. Bodies could not be considered for themselves; they represented a material bodily whole and therefore transgressed the limits of their isolation. The private and the universal were still blended in a contradictory unity. (1984b: 23)

In contrast, again, to the modern body or the new canon, 'the events of the grotesque sphere are always developed on the boundary dividing one body from the other and, as it were, at their points of intersection. One body offers its death, the other its birth, but they are merged in a two-bodied image' (1984b: 322).[31]

For Bakhtin, a perfect example of this 'two-bodied image' can be found in the Kerch terracotta figurines, the senile, laughing, pregnant hags. He writes: 'This is a typical and strongly expressed grotesque. It is ambivalent. It is pregnant death, a death that gives birth. There is nothing completed, nothing calm and stable in the bodies of these old hags' (1984b: 25). Of course, there are other ways for the grotesque to be expressed than this 'two in one' figuration. Bakhtin locates merging also in the androgyne, pictured, for instance, on Gargantua's hat: 'Against a base of gold ... was an enamel figure ... [which] portrayed a man's body with two heads facing one another, four arms, four feet, a pair of arses and a brace of sexual organs, male and female.'[32]

Merging, too, does not have to be an intercorporeal undertaking, as Bakhtin notes. The grotesque body achieves its cosmic proportions not because it makes only a total human engagement, but because it merges with *all* the world's elements, flora, fauna, and other ('things'). Encounter and merging with the earth is most evident in the act of eating.

> [T]he body transgresses here its own limits: it swallows, devours, rends the world apart, is enriched and grows at the world's expense. The encounter of man with the world, which takes place inside the open, biting, rending, chewing mouth, is one of the most ancient, and most

31 Bakhtin 1984b: 322. Perhaps one of the finest, and most often quoted examples of this open, unfinished body can be seen in Rabelais' description of the birth of Gargantua. There, the blending of eating, digesting (a double blending, since Gragamelle has gorged herself on tripe, the intestinal material of cows which have been extravagantly fed – in meadows that bore two crops per year), excreting, birth and death (Bakhtin 1984b: 225–6).

32 Bakhtin 1984b: 323. Interestingly, Rabelais still describes this as a man's body. It is left to later critics (Russo 1994; Miles 1991) to explore gender implications for the grotesque.

important objects of human thought and imagery. Every man tastes the world, introduces it into his body, makes it part of himself. Man's awakening consciousness could not but concentrate on this moment, could not help borrowing from it a number of substantial images determining its interrelation with the world. Man's encounter with the world in the act of eating is joyful, triumphant; he triumphs over the world, devours it without being devoured himself. The limits between man and the world are erased, to man's advantage. (1984b: 281)

The gaping mouth is thus a familiar symbol in grotesque figuration, not only because it is the eating mouth, but because 'it is the open gate leading downward into the bodily underworld. The gaping mouth is related to the image of swallowing, this most ancient symbol of death and destruction.'[33]

Whereas Bakhtin is primarily concerned with the grotesque body's merging with the earth in cosmic terms, either through eating or intercourse (or giving birth), there is one other aspect that needs to be mentioned here, hybridization. Stallybrass and White in effect see that Bakhtin's work really espouses two definitions of the grotesque: one works through the grotesque/classical binarism that we have so far been examining; the other is the notion of hybridization, which, as they note, actually has the potential to subvert the first. It is their opinion that the latter is actually a more useful definition (for their project),[34] since it also incorporates the high–low duality on which carnival operates. Stallybrass and White define hybridization in Bakhtin's work as 'inmixing of binary opposites, particularly of high and low, such that there is a heterodox merging of elements usually perceived as incompatible, and this latter version of the grotesque unsettles any fixed binarism' (1986: 44). Bakhtin does not, in truth, discuss the grotesque body as the hybrid body as much as he might, and when he does mention it, he certainly does not foreground it.[35]

33   Bakhtin 1984b: 325. See Miles 1991 for an exploration of the relationship between the gaping mouth, hell and the womb or vulva.
34   Their project is a 'rigorous and historical introduction to carnival as political discourse' (Russo 1994: 196 n. 2). In this case, I happen to agree with their evaluation, though I do not want to privilege one of Bakhtin's definitions over the other, because both will be useful. In fact, as will become evident below, the two aspects of the grotesque body actually set up a potentially compromised space which may be exploited in alternate readings.
35   There is some inclusion of hybridization in Bakhtin's treatment of the lower bodily stratum that could be included here in support of this concept. This is his discussion of the text where Gargantua relates to his father the best type of swab. Rabelais treats us to a lengthy discourse on the merits and demerits of various items for arse-wiping. These range from a velvet scarf to a March cat, a variety of herbs and plants, a slipper, a basket, and so on. Throughout, there is a brilliant play on words that melds the swabs with the anus and faeces, as well as the explicit description of the effects of applying each particular swab. Gargantua in effect becomes united with the world's elements (which, as Bakhtin explains,

By grotesque bodies, therefore and in sum, one can understand ever-changing forms whose digestive, excretory and reproductive functions are emphasized, and which, moreover, disclose the bodies' intimate connection with each other and the world in which they exist. A final reiteration of the carnivalesque setting in which Bakhtin locates the grotesque body provides a reminder that though carnival has the serious task of subverting hegemony, and though its bodies are implicated in that task, grotesque forms are for Bakhtin inherently positive, entertaining and hilarious.

Raining on Bakhtin's Parade: Three Major Criticisms

Three significant and interrelated objections to Bakhtin's view of the grotesque body appear in criticism of his work. The first objection is that his conception of the carnival in which the grotesque body is located is an overly positive and idealized one, and this brings into question its liberatory or utopic potential. The second objection is that Bakhtin's work neglects to observe carnival's implications for the bodies which are so exuberantly and flamboyantly used and displayed. Indeed, the politics of carnival mean the condoned or even enforced oppression of a particular group by the establishment: someone or some group always bears the brunt of the joke, with very real consequences for personal safety and autonomy of the body. Finally, a third and related objection to Bakhtin's work is that his idea of the grotesque underestimates the force of alienation in it. This has implications for the bodies involved in grotesque figuration, and also those who engage with it as viewers and readers.

Allowed Fools

Bakhtin's affinity for carnival and the Renaissance period was, as we saw above, due to his appreciation of its transitional and revolutionary nature. The carnival, it turns out, had affinities with his own experiences of pre-revolutionary Russia; both were worlds on the verge of change (Clark and Holquist 1984: 296). In the wildly fantastic and delightfully perverse texts of Rabelais, Bakhtin could locate some hope for his own time. His conception of carnival may thus be viewed as utopic, a liberating impulse against the strictures of Stalinism which affected the world in which he

---

display their own logic as they are presented according to a downward or degrading order), as they cut, irritate, clean and soothe him – all, ironically, as he attempts to rid himself of the world which he has swallowed and digested. Certainly, there is visible here the 'heterodox merging of elements usually perceived as incompatible' of which Stallybrass and White write. Moreover, this merging disrupts the grotesque/classical binarism of open/closed bodies, or perhaps, continues as an alternative discourse alongside it.

was writing (Eagleton 1981: 144).[36] Bakhtin was interested, particularly, in finding a new world order that subverted hierarchy and followed the more horizontally organized world of the carnival (Clark and Holquist 1984: 310).

As Eagleton points out, however, the carnival world may not have been so effective in meeting Bakhtin's needs. In fact, he observes, the carnival–utopia is 'a *licensed* affair in every sense, a permissible rupture of hegemony, a contained popular blow-off as disturbing and relatively ineffectual as a revolutionary work of art' (1981: 148). There is, as he adds, quoting Olivia in *Hamlet*, 'no slander in an allowed fool' (1981: 148). Hence, Eagleton's answer to his ruminations about the political efficacy of carnival is mixed:

> Carnival laughter is incorporative as well as liberating, the lifting of inhibitions politically enervating as well as disruptive. Indeed, from one viewpoint carnival may figure as a prime example of that mutual complicity of law and liberation, power and desire, that has become a dominant theme of contemporary post-Marxist pessimism. Bakhtin's carnival, however, is so clearly a licensed enclave that the point almost makes itself; and its utopian aspects are thus largely subordinated to its satirical functions. Though it is in one sense a thoroughly 'corporatist' culture, and thus in some danger of being undialectically translated into an image of the future, in another sense it exists only through its subversive engagements with historical hegemony, wholly constituted by its contradictory relations to ruling-class culture. This makes it difficult to disengage as a self-contained image, in contrast, say, to the anarchic circus image of *Hard Times*, which blithely ignores its enclosing hegemony. It is, in effect, a kind of fiction: a temporary retextualizing of the social formation that exposes its 'fictive' foundations. (1981: 148)

Stallybrass and White would agree with Eagleton's assertions that carnival politically enervates as well as disrupts. They further refine his perspective by discussing the socioeconomic aspects of the carnival/fair. It is, they argue, a grave oversimplification and abstraction to see it only as the location of 'communal celebration'.[37] The position of the fair was

36   '[I]n what is perhaps the boldest, most devious gesture in the history of "Marxist criticism", Bakhtin pits against that official, formalistic and logical authoritarianism, whose unspoken name is Stalinism the explosive politics of the body, the erotic, the licentious and semiotic. Rabelais is the memory that Bakhtin seizes hold of as it flashes up at a moment of danger' (Eagleton 1981: 144).

37   Bakhtin 1986: 29. Stallybrass and White explain that the bourgeoisie actually tried to separate the economic from the social, to invent, in effect, a purely pleasurable or purely economic fair, but were unsuccessful. They were in fact disturbed and scandalized by the mixing of both, especially since the notion of 'work' was in the process of becoming distinct from that of play. But, as Stallybrass and White note, such labours were in vain:

more complex than this because it was actually situated at the 'intersection of economic and cultural forces, goods and travellers, commodities and commerce' (Stallybrass and White 1986: 28–9). It worked as an 'agent of transformation', since it 'brought together the exotic and the familiar, the villager and the townsman, the professional performer and the bourgeois observer'. As such, the fair 'actually promoted a conjuncture of discourses and objects favourable to innovation' (Stallybrass and White 1986: 36) and, what is more to the point, it 'played a crucial part in the formation and transformation of local socioeconomic relations and the State' (Stallybrass and White 1986: 35).

In this respect, carnival might be seen not as the populist environment that Bakhtin envisioned, but as the 'point of economic and cultural intersection, of hybridization' (Stallybrass and White 1986: 38). Stallybrass and White observe that if the fair could be viewed as the site where official ideologies could be opposed (as Bakhtin would have it), it was 'also the means by which emergent mercantile interests could stimulate new desires' (1986: 38). This meant that the fair became a 'kind of educative spectacle, a relay for the cosmopolitan values of the "centre" (particularly the capital and the new urban centres of production)' (1986: 38). In other words, the fair shifted boundaries, and by stimulating new desires, created new contexts for the centre to take hold and exert its influence and authority.

Not only, however, can we speak of carnival's political enervations and suppressions: carnival is also in Bakhtin's work, as Stallybrass and White are at pains to point out, a *literary* affair. Thus its efficacy in real terms (as a socially transformative force) must further be questioned (Wills 1989: 130). Stallybrass and White criticize Bakhtin for making the Rabelaisian texts and the carnival homologous. Whereas they believe that Bakhtin's move to liberate Rabelais from a 'literary history which read the past only in terms of its "official framework"' is warranted, they are not convinced that he succeeds. This is because he 'never sufficiently clarified the key issue of *distinct discursive domains*, and the connection that these domains – each with its own languages and symbolic practices – had with each other' (1986: 60). For Stallybrass and White, the historical carnival and the literary carnival speak fundamentally different languages.

This brings us to the body. A politically suppressive and repressive context that masquerades as a liberatory one would doubtless have implications for the playing and displayed bodies of the fair. This is all the

---

Such an attempt to clean up the fair's hybridization was a paradoxical, even contradictory ideological project, for the labour of conceptual separation was itself subject to the seductive power of the hybrid. As these boundaries were constructed they were haunted by the play between the oppositions which had been formulated. (1986: 31)

more so for a written text about such a context, since, as Stallybrass and
White observe, the relationships between participant and observer are
constantly shifting. Clark and Holquist have argued that the particular
somatic aspect of Bakhtin's carnival is more than a 'defiant stand against
the prevailing idealism [about the body] of his day or a sally against the
puritanism of Stalinist society' (1984: 311). It is, instead, they argue, a
subversion of a particular ideology that intends to keep the body – the
individual body and the body as metaphor for the state – closed and free
from the influences of the outside (1984: 311–12).[38] But if the fair is not a
fundamentally free space, but in fact only 'licenses' revolution, then it
follows that the bodies that are involved in the carnival are being
implicated despite themselves in the mock-liberation, either as mock-
oppressors or as the oppressed. In short, these bodies would be
undergirding the ideological structures (moral, political, theological) of
the state, rather than acting against them.

Who's Laughing Now?

If the liberatory potential of Bakhtin's carnival is in doubt, so, too, is the
reputed celebratory and free nature of the grotesque body in it. In other
words, if carnival is a licensed affair, as Bakhtin's critics suggest, then it
must be that its universality is rendered suspect, and furthermore that
there *is* a division between spectator and performer after all, between
those on the 'inside' and those on the 'outside'. Moreover, it would be the
case that those on the 'outside' do not naturally find themselves there, but
are put there because they have been chosen by those on the 'inside' to
occupy a marginalized position. As 'performers', they are selected to
entertain those who represent the status quo, be that moral or religious or
political. And what is entertaining, in the carnival milieu, is that which
deviates from normality, from polite behaviour or the usual or acceptable
physical profile of the body. Those whose behaviour or bodies are not
normal are selected to perform for those who are. This is why the carnival
became the home of so-called 'freaks'.

Of particular use and interest in this regard is Stallybrass and White's
discussion of the role of the pig in European culture. After a lengthy
treatment on the semiotic function of the pig over a number of years
(namely, with reference to its repudiation and marginalization, largely due
to the position it held at the threshold of the farm, the dinner-table, etc.),
they give the example of the pig's place at the carnival, which was
ostensibly one of levity and celebration ('Carne-levare'). So far so good
for the pig (except that it is soon to be eaten). However, Stallybrass and

---

38   For a more detailed discussion of Bakhtin's work as a response to Stalinism, see Clark
and Holquist 1984: 307–16.

White note that the pig was also used to promote racist violence. They compare two carnivals, those of Rome and Venice. In the latter, pigs were chased across the town square and stoned, presumably as part of the pre-feast activities. In Rome, by contrast, Jews were treated in this manner, thereby made to replace pigs semiotically and all they stood for, both within and outside of the carnival context. Stallybrass and White observe that the pigs become the tool of 'displaced abjection', the 'process whereby "low" social groups turn their figurative and actual power, *not* against those in authority, but against those who are even "lower" (women, Jews, animals, particularly cats and pigs)'.[39]

The matter of marginalization occurring within the already margin-alized is one which is also of significance for the grotesque body and the subject of gender. As Stallybrass and White point out, women are among the list of the 'already low'. Because of this status, their implication in the carnival context puts their freedom and autonomy there at risk, more so than if they were not already marginalized. For instance, in the Wiltshire enclosure riots of 1641, rioters were accompanied by cross-dressing men known as 'Lady Skimmingtons', presumably for the skimming ladles that they carried, which could be used to beat henpecked husbands (Russo 1994: 58–9).[40] As Russo notes, the 'projection of the image of the fierce virago onto popular movements, especially a movement such as this one, involving the transgression of boundaries, is suggestive from the point of view of social transformation' (1994: 59). However, it is questionable whether and how the cross-dressers were actually able to effect that transformation.

> The carnivalized woman such as Lady Skimmington, whose comic female masquerade of those 'feminine' qualities of strident wifely aggression, behind whose skirts men are protected and provoked to action, is an image that, however counterproduced, perpetuates the dominant (and in this case misogynistic) representation of women by men. In the popular tradition of this particular example, Lady

---

39 Bakhtin 1986: 53. Stallybrass and White explain further:

> The Jews, usually a 'low' and marginal group within European cultures, had been defined in popular Christian mythology as the *antithesis* of the pig (following Levitical law; Lev. 11.7-8) ... By eliding the Jew with the pig the carnival crowd were producing a grotesque hybridization of terms expressly antithetical to each other according to the dietary rules of their victims, who, at carnival time, would be self-excluded from the great pig-feast. This offensive transgression through 'grotesque realism', though in formal accordance with the symbolic procedures identified by Bakhtin, simply reaffirmed the existing dominance of Christian laws: *it was far from challenging the dominant*. (1986: 53, second emphasis mine)

40 The riot was not a carnival proper, but its form of protest is carnivalesque in Russo's and Stallybrass and White's views.

> Skimmington is mocked alongside her henpecked husband, for she
> embodies the despised aspects of 'strong' femininity, and her subordin-
> ate position in society is, in part, underlined in this enactment of power
> reversal. (Russo 1994: 59)

Russo appropriately asks whether or not this 'comic female style' actually
works to free women from a 'more confining aesthetic'. 'Or, are women
again so identified with style itself that they are estranged from its
liberatory and transgressive effects as they are from their own bodies as
signs in culture generally?' (1994: 60).

Women are symbolically at risk in Rabelais too. Consider his
description of the building of the walls of Paris, which uses the inversions
and genital emphases of the grotesque body to build a fanciful wall for the
city and as a satirical tool:

> I have observed that the pleasure-twats of women in this part of the
> world [Paris] are much cheaper than stones. Therefore, the walls should
> be built of twats, symmetrically and according to the rules of
> architecture, the largest to go in front. Next, on the downward slope
> like the back of an ass, the medium-sized, and last of all, the least and
> smallest. These should all be made to dovetail and interlace, like the
> great tower of Bourges ... (Bakhtin 1984b: 202)

There are, however, actual as well as symbolic risks for the autonomy
and safety of women in the carnival setting. Russo observes:

> Other social historians have documented the insight of anthropologist
> Victor Turner, that the marginal position of women and others in the
> 'indicative' world makes their presence in the 'subjunctive' or possible
> world of the topsy-turvy carnival 'quintessentially' dangerous ... In
> other words, in the everyday indicative world, women and their bodies,
> certain bodies, in certain public framings, in certain public spaces, are
> always already transgressive – dangerous and in danger. (Russo 1994:
> 60)

For women and other marginalized groups, life is a double risk. The
'indicative' world, as Russo calls it, is dangerous, and that danger is
played upon and compounded in the carnival world.[41] And, though Russo
does not explicitly say this here, the process must also have been cross-
fertilizing. Women in the indicative world would have been equally
suspect because of their subjunctive status among the freaks at the fair.

---

41   The danger to which Russo refers is a real, physical one. There is significant evidence,
for instance, that women were regularly raped during carnival (Russo 1994: 60).

Carnival Meets the Uncanny

The third and final major criticism of Bakhtin's work has to do with its failure to acknowledge some of the more sinister aspects of the grotesque. Here, we move away from the political and edge toward the psychological. Since this psychological or 'inner' aspect of the grotesque is not primarily taken up with the physical body, its use here may not be immediately obvious. It is helpful, however, in that it offers some understanding of the emotional atmosphere in which the grotesque body (and readers' responses to it) might be better understood (as, for example, I discussed with reference to Arcimboldo's *Winter*, above). And, in fact, the reverse is also true: in Russo's words, despite its difference, this 'inner' grotesque nevertheless needs the body image as a 'prop' (1994: 9).

In recent studies, critics have differentiated between two types or avenues of the grotesque. Some have simplified them as a 'negative' and 'positive' grotesque (Harpham, Thompson), or 'comic' and 'tragic', while another (Russo), observes that one is a somatic grotesque, and the other an inner grotesque, devoted to the investigation of the 'psychic register and to the bodily as cultural projection of an inner state' (Russo 1994: 9). The differentiation, whatever its labels (Russo's are the most convincing), stems largely from the existence of two great works on the grotesque, Bakhtin's *Rabelais and his World* and Wolfgang Kayser's *The Grotesque in Art and Literature* (1963). The spirit of the two works is drastically different, and one can easily see how critics have tended to polarize them. As we saw, Bakhtin sees the grotesque as liberating, comic, always positive; Kayser, on the other hand, views it as dark, sinister and alienating.

The Grotesque in Art and Literature keeps its readers in suspense for a definition of the grotesque until the very end of the book. In the last ten pages, Kayser attempts to draw together the many threads unravelled in a very broad selection of material. He comes upon his definition by asking if the literary works throughout the last three centuries that he has considered have anything in common. He eventually settles on three theses: (1) 'The grotesque is the estranged world' (1963: 184), whereby our world is transformed. It takes us by surprise, fills us with suspense. It is full of tension, a 'pregnant moment';[42] (2) 'The grotesque is a play with

---

42   Kayser 1963: 184. Kayser explains:

> We are so strongly affected and terrified because it is our world which ceases to be reliable, and we feel that we would be unable to live in this changed world. The grotesque instils fear of life rather than fear of death. Structurally, it presupposes that the categories which apply to our worldview become inapplicable. We have observed the progressive dissolution which has occurred since the ornamental art of the Renaissance: the fusion of realms which we know to be separated, the abolition of the law of statics, the loss of identity, the distortion of 'natural' size and shape,

the absurd';[43] (3) 'The grotesque is an attempt to invoke and subdue the demonic aspects of the world.'[44]

There was actually no great debate between Bakhtin and Kayser over the nature of the grotesque: Bakhtin simply had a few comments to make about what he thought was Kayser's limited purview. Bakhtin's disagreement with Kayser – if it can be called that – is based on laughter. He does not think that Kayser's work, which he believes reveals the critic's twentieth-century modernist glasses, can capably account for the ethos of the pre-Romantic era.

> Kayser's definitions first of all strike us by the gloomy, terrifying tone of the grotesque world that alone the author sees. In reality, gloom is completely alien to the entire development of this world up to the romantic period. We have already shown that the medieval and Renaissance grotesque, filled with the spirit of carnival, liberates the world from all that is dark and terrifying; it takes away all fears and is therefore completely gay and bright. All that was frightening in ordinary life is turned into amusing or ludicrous monstrosities ...

> Fear is the extreme expression of narrow-minded and stupid seriousness, which is defeated by laughter. (Bakhtin 1984b: 47)

---

the suspension of the category of objects, the destruction of personality, and the fragmentation of the historical order (1963: 184–5).

43   'Laughter', Kayser notes,

originates on the comic and caricatural fringe of the grotesque. Filled with bitterness, it takes on characteristics of the mocking, cynical, and ultimately satanic laughter while turning into the grotesque ... Perhaps still another aspect of laughter in the grotesque should now be added. I refer to Fischart's description of the dance of the giants which began as a simple play with words but progressed to a point where language itself seemed to come to life and draw the author into its whirlpool ... (1963: 187)

44   Kayser 1963: 188. As Kayser explains:

It may begin in a gay and carefree manner – as Raphael wanted to play in his grotesques. But it may also carry the player away, deprive him of his freedom, and make him afraid of the ghosts which he so frivolously invoked ... In many grotesques, little is to be felt of such freedom and gaiety. But where the artistic creation has succeeded, a faint smile seems to pass rapidly across the scene or picture, and slight traces of the playful frivolity of the *capriccio* appear to be present. And there, but only there, another kind of feeling arises within us. In spite of all the helplessness and horror inspired by the dark forces which lurk in and behind our world and have power to estrange it, the truly artistic portrayal effects a secret liberation. The darkness has been sighted, the ominous powers discovered, the incomprehensible forces challenged. (1963: 187–8)

Bakhtin sums up Kayser's grotesque as particularly stressing alienation (the grotesque is 'something hostile, alien and inhuman'; Bakhtin 1984b: 47), and whereas he does acknowledge that the grotesque has something to do with it, he avers that its otherworldliness must be interpreted along the liberating, utopic lines discussed above:

> Actually the grotesque, including the Romantic form, discloses the potentiality of an entirely different world, of another order, another way of life. It leads men out of the confines of the apparent (false) unity, of the indisputable and stable ... The existing world becomes alien (to use Kayser's terminology) precisely because there is the potentiality of a friendly world, of a golden age, of carnival truth. (Bakhtin 1984b: 48)

Bakhtin also makes a few other points in response to Kayser. In the latter's concept of the grotesque, there is no 'room for the material bodily principle' and no acknowledgment of time, in terms of change and crisis – with respect to carnival (1984b: 48). Finally, Kayser's understanding of death as an opposite of life must be countered, according to Bakhtin, since in the grotesque system, death is merely an extension of life and wrapped up in the cycle of renewal and change (1984b: 51).

The kinds of themes Bakhtin touches on in his response to Kayser extend beyond the purely physical boundaries of the grotesque body; they incorporate worldview and acknowledge the power of laughter to overcome fear, definitely material for the 'psychic register' to which Russo has referred. Nevertheless, Bakhtin's analysis of the psychological causes and effects of the grotesque stops somewhere near these lines, and Kayser's work is invaluable for adding to the gap he leaves.[45]

Kayser's analysis of Romantic and modern literature is thorough. In psychological terms, however, his analysis of the alienated world he identifies is wanting. Russo provides some of what is missing in her overview of Bakhtinian and 'Kayserisch' grotesques by mentioning Freud's concept of the *Unheimlich*. Freud's by now classic text seeks to give some form to 'all that is terrible – to all that arouses dread and creeping horror' (Freud 1925: 368). For Freud, the root of the uncanny lies within us; it is a recurrence of the repressed. He summarizes thus:

---

45 It would be wrong to give the impression that the idea of the liberatory aspects of laughter in grotesque figuration ended with Bakhtin. What is under question is his failure to explicate the alienation that is part of the grotesque. More recent literature struggles with the place of laughter with respect to fear; see, e.g., Clark 1991; Kahane 1979. One might also involve Freud (1960) in the discussion. His observation that laughter is a 'psychical factor possessed of power' (1960: 133) can be pursued in a number of different directions on a psychoanalytical level. For instance, he suggests that laughter assists in the lifting of suppressions and repressions (1960: 137); that it occasions a pleasurable recovery of what is familiar (1960: 120); and that the pleasure derived from laughter results in a cathexis (1960: 148–9). See the chapter on laughter and pleasure for more (1960: 117–39).

> In the first place, if psycho-analytic theory is correct in maintaining that
> every emotional affect, whatever its quality, is transformed by repres-
> sion into morbid anxiety, then among such cases of anxiety there must
> be a class in which the anxiety can be shown to come from something
> repressed which recurs. This class of morbid anxiety would then be no
> other than what is uncanny, irrespective of whether it originally aroused
> dread or some other affect. (1925: 394)

Moreover, it can be said that the *Unheimlich* is never far from the
Heimlich, or familiar, since that which is repressed was once 'something
familiar and old-established in the mind that has been estranged only by
the process of repression' (1925: 394). Freud adds that the uncanny is
'easily produced by effacing the distinction between imagination and
reality' (1925: 398). This means that it is particularly at home in literature,
where an author can manipulate readers and 'guide the current of our
emotions' (1925: 406).

Kayser's (and Freud's) insights fill out Bakhtin's essentially comic view
of the grotesque. Ultimately, however, it is not useful to insist on the
division of the grotesque into the two types discussed here (positive and
negative; somatic and psychological, etc.); these have too quickly and
unhelpfully become binary opposites. The refusal of the grotesque to
occupy entirely one realm or the other is surely a key to its existence and
continuance. For the purposes of this study, and in light of Kayser's
critique, it is more appropriate to conceptualize a context for the
grotesque body that allows the hilarious and the terrifying uneasily and
provocatively to coexist. We are reminded, too, to bear in mind Kayser's
final and perhaps frustrating observation: the 'grotesque is experienced
only in the act of reception' (1963: 181).

The Female Grotesque, or, 'A Cunning Array of Stunts'[46]

The matter of gender has already been mentioned, above, with respect to
the implications for carnival's marginalized body. Broadly speaking,
though, this is a subject that has largely gone uncommented upon in
studies of the grotesque, until some fairly recent work by feminist
theorists. Whereas scholarly discussion of the grotesque *has* included the
subject of sexuality, it has been heavily criticized for its neglect of the
subject of gender. As Margaret Miles pointedly observes, '[S]exuality is a
prominent part of both Bakhtin's and Harpham's descriptions of the
grotesque, but gender is not.'[47] In Bakhtin's analysis, the sexual or

---

46 The anagram is Russo's (1994: 13). Its form speaks of inversion, the feminine and the
spectacle, all of which are key issues in the investigation of gender and the grotesque.

47 Miles 1991: 155, 221 n. 24. Stallybrass makes a similar point: 'But because these
connections [between politeness and politics] are never simply given, the body can itself

reproductive activities of the body have a distinct role to play in its grotesqueness, since in its sexual capacity, aspects such as permeability, volatility and merging become primary. However, what Miles, Russo and others like them find missing in Bakhtin's work is any analysis of the implications of identifying bodies as grotesque *because* of their sexual function or activities.[48] More particularly, since most of these activities are specifically female, the implication that the grotesque has an intimate relationship with the female body must be taken into account. This, then, is the project of two of the three writers considered below (Miles and Russo), each with its unique focus, of course. The third, Kristeva, addresses the theme via her work on the abject, through an alternate, but related, avenue of psychoanalysis.

The Volatile Body

In *Carnal Knowing: Female Nakedness and Religious Meaning in the Christian West* (1991), Miles is interested in the gender-specific associations of nakedness with subjectivity, particularly how it is that representations of the naked female body are used as a 'cipher for sin, sex and death' (1991: 12). Grotesque figuration seems to be an important key. Miles launches her discussion by using Bakhtin's treatment of a scene in the Italian *commedia dell'arte*, where Harlequin encounters a stutterer who is having difficulty 'giving birth' to a particular word:

> A stutterer talking with Harlequin cannot pronounce a difficult word; he makes a great effort, loses his breath, keeping the word down in his throat, sweats and gapes, trembles, chokes. His face is swollen, his eyes pop; 'it looks as if he were in the throes and spasms of childbirth.' Finally Harlequin, weary of waiting, relieves the stutterer by surprise; he rushes head forward and hits the man in the abdomen. The difficult word is 'born' at last. (Bakhtin 1984b: 304)

Bakhtin comments that the 'highly spiritual act' of speaking is here 'degraded and uncrowned by the transfer to the material bodily level of childbirth' (1984b: 309). In response, Miles observes:

> Unremarked by Bakhtin, the debasement of the act is brought about by a gender inversion, by the simple placement of the production of a word in a reproductive body. Thus the 'highly spiritual act' is that of a man, while its conversion to the comic occurs – must occur? – in the body of a

---

become a site of conflict. In *Rabelais and his World*, Bakhtin attempts to map out that site, although he concentrates on the body as the *locus* of class conflict to the exclusion of gender ... ' (Stallybrass 1986: 123–4).

48 Most of the work on the grotesque mentioned above can be included in this group with Bakhtin and Harpham: Kayser 1963; Burwick 1987; Barasch 1971; Clayborough 1965. The exception is Kuryluk 1987.

woman. The association of the female body with materiality, sex, and reproduction makes it an essential – not an accidental – aspect of the grotesque. The socially constructed *différance* which means that male and female bodies are not only physically different, but also hierarchically arranged and asymmetrically valued underlies the literary use of woman's body as the primary figure of debasement. (1991: 150–51)

Miles's is a conclusion shared by other critics as well. Russo makes a related observation of Bakhtin's discussion of the Kerch terracotta figures, the senile pregnant hags:

> But, for the feminist reader, this image of the pregnant hag is more than ambivalent. It is loaded with all of the connotations of fear and loathing around the biological processes of reproduction and of aging. Bakhtin, like many other social theorists of the nineteenth and twentieth centuries, fails to acknowledge or incorporate the social relations of gender in his semiotic model of the body politic, and thus his notion of the Female Grotesque remains in all directions repressed and undeveloped.[49]

Both Miles and Russo perceive that the female body is especially implicated in grotesque figuration because of its particular associations with sex and reproductivity. In pregnancy, menstruation and intercourse, the female body loses its integrity and ceases to be the ' "closed, smooth and impenetrable" body that serves as the symbol of individual, autonomous and "perfect" existence' (Miles 1991: 153). Bodies of women who were perceived to be perpetually engaged in sexual activity, such as those of prostitutes, were thus quintessentially grotesque; they 'epitomized the penetrable body, the body shaped by lust, the permeable body that produces juices and smells' (Miles 1991: 153). By contrast, perpetual and/or paradigmatic virgins, such as the Virgin Mary and Queen Elizabeth I (both key figures in the Renaissance period), were considered impenetrable, 'gardens enclosed' (Miles 1991: 153; Stallybrass 1986: 130).

The contrast being made between these 'two kinds of women', marked by the leaking body and the closed garden, is instructive.[50] Because of the body's possibility to slip from the desired state to the undesired one, it had to be subjected to constant surveillance. This focused on three specific areas, 'the mouth, chastity, the threshold of the house'. All of these 'frequently collapsed into each other' (Stallybrass 1986: 126). Thus a 'harlot' was linguistically promiscuous and she frequented public areas, whereas a 'good wife' (or good daughter) kept quiet and was kept at home, the sexual property of one man only. The latter woman is,

---

49   Russo 1994: 63. Russo does concede that Bakhtin's description is 'at least exuberant' (1994: 63).

50   It is also relevant to the Song of Songs (and draws on its imagery), where gardens, mothers' houses and the like are constantly intermingled.

Stallybrass notes, 'rigidly "finished"': her signs are the enclosed body, the closed mouth, the locked house' (1986: 127).[51] Woman, thus, was ambiguous: she was 'both a symbolic map of the "civilized" and the dangerous terrain that had to be colonized' (Stallybrass 1986: 133). This system of surveillance and control, moreover, had political correlates: '[T]he normative "Woman" became the emblem of the perfect and impermeable container, and hence a metaphor for the integrity of the state. The state, like the chaste woman or virgin, was a *hortus conclusus*, an enclosed garden walled off from enemies' (Stallybrass 1986: 129). Thus we find Elizabeth I celebrated in poem and in painting as 'imperial virgin',[52] *hortus conclusus*; she was at the same time both the sustainer of paradise (England and all its lands) and indicative of that edenic paradise.[53]

Miles makes a similar observation to Stallybrass's with respect to the bodily control of women, only she sees that grotesque figuration acts as an additional stabilizing force against the uncontrollable and unpredictable woman:

> Figured as Eve, the perversely bent rib, every woman was seen as essentially grotesque, though the revelation of her hidden monstrosity could be prevented by her careful adherence to socially approved appearance and behavior. The function of this figuration was to identify, define, and thus to stabilize a feared and fantisized object. Grotesque figuration contributes the bonus of laughter, permitting relief of tension; the simultaneously feared and desired object becomes comic. For women, in societies in which they were defined as 'Eves,' the perpetual threat was that their 'true nature' would emerge. Only by constant labor could women establish and maintain their identification with images of the 'good' woman, the docile, nurturing, obedient woman. Since the grotesque threatened to bleed into public view at any moment, constant vigilance was required, primarily by women, but also by the husbands and fathers responsible for them. (1991: 152)

In order to demonstrate how grotesque figuration works to stabilize women, Miles proposes that there are three rhetorical and pictorial devices in operation in the art and culture of the Christian West (hybridization, caricature and inversion). Of these, caricature receives the

51 Other restrictions can be found in manners and clothing. See Clark 1985.

52 Stallybrass notes that Elizabeth I still had a place in the ideology of a state that was heavily based on family values because, despite her unusual status as virgin queen, she was both virgin and 'mother' (of the people; 1986: 133). He also speaks of the connection between patriarchy and monarchy (1986: 131).

53 Not surprisingly, the Song of Songs and other biblical references were borrowed for this figuration of the Queen. Stallybrass cites John King who preached a sermon on the Queen as a 'several, peculiar, enclosed peece of ground ... [that] lieth within a hedge or a fense ... [marked off from] the grape of Sodome or cluster of Gomorrhe' (1986: 130–31).

most detailed attention and convincing treatment in her study.[54] It 'reveals a social consensus on what is to be avoided' and 'isolates and fetishizes parts of the body' (Miles 1991: 155). Miles observes that a number of medieval images of hell, for example, covertly depict the vagina as its opening, into which all kinds of profligates and evildoers tumble; hell may additionally appear uterus-shaped.[55] Caricature is also evident in the many examples of what Miles calls 'religious pornography',[56] that is, hagiographic texts complete with illustrations that violently target and fetishize various parts of women's bodies. As might be expected, in this conceptualization of caricature there is little acknowledgement of any humorous element, even though the word does imply it, and it is an obvious factor in Bakhtin's analysis. Miles is, of course, trying to point out that grotesque figuration (including caricature) has a misogynistic aspect and is therefore definitely unfunny. In omitting humour, however, she misses an important tool whereby grotesque figuration is accomplished.

Miles's third rhetorical and pictorial device, inversion, is not developed to a great extent in her study, but it does bring up an important issue. Broadly understood, inversion is the 'reversal of an expected and pleasing appearance to produce a disturbing image' (Miles 1991: 159). Miles's focus is specifically on the normativization of male genitalia in ancient, medieval and Renaissance perceptions of the human body. In the female body, however, these are inverted, a biological 'mishap' caused by and indicative of woman's moral and spiritual inferiority to man.[57] As a result,

54 Hybridization ('a random combination of disparate parts, without functional integrity'; 1991: 161) is barely touched upon, except to recapitulate what Bakhtin has already said. In this case, Miles recasts Bakhtin's discussion of the Kerch terracotta figurines, through which he identified the conflation of various life stages into one body. Her notion of hybridization *genders* Bakhtin's by emphasizing the female aspects of the body that outgrows itself and transgresses its own limits. Inversion is also little discussed in Miles's analysis, and not at all manifested in examples of Christian art in her book.

55 I do not find Miles's pictorial evidence all that convincing, particularly the examples of the uteri and vulvae as the 'mouths of hell'. My view need not negate Miles's point, though, for as we have been seeing, recognition of the grotesque depends in large part on its reception in the perspective of particular viewers.

56 Caution is needed in using such a term, which incidentally Miles contrasts with 'secular pornography', which she notes appeared in the modern period (1991: 156). Pornography has a particular relationship with popular culture and censorship, and it would be hard to justify the term with respect to Christian hagiographies which, it must be observed, are very much mainstream and not intended to be subversive (though that they have a particular *rhetorical* function cannot be denied). That the images are eroticized and violent (frequently involving bondage), however, is certainly true, and in this respect, Miles's nomenclature is understandable.

57 A woman's genitals were once considered homologous to a man's, only they were reversed, since women lacked the heat to turn them the 'right' way. This lack of heat was not immediately allotted to woman's spiritual and moral inferiority, but of course this quickly

in terms of Miles's study, the female body must naturally and always be grotesque due to its inability to be male. In fact, this gendered grotesque, or, as Russo has called it, female grotesque, threatens to become a tautology (Russo 1994: 12).

Gender lines are not so easily demarcated in terms of the grotesque, however, and this is to be expected. That is, the gender implications for grotesque figuration cannot really be reduced to the simple aphorism that a woman is grotesque because she is not a man, or, because she does not have a man's body/genitals. It is too simplistic, for instance, to say that all female bodies are grotesque and that all male bodies are not. As Russo puts it, 'the category of the female grotesque is crucial to identity-formation for both men and women as a space of risk and abjection' (Russo 1994: 12). If Bakhtin's carnivalesque bodies are anything to go by, it is the merging of categories and lines that are of significance to grotesque figuration.

In terms of gender, one such merging is touched on briefly by Bakhtin in his treatment of Rabelais on the androgyne, as I noted earlier. For Bakhtin, the point of the figure is that it exemplifies the blending of bodies or parts (Bakhtin 1984b: 323). The usefulness of this body for discussions of the grotesque is that it remains ambiguous. The body is one – a one-unit body – which is dissected or split upon the explication of its two natures.[58] As such, it could indicate a 'monstrous' creation of a 'mixed'

---

became the moral explanation for what was perceived to be a physiological failing. See Laqueur 1987 (also cited by Miles); Rouselle 1988; and Foucault 1990 for, variously, a discussion of this genital inversion in women, the Galenic legacy in histories of female reproduction and sexuality, and the politics of the female orgasm and reproduction. Miles does get somewhat sidetracked by this one issue, in that the category of inversion seems promising quite beyond images of genitalia. It could be used to her advantage in a general discussion of gender and pictorial or rhetorical devices.

58   So argues Freccero (1986: 151), who counters readings of this image as an echo of Aristophanes' third sex, or original, androgynous man–woman with the suggestion that it could also be a hermaphrodite (the distinction would be that an androgyne is a spiritual uniting of the two sexes, while a hermaphrodite is taken as a monstrous combination of the sexes that involves the deformity of both [1986: 149]). Interestingly, the phrase 'a brace of sexual organs, male and female' does not appear in her translation of Rabelais. Hers reads only 'two rumps' (1986: 146). The image is therefore somewhat ambivalent and could have been taken in two distinct ways: one glorifies Renaissance syncretism; the other harks back to mythical monstrosity. Freccero later observes that whatever the conclusion (androgyne or hermaphrodite), the figure in Rabelais is assumed to be male, even though both sexes are discussed. 'If difference is being asserted, it is within a context of sameness, further emphasized by the lack of features distinguishing one body from the other. The description proceeds by doubling or, inversely, halving a single entity' (1986: 51). Frecerro's point is that this is a figure that represents the two halves of a man, or is indicative of the merging of men (as in the bonds of friendship – though the homoerotic overtones should not be ignored). As such, it carries double weight: it is both magical or of religious significance, and monstrous (1986: 151).

person.[59] On the other hand, however, the figure might also be suggestive of two people copulating (grotesque in and of itself, according to Bakhtin's analysis). Either way, it serves as a figure for the blending of lines and the crossing of boundaries that seems to be so important for the maintenance of the grotesque.

Gender-mixing in grotesque figuration can also be subtler, to include women who masquerade as men, for example, or vice versa. As we saw with Stallybrass's work on the body in Renaissance texts, there were various ways to limit the monstrous possibilities of woman. Miles observes that dressing provided another such stabilizing tactic, and further, that cross-dressing was inherently threatening because of its transgression of social norms and the fact that its wearers masqueraded as that which they were not and never could be: men.[60] As we saw with Russo's discussion of the 'Lady Skimmingtons', though, the relationship between reality and the imagined is not so straightforward: cross-dressing brings with it real risks for the players as well as the targets of their satire.

Subtle gender mergings would also have to extend to the more complex practices of fetishization and hysteria. Since fetishization depends on positing and denying a castrated maternal phallus, in a basic and Freudian application there is inherent in it from the beginning a confusion of gender identity – a longing for the phallus in woman and a denial that it exists. But the discussion does not end here, of course. That which is fetishized blurs the lines between imagination and reality, or that which is desired and that which is attainable. The phallus is imposed upon that which it is not, and in the case of the body, parts – not only genital – intermingle and become confused. In hysteria (what some have simplified as an 'opposite' of fetishization), one might also point to a similar blurring of the lines mentioned above, only in this case the one affected would be a woman. Hysteria is particularly interesting here because, as is clear from the history of female sexuality, it was frequently used to explain and control women's 'aberrant' behaviour.[61] Russo, moreover, explicitly sees a correlation with the grotesque: 'The figure of the female hysteric, ungrounded and out of bounds, enacting her pantomime of anguish and rebellion, is as foundational to psychoanalysis as the image of the "senile, pregnant hags" is to the Bakhtinian model of grotesque realism.'[62]

---

59   The terminology is not mine, it is Freccero's; the choice of phrase is in keeping with the ambivalence over the anatomically unusual figure that Freccero sees in the Renaissance material she studies.

60   For more on the Renaissance controversy over masculine women, see Clark 1985.

61   Showalter's investigation of madness in English culture is but one example of many studies that trace the connection between female autonomy and suppression by 'illness' (1987).

62   Russo 1994: 9. Hysteria would fit into the 'inner' grotesque that Russo identifies over against the carnivalesque grotesque.

Gender mergings, overt and subtle alike, can be linked with Miles's initial forays into the idea of inversion, which has the potential to be expanded to create a powerful category (or 'rhetorical or pictorial device' as Miles termed it) for envisioning gender implications of the grotesque. The notion of a 'pictorial device' brings the discussion back to the other aspect of Miles's definition of inversion mentioned earlier, the reversal of a pleasing image to create a disturbing one. Miles was speaking particularly of the image of genital reversal, but it should also be pointed out that androgyny, cross-dressing, hysteria and fetishization, mentioned above, have some implications for looking at or viewing the body in addition to their broader implications for gender, subjectivity and so on. Gargantua's emblem on his hat of the androgyne is, after all, itself an *impresa*, a pictorial device with an accompanying motto (Freccero 1986: 146) meant to give some account of the person who wears it. In this case, the figure chosen was intended to confuse and mislead (as it seems to have done in critical writing on the passage as well – so argues Freccero).

The diversionary (in terms of diverting expectations) – or dissembling – aspect of gender merging is critical here. Cross-dressing women, as Miles observed, were deemed particularly odious in medieval culture because of the fallacious impression of themselves that the women tried to convey. And hysteria in its original clinical manifestations had an overtly performative or spectacular aspect. As Russo notes, the so-called hysterics of Charcot's (photographic) study at Salpêtrière were frequently paid performers who acted and posed in outlandish manners for the entertainment/study of an almost entirely male audience (1994: 68). One does not want to ignore the gendered politics of such 'diversion', of course, especially where they work to separate and control women's bodies and their subjectivities. It should be noted that those politics, however, also include the possibility for the visual or the spectacular to open up an ambiguous space, where performance might allow for the looked-at to contend for agency. As Russo rightly observes, in the hysterical there is a chance for discursive freedoms and possibilities (1994: 67–9).

Making a Spectacle (of ... ?)

These freedoms and possibilities are the background to Russo's interrogation of the idea of grotesque as spectacle. Because of the acknowledged normativeness of the male body and the tautological potential of the idea of the 'female grotesque', referred to above, there is an inherent misogyny in the concept of grotesque figuration that must be acknowledged (in Russo's words, 'the misogyny which identifies this hidden inner space with the visceral'; 1994: 2). It was indeed part of Miles's project to expose this bias against and hatred of the female body. Can one, however, escape the equation that the female body equals the grotesque body? If not, is there any recourse for the female body to regain its autonomy through grotesque figuration? Russo suggests that indeed there are possibilities for liberation and autonomy in the grotesque: these are evident in its visual or spectacular qualities.

Russo launches her study of the female grotesque with an introduction of the concept of the 'aerial sublime'. It is meant to bring, as she says, 'a principle of turbulence into the configuration female/grotesque' (1994: 29). The female grotesque is, as we have discovered, often associated with the 'symbolically low', and the lower bodily stratum, particularly the cave-like or grottoesque space of the female anatomy. 'Up there, out there' in the air, by contrast, Russo locates a more promising theme for the female grotesque, that of stunt-flying or stunting. She observes that 'the stunt bears a special relationship to groups who are exceptional or abnormal in relation to the "normal activity"' (Russo 1994: 19). Women stunt-flyers, such as Amelia Earhart, are 'stunts within stunts', since in their status as women, who then deviate from the practice of normal flying, they are 'doubly suspect' (Russo 1994: 20).[63]

The appeal of female stunt pilots or of women up in the air (aerialistes, acrobats, etc.), indeed for women as creators of spectacle, is 'not just their similarity to other women, but rather their dissimilarity from themselves': they are 'different from their own femininity' (Russo 1994: 44). In effect, they 'put on' or masque the 'effortless mobility' of the acrobat/stunt pilot. In the identification with and attraction to the flying female spectacle Russo sees 'a fantasy of femininity which defies the limits of the body, especially the female body' (1994: 44). Woman's status as creator of the spectacle is a site of progression and possibility.

There are also, however, risks to such stunting – literal and symbolic. As feminist film theorists, for instance, have capably pointed out, women are spectacular creatures, that is, they are seen as objects of the male gaze, and in a sense are constructed in accordance with this status.[64] Russo observes, as I discussed above in relation to the risks of carnival for the already marginalized, that woman experiences an impasse in this capacity: 'There is only one way out: death, whatever its representation – hysterical breakdown, unconsciousness, loss of visibility, or more literally loss of life' (1994: 44–5). Women, therefore, have a twofold relationship to the spectacle, each aspect tempering the other. On the one hand, the risks are

---

63   We saw this above with respect to the issue of displaced abjection in carnival, as discussed by Stallybrass and White. Here, the difference is that Russo wishes to explore the regenerative and liberatory possibilities of that double space.

64   The classic essay in this light is Laura Mulvey's 'Visual Pleasure in Narrative Cinema', *Screen* 16 (1975): 6–18.

pervasive and have finite consequences. On the other, however, the spectacle may also be a source of power.

In her final chapter, Russo returns to the aerialiste theme, this time with the aid of Fevvers, the protagonist of Angela Carter's *Nights at the Circus*. Russo uses Fevvers' story to problematize the connection between spectacle and femininity. As she points out, the novel is 'unique in its depiction of relationships between women *as* spectacle, *and* women as producers of spectacle' (Russo 1994: 165).[65] Whereas the novel has been seen as an ultimate celebration of a female counterculture (Palmer 1987), Russo tempers any hasty celebration with an observation about the power structures of spectating/spectatorship: 'One body as production or performance leads to another, draws upon another, establishes hierarchies, complicities, and dependencies between representations and between women' (Russo 1994: 166). The counterculture implied by Fevver's winged escapades are only, she thinks, a 'prefigurative possibility' (Russo 1994: 221 n. 44), since representations and relations between women are implicated in the 'histories and metahistories of violence and oppression by and of women' (1991: 221 n. 44).

More promising for Russo is the grotesqueness of Fevvers, the ambivalence that her large performing body exhibits. In the novel, she sees that Walser, a 'model spectator', is perpetually confused by gender (Fevvers') and generation (i.e. the relationship between Fevvers and Lizzie, her 'stepmother'). Russo finds in the intergenerational connections of Lizzie and Fevvers (which she has compared to the grotesque mergings of the Kerch terracotta figures) a transgressive and ultimately liberatory space:

> What appeals to me about this vamping onto the body (to use the word in a slightly archaic sense) is that it not only grotesquely de-forms the female body as a cultural construction in order to reclaim it, but that it may suggest new political aggregates – provisional, uncomfortable, even conflictual coalitions of bodies which both respect the concept of 'situated knowledges' and refuse to keep every body in its place. (Russo 1994: 179)

She is tempted, she says, to read the novel as a progression from 'the alienation of the femininity of the "coded mannequin"[66] to the liberatory aspects of the woman with wings' (Russo 1994: 179), but decides that a more realistic approach is to 'read their differences as part of an ongoing dialogue, filled with conflict and repetition – a difficult friendship and an improbable but necessary political alliance' (1994: 180).

65 Susan Swan's *The Biggest Modern Woman of the World* (2001) should be added to that list. It is, in some ways, even more provocative because it foregrounds issues of autobiography and subjectivity in its creation of the protagonist's countercultural space.
66 Woman as puppet is a similar category (see Palmer 1987).

> Like Fevvers' excessive body itself, the meaning of any possible flight
> [spectacle] lies in part in the very interstices of the narrative, as the many
> vectored space of the here and now, rather than a utopian hereafter. The
> end of flight in this sense is not a freedom from bodily existence but a
> recharting of aeriality as a bodily space of possibility and repetition.
> (Russo 1994: 181)

Whether a female counterculture or only prefigurative possibility of one
– or somewhere in between – the world of Fevvers is instructive for
gauging the liberatory potential for the female grotesque. It would not,
however, be appropriate to allow this potential to eclipse all that has been
discussed above: Russo's and Miles's insights are crucial to a twentieth-
century investigation of the grotesque body and to its use as a heuristic for
reading. What Russo's suggestion allows, though, is a way to escape from
a potentially oppressive state in which the female body is implicitly and
irrevocably tied to the grotesque.

Prefigurative Possibilities and Kristeva's Abject

Kristeva's work on the abject is not explicitly the subject of this book, but
it does have some bearing on the previous discussion, especially in terms
of gauging the transformative possibilities for the female grotesque and
the thorny matter of essentialism. There is, after all, a rough but
important parallel between the abject and the grotesque, especially in its
identification with the material bodily lower stratum, its interest in the
'cycle of life' and its relation with the female reproductive – here maternal
– body. Russo, moreover, mentions it throughout her work in what seems
to be an effort to nuance the female grotesque, to give it a significance for
the inner body, the 'psychic register and ... the bodily as cultural
projection of an inner state' (1994: 9). The abject is thus less concerned
with the appearance of the physical body that I have been discussing up to
this point, but it provides some context for it, as well as exploring its
implications.

   Though a simplification, it is helpful to think of the abject as a kind of
psychoanalytical elaboration of the grotesque. In Kristeva's analysis of
the pre-Oedipal phase, the undifferentiated subject exists in the realm of
the semiotic (roughly equivalent to the Lacanian 'Imaginary').[67] In this
phase, the child identifies wholly or completely with the mother (and
hence, the semiotic can be associated with the maternal and the female).[68]

---

67   Kristeva's work on semiotics (the discipline) should not be confused with her
theorization of the realm of the semiotic (a noun which remains uncapitalized in her analysis,
unlike the correlates in Lacan's work). The latter refers to the pre-symbolic (pre-Oedipal)
stage in Kristeva's conceptualization of the formation of the subject.

68   It is important to note that Kristeva is not *identifying* the one with the other, however.
Some have accused her of essentializing the feminine because of her identification of the

At the moment of differentiation, however, the child must separate itself from the maternal body, it must 'pursu[e] a reluctant struggle against what, having been the mother, will turn into an abject' (Kristeva 1982: 13), that which is to be repelled or rejected. At the time of this struggle – the development of subjectivity – the child ceases to be united with the mother, but is not yet a differentiated self. Encounter with the abject in this transition is thus a 'kind of narcissistic crisis' (Kristeva 1982: 14; Oliver 1993: 57). 'It is the "realization" that the primary identification with the other is a "seeming," a fake' (Oliver 1993: 57). The abject is thus neither subject nor object; it is better understood as a condition or an encounter that makes subjectivity possible. It is the jettisoned object, that which must be expelled in order for the subject to exist.[69]

In the first instance, the jettisoned object is the mother (or the pre-self that has identified with the mother). Once differentiation occurs, however, and the subject has had to repress its desire to remain one with the mother, its identity is continually threatened by what has been excluded. Thus Kristeva's unique contribution to the discussion: 'What is excluded can never be fully excluded, but hovers at the edges or borders of our existence, haunting and inhabiting regions supposedly clean and free of any influence or contamination' (Grosz 1987: 108). Once the child enters into the realm of the symbolic, then, the abject – the offending matter to be jettisoned – is represented by not only the maternal, and horror/fear of the feminine, but by anything that comes to represent the border between the two realms of the symbolic and the semiotic. Commonly identified as food matter,[70] excrement, death and the signs of sexual difference, the abject is 'not lack of cleanliness or health ... but what disturbs identity, system, order' (Kristeva 1982: 4). Thus we can say that the abject is 'what is on the border, what doesn't respect borders. It is "ambiguous," "in-between," "composite"' (Oliver 1993: 56). Kristeva explains the subject's reactions thus: 'Loathing an item of food, a piece of filth, waste or dung. The spasms and vomiting that protect me. The repugnance, the retching that thrusts me to the side and turns me away from defilement, sewage, and muck' (1982: 2). The abject and abjection are hence 'safeguards', 'primers of culture' (1982: 2).

Two instances exemplify the abject. In them, Kristeva depicts the subject's visceral reaction to the manifestations of the abject and clearly

---

chora (the undifferentiated space of the womb/matrix where mother and child are united which makes the semiotic possible) with, among other things, the maternal body and woman (Oliver 1993: 48).

69   See Grosz 1987 for a discussion of the abject in relation to the acquisition of language, that is, the creation of the speaking subject.

70   Food is a sign of the abject, Kristeva explains, only when it is 'a border between two distinct entities or territories' (1982: 75), for instance, between nature and culture, or the human and the non-human.

shows the implications that the abject has for the boundaries of the subject.

> When the eyes see or the lips touch the skin on the surface of milk – harmless, thin as a sheet of cigarette paper, pitiful as a nail pairing – I experience a gagging sensation and, still further down, spasms in the stomach, the belly; and the organs shrivel up the body, provoke tears and bile, increase heartbeat, cause forehead and hands to perspire. Along with sight-clouding dizziness, *nausea* makes me balk that milk cream, separates me from the mother and the father who proffer it. 'I' want none of that element, sign of their desire; 'I' do not want to listen, 'I' do not want to assimilate it, 'I' expel it. But since food is not an 'other' for 'me,' who am only in their desire, I expel *myself*, I spit *myself* out, I abject *myself* within the same motion within which 'I' claim to establish *myself*. (Kristeva 1982: 2–3, original emphases)

> The corpse (or cadaver: *cadere*, to fall), that which has irredeemably become a cropper, is cesspool, and death; it upsets even more violently the one who confronts it as fragile and fallacious chance. A wound with blood and pus, or the sickly, acrid smell of sweat, of decay, does not *signify* death. In the presence of signified death – a flat encephalograph, for instance – I would understand, react, or accept. No, as in true theater, without makeup or masks, refuse and corpses *show me* what I permanently thrust aside in order to live. These body fluids, this defilement, this shit are what life withstands, hardly and with difficulty, on the part of death. There, I am at the border of my condition as a living being. My body extricates itself, as being alive, from that border. Such wastes drop so that I might live, until, from loss to loss, nothing remains in me and my entire body falls beyond the limit – *cadere*, cadaver. (Kristeva 1982: 3, original emphases)

What, though, does this have to do with the grotesque? Kristeva's analysis and her vivid portrayal of the subject's encounter with the abject are reminiscent both of Bakhtin's work on the grotesque body and some of the subsequent criticisms of that work that we have been considering thus far. The correspondences with Bakhtin's work are to be found in the material bodily elements (food, sex, death, waste). These are reorganized here into a system which accounts for their place in the development of the subject and the work that must be undertaken to maintain his or her integrity. As such, Kristeva also expertly captures some of the emotional and visceral effects of engagement with the material bodily element. This has much sympathy with the work of Kayser and Freud, who, as we saw above, provide a counterbalance to Bakhtin's idealized and overly positive context for the grotesque body. Encounter with the grotesque/abject shows itself to be more than just a humorous and utopian event.[71]

From this brief exposition, it is clear that the abject has important connections with the feminine – or better, the maternal – which are always reiterated, even though the beginnings of the separation of the child from the mother happened long in the past. This reiteration continues because the act of separating is never fully completed, but rather is played out again and again in different guises in the subject's relations with other subjects and with the world around him/her. In place of the mother are the other abjects – food, sex, excrement, death – all of which are inadequate substitutes, just as those objects onto which the child projects its desires for the mother are inadequate. By virtue of their inadequacy, and the subject's need to keep abjecting them, the maternal is repeatedly but obliquely invoked.

In its associations (but not identifications) with the feminine, Kristeva's analysis might be understood to be somewhat contiguous with Miles's and Russo's. Its sophistication in interrogating the 'inner' grotesque establishes a greater context for understanding the visceral nature of responses to the grotesque, and also the compulsion to keep looking, to fetishize the body while responding to its grotesque figuration. Kristeva's work might also provide a useful critique of Miles (and to some extent Russo), in that it closes up a gap created in her identification of the female body with the grotesque (to the point where it almost becomes tautologous). For, any detractor of the idea of the grotesque might easily point out that male bodies also change, shift, leak and otherwise exhibit signs of instability. (Even Bakhtin refers to the phallus in these terms, though Miles and Russo are quite right that he seems drawn – and uncritically so – to female-gendered images as good indicators of the grotesque.) What Kristeva offers in response is a conceptualization of developing subjectivity that takes account of gender differences in its system, and at the same time explicates an archetypal relationship to the female body. That relationship is not essential, but referential: its limits may contain and define the subject, but they may also be transgressed.

In this light, Kristeva's work also fits with Russo's location of the 'prefigurative possibilities' of the female grotesque as spectacle. In Kristeva's analysis one can find transformative or liberatory possibilities,

71 Kristeva does not explicitly analyse the Song of Songs in the context of this study, though she does elsewhere (1984). She is, however, interested in biblical material with reference to the abject, specifically Levitical law (1982: 90–112). She observes that 'abjection accompanies all religious structurings'; it 'persists as *exclusion* or taboo (dietary or other) in monotheistic religions, Judaism in particular' (1987: 17). In Leviticus (and in the prophetic material, especially Ezekiel), Kristeva finds evidence of the religious systematization of the abject, notably in its prohibitions concerning food, bodily effluvia/waste, sexual conduct (incest) and death.

which means that the grotesque/abject again exhibits potential as a positive and empowering source in some respects, instead of being wholly a source of oppression. Briefly described, these transformative aspects take two forms: In the first instance, the semiotic (the realm wherein the drama between the maternal and the abject is played out) is for Kristeva the locus of art, poetry, music and other 'affective' utterances. She also aligns it with nature, with emotion, spontaneity, and the like – that which cannot be controlled or rigorously systematized. As will become clear, many of these features belong in the Song's province. Once the subject is formed and enters into the symbolic realm, the semiotic is never dispensed with fully, but punctuates the symbolic at unexpected and uncontrolled moments. These moments may appear to threaten the integrity of the symbolic, but in reality, the continued influence of the semiotic on the subject is crucial to his or her survival. Second, Kristeva locates in the abject a vital condition for the subject's ability to love. Without it, the subject would be, in effect, dead. Contrary to its appearance as a disruptive, polluting force, then, the abject is in Kristeva's view a positive entity. To limit something to the margins, then, is not to limit its effects. The marginal is, to the contrary, a source of life-affirming and transformative power.

The Grotesque Body and the Not-So-Sublime Song?

It remains here to collect the grotesque body's scattered pieces into some kind of unified form, however corpulent and disjointed that may be (and however much it might resist the exercise). Briefly put, one could say that the grotesque body is the body in process, the body undergoing change. There is a particular emphasis on its mechanics, that is, its digestive, excretory and sexual/reproductive workings. The grotesque body is integrated with life, with nature, with the world around it. As such, it is often represented as hybridized, a mixture of a variety of natural and human-fashioned elements. Mixing, too, can sometimes refer to the combination or confusion of gender. The grotesque body is meant to be viewed; it is itemized, consumed, and sometimes, thus, fetishized. In this capacity, there are attendant, pressing issues to be considered, issues about the objectification and autonomy of the lookers and the bodies being looked at. The spirit behind grotesque bodily figuration is, moreover, as mixed as the bodies themselves. The grotesque body can be inherently playful and comical, but as we have seen, it may also develop into the repulsive, that which is transgressive, alien and vile. In light of its status as spectacle, it carries also the potential for unease and discomfort in viewer and body.

This collection of grotesque parts into a manageable package (designed with the Song in mind) aims to draw together the threads that I have been unravelling throughout this chapter and to identify the heuristic that will be used in my reading in the next chapter. Again, the intention behind this more global definition is not to build a rigid 'model' that will be 'applied' to the biblical texts; nor do I hope to investigate those texts so as to find in them one specific, unchangeable entity called 'the grotesque body'. As I have been indicating, such a creature does not exist. In using the grotesque body heuristically, my intentions are to discover how it might elucidate the dynamics of the imagery in the text, and later, how it might shed light on related issues such as the book's gender politics, its presentation of desire, and readers' responses to these.

Chapter 3

REVEALED AND CONCEALED: THE GROTESQUE BODY IN THE SONG OF
SONGS

The variations and mutability of the grotesque body – at times playful and
at times sinister – allow for a range of interpretive possibilities. As it
happens, the Song has its own shifting qualities, which are noticeable
through the dialogical nature of the poems and the quick scene changes
and intermittent movements of narrative found in the book. The bodies in
the Song are variable, too, because they are frequently referred to,
sometimes displayed and sometimes made to vanish when their presence is
most desired. Moreover, the images that describe them are incomplete,
random, almost serendipitous. The result is a piecemeal portrayal of the
beloved body, which is in turn complicated further by scholarly
contestation over the meaning of the images. There is, therefore, a
kinship among the grotesque body, the Song's text and its lovers' bodies
in terms of their capriciousness and mutability. That is to say, this kinship
indicates a shared degree of indeterminacy among these players, and,
further, it is one that both presents challenges for the Song and opens up
vast possibilities.

It is the project of this present chapter to explore some of these
possibilities and challenges via a close reading of key body texts and
through the lens of the grotesque. My approach is to consider, in various
capacities, the four main descriptive texts of the body in the Song (4.1-5;
6.4-7; 7.1-10; 5.10-16), one other extended discussion (4.9-16), and, where
pertinent, some of the scattered or incidental references to the body (e.g.
1.15). The reading begins with an indication of the range of metaphorical
play in some of the images, as well as some of the more general areas in
which the grotesque body might more obviously be identified. These are,
in other words, initial visual impressions that readers probably construct
when they encounter the imagery. Next, my discussion moves to
investigate in more depth the connections that even these initial glimpses
begin to make with the rest of the book. Following this, it will be
important to look at some of the grotesque themes that I identified in the
last chapter, such as the hybridization of the body, its connection with

nature and the cycle of life, sexuality and permeability, and so on. To this end, I read some of the images more specifically in concert with the work of various readers of the grotesque, such as Bakhtin and Russo. Additionally, those who do not explicitly theorize the grotesque, but whose work, as I have shown, is pertinent to it, such as Wittig, Barthes and Certeau, are also useful here. Finally, this reading culminates in an investigation of some of the strategies of grotesque figuration that I have explored in the previous chapter. Once again, Certeau proves an invaluable reading companion as do some other unexpected readers of the Song, such as the sixteenth-century mystic and saint, Teresa of Avila.

Because the grotesque relies on what is different or counter-iconic for its success, one might initially be tempted to look for a normative biblical body to use as a measure in this investigation. (The margins at which the grotesque body operates imply a 'centre', as I pointed out earlier in initial discussions of grotesque art.) One might ask, therefore, if there is a biblical aesthetic for the human form: this, presumably, could be used as a literary context in which to study the Song's bodies and evaluate their grotesquerie. Unfortunately, the biblical record does not yield such an opportunity. Though it does occasionally mention the beauty of individuals, it refrains from explicating what that means, exactly.[1] The remaining possibility, that the Song of Songs might be that aesthetic, has been suggested by at least one reader (Brenner 1997b: 46–8). It is, however, an option that is not entirely satisfactory for a number of reasons.

Most troubling, from my perspective, is that to mandate that the statements about beauty in the text are meant to be explicated by what follows them is something of a terminal option for interpretation: it provides for no other alternative in reading than that these perplexing images are aesthetically complete, or, that they explicate (perfect) beauty. It is precisely the perplexing nature of the imagery, however, that demands that readers at least *consider* other alternatives. Second, and more to the point, it is only the first complete description that provides a straightforward connection between a statement or statements about beauty and the description of the body. Neatly, it opens and closes the description with general admiration of the woman's (total) beauty (Song 4.1, 7). The other statements, however (Song 6.4; 7.2, 7), either omit entirely, or else

---

1   Three adjectives are typically used as general evaluations of beauty, but are not usually expanded into explanations of what this beauty might mean: (1) יָפֶה: Gen. 12.11, 14; 29.17; 39.6; 41.2, 4, 18; Deut. 21.11; 1 Sam. 16.12; 17.42; 25.3; 2 Sam. 13.1; 14.25, 27; 1 Kgs 1.3, 4; Jer. 11.16; Ezek. 31.3, 9; 33.32; Amos 8.13; Ps. 48.3; Job 42.15; Prov. 11.22; Song 1.8, 15, 16; 2.10, 13; 4.1, 7; 6.1, 4, 10; [note: the verbal form, יָפָה, to be pleasing, might also be added to this list in the Song: 4.10; 7.2, 7]; Eccl. 3.11; 5.17; Esth. 2.7; (2) נָאוֶה: Jer. 6.2; Pss 33.1; 147.1; Prov. 17.7; 19.10; 26.1; Song 1.5; 2.14; 4.3; 6.4 [again, in the Song, note a verbal form, נָאָה, to be comely (Pi.) in 2.10]; and (3) נָעִים: 2 Sam. 1.23; 23.1; Pss 16.6, 11; 81.3; 133.1; 135.3; 147.1; Job 36.11; Prov. 2.18; 23.8; 24.4; Song 1.16.

comment on (elaborate, parody, refute) that earlier convention in Song 4, thereby raising significant and global questions about the relation of the Song's body descriptions with the ideal of beauty.[2] Thus, to insist that the descriptions explicate biblical ideals of beauty seems rather to limit the possibilities for these descriptions.[3]

What will be undertaken here, therefore, is an opportunity to take the puzzlement that readers seem to exhibit over the images as a sign that it is not completeness or wholeness, perfection or idealization that *must* be pursued in reading – and at all costs. Instead, the puzzlement signals that difference, even subversion, in the Song's presentation of the body are viable options for reading. As a consequence, the point of this reading is not about following a checklist or determinedly affixing a grotesque label on imagery (or, for that matter, about deciding on one definite meaning for the images). Rather, it is about undertaking a *reading with*. It will be important, therefore, to resist an either/or (grotesque or not grotesque) binary opposition for the body images, but to embark, instead, on an enquiry into dissonance. So, I am not looking for a measure against which to compare the Song's bodies, but for opportunities to read them in light of a heuristic that privileges the unexpected, variability and difference.

There is another context that may be considered to be absent in my analysis: the sociohistorical setting of the grotesque body as delineated in the previous chapter. A rather evident question to ask, to be sure, is whether or not the results of artistic and literary developments of the last 500 years can serve as a lens through which to view a text from an entirely different historical and cultural context. Related to this, and more particular to the manifestations of the grotesque body as Bakhtin represents it, is whether or not it must be considered within one of its posited historical contexts, the carnival.

Both issues are historical, and related. Using the grotesque body heuristically to read a biblical text might be perceived to be glaringly anachronistic. Though many might argue that the grotesque existed long before it was actually named, before the paintings and literary texts with which I began this study (e.g. see Harpham 1982), it remains that that material is probably well over 1500 years younger than the images I propose to examine in the Song (depending, of course, on exactly when

---

2   The next description (almost a verbatim quotation of that in 4.1-5) begins not with a general evaluation of beauty, as in 4.1, but a statement that the woman is as beautiful as Tirzah and as lovely as Jerusalem. These observations are then followed by an enigmatic statement that describes the woman as terrible as an army with banners. No summarizing statement follows this description. In 7.1, in what could be taken as a parodic manner, the man makes only the observation that her feet are beautiful. No statement summarizes the body description, but one does intervene in 7.7.

3   This does not mean, however, that the statements about beauty will be ignored. They merit consideration and will dealt with at a later stage.

the Song is dated). Quite apart from the fact that all literary-theoretical interpretation of the Bible is in some manner anachronistic, how can this particular marriage be justified?

The simplest response to this query is to reiterate that my project is ultimately not interested in asking historically bound questions for the Song of Songs, such as what a particular image meant for those who used it. It is clear, as we saw in the previous chapter, how this kind of conjecture results in a multitude of interpretations, but ultimately with little satisfaction. Neither is this work interested in pondering the identity and intentions of the Song's 'author' ('what did he or she mean when he used a particular image?'). So, my intentions are not historical, but does it matter that the heuristic I use could be considered to be historically bound? Since the grotesque does develop with respect to sociohistorical norms, and since a large proportion of my analysis uses modern criticism of Renaissance texts, one could argue that indeed it does matter. The issue, however, does not end there. In reality, the grotesque body as it has been presented in this chapter is developed through the eyes of twentieth-century literary critics, and it is, moreover, a selective view of it that is not insistent on a particular historical context.

The same can be concluded for the literary and sociohistorical context of the grotesque body, the carnival. We have already seen how Stallybrass and White have separated the two aspects of grotesque figuration in their analysis of Bakhtin. More compellingly, as the work of Harpham (1982), Kayser (1963), Miles (1991), Russo (1994), and others have shown, it is perfectly possible and allowable to envision the grotesque body without the carnival. To insist on their unity would be to insist that the grotesque body is only locatable within one particular sociohistorical context. To be sure, it is plausible to approach the Song from the perspective of the carnival, and I may make some cursory concluding comments to that effect.[4] It is better at this juncture, though, to avoid setting limits on the grotesque body in terms of context, but rather to allow it to float free and entangle itself where it may.

To this end, and in keeping with the nature of the grotesque, my study of the texts in question will involve a certain amount of reading at the margins. That is, in addition to looking at the texts and making use of the work of mainstream commentators, I will also explore various intertexts, look at word-plays, take seriously the ostensibly questionable theorizing about the meaning of puzzling texts in scholarship, and investigate critics' exploration of cognates to settle the meaning of various *hapax legomena*. In other words, I am just as interested in what follows in the possible 'marginal meanings' of the Song as I am in what has been the general

---

4   Stephen Moore has entertained a reading of the Song of Songs alongside the carnival (2001: 66ff.).

consensus of scholars. In this instance, there will be another chance to consider the unease that scholars appear to have with the body imagery in the Song.

First Impressions

As we saw in Chapter 1, the cartoon rendering of the woman in the Song of Songs depicted in Figure 1 hyperbolizes the body descriptions, making them comical by their literal representation and by their conflation into a single body at one time. Such a reading would probably engender *at the least* the disapproval of many commentators of the Song, who would urge that to read the imagery literally in this way is to miss the point, to show oneself ignorant of poetic language, even to be unaware of the sophistication of literary technique that is evident in the Song's metaphors.[5] Another objection that could be made would be that poetic descriptions are not visual, that it is not an actual picture of a woman that results, but an impression (or emotion, etc.). This is the repeated claim of Brenner (1993a: 235; 2003: 296; 2005: 166), and it is certainly behind such readings as Soulen's and Falk's.[6]

It is probably true that the lovers who image their loved ones in the Song would be surprised to see the cartoon's rendition of their words. To be sure, if it were possible to determine the lovers' intentions, an entirely plausible assumption would be that they were not dictating their descriptions with the expectation that they would be translated into *actual* pictorial form. This begs the question, though, as to whether or not there is to be a natural and expected interpretive outcome for poetic description of the body. If there is, what is it to be? Who decides what is effected? A speaker/lover? A recipient of the praise? A third party – a reader? Furthermore, should it be insisted that images carry with them the prescription for one (and one particular) mode of interpretation? If not, why not interrogate the possibility that each lover could have in mind – and intend to convey – something visual in his or her figuration of the loved one's body (even if that is to be imagined)? And would this not be especially the case when the descriptions move away from the general (such as 'your eyes are lovely'; or 'you are beautiful'), towards the particular ('your hair is like a flock of goats')? If the creation of a visual

---

5 Fox's evaluation of one image, for example, as 'incongruous enough to forcefully convey unexpected attitudes and overtones' and his expectation of 'losing some readers' who find the images abrasive (1985: 226–7) is a case in point, and but one example of many.

6 Comments by commentators such as, most recently, Exum, reveal a similar perspective: 'Clearly the description here in [Song 4] vv. 1-5 is not meant to inform the reader what the woman looks like, for it does a very poor job of that' (2005a: 159). See also 2005d for some preliminary comments about Hart's cartoon.

impression is not a reasonable assumption, as some have indeed argued, then are we to imagine that a poet or a lover might pen these words without ever perceiving the possibilities for how image and referent *appear* when brought together, that is, without forming a picture in his or her mind of what is being written? Would we determine, furthermore, that he or she might be unaware that others will do so?[7]

It is, of course, difficult (and questionable practice) to posit authorial intentions for the words of poets – and especially for lovers. Naturally, even if their intentions could be detailed, authors could not necessarily control how these words were received by their intended target or by the audience who hears/reads them. Experience of reading, however, indicates that readers *envision* descriptive language in addition to making other moves.[8] The imaginative response that is elicited in the reader is synaesthetic, after a fashion, implicating the visual senses in addition to others – be they the actual senses of hearing or smelling, or the evocations (sense-impressions) of which Soulen (1993) writes. The point is, of course, that that response is highly subjective: it was for the lover, no doubt, so one would not expect specificity (or uniformity) from readers, either.

The question I raised in Chapter 1 with respect to Hart's cartoon, therefore, was whether or not the visual impact of the cartoon need be summarily dismissed by serious readers because of its hyperbole and/or its context (a satirical magazine). Quite the contrary, it seems that the cartoon proffers a challenge to readers of the Song by forcing them to confront issues around the status and politics of interpretation. The challenge concerns, in the first instance, the practice of literal reading

---

7   Brenner's recent insistence that '[t]he physical properties attributed to the lover are mostly obscured rather than revealed by the practice of using metaphors instead of direct descriptions' and that 'what is attempted … is *not* a physical description per se, but conveyance of impressionistic emotions engendered by the presence of the female beloved [in Song 7.1-10]' (2003: 296, 299) needs to be addressed further. Truly, I do not imagine that these texts provide technical, detailed and complete renditions of the body as it is being observed ('your eyes are almond-shaped, well-spaced, and brown … '). Brenner also makes an excellent observation about the playfulness of the images, where they hide and reveal the body to varying degrees. However, I cannot agree that we are only dealing with 'impressionistic emotions', rather like Soulen's argument, in these texts. Most importantly, Brenner's reading does not account for the variability of readers' interpretations of the images; it is, moreover, very difficult to evaluate a poet's intention from a text. And what of the possibility that a recipient of these words, or a reader of them, would probably construct a visual impression as much as he or she might create an emotional one – especially when the imagery is as unexpected and jarring as this is? This is a good place to start a counter-iconic or non-traditional reading of the type that I am suggesting: to be sure, it is not the end of the discussion, but it cannot be ignored.

8   I can only competently comment on my own experience of reading. However, the numerous readers who mention that the images might be perceived as grotesque (see Ch. 1), but who argue against that conclusion, do suggest that my experience is a common one.

(which has generally had a bad rap since the early days of allegorical interpretation). Secondly, it occasions broader questions about how readers work with the images to determine their meaning. These questions range from the subjectivity of individual readings (envisionings) to the permissibility of readers' interpretations, which are a consequence of their intrusion into the 'privacy' of the lovers.

If reading and envisioning the Song's images may be more interrelated than might initially be acknowledged, it also stands to reason that the results of reading in this way should be more accurately viewed not as a matter of reading more competently (or less so), but *reading differently*. The hegemony of traditional readings in the study of the Song's imagery (and in biblical scholarship generally) is challengeable on these terms. So whereas 'sophistication' for the biblical scholars that I mentioned above has meant a particular type of reading, I want to challenge that it should mean much more. Sophistication should mean perceiving or understanding the *range* of meaning that is possible in one's engagement with the images, for example, their volatile, elusive, dissonant nature, as much as their holistic, beautiful or otherwise positive aspects. More specifically, sophistication might mean acknowledging a variety of modes of reading: it might mean, for instance, following cues that originate, paradoxically, in literal reading, a mode that is often considered simplistic or facile – in short, unsophisticated.

A further word must be said about literal reading. It is curious that in its desires to get away from allegory, biblical scholarship has insisted on the *literal* reading of the Song as an erotic poem that declares the love of two human beings – that is to say, not as a cosmic affair between the soul and God (or Israel and Yahweh, or ...). Interestingly, scholarship also seems to have its limits where literalism is concerned. Why stop at the visible body, though? If the erotic context for the characters, veiled as it is in figurative language, can be insisted upon as the literal meaning for this text, why not initially entertain, *as part of the poetic process*, a literal reading of the figurative language that describes their bodies?

By part of the poetic process I do not mean that (simple) literal reading is the final goal of a grotesque reading, but that we might entertain the literal as part of our consideration of the figurative – that we might use the initial impressions (envisionings) that some might discredit because they are literal, as a stepping-stone on the way to an evaluation of *how* a particular image means. To step off into the world of the grotesque from this point, would not be, I think, to limit interpretive options, but rather to expand them. This is an observation that Nicholas of Lyra, a twelfth-century interpreter influenced by Rashi, uniquely realized in his own rendering of the Song. Even though the erotic relationship of Solomon and the Shulammite proved to be too much for him to reconcile, he was convinced that his contemporaries' tendencies to immediately allegorize the book were detrimental to its overall transmission.[9]

Perhaps, however, to observe scholars' predilection for one kind of literalism (the Song as erotic text) and its rejection of another (the body images), is to be pedantic. After all, the first type of literal reading seems a judgment of ideology, genre and, vaguely, narrative,[10] while the other is a decision about how to interpret poetic devices. Is there a considerable distance between both literalisms? I wonder. To be sure, 'literal' in these two contexts has meant different things: the first really indicates non-allegorical (non-theological, secular) reading, while the other seems to be both a recognition that the descriptive language is comprised of similes and metaphors – it is figurative speech – and a response to dealing with difficult language that is targeted at the body in 'love poetry'. It is worth pointing out, however, that these categories and distinctions are not rigid; moreover, their terms are actually confusable. Decisions about genre (the *wasfs*) have influenced the way readers view these poetic texts by giving them a specific setting; similarly, poetic decisions about context, such as pastoral setting, the relationship of the characters (two lovers, perhaps even beset by difficulties), etc., have affected readers' decisions about the overall shape of the book and how it is to be understood. There appears to be an impasse here, but I wonder if it is as untraversable as it appears. If it is forgivable to excuse allegory from the picture in order to read the Song of Songs as eroticism, why not allow 'poetry' a fuller range of meaning that incorporates literalism as well as evocation, impression and more?

So, if we may – unabashedly and without remorse – read the Song's bodies initially alongside Hart's literalistic cartoon, what will we see? At this juncture I am only interested in taking an initial look – a first impression – of what these bodies are like in terms of grotesque figuration as I have discussed it so far. The first of the images, Song 4.1-5 provides such an opportunity. It is not the most involved of all the images, but there is enough here to get an impression. In addition, the description illustrates some important matters about the politics of looking and describing the body that should be introduced. These affect all the images that will be investigated in this chapter.

Song 4.1-5 is uttered by the man, who addresses his lover after she has been watching and describing his approach from the wilderness in a glorious procession (3.6-11). In 3.6-11, hers is a highly publicized address,

9 See especially Turner's discussion (1995: 83–125), though note the difficulty in defining both 'literal' and 'metaphor' where the history of allegorical interpretation is concerned (see 93ff.). Mary Dove's contributions to this dicussion are both insightful and provocative (2000, 2001).

10 Elsewhere, I have argued that readers impose a narrative of sorts on to the Song's poems. This is a response to readerly drives for completion of the lovers' 'story' (1999). I take this up further in Ch. 4.

and strictly speaking, the litter, and not the lover, is the target of her praise.[11] By contrast, the ensuing shift to the private[12] and particular for Solomon is a marked one; here he embarks on the first of what is to be a series of intimate itemizations of his lover's body. Issues of the private and the particular, as well as the intention of the lover in his description, come immediately to the fore in this text. Are his words intended for her ears alone? Do they respect some private communication of which we are unaware? If so, should this alter any evaluation that readers might make of the descriptions? Furthermore, the lover begins his description with an acclamation of his love's beauty. How might this affect readings of this text? These are not questions that are easily answered – especially in this first stage of reading – but it is important to observe that what we determine the speaker's intentions to be and how we perceive the textual context of his or her words naturally have a bearing on what is read. I will return to these matters below.

A first *glance*, then, reveals a series of hybridized forms, integrated with the natural and architectural world around them. So, for the reader of the Song, perhaps already bemused by some of the brief descriptions of the lovers that have appeared so far in the book (mare among Pharaoh's chariots, rose of Sharon, apple/fruit tree), the picture in 4.1-5 is not entirely unexpected, but it is startling in its concentration of these kinds of descriptions. The text offers a detailed but rather cryptic examination of the woman's body. Described here only from eyes to breasts, this incomplete woman is an odd and fanciful hybrid, an assortment of natural and human-made elements. Imposed on her body are fruit and animals, along with the physical lines of the land and its marks of human habitation and destruction.

From what little is presented of the woman's body, it is clear that her lover envisions that she is inextricably connected with nature. In fact, she has already suggested this identification herself earlier in the Song (2.1), as has he (1.9; 2.2), and it is a connection which we will see featured more and more as the images continue. Here in 4.1-5, her eyes are doves, her hair is like goats, her teeth are like sheep, her temples[13] are like

---

11 His presence, of course, is no incidental detail, but the woman is clearly taken with Solomon's wealth, his power and the impression that his arrival makes. The litter may in fact be metonymic for Solomon, but the contrast created by her praise of accoutrements and his of body-parts is too striking to ignore. For an in-depth discussion of the poetic contours of this text, see Exum 2003a.

12 The description is private in one sense, that the lover does not acknowledge that anyone else is present for it (as opposed to the woman's descriptions of him, which are prepared for the daughters of Jerusalem: 3.5 [if read as the same context as Solomon's approach]; 5.9). In another sense, though, it is very public, for we are spectators of it.

13 There is some discussion about what this word, רַקָּה, means. The temple as an object of beauty (or as visible behind a veil) is presumably perplexing for many readers in this

pomegranates, and her breasts are like gazelles. Eyes like doves is a popular refrain of both lovers (1.15; 4.1; 5.12; the man also calls his lover 'my dove': 2.14; 5.2; 6.9). Some of the other images we will also see again in the book, either verbatim, or with subtle changes.

Four of these images are not static, but imply or explicitly mention movement, either wild and natural (doves, gazelles), or domesticated and controlled (goats, sheep). A fifth, the pomegranates, suggests the byproduct of the domestication of nature, perhaps, in its incorporation of food. Whereas commentators have been apt to see these first descriptions as pastoral and idyllic, one cannot say that nature is always benign. The poet's descriptions imply hardship at times, and the movement of the animals refuses a static vision.

The alignment with the natural world is not, however, exclusive. This body also has particular military and architectural connections, notably in the case of the neck, which is compared to a tower of David. The exact location and appearance of this tower is unknown, but the poet does furnish us with several descriptive aspects. First, it appears to be built with a particular architectural feature, תלפיות. Often translated as 'courses' (Murphy 1990: 155; Fox 1985: 131; Keel 1994: 147; Pope 1977: 466–7; Goulder 1986: 33–4; Exum 2005a: 153), the word is a *hapax* that has been understood as anything from a proper name (LXX), to weapons (as in the RSV, presumably taking a cue from the following features in the description) to masonry arranged in rows (Bergant 2001: 47; Goulder 1986: 34).[14] The lover details the comparison further by noting the shields that hang on the neck, typically read as a metaphor for jewellery, but doubtless functioning as reminders of victories in battle, or the prowess of soldiers.[15] In the scholarship there is a range of attempts to come to terms with this odd image, especially in light of the perplexing dimensions imposed on the human form. For instance, Exum paints a romantic picture of how the lover might come to such an impression (while lying beside her, his vision distorted, he sees a lengthened neck; 2005a: 165); by radical contrast, Pope insists that we may be forgiven for thinking that it is odd for a human body, but urges that it is not unexpected if the body is divine (1977: 465). The initial impression, however, persists: the image is startling and somewhat grim in its dehumanizing of the body through architecture and the gore of war.

---

context. Some prefer 'cheeks' (Goulder 1986: 33; Murphy 1990: 155; Fox 1985: 131; Exum 2005a: 153), others 'brow' (Pope 1977: 462). Keel appears to be alone in proposing the inside of the mouth (1994: 146), though Bergant does show some sympathy with the idea (2001: 47).

14   See the interesting alternative proposed by Bloch and Bloch that the word is meant to be taken adverbially, conveying something like 'to perfection' (1995: 171–2).

15   Scholars understandably are puzzled as to what the nature of the comparison with the shields/bucklers is: For example, is their significance that they are shiny? Or round? Do they therefore suggest jewellery?

In this vision, we also have a chance to see some of the strategies of the grotesque at work, such as the juxtaposition of unexpected elements on the body. So, for example, the comparison of the lips to a crimson thread is decidedly odd. One might easily excuse its oddity by protesting that failure to understand is due to a loss of cultural context on our part – a common excuse for many of the Song's images, actually – but perhaps there is an unusualness to the comparison that does not only jar with contemporary readers' experiences of it. Are these lips – as thread – even visible? What does the lover find appealing in their sparseness? The comparison is most awkward when presented with the lover's ensuing statement: 'your mouth is lovely'. Is what is unexpected the size of the referent – its particularity and finitude? Or is the praise of the mouth as lovely ironic, given how the poet has just envisioned it? The incongruities of size in lip and thread are but one of a number in this text: neck to tower, hair to goats, sheep to teeth, are others. When viewed together, there is a disruption of scale that makes the woman impossible in her total form, in addition to her particular parts. In sum, the poet caricatures with these incongruities, and caricature produces humour.

Sometimes, however, these juxtapositions are strange enough that they actually unsettle, as in the case of the neck as tower. To my mind, the unsettling comes through both the extreme size and the specific referent chosen, which has combined the materiality of a building structure and its components with the harshness of war. Not only does the first imply the second (kingdoms are fought over and lives are lost in the process), but the second transgresses the first, as if human life is the price, the *decoration*, of humanity's marking off and defending land that it has claimed for its own. All is displayed on an enormous scale, and elaborately, as if to make a provoking and alarming statement.

In our first glimpse of this body, then, the grotesque makes itself known in a number of ways. There is, first, the hybridity of the body, its incorporation of incongruous elements that combine to make an impossible and comical creature. The comedy is in the unexpected and the hyperbolic; it is also in the problematization of statements about the loved one's beauty that frame the descriptions. Thematically, the body also reveals an intimate connection with the grotesque. This is evident in the merging, even interdependence, of the human form and the natural world. In movement, hunting, killing, eating, even washing, the woman is closely tied to what we saw in Bakhtin's grotesque body was the cycle of life. The connection with the grotesque is also evident in the estrangement or dehumanization of the body through the imposition of the architectural world on it, and the grim reminders of war. There is, moreover, material here, facilitated by commentators' own sometimes awkward readings, to create unease, to provide an edge on which the grotesque may take root and assert its influence.

Metamorphosis: Barthes' Heads on the Lovers' Bodies

I want now to explore the grotesque body further by reading it alongside the curious representations of Arcimboldo and the ensuing literary explanations of Barthes, discussed in the previous chapter. Barthes' article helped to investigate Harpham's claim that the grotesque prompts a 'struggle for sense' in the viewer. His study of the Arcimboldo heads aligned this struggle for sense with language, where analogy is exploited and where an image holds multiple significations. Moreover, all exist at the same time, and this multiplicity is never able to be fully reconciled by the viewer.

Reading the body images alongside the Arcimboldo heads may raise some objections: to compare painted images with literary ones might appear unorthodox.[16] It is not, however, a strict comparison (and one on artistic terms) that I am after, but one that appeals to the process of signification. The compendium of natural and man-made features written on the body in 4.1-5 is reminiscent of the heads Barthes studies in his essay. The similarities go beyond the mere fact that both undertake a likening of a particular body-part to a foreign element in order to conceive the body anew. I also see similarities in the audacity of the elements chosen and in the endlessness of signification offered. Additionally, one might identify connections in the expectations that the analogies place upon the body and on the viewers/readers. Barthes wrote of compositional excess and a malaise generated in the viewer: these, too, are present in the Song's bodies. Moreover, as readers read on through the Song, the excess and its related malaise increase as image piles on top of image. These broader themes (what we might call the implications of grotesque figuration – the expectations and malaise) will be dealt with below, once further study of the images has taken place and I return to the matter of strategies and implications of grotesque figuration in the Song. At this juncture, I want to give a sense of analogy and multiplicity of meaning: these are best illustrated by discussing a key feature of Barthes' analysis: metamorphosis.

I return to Song 4.1-5, where we see immediately that the organic components of the woman's body are dynamic. The lover does not make the comparison without elaborating on it. Doves are (visible? moving?) behind the veil; sheep move up from the wash; goats stream down a mountainside; pomegranates are cleft in two, and again, appear from behind a veil; breasts resemble (move like?) gazelles, feeding among lilies. The movement explicated here implies not only that life is doing what life

---

16   Even despite my insistence that readers may *envision* descriptive texts such as these, it is still another step to posit them as actually *illustrated*. Hart's cartoon, however, bridges the gap a little.

does – lives, eats, breathes, is active – but also that it shifts, that change is
always imminent. The changes (or metamorphosis) in question are not
only those expected with movement of wild creatures, but also with the
cycle of life in which these organic components find themselves – as
Bakhtin so painstakingly pointed out. Moreover, the images move off the
page, as it were, by metamorphosing into other images and through a
range of interpretations.

Thus, goats stream down from Mount Gilead, and newly washed sheep
come up from the water; each mirrors the other in action, so that
opposing movements are held within the woman's frame. Sheep[17] newly
up from the wash evoke the muck and waste from which they came. The
explicit mention of their offspring is here combined with the success (and
chance) of twinning, and at the same time tempered by the possibility of
bereavement. Fox asserts that the sheep in this verse help 'create an
atmosphere of health and fecundity' (1985: 129), but surely this cannot be
the entire content: present here too are the trials and hardship of birth and
the risk of loss (Fox's translation of שׁכּל as 'miscarries' says as much).[18]

The twinned sheep are recalled in v. 5 (and again in 7.4) by the two
gazelles to which the woman's breasts are compared (the breasts are
paired here, but not always; see 7.8, 9). The Song frequently mingles and
plays with its images, too: tempted by its resistance to concise and finite
displays of images, we see that the teeth of v. 2 gnaw through the rest of
the description. They are contained in the thin, blood-red line of the
mouth – bright and bleeding as if they have bitten the lip – and they taste
and masticate the blood-red pomegranates that characterize her temples
(v. 3b). Even the lions and leopards of 4.8, the dens of which are, in the
lover's view, the lair of his mate (and metonymically, they become her),
are prefigured by the teeth. Lions and leopards lie in wait for their prey:
are gazelles feeding among the lilies themselves to be food, as sheep and
goats might be?

In this way, image piles on top of image. The blood and death, which I
suggested are intimated in the natural images, for instance, appear
elsewhere in 4.1-5. Jutting up awkwardly and incongruously, the woman's
neck is compared to the tower of David in v. 4. Shields and spoils adorn it,
as grim, gargoyle-like reminders of injury, blood spilt, death and loss. The
teeth of 4.2 might even gnash in anger and hatred (cf. Job 16.9; Pss 35.16;

---

17   עדר is in construct with הקּצוּבות, 'shorn ones', and not the expected רחל ים 'sheep',
seen in the parallel text in 6.6. קצב appears only elsewhere in 2 Kgs 6.6 ('cut off'; Murphy
1990: 155). Pope figures this is a 'poetic equivalent' of the more usual רחל ים (1977: 461), but
he offers little evidence for this evaluation. As it turns out, the diversion from the expected
heightens the image's grotesquerie (see below).

18   מתאימות ('bearing twins') is a hiphil participle (f. pl.). Fox sees שׁכּל as antithetical
to מתאימות; it is accordingly translated as 'miscarries' by him (1985: 129). שׁכּל has this
meaning in the Pi. and Hi. stems.

37.12; 112.10; Lam. 2.16). Here, of course, there is also the triumph of human architecture and the glory of war, but it is always tinged red. The cutting or splicing of the pomegranates in v. 3b convinces us as much, as do the temples they describe – elsewhere the site of Sisera's violent demise (Judg. 4.21-22; 5.26).[19] Here, too, the power and might of the lion in 4.8 are prefigured (Isa. 15.9; 31.4; 35.9; Jer. 2.30; 4.7; 5.6; Amos 3.4, 8; Hos. 11.10; Joel 1.6; Pss 7.3; 10.9; 22.14, 22). Even the sheep are not explicitly called sheep, but are instead the 'cut' or shorn ones.

Then another transposition: if the woman's body is represented by the animals and buildings of the land, it also comes to be identified with the land itself. On her, animals are herded (4.1, 2); on her, animals feed and might be hunted themselves; on her are built the structures that both decorate and aid in her defence. Sometimes, the semantic range of the words used in the description presents other grotesque opportunities. For instance, the noun used for her lips (שָׂפָה) might also be translated as 'edge', as in the bank of a river, or shore of a sea (e.g. Aroer on the edge of the Wadi Arnon [Deut. 2.36; 4.48; Josh. 12.2] or the border of Abelmeholah [Judg. 7.22]);[20] in short, they are the markers of territories that are being challenged or that need defence, and in whose interest blood is sometimes spilt.[21] This edge of the land, written onto her lips, appears elsewhere in her lover's identification of her as a mountain of myrrh or hill of frankincense.[22] She has already used a similar image to describe herself in Song 2.17 (mountain edges), and will do so again in 8.14 (mountains of balsams/spices). In 4.3 מִדְבָּרֵיךְ is used to describe the woman's mouth. There is a pun here, for the noun also means desert or wilderness.[23] In 4.8, as I have also mentioned, her lover calls to her to

---

19   As mentioned above, רַקָּה means 'temple' (of the head) here; it is used also in Judg. 4.21, 22; 5.26 of the part of Sisera's head through which Jael drives the tent peg. Interestingly, commentators often choose 'brow' or 'cheek', as most recently Exum has, based on what might be most logically viewed under a veil (2005a: 153), and, I wonder, on the desire to avoid any connection with the only other HB text where that word appears and refers to the temple, Judg. 4.21-22.

20   See also Gen. 22.17 (the promise to Abraham about the creation of the nation Israel) and 41.3 (Pharaoh's dream of famine). These intertexts repeat the themes of eating and consumption – or lack – and national beginning and identity. The tower of David is likely a tribute to the latter, or is in service of its defence.

21   One also thinks of the related expression, 'edge of the sword', פִּי חֶרֶב (Josh. 6.21; 8.24; 10.28, 30; 1 Sam. 15.8; 2 Sam. 15.14; Jer. 21.7; Job 1.15, 17), here, which is literally 'mouth' of the sword.

22   It is possible to take this as a metaphor for the woman or as an actual (still metaphorized) destination to which he will go. If the latter, the logic is hard to follow – why would he run away from his love? – unless, of course, he realizes he does not fancy the one whom he has just described!

23   Most commentators point out the relation of the *hapax* with speaking (דָּבַר), (Bergant 2001: 45; Keel 1994: 143; Longman 2001: 145; Exum 2005a: 153), but are not

descend from the mountain peaks and the dens of animals, with which she is identified.

Next, as if in a gallery, the description may be looked at from yet another angle. Animals and food have already been mentioned here, in terms of how the two might fit together, as in the bloody and violent hunter–prey connotation, with lips, teeth, lions and prey. This body, however, is also delicious and comestible. Eating – be that by wild animals or by ravenous lovers – is an important grotesque theme, as Bakhtin so clearly demonstrated in Rabelais' work. The pomegranates in v. 3 make the initial reference to human consumption in this description, juxtaposed with the mouth and lips in the first half of the verse.[24] Are the lips blood-red because they have feasted on pomegranates? Is the mouth lovely because it is dripping with juice (see 4.11)? Or are the cheeks splashed red from exuberant feasting? A little incongruously, the gazelles that feed on lotuses or lilies are also present, painting a plush and tranquil picture. Food in these instances is clearly for enjoyment: it is delectable, savoured, a gustatory delight. But the connection of the woman's body with food is merely begun here. We will have to wade further into the Song's imagery for more, and it becomes rich and plentiful. The Song manifests well the familiar cannibalistic murmur of lovers, 'I could eat you up!'

In this way, image bounces from image to image, and in this movement, the grotesque is able to take root and thrive. The metamorphoses occur not just in what we have seen, but from broader text to text as well. Without stopping here to trace these initial images from 4.1-5 throughout the entire Song, it is possible at this juncture to see a little of this larger-scale movement in the progression to the next major description, 6.4-7. Almost a verbatim repetition of 4.1-5, this second image contains some important changes that illustrate the way that the descriptions shift in front of the lover's eyes. Such movement has already taken place, actually. Song 4.1 was a partial repetition of 1.15, 'your eyes are doves', but already

---

concerned with the potential desert pun, except for Bergant, who hints at it with the observation that '[i]t might be that a concrete visual noun is not used because of the double meaning of *midbār*' (2001: 47). See, however, Fox 1985: 204, who identifies a double pun: the first is as I have located it above; the second is with נאות, which he notes can be read as a pun of נוה, 'habitation', which in conjunction with מדבר means 'oasis' (as in Isa. 27.10). Fox's interpretation of the puns does not appear to be grotesque, though. He concludes: 'Thus the youth is saying in playful hyperbole, you are so lovely, so flawless, that whatever part of you might be reckoned as a desert, as somehow defective, in comparison with the other parts – that "desert" is really an oasis, fresh and refreshing' (1985: 204).

24   In Rozelaar's view (1988), the noun used to describe the temple, רקה, does not refer to the temple at all, but to the mouth. If we followed this reading (which most would not, because it is based on sketchy semantic evidence and the author's reconstruction of Sisera's death), רקה could also lend support to the eating theme; there, mouth and pomegranate would be merged, in typically grotesque fashion. Keel agrees with this interpretation of רקה (1994: 146).

the lover has added more ('behind the veil') to augment the sense-impression.[25] It should not be a surprise, then, that the description in 6.4-7 carries on the practice, only it ups the stakes by increasing the intensity of the metamorphosis. The resultant shifts, moreover, serve to heighten the figure's grotesquerie.

The slight variations between the two poems provide a good starting-point for discussion.[26] The lover quotes himself (4.1b-3), but not entirely accurately.[27] The most obvious omission is that of 4.3a ('Your lips are like a crimson thread, and your mouth is lovely'). Another visible slip of his tongue is over the sharp edges of הקצובות in 4.1 (a flock of shorn/cut ones), which he replaces here in v. 6 with הרחלים (a flock of sheep), רחל being the more usual word for sheep. Missing, too, is the noun הר which modifies גלעד in 4.1b. So the lover has excised the mountain and the shearing/cutting from his previous words; he has, moreover, replaced one excision with a more 'normal' or expected noun. Are the changes significant? With this pared-down version of the description, one wonders what it was about the lips and mouth that caused a change in perspective: perhaps they seemed odd, as I found them, on repetition.[28]And for the teeth and hair, the emphasis would apparently be on the sheep rather than the shearing, and the Gilead, rather than the mountain. But the omissions are noticeable and they prompt questions. Has the lover changed his mind about what he sees, so that these sheep – these teeth – are not the ones he has seen before? How do they differ? Are they less white, less straight, less smooth (what was the basis for the comparison with shorn ones)? And does the hair still move in the way anticipated by the lover? Or has he changed his mind about the impressions his lover gives?

The complete picture of 6.4-7 is not only a matter of what is missing,

---

25   This is not the extent of the movement of the eyes. As I will have cause to discuss below, there is actually quite an interesting progression that takes place with this one image.

26   The underlined text in 6.4-7 represents the quoted material of 4.1-5:

4 יפה את רעיתי כתרצה נאוה כירושלם אימה כנדגלות:

5 הסבי עיניך מנגדי שהם הרהיבני שערך כעדר העזים
שגלשו מן־הגלעד:

6 שניך כעדר הרחלים שעלו מן־הרחצה שכלם מתאימות
ושכלה אין בהם:

7 כפלח הרמון רקתך מבעד לצמתך:

Note also the slight difference between מהר גלעד in 4.1 and מן־הגלעד in 6.5.

27   These alterations may also be taken as evidence of the textual play (puns, *hapax legomena*, repetition, rhyme), here shown in a small dose, that is visible throughout the Song. In the Song's punning, quotation and repetition of itself, and in a number of other features, it is possible to detect a kind of textual hybridization, which I will later explore as grotesquerie on a textual level (the textual body).

28   Many comment on the omission of this phrase, and it is plausible – and easy – to explain it as scribal error. Exum, for example, adds it back into the text in her translation, reading with a number of mss (2005a: 212).

but also what has been augmented. The augmentations are not in the form of body parts added to the list, but in general statements that colour the entire description. So, for example, the lover also makes an initial statement about his love's beauty, only here it is alarming and perplexing and not at all the general and beneficent statement that it appeared to be in 4.1-5. The lover also chooses to describe the eyes – but not as doves. He merely asks that his lover turn her eyes away. The reason? Not that they remind him of doves, or that they are hidden behind her veil (1.15, 4.1), but that they are a source of disturbance: they alarm him. These augmentations serve to cast an entirely different mood over the quotation of the initial description in 4.1-5, and it is one that is potentially troubled and unsettling. This implies to me not that the lover (or the poet) is building an increasingly sinister picture as the book progresses, but that depiction of the body and the relationship that this depiction purports to encapsulate become increasingly complex the more we read.

By looking at these two augmentations for a moment – the eyes and the statement about beauty – it will be possible to explore some of this complexity. In the process, we might also move more into the territory of grotesque themes and devices, having seen how the unfolding and repetition of the images is evidence of their metamorphosing, teeming nature. To be sure, the images continue to unfold in this way, well past 6.4-7, and indeed, throughout the Song. The eyes and the statement about beauty, though, indicate well some of the trouble that the grotesque causes as it is unleashed on the Song's bodies.

Scholarly debate over what the disturbance of the eyes might convey signals the trouble that the lover's request causes for the description (is it, for example, that the eyes arouse him [Pope 1977: 564]? If so, why ask her to turn away?). The NRSV gives 'overwhelm' as the meaning for רהב, which generally means to alarm or awe one (Hi.). LXX and Vg. generally give the sense of fleeing or moving away (*avolare*, 'hasten away'; ἀναπτερόω, 'raise, set up', 'excite'). Some see that the awe is in fact a kind of arousal that prompts fear, intimidation or confusion (Bergant 2001: 77; Bloch and Bloch 1995: 189; Keel 1994: 215; Murphy 1990: 178; Snaith 1993: 89). Longman cannot quite decide what sense to give it: 'overwhelm, overpower, excite, *unsettle*' (2001: 180). Exum uses the description to add to her case that the woman causes a certain anxiety in overwhelming feelings for the man; here he must ask her to look away (2005a: 160, 217). Fox's reading is more extreme: he believes that the woman is quite simply frightening (1985: 152). From these various readings, it is clear that the eyes are troubling, and surprisingly, commentators do not shy away from pointing out that the woman is a source of fear and anxiety.[29]

The difficulty with the eyes is, moreover, trouble that has already been started by the preceding verse and its evaluation of the woman's beauty. The man states that she is beautiful (יָפָה) as Tirzah and as attractive (נָאוָה) as Jerusalem. So far, on the face of it, the similes seem quite innocuous, albeit somewhat incomprehensible, but the real punch comes in the next half of the verse, where the lover adds אֲיֻמָּה כַּנִּדְגָּלוֹת. This phrase has been problematic for readers, and something like the NRSV's 'terrible as an army with banners' might be a possible translation. If so, the military language of the previous description is immediately invoked, along with the blood and war that was suggested there. Of all, it is the adjective אֲיֻמָּה that seems most disturbing. Found only elsewhere in Hab. 1.7, it there describes the fearsome Chaldeans, whom Yahweh will rouse to seize dwelling places which do not belong to them (1.6), and who 'come for violence, gathering their captives like sand' (1.9). True, the protagonist in the Song is not the devouring and rampaging instrument of Yahweh, but this phrase does recall something of her might and fearsome nature that I pointed out in Song 4.[30] Along these lines, various options have been suggested for the meaning of נִדְגָּלוֹת.[31] Are the standards referred to

---

29 I would be remiss, too, if I did not mention that the verb in question has a nominal parallel in Rahab, the monster of the deep, against whom battle is waged by Yahweh in texts such as Isa. 51.9; Ps. 89.11 and Job 9.13 (Pope mentions this as well: 1977: 564). This would make the woman not only fearful, but monstrous, and cosmically so.

30 Keel seems to agree:

> Something that truly fascinates humans also engenders respect and awe – even anxiety; in the same way something that inspires respect and awe almost always fascinates humans. Both elements are contained in the picture of the city and its mighty walls and towers. Verse 4c now unfolds the other side, saying of the beloved that she is as 'terrifying as an army with banners'. ... This hauntingly beautiful woman commands respect, for she exhibits the inner order, the strict discipline, of an army grouped around banners in battle formation; the loving admirer is rendered shy and reserved in her presence. (1994: 215)

Murphy also points out the dangerous and threatening aspects of the woman (1990: 177).

31 The meaning of נִדְגָּלוֹת (דגל) – 'those who set up standards' (BDB 186a); 'gathered around banners' (*HALOT* 203) – is contested as being related to דגל ('to lift banners') or דגל ('to look'). As such, it has been taken variously as: 'army with banners' (Keel 1994: 215); 'visions' (Murphy 1990: 175); 'trophies' (Pope 1977: 560–1; the visual references by Pope and Murphy follow the Akkadian cognate *dagālu*, which has connotations of looking or seeing); vaguely, as 'the most eminent' (Fox 1985: 152); 'heavenly pictures' (Rudolph 1962: 162; *Himmelsbilder*, owing to the repetition of the phrase in 6.10 and the context of the sun and moon there); 'brilliant stars' (Goitein 1965: 221), which insists the paralleling of sun and dawn be repeated for dawn and נִדְגָּלוֹת; 'daunting as the stars in their courses' (Bloch and Bloch 1995: 191, who appear to agree with respect to 6.10, but who cannot offer the same reading for this verse); and so on. See Exum 2005a: 218 for an even more detailed list.

in the noun the trophies of war, like the shields that adorned her neck in
4.4? And will they, like the shields, not only speak of the glories and
triumph of war, but also its violence and loss? Pope's reading includes
intertexts of parallel Ugaritic materials, notably the gory 'Anat Text',[32]
which are apt for this discussion. There, the goddess, 'distinguished for
her violence and her beauty' (1977: 562, 606) wears trophies of severed
hands and heads as she wades through the remains of her human victims.
We have come some distance indeed from the demure woman who flutters
her dove-like eyes behind her veil (cf. Goulder 1986).

Where exactly, then, have we arrived? As Pope observes,
'[c]ommentators have been sore abashed to explain the collocation of
beauty and terror' (1977: 560).[33] This is precisely the difficulty of such a
comparison made by the lover. As did the first general attestations of
beauty in 4.1 and 7, this one makes us question not only what beauty is
supposed to mean to the lover who speaks of it, but also for the body
descriptions that follow, which now do not seem to be very appealing at
all.[34] Moreover, they make us wonder what is the motivation on the part
of the lover (conscious or unconscious) for speaking about the woman
whom he loves in this manner. Ultimately, too, the phrase prompts the
reader to look again more closely at the first half of the verse (the
comparisons to Tirzah and Jerusalem), which might have been skipped
over as cryptic, or excused, as some commentators have done, as homages
to the cities' beauty.

Cryptic Tirzah seems to have caused some puzzlement. Looking back
on it after reading אֲיֻמָּה כַּנִּדְגָּלוֹת, as I have above, there is material here
to support the more disturbing military image, and therefore the presence
of the grotesque. The noun's parallel with Jerusalem suggests it be read as
a place name.[35] The beauty of Jerusalem is a given for most commentators, and many anticipate the same for Tirzah (its likely connection to

---

32   The text is cited by Pope as 3 ['NT].2.3-41 (1977: 606). See J.C.L. Gibson for the full
text (1977: 7–8).

33   Cf. Murphy, who notes, 'the poet obviously sees no conflict between attraction and
fear' (1990: 177).

34   If read in conjunction with the parallel text in 6.10, which many seem to argue it
should be (see esp. Long 1996), the cosmic elements to which the woman is likened raise
additional questions. From a grotesque perspective, the linking of the woman to the sun,
moon and the dawn would be the ultimate tying of her body to nature, on a great cosmic
level. And juxtaposed with these, the phrase 'terrible as an army with banners' seems odder
than before. For Keel, the host of heaven and cosmic battle are envisaged here (1994: 220).
The scholarly impulse to interpret the phrase as 'awesome as the sights', or something similar
seems warranted. As I have so far been arguing, however, here is the place to resist such
smoothing over of potential difficulties and see what transpires if we emphasize difference.

35   תִּרְצָה refers to the city, Tirzah, as the parallelism with Jerusalem indicates, but some
of the versions do not acknowledge it as a place name. Pope translates the noun as 'verily
pleasing', in recognition of the noun's relation to רָצָה; the כ is then taken as asseverative

רצה, 'to be pleasing', assists in this interpretation; Exum 2005a: 217; Keel 1994: 213; Longman 2001: 179). The biblical record of Tirzah, however, notes it to be a place of political unrest (Josh. 12.24; 1 Kgs 14.17; 15.21, 33; 16.6, 8, 9, 15, 17, 23).[36] It is the site of brief reigns of various kings of Israel, and also of sieges and takeovers; at Tirzah, the son of Jereboam dies at the hand of Yahweh as a sign of his anger against the nation. Jerusalem, though typically praiseworthy (Ps. 50.2; Lam. 2.15; so Pope 1977: 558), is also the site of desolation and mourning in the biblical record (see particularly, and most obviously, Lamentations). The implications in terms of the grotesque would be twofold. The first is that here is yet another instance where the woman is connected with the land, here with two cities, and this despite objections from earlier scholars (e.g. Stephan and Cheyne, so Pope 1977: 558), who insist that women cannot be compared to cities. The second is that in these two cryptic similes, 'beauty' remains enigmatic and troubled by the death and violence (here unrest) that we have seen already in 4.1-5.

In this light, the eyes, then, continue the theme of the previous verse. With Tirzah, Jerusalem and the אימה כנדגלות in mind, they sharply contrast with those we saw in 4.1. Moreover, instead of being items to look at, they look out at the lover and the reader/viewer, resisting his or her gaze. The expected images from the first description in 4.1-5 here follow the eyes, but they and the woman's beauty, troubling as they are, cast a pallor over what comes next. Instead of the predominance of the natural world as the central focus, the sheep, goats and pomegranates become wild, unruly, the sources of unease. Do the hair and the teeth also unsettle? Will the lover want to stop looking?

As we have been seeing so far in the metamorphosing of one description into another, the imagery is not finite, not even as it reaches the end-point of the second description in 6.7. Several components – as it happens, the additions made to this second description – reach beyond themselves and pervade the rest of the Song. In the case of the eyes, we see them again in Chapter 7, where they are placid pools (7.5). How can this be reconciled with what has been seen earlier? Is a reader meant to prefer one version over another, or to hold all three in tension in his or her mind? Is the Song insistent on this kind of consistency? The banners of 6.4 flap back almost immediately, in 6.10, and there they have cosmic implications. Does one then read the cosmic onto the military? Does the woman exhibit a beauty

---

(1977: 558). Many recognize the relation of the two words, however, without adopting Pope's translation: see Bloch and Bloch 1995: 188; Exum 2005a: 217; Fox 1985: 181; Keel 1994: 213; Longman 2001: 179; Murphy 1990: 175.

36 Longman mentions the problem of it being likely at odds with Jerusalem because of its location at the time of the Song's creation (Longman 2001: 179). He surmises that it may have been of great enough renown to overcome the political difficulties, however. The noun is also a proper name: Num. 26.33; 27.1; 36.11; Josh. 17.3.

beyond all earthly description? I will continue to comment on the unfolding of the images as I proceed with my reading. Discussion of the eyes and the military banners, however, brings us more fully into the nature of the grotesque themes that weave themselves through the lovers' words.

The Themes

As Bakhtin, Kayser, Miles, Russo and others have made evident, the grotesque works particularly well in concert with various themes, among them nature and the cycle of life, the body (bodily functions) and sexuality, war and violence – and other alienating forces – and so on. In this section, I want to trace some of these themes as they are able to be perceived in the Song's descriptions. Logistically, there might be a number of ways to discuss these. The poems in their totality (such as they are) are an attempt to render the body within a specific set of parameters and at a specific moment. At times, they do manage to encapsulate a theme rather succinctly, despite their piecemeal approach to the body, as in Song 5.10-16. Because, however, the descriptions do depict the body part by part, and referent by referent, it is more often the case that a particular poem will house several themes; these may then be elaborated by similar texts in other poems/descriptions. It might, therefore, be more expedient to discuss the themes without recourse to their boundaries within the poems, and irrespective of the relative totality of the bodies that house them – even though to do so risks further fracturing the forms.[37]

In light of these two options, and the problems they suggest, I will undertake to do a little of both. My reading will 'collect' imagery that is pertinent to a given theme, but then also discuss it on a broader basis, in the context of the extended descriptions. Sometimes, too, thematics are achieved by poetic device and effect as much as by singular metaphors, as in the case of the architectural, a theme considered here in its own right, but then also applied to the 'constructed' body of Song 7.1-10. My work in this section is not intended to be exhaustive, but to give a (detailed) indication of where and how grotesque figuration works. In what follows, I then turn my attention more fully to the mechanics and strategies of grotesque figuration, as well as its implications.

Nature/Cycles/Life/Cycles ...

Bakhtin's analysis of Rabelais revealed the grotesque body to be intricately tied with nature. What Bakhtin was at pains to point out

---

37 Such a reading strategy would, it has also to be pointed out, have political implications for the body (typically the woman's) that is being described.

was that this was not a matter of mere associations, but that boundaries between subject and nature were often indeterminate: in short, they were *merging*. The present participle is appropriate here because it is the active, changing body that is at issue, just as much as it is the body in contact with the world around it. As we have already seen with respect to Song 4.1-5 and 6.4-7, the interpolation of the land or the natural world into the body is a popular means of envisioning a loved one. Even so, to speak of nature or the cycle of life as *a theme* is misleading here. In this context, natural or cyclical elements are complexly bound up with other matters (as they were in Rabelais), such as eating or consumption, the senses (smell, taste and touch, predominantly) and perhaps unsurprisingly, sex. So nature, as prominent as it is, must be seen to be at the core of a series of interrelated ideas, and not merely a unique theme.

Commentary could be made on the prevalence of natural imagery in the main body descriptions. In Song 4.1-5 and 6.4-7, it was the physical contours of the land and its rich, comestible produce that assisted the lover in explicating his feelings for his love. The grotesque was readable in these texts because of the collocation of various forms of wildlife in the descriptions (e.g. doves, goats, sheep, gazelles) with the themes of eating (gazelles grazing, the pomegranates, cut and ready for eating) and the references to the mouth and lips. As I indicated earlier, these themes continue throughout the Song and are quite evident in another of the body descriptions, 7.1-10. In that text, it is particularly wine in two forms, in the navel or vagina, and as kisses, gliding over lips and teeth, that is reminiscent of what has already been seen in the earlier texts in Song 4 and 6. Further consideration of the extended descriptions could explore these connections, as well as those made by other animal imagery – with its concomitant themes of the hunt – by agricultural images (the belly as wheat), and by comestibles, particularly fruit.

One particularly nice, concentrated sequence of images found in 4.9-16, however, establishes an even better context to begin the exploration of natural imagery. This is not a text that is traditionally identified as a *wasf*, thus its significance for depictions of the body in the Song is often overlooked. The body in this text is not displayed and itemized in the same manner as we have seen in 4.1-5 and 6.4-7, but there is, nevertheless, a protracted rumination on the body in certain of its aspects; this easily justifies its inclusion here. Song 4.9-16, then, presents a picture of the woman that is comprised of a few brief references to several body-parts and an extended dual metaphor of a garden and a fountain. For my purposes, what is so provocative about this text is that it easily and naturally shifts from nature as abstract to nature as particular and intimate; this can indicate the personal, but in this example, also the sexual. As we also saw from Bakhtin (and Miles's and Russo's critiques of him), the latter frequently comes as part-and-parcel of the former.

I begin with v. 6, which establishes the setting for the description. The woman's lover does not explicitly identify her as the mountain of myrrh and the hill of frankincense to which he announces he will hasten.[38] There is significant cause to perceive that these are metaphors for her, however, not least of which is that he has just been addressing her and describing her body in detail (vv. 1-5). Then, he addresses her again in v. 7 to praise (?) her beauty, so that we can see that the puzzling v. 6 is framed by speech directed towards the woman, and could plausibly be considered part of that same line of discourse. There is no reason to assume consistency of speech or speaker anywhere in the Song – it changes tone and speaker often and without warning – but it would be odd for the lover to interrupt himself at v. 6 and mundanely announce a travel itinerary before he resumed his praise, as if his words to her and the feelings that they purport to demonstrate were of no consequence. This would, if nothing else, indeed be bad courting technique. There are other, more compelling reasons for suggesting that v. 6 refers to her, too. The verse seems to be a rejoinder to her own words in 2.17 (in fact part of the verse is quoted), where she invites him to the 'cleft mountains'. Next, the spice-laden imagery with which he continues in 4.12-15 (and which she echoes in v. 16) also suggests that the mountain and hill metaphors in v. 6 represent her. To this end, it could also be that her later reference to herself (?) as the mountains of spices in 8.14 continues the identification. Ultimately, though, whether the lover's identification of the woman as mountain in v. 6 is inadvertent or intentional is immaterial. The connection is made, then reinforced, by the fact that he seems to identify her with the land and then takes up these images again to describe her body in vv. 12-15.

The garden constitutes the main description of the woman in vv. 12-15. Before it, her lover mentions briefly her eyes (v. 9), lips and tongue (v. 11). These, together with her caresses (or 'loving' – or breasts, see below; v. 10) and genitalia (v. 13), hidden in the garden image, will be all that will comprise her odd body in this text, making for the third incomplete register of her form so far in the Song. The combination here is intriguing, highly erotic, and wonderfully grotesque. The mouth, the tongue and the luxuriant foods are not forgotten after their first mention, either. In the extended metaphor of vv. 12-15, her sex is combined with food and spices, and if we miss the equation of eating and sex – meaning its oral forms –

---

38   Many commentators read the reference generally as I do (Bloch and Bloch 1995: 173; Murphy 1990: 159; Longman 2001: 147), but others think of specific body-parts, usually the woman's breasts, which, I surmise, might have had its origins in allegorical readings, though there is a 'case' that can be made from related references in the text (1.13, 3.6). See, for example, Fox 1985: 132; Bergant 2001: 48; Exum 2005a: 166; Pope seems to have some affinity with the idea (1977: 472), though he cites Gerleman who disagrees; actually Pope proposes that they (the breasts) represent the fantastical land to which Gerleman refers (Keel agrees: 1994: 153).

the lovers make it overtly for us in 4.16 and 5.1, when she invites him to her garden to eat her fruits, and he accepts.

This version of the body is harder to capture than the others: against their hardened, sharp edges and faunal aspects, it is liquid and drips with luxuriant scents and foods. Reading with the LXX, Vg. and other versions, the breasts in v. 10 are described as better than wine.[39] The image is gustatory. Wine and breasts are compared, but it is hard to keep the two separate, and they are easily conflated, so that it becomes the breasts that exude the wine to which they are compared.[40] Then, in v. 11, the lips are put on show again, though this time they are not the bleeding line we saw in 4.3, but remain excessively wet, here described as dripping with honey (נפת). Finally, the tongue makes an appearance. Under it, the lover finds liquid honey (דבש) and milk.

Suddenly, the woman in the Song has become the leaking, permeable body that Miles (1991) describes. She exudes scent too, from her clothes (11b) and from her body (10b). All, for the moment, is sweet and delectable. One cannot miss, however, the similar texts of Prov. 5.3 and 16.24, where the same image of honey in the mouth and on the lips describes something altogether different. In 5.3, נפת drips from the lips of the strange woman (the permeable body, sexually uncontrolled), and in

39   To read with these versions is to depart from the scholarly consensus on this text. There are other places, to be sure, in my reading for the grotesque where I make similar departures, but I suspect that this one might be resisted by most readers, even though historically influential interpreters such as Luther have followed these alternate versions. My rendering may be especially queried because I unapologetically read with the MT in a later section. I reiterate that it is precisely this fluidity of imagery that I want to foreground here, as well as the possibility of reading at the margins. (Despite Pope's observations, the matter of logic of gender and pronouns is a small one, frequently transgressed throughout the Song [1977: 298]. A greater issue for him [and others] seems to be whether men might have breasts.) Moreover, in this particular text, I also want to bring to the fore the apparent mixing of caresses and breasts in other texts in the tradition (a scribal error [?] that is easily understood, given the ostensible, though probably androcentric, relationship between the breast and the caress), such as in Prov. 5.9 (see Camp 2000: 76). This is of especial significance with regard to a book such as Proverbs, where the offering of דדים has such grave implications for a person's (man's) well-being. Of interest, too, is the intertext in Isa. 60.16, where Zion drinks the milk of nations and nurses from the breasts of kings. Pope's protestation (following Ginsburg) that '[t]he figure ... relates to economic nourishment and exploitation and it would be preposterous ... to appeal to this catachresis in support of the LXX and Vulgate rendering "breasts" in the present passage' should not be ignored in our pursuit of the grotesque.

40   Elsewhere, the Song suggests a connection for us. In 2.9, the lover is likened to a gazelle, and in 2.16 we see him feeding among the lilies. (רעה may be a transitive or intransitive verb, so 2.16 might refer to him feeding himself.) In 4.5, the woman's breasts are described as gazelles that feed among the lilies. In the Song's use and reuse of imagery, man, breast and feeding become conflated; we need not, moreover, rely on a straightforward analogical relationship (breast = lily; man = gazelle) to perceive the merging of subjects and parts.

16.24, צוּף־דְּבַשׁ describes אִמְרֵי־נֹעַם, the pleasant words (of a wise person; cf. v. 23). Honey has both bad and good connotations, then, and they might both be written here in this mouth. The insight on these images that Proverbs affords does not end here, however. The strange woman is to be the subject of caution, and she is contrasted with the faithful wife, who is described using very fluid imagery, as a well or a cistern from which the prudent man is encouraged to drink (Prov. 5.15-20).[41] This becomes a pertinent image for Song 4.12-15. Then, the strange woman appears again[42] in Prov. 7.10-27, where, in v. 18, she offers the impressionable young man דֹּדִים.[43]

In Song 4.12, with the introduction of the garden, the lover changes gears and returns to the thematics he began in v. 6, though the liquidity of the form is never far away. The garden that describes the woman in vv. 12-15 is replete with the spices mentioned in v. 6 (מוֹר and לְבוֹנָה), and more besides. Verses 12-15 are framed by two parallel metaphors in various manifestations, the locked garden and the fountain/pool/spring. Within this locked space, there are שְׁלָחִים (channels/sprouts), which are themselves an enclosure or grove of pomegranates, laden with a whole host of the very best of exotic spices: henna, nard, saffron, cane, cinnamon, incense, aloes, myrrh.[44] Pungent and fluid images are heavily layered on top of each other here: garden, spring, then channels, then enclosure, then pomegranates, then spices, and back, finally, to fountains and springs again. The woman is intricately connected with the natural world, its flora (spices and aromas) particularly. Though downplayed, the land in a broader sense is also visible here, in the form of the rivers that flow from Lebanon. So elaborate is the description of the garden and its springs that the woman almost ceases to exist (Murphy 1990: 160); nature and body collapse into each other. The connection is, too, perhaps more intimate than we initially realize.

41   It is this woman whose breasts are described (in the wish that the prudent man may be satisfied with them) using דַּדֶּיהָ.

42   The terminology is different; the woman to be avoided here is described as אִשָּׁה לִקְרָאתוֹ שִׁית זוֹנָה. There is some debate as to whether the two women are the same figure, or whether they are part of a more complex depiction of foreignness and adultery that appears throughout Proverbs. See Camp (esp. 2000: Chs. 1–2) for a sophisticated investigation of the strange woman and the trickster in Proverbs.

43   Given my observations and interests above (see n. 39), a different sort of connection might be made with Song 4.10, where, if one does not wish to read with variant versions, the MT reads דֹּדֶיךָ.

44   For discussion of the identity of these various plants, see especially Brenner 1983 and the discussion in Pope 1977: 491–5.

Sex, Naturally; or 'Pardon me, Have you Seen my Vagina?'

The noun שְׁלָחַיִךְ (v. 13, 'your shoots'?), located at the centre of the enclosed garden and pool, has been the source of some consternation for biblical critics. Though many have posited a range of meanings for the noun, as Pope observes, the possibility that it refers to a 'more intimate portion of the anatomy' has been suggested (1977: 490).[45] Keel explains further that a parallel term in Job 33.18, שַׁחַת (pit) has encouraged the interpretation of שְׁלָחַיִךְ as a [*sic*] 'vertical excavation or shaft' (1994: 176). Transferred onto the body, especially when commentators are convinced that the locked garden refers to the woman's virginity (Fox 1985: 137 ['modesty']; Goulder 1986: 28;[46] Pope 1977: 488), the anatomical choice for שְׁלָחַיִךְ seems obvious. Keel also observes that the Arabic cognate *shalch* can mean vagina, and refers to various associations in Egyptian and Sumerian poetry of garden, canal, womb and vagina. Moreover, Lev. 12.7 and 20.18 use spring and fountain for vagina (Keel 1994: 176).

The enclosed garden has a part to play in this genital interpretation, for it suggests a context for it. Whereas commentators frequently assume the enclosed garden refers to the virginity or the inviolability of the woman, she herself suggests a more specific and anatomical meaning in 4.16, when she picks up on her lover's imagery and invites him to come into her garden (the sexual connotation of בּוֹא should not be ignored). Subsequently, in 5.1, he declares that he has done so. Many have taken this as a reference to consummation, in which case, the garden would represent the woman's body, and שְׁלָחַיִךְ expands on the previous image (enclosed garden, v. 12 / enclosure of pomegranates, v. 13).[47]

The גַל of v. 12b[48] must also be mentioned here in support of this reading. E. M. Good observes that the Ugaritic noun *gl* means 'cup', and so believes that the Hebrew noun here refers to a cup-shaped pool (1970: 94). The uterus is an obvious choice, especially if we have just been

45 Pope himself translates it as the singular 'groove' (1977: 490). Fox decides on irrigation channels (1985: 137). Görg debates between 'canals' (*Kanäle*) and 'branches' (*Zweige*) (1994). Keel selects 'canals' (1994: 174–8). Rudolph chooses *Frische* (1962: 150–51; 'freshness'). Exum renders it 'watercourses', though she acknowledges that it probably means 'shoots' or 'branches' (2005a: 155, 176). Longman decides on 'shoots', though in a logical conundrum over the fact that he has understood the garden to be the woman's vagina, he wonders whether the noun might refer to her pubic hair or legs (2001: 156); the NRSV renders it 'channel'.

46 Goulder's translation of גַל נָעוּל as a 'forbidden mound' emphasizes the reading. He sees this as her 'mound of Venus', later, a spring sealed by her hymen (1986: 36, 38).

47 The difficulty with these vaginal readings, of course, is that שְׁלָחַיִךְ is a plural noun, so the correlation of body–vagina is not supported literally; there is enough *fluidity* in images in the Song, however, that this does not have to pose a considerable problem for this alternative, but apparently popular, reading.

48 Reading MT. Some read with LXX and Vg., and some Hebrew versions, to repeat גַן. See, for example, Exum 2005a: 154.

interpreting the enclosed garden as referring to virginity. Pope agrees with Good's explanation, but does not here anticipate his own reading of another text, 7.3 ('your vulva [שָׁרְרֵךְ] a rounded crater [אַגַּן]'; 1977: 617–18), which is also provocative. Though the nouns for both the female genital and the bowl-shaped item to which it is compared are different from those in 4.12b, the proximity of these two themes is instructive, especially if we are not insistent on a linear reading for the entire Song. Influenced by 7.3, therefore, the enclosed pool in 4.12 can be seen nicely to prefigure שְׁלָחַיִךְ in the following verse.

Playfully, then, the extended metaphor heaps image upon image, tying the woman to the land, but it also reveals, for those looking, the concealed female genital. Let us read outwards again to the enclosed garden and running springs. Boer's provocative rendering of שְׁלָחַיִךְ as 'ejaculation' (1999: 68) picks up on the Vg. and LXX (Vg.: *emissiones tuae*; LXX: ἀποστολαί σου), and also plays in a sexual sense with another meaning of the noun, 'weapon' or 'missile'.[49] What is being sent out/ejaculated? Pomegranates? The image is delightfully ludicrous.[50] But spices and fluids seem more appropriate, and they are plentiful; indeed they once again invoke Miles's description of the female grotesque body, the 'permeable body that produces juices and smells' (1991: 153).

Volatile and thus grotesque, the body here is fluid, leaking and heady with scent. There is much to suggest from the imagery that this body is sexually aroused or even actively engaging in intercourse. The abundance of liquid suggests sexual fluids and their accompanying odours.[51] But the

---

49 With these two possible meanings of the noun, the obvious military imagery that goes along with שְׁלָחַיִךְ must also be mentioned. (But not always to the exclusion of sex: interestingly, for Boer, it is the connotation of the word as 'missile[s]' that makes him render it 'ejaculation' [1999: 68].) The military theme is not picked up elsewhere in the poem, but one has cause to think of the military might we have seen exhibited elsewhere (4.4; 6.4).

50 Or, distinctly appropriate, if we take Goulder's rather clinical interpretation, which appears to share a certain interest with that of another reader, Lyle Eslinger (1981) (see below):

At the head of the 'conduit' is the cervix, a firmfleshed protuberance round which the vagina broadens ('like a rounded cup', 7.2), with a small depression in the centre for the cervical canal; it bears a striking resemblance, when one comes to think of it, with the end of a pomegranate, which is similarly curved, firm, and with a depression. (Goulder 1986: 38)

Given such elaborations, one does have some sympathy with writers like Exum, who urges a 'delicate lack of specificity' (2005a: 176); indeed, it is odd to find this reading in Goulder, who had remarked, just sentences before, that שֶׁלַח is plural in the text 'for delicacy' (1986: 38).

51 The 'ejaculation' (or flow) of other fluids is of course also possible, such as blood (see my discussion of 7.3, below). The Levitical intertexts mentioned above (Keel) might further fill out this reading. That the Song invites incongruous material into its midst has already been noted, especially in the case of 4.7, which I suggested could be evocative of prohibitions against physical uncleanliness. Here, the connection is more elaborate. In Lev. 12.7 and

locked garden? It seems to challenge the assertion that the body is permeable, especially in the sense of penetrable. The image may refer to sexual conduct – why not? – but who is to say that the locking is against all who seek entry? After all, the lover is invited to enter at the end of his description in 4.16, and he does so (or will imminently) in 5.1. Locking here may intimate sexual allegiance or even ownership, rather than, simply, chastity.[52] Alternatively, argues Lyle Eslinger, the image may not have anything to do with sexual conduct at all, but might be part of a detailed anatomical reference to the woman's vulva that extends to various texts in the Song. The verb נעל and its derivatives might, in fact, be signifying the 'bulbospongiosus muscle as the locking or barring mechanism' in the vulvic cavity (Eslinger 1981: 276). In this case, the locked garden poses no problem at all, but only reiterates the genital theme of this text.[53]

Locks and lovemaking appear once again in the Song, and this instance is worth mentioning here, though it does not appear in the context of a description of the lovers' bodies. The mystifying 'dream scene' of 5.2-7 mixes spices, fluids, locks and sex in an enigmatic nocturnal episode. Here the woman is again intimately equated with spices (myrrh) and liquid: her hands drip with myrrh, in fact, liquid myrrh, and she puts them on the 'lock' in order to open to her beloved. A variety of readings have been suggested for this passage: a masturbatory fantasy (Pardes 1992: 132); coition, or coitus interruptus (reading from v. 4, 'my beloved put his hand through the hole . . . '; Pope 1977: 519, 521–4; Snaith 1993: 73–4);[54] even a more literal and non-sexual interpretation, that the woman gets up to answer the door (hands suitably anointed for the night), and finds her lover absent (Bloch and Bloch 1995: 181; Gordis 1974: 90; Gerleman 1965:

20.18, Keel observes, another general noun for spring, מקור, serves to refer to the flow of blood after childbirth (12.7), or during menstruation (20.18). The nouns used in Leviticus and the Song are clearly different, yet the vaginal flow of liquid is thematically related. Leviticus, with its prohibitions against menstrual sex especially (20.18), makes for a grotesque intertextual reading, and also reminds us of Kristeva's abject. Is she sexually ready/ active, or perhaps unavailable? Song 7.3 brings the issue even more sharply into the foreground, as we shall see, below.

52   Cf. Bloch and Bloch 1995: 176; Delitzsch 1877: 84; Fox 1985: 137; Murphy 1990: 156; Rudolph 1962: 132; Snaith 1993: 67; but compare Gordis 1974: 88; Keel 1994: 176; Longman 2001: 155 and Exum 2005a: 175, who believe that the metaphor refers to the woman's inaccessibility, and Gerleman, who sees only a garden locked with a gate (1965: 159).

53   Eslinger's enquiry in his article is directed at the כפות המנעול of 5.5. The גן נעול of 4.12 is referred to because of the verb נעל.

54   Murphy could be provocatively read in this instance, as Boer does (1999: 165 n.56): 'The myrrh on the lock *comes* either from the man or from the woman' (Murphy 1990: 171; emphasis added, assuming I read Boer correctly).

167; Goulder 1986: 41; Fox 1985: 144–5; Murphy 1990: 171).[55] As Pope notes, however, hand is used euphemistically elsewhere in the Hebrew Bible for penis, and this makes this text at the very least ambiguous, a clear case of *double entendre*.[56]

Liquid gardens bring us full circle to the first of the descriptions in this set of images, the tongue and lips of 4.11, which are connected with honey and milk. Lush gardens are meant to be enjoyed, even this *utopischer Phantasiegarten* (Gerleman 1965: 159), but they are also replete with exotic plants that yield foods and spices, which means that their enjoyment may be of a gustatory as well as a visual nature. I have already considered the translation of food onto the body in the previous descriptions, and, in reverse, the description of sexual conduct via food. Here, however, these themes have a more detailed quality, and so the blending of incongruous elements and the consumption of the body as food are easily more visible.

The *consumption* of the woman that is enthusiastically declared by her lover in 5.1 is nicely (and grotesquely) anticipated throughout this description of her in 4.9-15. Milk and honey are under her tongue (her edibility here doubly emphasized by conflating the comestibles with these parts of her that do the eating). Her breasts are better than wine. Her 'garden-shoot' offers pomegranates and fluids flow plentifully and fast. And the spices, some of which flavour food as well as scent the body (see Keel 1994: 178–80; Pope 1977: 493–5), make her so delicious that she invites the winds to waft her smell abroad. She is indeed an incredible, edible woman. In 4.16 she invites her lover to come and eat. And he does (5.1), exhibiting a *tendresse cannibalistique* (Lavoie) as he plucks, mixes and savours every morsel.

It is worth mentioning that, although relatively concentrated in Song 4.9-16, this patterning of natural images around food and the erotic body is repeated again in the description in 7.1-10. The natural world quickly becomes the comestible world in this description, as in the previous. Date palms (and presumably dates) and clusters of the vine imply that the lover expects to consume her – her breasts at least.[57] And there is certainly more. Enticingly (the scent of) her nose is said to be like apples. Earlier, in v. 3, he describes her stomach as a heap of wheat, fecund – and edible? He

---

55   Keel argues for another interpretation, that this and the scene in 3.1-5 do not represent actual events, or dreams, but are 'formulations of a typical relational fantasy describing the missing of the opportune moment, the painful recurrence of feelings out of phase: when he wants to, she does not; when she wants to, he does not (any longer)' (1994: 186; see also 119–21).

56   See, most recently, Exum 1999, with further elaboration in her commentary (2005a: 190–96).

57   This recalls the breasts (דדים) in 4.10 (LXX and Vg.), and my observation that other Song texts conflate woman, breast and eating.

also compares her vulva or navel to a bowl that never lacks wine. Her palate too is like the best wine (v. 10), going down over the lips of sleepers, or, as some versions have it, lips and teeth. Her body exhibits the harvest, the finest of the land's yield, all to be delicately and deliciously consumed.

Wine and the grape draw together a provocative, perhaps disturbing, combination of body-parts, seen already in 4.9-16: breasts, vulva and mouth. In 7.3, the woman's שֹׁר is described as a bowl (אַגָּן) that never lacks wine. With Pope and others, I take the word to mean 'vulva', even though its usage elsewhere in the Hebrew Bible denotes umbilical cord or navel (Prov. 3.8; Ezek. 16.4; Pope 1977: 617). Pope bases his reasoning on three issues: the related Arabic term *sirr*, denoting secret or pudenda, or even coition and fornication; the direction of the description (foot to head); and the text's habit of portraying each body-part only once (the stomach is mentioned directly afterwards) (Pope 1977: 617). He also observes that the navel is not known for its capacity to hold liquid.[58] Other commentators agree (see, for instance, Goulder 1986: 56, 'womb';[59] Haupt [so Fox 1985: 158]; Keel 1994: 234–5; Krinetzki 1981: 194, 'Die Nabelwust steht ... als pars pro toto, für die ganze weibliche Genitalzone'; Lys 1968: 258, *sexe*;[60] Murphy 1990: 185–6, with 'valley' as a euphemism for pudenda; Rudolph 1962: 169).[61] The מֶזֶג, or mixed wine with which it is hoped her vulva is never lacking, is thought to evoke her sexual fluids or possibly semen,[62] or menstrual blood. The latter seems unlikely, since it would be odd that the woman be *urged* to be continually menstruating (and therefore sexually inaccessible), but the noun אַגָּן,

---

58   Fox disagrees with both assertions, saying that the description does not rigidly follow a particular direction, also that the liquid would be held in the bowl not the navel (1985: 159). With respect to the latter objection, it seems to me that both Fox's and Pope's demands on the imagery are rather rigid: navels cannot hold liquid; liquids must be in bowls. In both cases, the demands seem rather to collapse the simile.

59   Goulder's study is once again startlingly detailed and clinical: 'The entrance of the womb is shaped like a rounded cup, the vagina being at first like the thin stem, and then broadening out into a hemispherical bowl round the cervix ("pomegranate") ... The lilies are the curling hairs [why the delicacy here?] on its lower side, as at 4.5' (1986: 56).

60   Lys explains his translation: 'On pourrait garder un certain euphémisme en français en traduisant non par "vulve" mais par "pubis" ou par "sexe". Ceci n'a rien d'obscène' (1968: 258).

61   Cf. Bloch and Bloch 1995: 201; Fox 1985: 158–9; and Gerleman 1965: 197. Bloch and Bloch's objections to Pope's translation (he is never named in the objection) are that many modern renderings of the Song verge on crudeness and are 'out of place' in the Song's 'delicately allusive language' (1995: 41). The objection may also be taken as evidence of these commentators' own sensibilities, however. I agree with Bloch and Bloch that the Song differentiates between eros and sex (1995: 41); however, I do not think the differentiation is by any means clear. In fact, I think the Song wishes to blur the boundaries. See also Black 1999 and Exum 1999.

62   Pope raises the possibility that מֶזֶג might refer to semen, but ultimately rejects it in favour of 'love water' (1977: 620).

referring to a dish used to throw blood at the altar (Exod. 24.6; so Pope 1977: 618), rather supports the bloody image. A reading by Rashi further fills it out.[63] Fox and Pope both suggest that the phrase אל־יחסר המזג is actually hortative, that is, it is an apostrophe to the woman's vulva (Fox 1985: 159; Pope 1977: 619). In this case, it would be rendered something like 'May it never lack wine!' or 'May it always be wet!'

There is, too, one other possible description of the vulva or part thereof, in 7.9. Though normally translated as 'nose', Pope notes that in Ugaritic and Akkadian the equivalent nouns to the Hebrew אף refer to a gate/ opening or a hole, respectively, and concludes that it 'may be an aperture or a tip other than nostril or nipple, perhaps the vulva or clitoris' (1977: 637). This solves, for him, the peculiarity of the reference to the scent of the nose (ריח אף), in that presumably, vaginal odour is more logical and appropriate to the Song's use of scent as an erotic stimulant.[64]

The image of wine flowing from the vulva in 7.3 does not disappear. It is echoed in v. 10. In the interim, the breasts are compared to the fruit of the vine – grapes – and we note that the lover wants to take hold of these to consume their effluviant. For provocatively, the breasts may be seen to exude wine, like they did in 4.10 (following variant readings of דדים). Fittingly in these gustatory images, the lover mentions the woman's palate in v. 10, and describes it as 'like the best wine going down for my love,[65] flowing smoothly over the lips of those who sleep'. For Pope and others, the reading 'lips and teeth', found also in LXX and Syr., makes more sense than wine descending down the throat of a sleeping person. Moreover, it is not a serious matter to make the emendation.[66]

---

63 In his discussion of vv. 2-3, Rashi inadvertently (?) emphasizes washing and cleanliness, then follows with the seemingly incongruous prohibition against penetration (for 7.3b), giving the example of a bridegroom who is confronted with a bride who realizes that she has begun menstruating (Schwartz and Schwartz 1983: 132–3). His interpretation of the thighs as the drainage pits of the altar further fills out the picture.

64 Fox (1985: 163) disagrees, on the grounds that the noun אף also appears in v. 5. He wonders if Pope would translate it similarly there, too. As has been my practice with other images, I am not insistent that nouns referring to body-parts be interpreted the same way each time they appear. I figure that variation is part of the Song's play with imagery. What does not make sense, however, is that the vulva would be referred to in v. 5 among the facial features in what is a rather strict uni-directional movement from feet to head in this text. In v. 9, it does not seem to pose as serious a problem, for strictly speaking, the foot-to-head description is complete; what we see here are appositives to what one might surmise are the lover's favourite parts.

65 Pope notes that דודי is not used of the woman elsewhere in the Song, and this has occasioned some confusion as to who is speaking (1977: 639). The possessive pronoun on the word חך, however, implies that the man is still the speaker here. Goulder figures the speaker changes mid-sentence (1986: 58). See also Murphy (1990: 183).

66 It would involve seeing the final *mem* of ישנים as an enclitic, emphatic particle. Another possibility is that the yodh of ישנים could be changed to a *waw* (not an unlikely occurrence in Hebrew), and the final *mem* left, so that the phrase reads 'lips and teeth' (Pope 1977: 641).

Wine brings together mouth, teeth, vagina and breasts, suggesting that they collapse into each other on the body's erotic sites. Written in this description, we see, then, the lover's erotic-cannibalistic feast as he drinks, tastes and eats (wine/fluids, the nipples, the clitoris, following Pope's reading of אף). Then, in v. 10, the horror of *vagina dentata* appears as wine becomes again blood in the mouth/vulva, flowing over lips and teeth.

In sum, this body is frequently 'ready' for or engaged in intercourse, but yet it is inviting/waiting and forbidden (menstruating? a hedged mound?) at the same time. The key to the grotesqueness here is the body-in-process (the uncontrolled body), with its liquidity and insatiability. Her sexual fluids or her menstrual blood never ceases – the wine is unending – she exudes scent; she is fecund. A confusion or melding of images continually reinscribes the body in process, for they themselves are not static or fixed and reappear in other contexts, inviting the reader to mix or pervert them (as in the bleeding vagina that resurfaces in 7.10).

War, the Land and other Alienations

All is not verdant, robust and alive in the natural body as the lovers configure it, however. As I indicated above in my initial impressions of the grotesque, nature implies not only fecundity, enjoyment and excess, but their opposites as well. Some of the images mentioned in connection with Song 4.1-5 and 6.4-7 (the hunter that threatens to devour its prey; the fuller implications of the reproduction of the sheep, and so on) revealed as much. Moreover, as we saw in the text just considered, though the garden was lush and exotic, even excessive, the progression of the vaginal imagery took 'nature' to a place beyond the pastoral, picturesque vision that commentators have often supplied. This section continues to explore natural imagery, particularly its 'other side', as connected with the land and human invention on it (architecture and war). Through these images, nature continues to merge with the world around it, this time harbouring such themes as foreignness, alienation and estrangement as it does so.

Though, as with the preceding theme, it is possible to follow these tracings through single images and poems throughout the book, it is more useful to pursue them primarily in one description, 7.1-10.[67] In this poem, we find the most detailed of all the descriptions of the woman. The poem

---

67   As I mentioned at the beginning of this book, there is some variation over where the boundaries for these poems (the so-called *wasfs*) lie. Commentators end this initial poem in Song 7 in different places. Brenner (1993a) considers vv. 1-10 to be the extent of the poem, as does Goulder (1986: 54); Keel sees a natural ending in v. 6, with a new poem constituting vv. 7-10. Falk follows much the same pattern as Keel (1994: 208–16); Murphy and Fox end it at v. 7 (1990: 185; 1985: 154–55); Rudolph (1962) delineates two poems: vv. 1-6, 7-11. These variations are not important. Most of the readers just mentioned divide the poem according to what they think logically belongs or makes sense as a unit, as I have done.

proceeds in the opposite direction from the others (foot-to-head), and here, for the first time, the body includes the thighs and the feet, thus presenting readers with an almost complete body – at least, a figure that stands, and, as we shall see, is on display for an audience. On the delicate base of two beautiful, sandalled feet, we find thighs like jewels, a vagina that flows continually with wine, a belly like wheat and two young gazelles (or a cluster of grapes) for breasts. Then, balanced on a tower of ivory is an oversized head – as big as Carmel – with purple hair, entrapping a king. The full(er) picture of the woman given in this description reveals a body that is intensely hybridized and disproportioned, an impossible creature.

Hybridization and disproportion are aspects that have to do with the physical composition and structuring of this body. It is, in short, a body whose relationship with the world around it is *built*; this is evident not merely through various architectural aspects, which give a constructed or manufactured impression, but also in its creation or assemblage, from the very first element (the feet), to the last, as image is piled – built – on top of image to render the whole. In all, the land provides the materials and the canvas for such manufacture. I suspect that both of these features (the building and the building*s*) trouble the body: they threaten to do much to estrange it; they border dehumanization.

In the descriptions already considered, we saw that natural imagery was primarily faunal or floral. There, the integration of the body with the land was made evident, especially through the playing-out of the cycle of life upon it (herds grazing, animals hunting, crops growing, etc.). These ideas are apparent in 7.1-10, too. Several images will remind readers of what they have seen already, for example the woman's breasts being likened to gazelles (7.4); these recall the twins of 4.2 and 6.6, and their accompanying threat of the hardship and potential losses (as well as the successes) of birth. Other connections are less obvious, but still build on the same ideas. For instance, in 7.6, the woman's hair is described as רהטים, in which the king is captured. A conundrum in this context, elsewhere the word means 'troughs', as in those that provide water for animals (see Gen. 30.38, 41; Exod. 2.16). Scholars generally render the word something to do with the hair ('tresses', Pope 1977: 630; Murphy 1990: 180, 182, though he questions it; 'locks', Fox 1985: 161; or simply 'hair', Bloch and Bloch 1995: 204), but when considered against the faunal imagery of Song 4.1-2 and 6.5-6, the goats and the sheep (hair and teeth), the comparison and the proximity of the troughs seem entirely logical: domesticated animals need to be fed and watered. Still other images speak of fecundity and food that is to be enjoyed from nature's efforts. Later in the description (7.8), the woman's lover compares her stature (קומה) to a palm tree, and her breasts to fruit clusters. The doubling of imagery for the breasts is intriguing in this description, and it is even extended further in the next verse from fruit clusters to clusters of the vine.[68]

On the whole, the natural images in this description are pleasing and uncompromised. As I have been suggesting in places, however, nature in the Song's grotesque body exceeds Bakhtin's 'gay and gracious' evaluation and appears to move in more disturbing directions. In this description, the shift seems to come in two areas. On the one hand, the land, which is the surface on which this body is built, sees the body stretched and dismembered as it aligns it with topographical features. On the other, the land also provides the canvas for the results of human design and invention. The latter, though not strictly definable as natural elements, do seem to speak to human industry, to the consequences of subsistence and colonization. They are, in a manner of speaking, the logical extent of humanity's presence in the natural world that the lover envisions.

In the earlier descriptions, there were one or two unique references to architectural or cosmopolitan features, such as the neck in 4.4 (a tower of David) and the woman's overall appearance being likened to Jerusalem and Tirzah (6.4). Here in 7.1-10, we see an increase of these kinds of connections. On the one hand, the lover seems to be drawing comparisons with certain (natural) aspects of the land, as in the eyes as pools in Heshbon (7.5) or the head as Carmel (7.6). These have sympathy with the other natural referents that appear earlier in the description (e.g. the belly like wheat or the breasts like fawns; 7.3, 4) and resemble the collection of natural elements evident in 4.1-5 and 6.4-7. Yet, on the other hand, the pools and Carmel also seem to take us in another direction, one that plots the woman's body across the topography of Israel, in effect merging her not only with certain features of geography, but mapping her body, as one might tread from place to place, as if on a journey.

André Robert's work (1963) takes such a practice to its extreme. Grotesquely, he applies physical locations onto the woman's body from each described part, theorizing that the descriptions are an allegory of (the land of) Israel. Robert's work cannot be considered in detail here, but a brief presentation will suffice. At the woman's feet, Robert sees an allusion to Yahweh's promised return of the exiled (Isa. 11.15), and so locates them at the Nile (1963: 255). The thighs (7.2) he figures are better understood as the hips of the woman, and nicely resemble the Palestinian coastline (1963: 257). In the woman's navel of 7.3, described as a rounded bowl, he locates an allusion to Jerusalem and describes its topography relative to the cities that flank it (1963: 258–60). In the stomach (7.3), he locates the mountain of Judah (1963: 260); in the two breasts, Mounts

---

68   The two may of course mean the same thing, but the juxtaposition of date palm and breasts as fruit suggests that it is the fruit of the palm that is referred to here.

Ebal and Gerizim (1963: 261–2), and in the neck (a tower of ivory), an allusion to a mountain called the Little Hermon (1963: 263). Eyes are linked to where the texts literally indicates, Heshbon, and the head to Carmel.

It is left to Pope to point out that Robert's construction of Israel through the body is on occasion physically impossible, or at least, it engenders some mixing or rearrangement of the woman's parts. The confusion that Pope points out comes in the latter images, namely, the eyes (pools of Heshbon). In insisting on Heshbon, Pope observes that Robert 'here ignored the considerable detour eastward from the south–north geographical sweep which results in placing the eyes somewhat out of line with the neck and head'. It would not help any, he continues, 'to adopt Winckler's reading "Helbon", for that would put the eyes above the top of the head' (1977: 626). Pope clearly thinks little of Robert's allegorical reading,[69] but his perhaps pedantic insistence on geographical accuracy highlights an interesting feature of interpretation of the Song's imagery. Robert's attempts to link the woman with the land in effect further tie her to it, and sometimes more grotesquely than the lover originally did. With Robert's reading, the body is cut up and spread across the land, a little like the victimized woman of Judges 19, and reassembled, Picasso-like, as the pieces are gathered into a geographical portrait.

The woman's association with geography is one matter, but many of the images suggest another: that her body is a foundation, a platform on which the triumphs of human ingenuity are constructed. In 4.4, we saw that the woman's neck was compared to a tower of David; grotesquely, it was 'decorated' with shields and signs of war. The lover was apparently so convinced of the applicability of this type of structure as a descriptor that he uses it again here – twice. In 7.5, the neck is like a tower of ivory; the nose, too, like a tower of Lebanon. Naturally scholars have wondered at the basis for comparison; some even suggest that these are not artificial structures, but refer to topographical features (see Gordis 1974: 96; Goulder 1986: 56; Pope 1977: 626–7; Snaith 1993: 104), for instance, the nose might be Mount Hermon. In the next verse, the man makes another striking comparison, here even more daringly specific: the woman's eyes are like pools in Heshbon, by the gate of Bath-Rabbim. Are these natural pools, or feats of human engineering (Pope 1977: 625; and perhaps Bergant 2001: 85 and Bloch and Bloch 1995: 202)?

A further grotesquerie – that of violence and warfare – makes the manufactured nature of these body-parts seem even more imposing and alienating. In 7.5, as in 4.4, the neck is portrayed as a tower, only here it is

---

69 'With sufficient devotion, however, it would be possible to find an allegorical explanation, geographical or otherwise, for eccentric eyes' (Pope 1977: 626).

not David's, but a tower of ivory. The noun שֵׁן (see also 5.14) is a pun (ivory/tooth), and if read as tooth conjures up the grotesque. Fang-like, the neck as tooth is evocative of that in 4.4, which glistened with the spoils of war.[70] The likeness of the nose to a tower in the next verse is not to ivory, but to what one assumes is a particular or specific construction, in Lebanon. Pope observes that some have posited a precise physical location for it (see also Murphy 1990: 183). Keel emphasizes its military importance ('the tower is a symbol of proud military preparedness') and its signification of the might and extension of the kingdom of Israel, emphasized by the reference to it overlooking Damascus in the following part of the verse (1994: 236). The pools in Heshbon that describe the eyes (7.5a) might also fit into this military theme, as Meyers has argued, if they are taken to be representative of military reservoirs (1993: 203). In all, we see the woman equipped, again, to fight, and capable of the destruction intimated in the description of 4.1-5. She has, moreover, political power, as the capture of the king in her hair in 7.6 suggests. Is she to be avoided, like the women described in Proverbs who have the power to destroy kings (Prov. 31.2-3)?

One might be tempted to pass these by – only a few have suggested the military implications of the eyes and the nose, after all – but for the initial setting of the description, which rather strengthens the connection. In this description, the scene is set by an invitation to the woman to present herself (7.1)[71] so that she may be the object of viewing. Then, someone asks a general question (is it the man or the woman herself?): What do you see when you look on the Shulammite, כמחלת המחנים?[72]

The dance of the *Mahănāyim* has generated quite a bit of scholarly discussion. מחנים is mentioned elsewhere in the Hebrew Bible to denote a proper place name (Josh. 13.26, 30; 21.38; 2 Sam. 2.8; 17.24, 27; 1 Kgs 2.8; 1 Chron. 6.65), or various encampments (Gen. 32.3, 8, 9, 11; Exod. 14.19-20; see Pope 1977: 603 for a complete list), but there is no connection made there with dancing. Pope's eleven-page discussion of the term (1977: 603–14) yields a number of options. Of the more interesting are

---

70   Truly, as evidence of the interconnectedness of the Song's imagery, this 'tooth tower' carries its own dangers, those of the hunting, fighting, wild animal, even evoking the bleeding mouth of 4.3 and the mighty lions of 4.8.

71   More specifically, the speaker is inviting or asking the woman to 'return', which many take to be some reference to the dance described in the second half of the verse: the sense would therefore be something like 'Turn, turn ... that we might look upon you'; cf. Rudolph ['turn'] (1962: 168); Murphy ['turn'] (1990: 181); Pope ['leap'] (1977: 595); Fox ['return' – he maintains the verb never means 'pivot' or 'whirl' and disagrees that the woman is dancing] (1985: 157); Exum concurs ['come back'] 2005a: 211). The question is then asked: 'What will you see in the Shulammite [as she dances? or as you see in?] the dance of the *Mahănāyim?*'

72   Contra Keel, who believes that the question in 7.1b 'indignantly reject[s] the request to make Shulammite the object of voyeurism' (1994: 228).

Delitzsch's Dance of the Angels (from Jacob's wrestling with the angel in Gen. 32), the sword-dance proposed by Wetzstein and Budde, and the foray into the 'Anat Text' and other parallel material by Pope himself (mentioned also in conjunction with 6.4-7, see above).[73] Despite Pope's lengthy digression on this phrase, he does not seem able to solve the conundrum of the term. Others generally concur that it is unsolvable (Murphy 1990: 181) and seem happy to assume that the dance has something to do with two 'camps' or lines/sets of dancers.[74] Whether the woman is dancing or not, the important factor for a grotesque reading is that, like the mysterious epithet אימה כנדגלות in 6.4, the woman seems once again depicted in an exercise that is reminiscent of military activity. Consider Longman's tribute:

> Watching her is as mesmerizing as watching two armies battling with one another ... As the two armies encountered one another, who could turn their eyes from the scene as they watched the strategic moves and countermoves of attack and defense? The beauty of the Shulammite draws the same kind of awestruck attention. (2001: 193)[75]

The land, then, when written over the woman's body, brings much. Nature, as we saw with the preceding sections, incorporates her into the topography, stretching her as if she might be a path to be trodden or a hill to be climbed. Moreover, this land is also a canvas, a platform on which the efforts of human engineering might be constructed. The imposition of buildings and the cold, impersonal elements of their construction and artifice – ivory, bricks and mortar? – paint an inhuman setting for the body. Certainly, one could interpret the imagery as many have done, as trading on the architectural and decorative feats of Israelite builders, but the images suggest another side to such trophies. These edifices take us out of the natural world and into the realm of the manufactured. If the association with nature and the cycle of life allowed, as Bakhtin might argue, the merging of the body with the natural world so that each becomes indistinguishable, then this conversion unites the body with that which is immovable and impenetrable, cold and devoid of life. When the violence and chaos of war is added to this picture, the results are

---

73   Pope uses a phrase in the Anat Text, 'between the two towns' to posit a parallel (with 'two camps'), cites 6.4, with respect to which he had cause to mention the Anat Text earlier, and concludes, 'There is no mention of dancing in this episode, but the references to the goddess's laughter and joy as she wades in blood and gore may be imagined to have choreographic aspects, amounting to a sort of victory dance' (1977: 607).

74   See Bloch and Bloch 1995: 199; Exum 2005a: 229; Longman 2001: 193; Keel 1994: 225; Murphy 1990: 181; Rudolph 1962: 168; Snaith 1993: 98. Compare Fox 1985: 144, 'camp-dancer'; Gerleman 1965: 188, *Lagertanzerin*; Goulder 1986: 54, 'choral dance').

75   Longman's tribute is not surprising. The connection between the female body and military propaganda is well documented in various cultures, throughout the ages.

compounded: to be sure, valour and victory are here, but these can never be achieved without estrangement and loss.

Playing with (his) Parts: Inversion and Song 5.10-16

The last theme for consideration, inversion, actually sits somewhere between theme and strategy. As I detailed in the last chapter, Miles incorporates three rhetorical and pictorial devices into her discussion of the female grotesque. One of these, inversion, is somewhat underdeveloped in her analysis and, as I noted, the category has limited usefulness for a more global understanding of the grotesque body, especially as she deals with it in the context of Renaissance art. Her analysis, however, is important for its specific beginning point of incorporation of Thomas Laqueur's work (1987; 1990), particularly his interrogation of Galen's understanding of female genitalia. Galen's theories about the genital inversion of men's bodies to create women's, along with the accompanying implications of seeing male bodies (genitalia) as normative, provide for Miles a way into talking about Renaissance figuration of women's uteri in art. In this case, the matter of 'appearance' is significant for her study – and mine – since Galen was at least implicitly dealing with the aesthetics of bodies when he was undertaking his examinations and theorizations. Later interpreters based their moral and spiritual evaluations of men and women in part on this issue – or, more accurately stated, the one (that biologically, women are 'hot', less rational, more emotional) came to serve the other (they are therefore less capable of moral and spiritual righteousness). In short, how women's bodies were formed, and how they were physically manifested – in fact, how they *looked*, internally at least – seemed to have implications for how they acted and how they were evaluated by men.

In her discussion, Miles eventually makes a general summation of the rhetorical device: inversion is the 'reversal of an expected and pleasing appearance to produce a disturbing image' (Miles 1991: 159). To be sure, the summation is general enough that it might be applied to anything; it might also come to mean anything, given its highly subjective nature. However, because of its Galenic origins, inversion might be incorporated here in my analysis, both as theme and, in part, as strategy. It is not so much genitalia that are at issue here (though I do have cause to consider these parts along with others – as I have above), but the matter of evaluating the body and one's relationship to it based on how it looks. The grotesque, with its hybridizations, confusions and inversions, demands a response of the body: both that which is being figured, and that which is observing, or figuring.

As we saw with some of the art considered (Bosch and Arcimboldo), and in some of the work of Bakhtin, inversion plays a unique role in the appearance and maintenance of the grotesque. In Bosch's and Arcimboldo's work, reversing expectations of viewers (a clam for an ear, a fungus for a nose), especially when the reversals carried emotive weight (a hunter for the hunted), was particularly useful as a rhetorical device in the grotesque body. Moreover, these reversals and/or mixings, had implications for gender, as in the cross-dressing 'Lady Skimmingtons' mentioned by Russo. In Bakhtin's analysis, it was these inversions that created surprise, a bright new way of looking at things, a change in vision to the euphoric and celebratory. In all cases, the reversals did not provide a one-to-one exchange (grotesque/non-grotesque), but really served to muddy the waters, to throw all into question. The androgyne in Bakhtin's discussion, then, or the aerialiste in Russo's, unsettled conventions, but they also proved subversive in some contexts.

From the very first verse of the poem in Song 5.10-16, it is apparent that we are dealing with something quite different from the descriptions of the woman. The two do share some features (the palm branches, the doves, the dripping lips), but the general appearance of this figure is, on the whole, unique. One would not want to call this an opposite – not strictly, anyway – of the descriptions of the woman, but there are differences enough here that would make any reader pause. Readers usually explain these away, as we saw with Soulen, who was harshly criticized for opining that the woman was less creative or imaginative than the man. Clines continues the practice by noting that there is something odd here and that its significance remains elusive (1995: 120). Even some more recent commentators are either dismissive of the differences, or uninterested in interrogating their presence.[76] However, as I have been arguing, differences such as these create an opportunity to investigate the Song's contours, especially in terms of issues around the gaze and the politics of love. What seem to be at work here, then, are inversions, the replacing of what might be expected figurations of the body with the unexpected. They serve to whip the rug out from under the body and its peculiar figurations, taking reader (and recipient) perhaps one step further into that which is uncertain, unreliable, even unmanageable.

The description in Song 5.10-16 is the result of a question posed by the daughters of Jerusalem to the woman. In 5.2-7, she reports a missed encounter of her lover that ends tragically for her. She goes out into the

---

76 Compare Murphy's terse comments that 'the style [of 5.10-16] is strange to our western taste, but it must be respected' (1990: 169) with his praise of the man's description in Song 4, which includes discussion of the problematic nature of the imagery and how it is to be understood (158–9). Similarly, Exum's evaluation that '[i]f, on the whole, his imagery is more vivid and animated than hers, hers is more relational than his' (2005a: 202) seems to account for differences in the lovers' language by attaching them to modern stereotypes; these also threaten to undermine her idea of mutuality (erotic not voyeuristic) in terms of the gaze in the Song.

streets looking for him and meets watchmen instead, who beat and strip her (unlike her safer search attempt in 3.1-4).[77] At the end of her tale, she appeals to the daughters to tell her lover of her current state of mind where he is concerned, and they reply rather oddly: 'What is your beloved more than another?'[78] Perhaps: What difference is there between your lover and any other? – as if any handsome suitor would do. The woman's answer consists of a purely physical, and highly stylized, description. In it, she is remote, speaking of him in the third person, albeit still admiring. Already, then, we see a major difference in this description and those of the man's: direct consuming engagement with the body does not seem to be part of the woman's figuring of her lover's body, not in the way it is in the man's descriptions. Also, the intention behind the representation appears not so much to admire and express feeling as to convince the daughters of the uniqueness of the appearance of her man. [79]

One notices immediately another, quite distinct, feature in the man's

77   Commentators have had difficulty with this scene in 5.7. After discussion about whether this is a literal/actual narrative event or a dream, many agree that there is violence occurring here, but often downplay or excuse it. (The interpretation of the noun רְדִידִי would also have some bearing on this enquiry. Was the woman deprived only of her cloak [and if so, to what end?], or was she completely stripped?) For example, Murphy (1990: 171) wonders if the woman's failure to find the man quickly accounts for the violence; Gordis believes she has been mistaken for a harlot (1974: 91); Snaith remarks only that this behaviour is 'unsuitable for the police' (1993: 76); Brenner tries to offset the violence by pointing out that at least she is not 'sexually molested for her immodesty' (1989: 83); Pardes, keeping the oneiric context of the scene in mind, suggests that the beating represents anxiety over the woman's impending exposure; Garrett posits that the beating signifies the woman's anxiety in her dream over her loss of virginity by her lover (1993: 409, 412); Longman seems to avoid the problem altogether with a reminder to his readers that the characters and the action are fiction (2001: 165). The exact details of what occurs here are not given by the text, but it is safe to say that the woman is outrageously treated (either actually or in her imagination), especially given her safe passage in a similar scene, 3.1-4. See Black and Exum 1999 for what I believe is the first study to recognize the scene as problematic for feminist readings, and Black 2001 for an in-depth examination of the scene in this light. Fontaine's recent thoughts on how to read this text are critical (2004). Burrus and Moore (2003) provide a unique response to Black and Exum, in part by engaging Boer (1999). Finally, see Exum's recent and thoughtful discussion of all of this (2005a: 197–200).

78   The daughters' response does not directly address the woman's request. It is often assumed that they are asking for a description of the lover, so that they can assist in the search (Keel 1994: 197; Murphy 1990: 171; Snaith 1993: 77; cf. Exum 2005a: 202, who sees that the help they give is to allow the woman in effect to conjure up the man). Perhaps, however, the information given is not all that helpful, and neither was the question, which would have been better phrased as 'What is your beloved like?' or, as Keel has it, 'Who is your beloved?' (1994: 197). One wonders if the daughters are actually all that helpful or interested in the woman's plight. Lys finds their comment hostile and ironic (1968: 217, 218).

79   This is not to say that makes no comment about her attraction to him: she does comment that all of him is desirable. As with the descriptions of the woman, though, we will need to ask exactly what that means – at a later point.

body. He is almost entirely static, like a statue. Not only is she set apart from him by her third-person address and her objective (?) representation of him, but what she renders for the daughters and readers is rigid and removed. It is not that these kinds of hardened images are absent from the man's description of the woman (e.g. 4.4; 7.5), but they are not the preferred means of communicating his vision, neither do they combine to give the overall impression of stasis that is visible here. The exception is the facial features, but even these fit into a hardened or moulded golden head. This decoration is then repeated throughout his body, in his arms and legs. The arms (hands) are golden rods. These are 'full' (i.e. bedecked) with jewels (jasper), or stones of Tarshish. Likewise, his belly, described as a plate of (smooth as?) ivory, is said to be covered in sapphires. His overall appearance is said to be like Lebanon, beautiful as the cedars. Towering, golden and jewel-encrusted, he is, then, really quite statuesque, rather like an idol. He is expensive and exotic, an amalgamation of the finest of decorative pieces from all over the world.[80] Moreover, he would make an excellent feature in his own palanquin, which seems similarly decorated (3.10). In this, the woman turns the dynamic, natural images of her man's words into something quite alternative: she matches him with his litter; she takes him outside of herself.[81]

The man's facial features, though, do seem to avoid the static and hard nature of the rest of him. His hair is wavy (waving palm branches), black as a raven. His cheeks and lips are described as beds of spices and myrrh-dripping lilies, respectively, and his eyes are doves. In this collection of images, we see some of the interrelatedness of the man's body with the natural world, and therefore with the woman's body: ravens, doves, spices, lilies. The elements selected, however, appear to be more random, a collection of what is exquisite. I could not say from them that the man is intimately connected with the cycle of life, or that his body is comestible, and that his lover waits to devour it – as I could with the figurations of the female body. What can be said, though, is that this appears to be again a recycling, or reconstituting of features of the woman's body into her description of the man's.

In some of the face, Pope locates various 'amative oral activities other than sweet talk' (he does not say what they are) (1977: 541). He rightly points out the collocation of lips and mouth here as part of a general interest in the Song (see 1.2 for kisses; 4.11; 7.10), and it certainly shares

---

80   As such, he would make a terrific attraction at the carnival or fair (Bakhtin's location for the grotesque body), the point of 'economic and cultural intersection' (Stallybrass and White 1986: 38).

81   This strategy of playing with descriptions, of turning words around, seems to be something at which the woman is quite accomplished. Elsewhere, I argue that the woman turns descriptions of the brothers into words that, rather than limiting her, actually give her autonomy in variability of description (2006).

imagery with the woman's oral features. Lips dripping with myrrh even hints at some of her volatility and fluidity. One could not read, though, the provocation here as I did with her body, notably, the wine and honey that dripped from her mouth in 4.11, and the desirable and dangerous elements of 7.3 and 7.10, the mouth and vulva that leaked with wine. In the first verse of the description, the woman calls her lover אדם, red. Most commentators settle on a meaning for this word that is more appealing, such as 'ruddy' (e.g. Murphy 1990: 164; Pope 1977: 531; Snaith 1993: 79), but it is used elsewhere to refer to the colour of blood (2 Kgs 3.22), or the grape (Isa. 63.2). Both of these (blood and the grape) are certainly elements we have seen before with respect to the woman's body, and the adjective could therefore be seen to be evocative of some of the military or comestible features of her form which I mentioned above. Bloch and Bloch propose that it is milk and wine that are being imposed upon the man's body by the two adjectives, אדם and צח (cf. 4.11, of the woman's mouth).[82]

In the hair and eyes we also see some familiar images cast for the man's body. The waving palm branches prefigure those that we saw describing the woman's general stature (7.8, 9), and doves are used elsewhere in the Song to represent eyes (1.15; 4.1). His eyes, it is said, are doves that bathe in pools of milk. Here we have a curious combination of food and fauna in the leaking eye, but it is not edible. Another curious combination occurs with the hair. Black and raven-like, it contains a paradox. Pope points out that black hairs are signs of health and purity from disease (1977: 536), yet the comparison to the raven is curiously conflicting. It is mentioned in the Hebrew Bible as an unclean animal, a scavenger (Lev. 11.15; Deut. 14.14; cf. also Isa. 34.11). Pope is quick to point out that it is only for the bird's blackness that the comparison is rendered, but the conflict is provocative. Is the man clean or unclean? And does the comparison affect his hair only, or his whole body? The other Levitical (and Deuteronomic) intertexts I mentioned with respect to the woman (Song 4.7/Lev. 21.17, 18, 21, 23; 22.20, 21, 25; Deut. 15.21; 17.1; Song 4.13/Lev. 12.7; 20.18) come to mind here, too. Could the man be implicated in the same system of purity that I suggested touched the woman? If so, how does he fare?

Other, smaller, features suggest themselves as possible links to the woman's body, and innovations on it. There is, next, something else in the

---

82 צח, 'dazzling' ('bright', 'clear', *HALOT* 800), is less frequently used in the HB (Isa. 18.4; 32.4; Jer. 4.11; Lam. 4.7). In only one of these instances (Lam. 4.7) is it used to describe people, and this is the verbal form, not the adjectival, as in Song 5.10. Rudolph translates both adjectives as colours (1962: 158, *weiss und rot*). Bloch and Bloch make their translation of milk and wine following the Lamentations text, where Israel's princes are described as milk and honey (1995: 184–5).

man to suggest the military in 5.10. There, the woman declares that her lover is outstanding/admired (דָּגוּל) by many. Brought to mind here are the banners of 6.4 (and 6.10), which it is recalled, described the woman, 'terrible as those who carry standards'.[83]

As with the descriptions of the woman, sexuality is certainly a predominant theme of this series of images. Again, though, it is differently constituted. It cannot be ignored that the man is sexually mature, in fact, perhaps even sexually aroused in his lover's portrait. There is also ample opportunity to argue for the presence of genital themes, though as with the woman's body (and quite unlike the bodies in Bakhtin's analysis), they do not seem to serve any procreative function. One might mention the euphemistic 'hands', phallically displayed as golden rods.[84] There are, too, the מֵעִים or loins of 5.14, though Pope vehemently (and a little suspiciously) denies their genital significance.[85] Further, the word שֵׁן appears here (see also 7.5), this time to describe the 'loins'. Tooth- or tusk-like, it is apparent that the image holds phallic currency. Goulder embellishes by pointing out the connection, and observing, as we saw in Chapter 1, '[a]nd to an enthusiastic bride ... a tusk might seem a very

83   דָּגוּל, 'outstanding' is problematic. It should be mentioned here for its likely relation to נִדְגָּלוֹת in 6.4 and 6.10, discussed above. It also appears in 2.4, in the nominal form as 'banner'. Here the word could be translated as 'bannered' or 'carried', following its use elsewhere in the Song, but it is difficult to make sense of this in relation to מֵרְבָבָה which follows, unless 'from [compared with] the multitude [or ten thousand]' could have a more figurative sense, as in 'outstanding'. It is sometimes translated as having to do with looking ('admired', Snaith 1993: 80; 'conspicuous', Pope 1977: 532), presumably as a Qal passive particle of דְּגַל (in its relation to the Akkadian word *dagālu*), which, like 6.4 and 6.10, some translate with the idea of looking ('vision', etc.; see above). Gordis makes a case for this connection, and links all forms in the Song (2.4; 6.4, 10) with the Akkadian word (1969: 2003–4). As discussed previously, usually, דָּגוּל is translated as 'outstanding' (Murphy 1990: 164; Rudolph 1962: 158), or with similar connotations, such as 'distinguished' (Keel 1994: 198; Longman 2001: 170), 'pre-eminent' (Fox 1985: 140; Gordis 1974: 63), or 'he stands out' (Exum 2005a: 202). Murphy's (1990: 164) observation that the versions (Syr., Vg., LXX) read something like 'picked out of a military unit' is useful, because at least the other, military connotation of דְּגַל ('carry banner, standard') is captured. Equally agreeable from this perspective is Keel's further elaboration, 'he stands out like a banner' (1994: 198).

84   As far as I am aware, no one has proposed that it is the penis that is being referred to (despite biblical Hebrew's usual euphemism in יָד), presumably because the word is in the plural. A curiosity: Pope (who would be likelier than most to find an erotic connotation of a phrase) gleefully jumps on the possible polymasty of the woman in 7.9, but would not dare suggest the man is polyphallic. Like most, he understands hands described as rods to be arms, even though he reads hand as penis earlier in the chapter (v. 4). As I noted earlier, it is also curious that the plural of 'shoots' in 4.13 did not deter authors from interpreting the word as vagina (singular).

85   Pope's translation for מֵעִים is 'loins', denoting not the genitals (despite his citation of 5.4, which he essentially interprets as the woman's genitals; 1977: 519), but 'the area below the chest and above the crotch' (1977: 543).

potent image' (1986: 6).[86] There is, finally, still more, for if the phallic nature of the man is not yet visible to onlookers, it is repeated again in the legs (pillars of alabaster), and even in his general appearance – surely cedars are of a commensurate shape. All this shows not necessarily that the man is construed as a giant phallus, or perhaps that his lover is preoccupied (or I am), but that there is also in this body, as we saw with the woman's, latent sexual imagery. Despite the imagery, though, there is not the accompanying threat of volatility or fluidity as we saw in the woman's body with her sexuality.[87] In his case, the parallel threat – loss of erection? – is merely a whisper among the cedars.

No doubt due to lesser frequency – in part – this series of images does not seem to itemize and scrutinize in the way that the man's images do. The use of the third person also contributes to this different effect, as does the fact that the description is for others (even if the woman might enjoy it too). How are the general differences to be accounted for? Is this description ironic, as I have just suggested? Is it parodic? Might we read satire here? Or does the woman appear to construct a lover who is not entirely accessible to her? Does she mean to elevate him, to show him removed, even to venerate him, as one worships an idol? If so, such a reading would have grave complications for feminist readings of the book that find an autonomous woman here, capable of articulating – and gratifying – her desires. In the next chapter I will have cause to consider some of the implications that the different visions of the man and the woman generate.

Strategies

I have been tracing the imagery as it unfolds throughout the Song, from text to text and theme to theme. In many ways such tracings could be endless, not only because of the complex way that the Song's descriptive texts interrelate but because the texts exceed the boundaries of the book to metamorphose in readers' interpretations. Moreover, there is a tension between the whole(s) and its parts that is not resolvable. The descriptions – alone or in their greater context of the entire Song – present one kind of picture (or a series thereof), but the elements that comprise them are not entirely containable; they threaten to exceed the body on which they are located and make their own connections and permutations. This dynamic multiplies the possible meanings for the Song even further.

Given these observations, it would be possible to continue some distance with the interpretive work as I have been going so far, tracing

---

86 Compare Longman (2001: 173).
87 Except maybe in the pun, שש, which could be read as 'linen' as well as 'alabaster'.

particular descriptions or themes, for example, as they move into the interpretive tradition. In this section, however, I want to move in other directions, not to the omission of the Song's interpretive history, but with a view to including it while I explore new avenues. As I have been indicating, at the heart of the problem of the imagery for the Song of Songs is – as Harpham phrased it – the struggle for meaning. Therefore, the question remains as to whether or not it might be possible to interrogate the nature of that struggle further. To be sure, part of investigating the grotesque body in the Song had to involve showing evidence of its presence, so it has been important to spend some time covering some of the grotesque themes encountered in the Song and tracing how the images metamorphose, how their multiplicitous nature, among other things, evidences their grotesquerie. However, to understand the struggle for meaning is to engage with how grotesque figuration actually works – what are its strategies and methods, and its implications. This is the subject of this section. As with the themes, this part of the study cannot be exhaustive, but will isolate three aspects that bear further exploration. These are: (1) analogy's descent into madness; (2) Barthes' idea of double articulation; and (3) speaking 'other-ly'.

Analogy Gone Mad

In showing the shifts and permutations of the Arcimboldo heads, Barthes (1980) discusses the artist's strategy of analogizing the body-parts. Part of the effectiveness of the heads, and indeed their success at the confusion and disorientation in readers which Barthes identifies, is their sustained use of audacious analogy. It is, as Barthes explains it, analogy that is radically exploited; it is analogy gone mad. Barthes seems here to be referring to a process whereby the effect of the comparison is so jarring that the viewer cannot help but be surprised by it – surprised enough to be unable to let go of either the object or the analogue. So, for example, as we saw with *Wasser*, an ear is painted to look like a clam; that is to say, a clam is put in place of the creature's ear. Yet, neither ceases to exist: the viewer holds both in his or her purview indeterminately.

How does one measure analogy? Can one point to it and evaluate it as audacious in one case and ordinary in another? By its very nature, analogy brings disparate elements into conversation, chiefly for the purpose of explicating at least one of these in a way that is new and enlightening. In the process, the communication of meaning as these connections are made is often jarring, unexpected, even shocking. Moreover, the meaning generated is not necessarily directed towards establishing a *singular* 'truth' – an essential identity. For instance, Arcimboldo's argument would not be that an ear is best understood in terms of the clam, only that it might be differently or radically so. Moreover, it must be observed that the success of a given analogy depends on its audience. Some, for instance, might find Arcimboldo's work so ridiculous or implausible that it makes no effect at all.

The strategies that Barthes is tracing are, therefore, generally the strategies of all analogical language. However, there are some distinctions to be made. Barthes is initially referring to the shift in complexity that he sees taking place from the initial analogy to something more sophisticated, where, as he says (for example of *Der Koch*), 'the helmut no longer is like a plate, the helmut is a plate' (1980: 20).[88] Second, he is investigating particularly successful analogy, which can be so deemed because of its enduring attraction – the paintings continue to hold the public's fascination and esteem (the metaphors, therefore, are not overused; they have not become tired and meaningless). Third, and related to this, must be that Barthes is also referring to the visual, to the fact that these analogies are visually transcribed, placed on canvasses for all to see. As such, they have what might be argued is a more immediate and intense impact.

If it is permissible to make an analogy about analogies, it could be said that there is a similar process underway here in the Song. In my initial readings of the images, I used terms such as 'envisioning' and 'glimpsing', partly in an effort to respond to critics that we cannot expect an *actual* description of the lovers' bodies in the Song's images. My intent has been to push the notion that readers picture what is being described, at least on some level, before they entertain the interpretive measures necessary to help them make intellectual and emotional sense of what they read. By 'sense' I mean that the images become comfortable to them, with respect to their particular ideas about the Song, about the language of love, and about these features as they are situated in the canon. So, assisted by the insights of Barthes, the analogy is that interpretation of this imagery is *painterly*. Readers consider the lovers' bodies as they might mark paintings. Later, they allow their visual impressions to be translated into impressions, affections and responses.[89]

In the matter of the bodies of the Song of Songs, it is entirely conceivable that the reason that scholars struggle to explain a particular analogy is not because they lack experience of the historical context with which to interpret it, or even the sophistication to perceive the correct meaning. Rather, the struggle would be because of the incredibly effective figuration that we encounter in the Song. It does what effective figuration

---

88   As Barthes illustrates, the shift resembles that of the difference between a simile and a more complex metaphorical comparison.

89   Mieke Bal's recent work in *Reading Rembrandt* (1991) might be an interesting conversation partner here, given her intentions to unsettle the word-image opposition in paintings, and to show how both influence each other in the interpretive process.

does: it eludes the reader just enough to keep him or her guessing. In other words, the struggle takes place because the analogy (or series thereof) is so audacious that it generates explanation after explanation after explanation. Neither a cheek nor a pomegranate ceases to be: both are carried about by the woman's body indeterminately. The impression made is so strong, so unexpected, that it is as if the reader has seen it on a canvas; it is hard to disperse from the mind. Furthermore, as I will come to argue in more depth below, this depth and elusiveness of figuration is needed to allow the Song to explore its global themes of love and eroticism effectively.

The ability of analogies to be audacious, moreover, goes much further in the Song of Songs than Barthes might have imagined for the Arcimboldo heads. What Barthes only alludes to, but does not fully investigate, is that the relation of one head to another might increase the impact and the endless referentiality of the metaphors – to make them more audacious, in other words. So, suppose that these were painted by the artist in close proximity (spatially or temporally), or that they are represented in a gallery side by side; or that a viewer might, in a study of the heads, wish to read or consider them together. Some of the connections formed might be more easily made than others and might consequently appear to be indigenous. For instance, *Herod* and *Wasser*, though seemingly unalike, are connectable by virtue of their subject matter, the first an overt depiction of the King, the second an oblique homage to a ruler of another time. One might ask, therefore, if the juxtaposition of Maximilian and Herod (and all that pertains to their respective 'heads' – in these cases, a jumble of sea creatures and human bodies) might intensify the effect of the analogical language. Other connections might be supplied wholly externally,[90] by viewers or readers who, for want of a better phrase, *read them together* to see what they come up with. In a similar fashion, the Song's images, housed as they are in extended descriptions of the body, which then find themselves in the company of others, bounce off each other, magnifying and refracting the body and its parts as they do so.

A series of analogies concerning the eyes is useful to consider briefly in light of these observations. The eyes (compared to doves in various guises, and water) might appear to be a fairly benign group of images when one is talking about audacity, but taken as a series, they show something of the

---

90 In truth, the ability to perceive and evaluate analogical language (ostensibly indigenous or alien) is a readerly activity, and therefore more external or constructed than readers probably like to acknowledge. My observation is that some connections between images appear to readers to be intrinsic to the Song (some might call this of authorial intent or derivation), while others appear to be applied to the images by readers as part of the reading process.

radical exploitation of language. They also illustrate its consequences, namely, what Barthes ultimately referred to as a malaise in viewers, or, to speak more generally, an affect of reading.

Song 1.15 – not even part of the composite body descriptions – contains the first mention of the eyes. The man remarks that the woman's eyes are doves. His words are an interjection, a reply, perhaps, to her description of him in the previous verse (1.14). There is no context for this image (especially not a series of itemizations of body-parts): it hangs in the air. What is the woman to make of it? And readers? Coming, as it does, after two identical statements that his love is beautiful, it might be that this is meant, at first, to be an elaboration. For the man, beauty may be first articulable with respect to his love's eyes. What, though, are doves to eyes? Is the comparison to be made based on colour? Shape? Movement of the lashes? Readers always ask such questions, and they usually find answers, as we have seen in Chapter 1. Exum, for one, addresses the matter at length – doves are chosen for a host of reasons:

> It is not surprising that he singles out her eyes for comment, since lovers say so much with their eyes... Hebrew ʿayin is a homonym, meaning both 'eye' and 'spring,' and the comparison to eyes may have been suggested by the woman's reference to En-gedi, 'the spring of the kid,' in the previous verse. The choice of doves for comparison suggests softness, gentleness, beauty, and perhaps shape (as Gerleman proposes on the basis of Egyptian art). The dove was used as a symbol of love in the ancient Near East ... For the range of romantic images it conveys by its aspect, movement, and behavior, as well as its association with the love goddess and with spring, the dove has attained a special status as a love bird in ancient and modern love poetry. (2005a: 112)

The implication, in fact, is that this is a very regular, almost routine image. Why, we might even ask, would doves *not* be chosen in this initial and most important statement about the woman's eyes?

Yet, despite the fact that we might find a rationale for the eyes-to-doves analogy in this list – each one entirely plausible and supportable from ancient literature – I urge that the image is unexpected, initially jarring, and especially so given its textual context of the initial verses of the Song. The lover rather blurts it out. Furthermore, though the woman has already mentioned her own appearance, this is the first time she (or any reader) hears how her lover perceives her physical body, in any aspect. Behaviour, movement and aspect of the dove do, as Exum indicates, allow a range of romantic correlations. In their mundaneness, however, they might also allow a range of not-so-romantic connections.

Then, if one looks to the surrounding verses for further elaborations, one does not find any, even though both lovers have previously evaluated their partners (n.b. not explicitly their bodies) with brief, general statements. The woman remarks that her love is a sachet of myrrh that lies between her breasts and a cluster of henna blossoms (1.14). The man has previously offered the almost incomprehensible 'I compare you to a mare among Pharaoh's chariots' (1.9). Given the complexity of that analogy and the range of interpretations that it has generated, one wonders where the comparison of the eyes to doves should fit. Will this be the stage that the man chooses to set for love-talk?[91]

The analogy of the eyes is, of course, one that pervades the Song. Intriguingly, it never remains the same as when it was first used; the lovers shift it slightly as it moves through the poems. (As such, it is a good example of the instability of the Song's imagery.) So, in the first descriptive poem, the man repeats himself: 'Your eyes are doves ... ' (4.1b). He has even repeated the statement that the woman is beautiful (4.1a). Yet here he embellishes on the doves, continuing with 'behind the veil', and further complicating the imagery. The idea of doves behind a veil presumably makes them less visual, or affects their visibility in a particular way. Correspondingly, commentators seem to become less sure of what is being conveyed here.[92] Playfully, the woman responds in 5.12. Her lover's eyes, she counters, are doves beside springs of water.[93] Next, he retorts that hers are pools in Heshbon (7.4). Each time, the banter builds on and/or alters the image, making it, I suggest, less and less accessible as it develops. By accessible I do not mean that doves are more

91   There is no question that the comparison to a mare among Pharaoh's chariots is one of the most difficult in the Song (definitely an audacious image in its own right). Pope's response to it is perhaps the most ingenious, and it is certainly the most often cited. His interpretation is that the woman's presence has the same effect as the sexual excitement, distraction and therefore confusion that introducing a mare (on heat) into a herd of stallions at the time of battle might have (an attested military strategy) (1977: 336–41). Longman is much convinced by Pope's theory (2001: 103), and Exum seems also to have some sympathy with it, though does not believe it to be the exclusive meaning (2005a: 109). Murphy believes the analogy to concern not her physical appearance but her adornments (1990: 134). Fox agrees, and finds Pope's proposal unconvincing (1985: 104). Bloch and Bloch argue against 'compare' for the verb דמה and prefer the sense of dreaming of her, or conjuring her; they also maintain the first-person possessive suffix ('my mare') (1995: 143–4).

92   For example, Longman observes that the veil 'both hides beauty and heightens desire'; in short, it 'heightens the woman's mystery' (2001: 143–4). Bloch and Bloch undertake an extensive discussion of the nature of this veil, reasoning that there is little semantic evidence that the word refers to an actual garment, and that there is, instead, a more compelling case that it refers to her hair (1995: 166–8). Bergant points out that the exact nature of the veil is difficult to determine (2001: 44), the implication being that if we knew, we might understand the exact meaning of the metaphor. Exum moves instead to a discussion of modesty and veiling, then considers further 'immodest' aspects of the description, such as the visibility of the breasts (2005a: 161).

93   If Exum's identification of the homonym spring/dove for 1.15 is to be followed, this might deepen the playfulness of the retort. Even without it, the woman can be understood to be building on the picture here.

comprehensible than water as a comparator for the eyes, but that each new analogy increases the distance between image and referent, that is, between dove and eye. Each time that the lovers embellish or alter, they bring new connections, but must also contend with the fact that the old ones linger. So, on hearing these words, a lover – or a reader – asks, despite him- or herself, how might water relate to the veil? Or the pool to the spring?

These are not the Song's final words on the eyes. Interspersed through these four images are three more references to them. These do not describe the body-parts, but they do elaborate on the eyes (and the doves?). The man adds, after his first description has been completed, that his love has 'ravished'[94] his heart with a glance of her eyes (4.9). Later, he will ask her to turn her eyes away from him, because they alarm (arouse?) him (6.5). Being so proximate to the body descriptions, one cannot easily separate these isolated statements from them; nor can one ignore what they convey. Neither verse constitutes an entirely pleasant or benign remark. Ravishment and alarm (or even arousal, if we allow for that in the translation) imply something that harms, that unsettles or alters the man – irreparably? Is he forever changed by this encounter? The final comment, that of the woman's in 8.10, is similarly unexpected, given what has just been said: she mentions her love's eyes in response to a dialogue that she has been having with her brothers. In his eyes, she explains, she has found peace, perhaps *riffing* on the name he gave her in 7.1 (a pun of his own name, a derivative of שׁלם).[95] The comment counters the energy and volume behind her lover's. It is a quieting of it; a negation, perhaps? Or is she playing around with (poking fun at?) his comments about her own eyes?

These images of the eyes are forgeries, as Barthes has elaborated in his study of Arcimboldo, by which he means they are complex in their artifice, yet also *manufactured*. In other words, this picture has been slowly and

---

94   Many commentators seem to be influenced by the KJV in their choice of 'ravished' (even the NRSV has not changed the translation from earlier versions). They often point out that the word means either 'hearten' or 'dishearten', but do not choose either): Goulder 1986: 36; Murphy 1990: 155, 160; Bloch and Bloch 1995: 174; Bergant 2001: 51. In agreement with Keel, and wanting to give a sense of the emotional excitement involved, Longman opts for 'drive crazy' (2001: 151). Pope prefers 'aroused' (1977: 479). Exum splits the difference and makes a case for 'captured', pointing out that 'a stolen heart is an enflamed, aroused one' (2005a: 170). I include this mention of ravishing here because, as Bergant points out (but does not address), '[r]avish is a good translation because it means "to fill with strong emotion" as well as "to carry off by force"' (2001: 52). I would add that the latter also has the sense of sexually violate, particularly of women. In this light, see Vg.'s translation: *vulnerasti cor meum*, which uses an image of wounding or penetration, though it does not seem to indicate sexual violation.

95   See Black 2006 for a discussion of שׁולמית as a proper name and its use in connection with the woman's subjectivity.

painstakingly built up or constructed by the lovers as they hear the other's words and respond.[96] And the eye has been built, too, taken from one simple analogy to another and another, until the final product is rich, dense, confusing, and at the same time so enticing that it cannot be ignored. The eyes, then, are audacious because they are not entirely able to be grasped; meaning changes and they shift about *before our very eyes*. Yet they are also audacious because there is a progression here, one that even if not linearly developed according to the verse order of the references might unsettle in its context of love poetry. For the man at least, the eyes move from attracting him with their beauty to ravishing him, to transgressing boundaries that have not, in the beginning of his encounter, been traversed.

Double Articulation: A Secret Language?

Barthes' observations about analogical language culminate in his evaluation of its implications. As we saw, he eventually determines that the Arcimboldo heads manifest what might be called singular or initial analogical relationships and more complex ones, where the relationship becomes excessive. For Barthes, the possibility for both the simple and complex to coexist is what he names double articulation. (This is similar to what Harpham was expressing in his observation that *Wasser* is both a collection of sea creatures and a head at once.) The paintings, he writes, become an actual language. Moreover, it is a language that is itself excessive, and as a result inaccessible or secret: it is, as he says of one image, a structural, hypertrophying monster (1980: 26).

Hypertrophying one understands; but monstrous? Barthes indicates two things by this term. On the one hand, he notes that in Arcimboldo's day, the monster was a marvel, a fairground attraction, something to be repeatedly gazed on and wondered at. As such, what is produced here is *drollerie*, a diversion. On the other, he is trying to bear witness to the fact that these multiplications, this 'spattering of meaning', is unsettling for the viewer/reader. It is not just a matter of too much information or too many stimuli for the eye. It actually turns the stomach, renders one nauseous and unable to comprehend, at once attracted and sick.

In this way, descriptive language about the body is affective. Barthes writes of the 'subtle (because intellectual) malaise' that is produced by these multiples (the composites and the myriad meanings generated in their production). He refers to the 'swarm', easily visible when one considers the jumble of fish and creatures of the sea in *Wasser*, but equally

---

96 I think here, too, of Wittig's desires to have the hearer/reader/other build the beloved body with her. There is a collusion between writer and other – between lovers – on which the figured body depends.

applicable to any assemblage, especially when written on to the close quarters of the face and head. Yet I find Barthes' analysis somewhat incomplete, as if he has been tricked by the images, or experiences something which he is not able to articulate. The unease he describes in relation to *Winter*, which we saw in the last chapter, seems to be about more than the failure of the mind (and spirit) to cope with multiples of forms, or the double-speak of the paintings. Barthes' obvious revulsion at *Frühling*'s pulverulences and *Winter*'s tumescence smacks of still other concerns.

Certeau's work on Bosch provides, as I discussed, another avenue to explore for understanding the struggle for sense; it also further fills out Barthes' work in some aspects. Certeau observes that Bosch's work provides an alternative space, in a sense, where conventional meaning is rendered inaccessible and entirely unsuitable: the painting organizes a loss of meaning; 'I lose my way in it', he writes (1992a: 50). At work here, as with the Arcimboldo heads, are strategies such as endless signification, the fabrication or manufacture of new forms from strangely recognizable features, and the use of items (a vocabulary) that already have meaning in a new space to create a new language. The viewer contends, Certeau observes, with difference and absence in this encounter. Certeau eventually moves to consider this the springboard for mystical discourse. I suggest, however, that these observations might also be added to the conceptualization of malaise that Barthes identifies. In addition to being confronted with the unsightly, the irregular, the unexpected, is he not also speaking of loss? The horror at *Winter* and the cringing at *Frühling* seem to me to be readable as fear or grief at the loss of wholeness (whole elements or forms, yes, but wholeness of body and mind also), of health and of completion.

In the Song, how might such a strategy of double articulation and its effects be measured? We might resume the discussion with respect to the eyes. Initially, Barthes' observations might be most easily understood when one considers the descriptions as a whole. Like the Arcimboldo heads, the reader is confronted with a human form, but at the same time comprehends the sum of its parts as separate entities. Because of the difficulty of the images chosen, I would argue that, like the paintings, one (the individual element or form) never quite disappears into the other (the body). Readers instead hold both in their minds at the same time, and the effect is confusing, disorienting and somewhat off-putting. As I showed, however, the eyes do not merely fit once into a single, strangely discombobulated form, but morph themselves as they roll from one description to another, shifting from side to side, in and out of the body texts. The effect is therefore intensified, leaving the reader with a dizzying array of choices and meanings with which to contend.

The malaise of the swarm is certainly here, though one does not normally think of the body and its multiple parts in this light. We might consider the effect, though, when the parts are themselves creatures from nature, or a dazzling display of precious jewels, or the materials of man-made structures. Perhaps, all of these, combined into one. The effect is not only achieved with the entire picture, but in the singular parts as well. Take the eye for instance: there is the fluttering of feathers, the flock of birds as they multiply from eye to eye; even the peck of the beak at the glassy orb. And there is the eye peering back at the lover who names it, altering, transgressing, demanding its own response and yet denying full knowledge of itself. As Certeau wrote of the central figure of the eye in the Bosch works (not coincidentally I think): 'This point, the eye, an object *seen* by the onlookers, begins to *look back* at them. It stops being a sign to be read and looks down on us. It perforates the pictorial sky and judges us' (1992a: 54; emphasis original).

Struggling for Meaning and Speaking 'Other-ly'

Despite Barthes' and Certeau's elucidation, Harpham's observation about the struggle for sense does not seem entirely addressed. For, if the grotesque prompts the viewer or reader to struggle to make sense of what he or she reads/sees, it begs the question as to whether that struggle is ever resolved, and if it is, then how it is resolved. Since, as I have been arguing, the efficacy of the grotesque depends precisely on keeping the viewer/ reader in a marginal state – between sense and nonsense, beauty and ugliness, attraction and repulsion, and the like – it is clear that as long as the grotesque remains, it would be unreasonable to expect the resolution of the struggle for sense. Yet can we not still speak of *something* being effected in readers and viewers as they experience the grotesque? I suggest that the outcomes of grotesque reading or viewing are not a termination of the interpretive process into a given and finite solution (not a confirmation of a new meaning), but a translation of the struggler into a new dimension. This dimension is one in which he or she is incorporated on an intimate level into the world of the Song.

We have already seen that the grotesque offers an alternative means of figuring the body. I want, now, to take this one step further and suggest that what it really indicates for the Song is an *other* discourse: an ulterior – or *alterior* – way of speaking. This mode of speaking applies both to the lovers who speak and to the text in which they speak. In short: the lovers communicate something of this alterity in their descriptions of each other. And, taken as a whole, the Song of Songs represents speaking *other-ly* in its presentation of love and desire.[97]

---

97   This idea of speaking other-ly, inspired by Certeau, could have some connection with Fontaine's recent work on the Song (2004), wherein she advocates reading otherly. Though

Thus, in the tradition of the metamorphosing of the Song's images that I have been explicating, it is useful to investigate yet one more shift. This time, the shift takes us through the translation of the imagery into the realm of the ideological and spiritual. In using these terms, especially the latter, I do not indicate that the significance of the body images must ultimately be theological, that they are about, for example, the soul's relationship to God (though some might reasonably conclude this, of course). Instead, prompted by Certeau's tracing of the spectacular images in the *Garden of Earthly Delights* to the structures and strategies of *mystics*, I follow the Song as it bumps unexpectedly up against the locale of mystical discourse. At the heart of both are the struggle for meaning and the language of love and eroticism.

The Eyes have it ... But What is it?

It should come as no surprise that, given the preceding discussion, and given our constant gazing at the lovers' bodies, the eyes also play a central role in this final step of reading. This time, they appear off the text in the context of an analogy made by the great mystic and visionary Teresa of Avila (1515–82), who was a discalced Carmelite in Spain, a prolific writer, and an important – but of course unrecognized – theologian of her time. Teresa is perhaps most widely known for a particular encounter with God, wherein she describes herself as being penetrated by God with an arrow (of love). This event was subsequently and somewhat notoriously interpreted by Bernini in sculpture (1652, Santa Maria della Vittoria, Rome). Because of Teresa's connections to the Song of Songs,[98] and because of her prominent appearance in Certeau's study of *mystics*, she makes an apt reading companion for this present section.

In her *Vida*, Teresa appears to draw on what will by now be familiar texts from the Song of Songs – not coincidentally about the gaze – to explain a recent vision of Jesus.[99] I quote §27.10 at length:

> Returning then to the discussion of this kind of understanding [a particular type of vision], it seems to me that the Lord in every way wants this soul to have some knowledge of what goes on in heaven. I think that just as in heaven you understand without speaking (which I

---

outside the scope of this present discussion, it would be useful to bring these two concepts into further conversation in the future, especially since, as Fontaine observes, one must wrestle with what is legitimately in the text and what might be added to it through the process of reading.

98   Teresa wrote a series of meditations on it (1976–85, Vol. 2), but also refers to it often throughout her other writings.

99   Teresa only refers generally to the Song of Songs; the specific texts are identified in a note provided by the translators (see below).

certainly never knew until the Lord in his goodness desired that I should see and showed Himself to me in a rapture), so it is in this vision.[100] For God and the soul understand each other only through the desire His majesty has that it understand Him, without the use of any other means devised to manifest the love these two friends have for each other. *It's like the experience of two persons here on earth who love each other deeply and understand each other well; even without signs, just by a glance, it seems, they understand each other. This must be similar to what happens in the vision; without our knowing how, these two lovers gaze directly at each other, as the Bridegroom says to the Bride in the Song of Songs – I think I heard that it is there.* (Rodriguez and Kavanagh 1976: 1: 177; emphasis added)[101]

In the reference to the Song of Songs, Teresa pretends that her knowledge of the book is hearsay. She does this to satisfy censors that she has not read (and is not interpreting) scripture, two activities that would be unacceptable for a woman in her position. Her posturing is indicative of what has been termed a 'rhetoric of obfuscation' by Allison Weber (1990: ch. 4 and *passim*). It features certain strategies, such as the insistence on the insignificance of her subject and the adherence to official ideology about women who, as a consequence of their weakness, need instruction such as that which she is writing (Perez-Romero 1996: 128). As a consequence, the reference to the Song remains intentionally vague.

Despite the imprecision of Teresa's reference, however, her text is footnoted by Kieran Kavanagh and Otilio Rodriguez (translators/editors of the collected works of Teresa of Avila, and of the quote, above), directing readers to Song 4.9 and 6.5 ('With one glance of your eyes you have ravished me ... ' and 'Turn your eyes away from me, for they excite

---

100   The vision about which Teresa is speaking is one where Jesus has appeared at her side, but was not seen, only felt. Prior to this discussion, Teresa undertakes to explain how she could know it was Jesus if she did not see him. This is part of an extended discourse where, in addition to revealing to her audience a practical means of seeking and connecting with God, Teresa is also attempting to provide a systematization of her visions, classifying them according to intensity, regularity and type.

101

Pues tornando a esta manera de entender, lo que me parece es que quiere el Señor de todas maneras tenga esta alma alguna noticia de lo que pasa en el cielo, y paréceme a mí, que así como allá sin hablar se entiende (lo que yo nunca supe cierto es [ser] así hasta que el Señor por su bondad quiso que lo viese y me lo mostró en un arrobamiento), así es acá, que se entiende Dios y el alma con solo querer Su Majestad que lo entienda, sin otro artificio, para darse a entender el amor que se tienen estos dos amigos. Como acá si dos personas se quieren mucho y tienen bien entendimiento, aun sin señas parece que se entienden con solo mirarse. Esto debe ser aquí, que sin ver nosotros como de hito en hito se miran estos dos amantes, como lo dice el Esposo a la Esposa en los Cantares, a lo que creo, lo he oído que es aquí. (1970: 163–4) [alarm] me ... '). Kavanagh and Rodriguez are quite correct: if we take Teresa literally ('as the Bridegroom *says* to the Bride ... ' and 'gaze directly'), these are the two significant verses that verbally acknowledge an act of looking and a type of communication being effected through that look.[102] These two texts, when combined with Teresa's explication about communicating with/understanding the divine, are provocative. For the Song, both imply sustained looking. Furthermore, they suggest that something has been achieved by the woman who visually pores over her love, or, as I noted above, that a transformation has been effected in the lover who is being subjected to the gaze.

In her urging to the sisters that they emulate her example, then, Teresa appears to be trying to convey a fairly straightforward message. Just as two lovers are able to communicate something of their love for each other without direct communication (signs or a word), so too might the soul and God have a special kind of relationship that is not based on words or outward signs, but a kind of inner knowledge. Moreover, Teresa points out that it is through God's grace or will alone that this communication is effected: 'only through the desire His majesty has that it [the soul] understand Him...'

The message seems simple enough, but a closer look at it in conjunction with the suggested Song texts brings to light a few problems. As I have already discussed, the Song texts are themselves troubled, in that they address the gaze of the woman at her lover as sites of conflict (the lover must ask that she stop). What does it mean, therefore, to say that this special inner knowledge between human and divine is so disquieting that it radically changes the lover who is being gazed at? To this troubled looking, furthermore, Teresa adds her own difficulties, for the word choices in the analogies that she makes seem rather to contradict each other. That is, Teresa speaks of earthly lovers twice: in the first instance, she compares the special relationship that she is trying to explicate to a glance between generic lovers; in the second, she refers to the Song's lovers gazing at each other. It could be that Teresa intends the glance and the gaze to be interchangeable, but their variable use here potentially undermines what she is trying to say. These choices bear looking at a little further.

The phrases in question, *con solo mirarse* and *como de hito en hito se miran*, both concern looking, but appear to be suggesting two different ideas.[103] The first, *aun sin señas parece que se entienden con solo mirarse*,

---

102 Song 7.1 is a third possible text, but what is going on here is slightly different, as I shall explain below. It should also be noted, of course, that the act of looking is also implicit throughout the Song, especially in terms of the physical descriptions of the body.

103 I am grateful to translator Montse Basté for her insights into the original text and the rich discussion that we have had about Teresa's words and her influence.

indicates that (generic) lovers understand something of each other with a brief glance, and without, Teresa opines, gestuality. She goes on apparently to explicate (?) her point with the phrase, *que sin ver nosotros como de hito en hito se miran estos dos amantes.* This Kavanagh and Rodríguez have translated as 'without our knowing how'[104] and then the somewhat tautological 'these two lovers gaze directly at each other', eventually intending the idea that concentrated looking renders the subject and object in a mutual position of knowledge of the other. Is the mismatch between the glance and the gaze a problem of translation? Apparently not, for another well-known version, that of E. Allison Peers,[105] seems to offer an equally inexact rendering: 'for, without seeing each other, we look at each other face to face as these lovers do ...'[106] Looking face-to-face seems still to imply an exposure that is more involved than that of a brief glance. Is the mismatch an issue?[107]

The confusion that I see in Teresa's two ideas lies, perhaps, with what comes between them, in the idea expressed by *que sin ver nosotros ...* ('without us seeing'). This phrase appears to be a pivotal one that offers a contrast with what follows it (the mention of the lovers gazing at each other). Teresa is saying that, just as *the lovers understand by looking at each other* (but without any other signs), so *without* looking at each other, we (God and the soul) understand. In other words, the intense gazing of

---

104   This is a sense that is not indicated by the verb *ver* (Basté).

105   Because the discussion of the Spanish and two translators might be confusing (especially given the confusing subject matter), the following table should ease comparison:

ORIGINAL	KAVANAGH AND RODRIGUEZ	PEERS
... *dos personas se quieren mucho* ...	two persons here on earth who love each other deeply	two persons of reasonable intelligence who love each other dearly
y tienen bien entendimiento,	and understand each other well;	seem able to understand each other
aun sin señas	even without signs,	without making any signs,
parece que se entienden con solo mirarse.	just by a glance, it seems, they understand each other.	merely by their looks,
Esto debe ser aquí,	This must be similar to what happens in the vision;	This must be so here,
que sin ver nosotros	without our knowing how,	for, without seeing each other,
como de hito en hito se miran	these two lovers gaze directly at each other	we look at each other face to face
estos dos amantes,		as these two lovers do:
como lo dice el Esposo a la Esposa	as the Bridegroom says to the	the Spouse in the Songs, I believe,
en los Cantares,	Bride in the Song of Songs –	says this to the Bride:
a lo que creo, lo he oído que es aquí ...	I think I heard that it is there.	I have been told that it occurs there.

106   Its apparent contradictions (without seeing ... we look) explain why Rodriguez and Kavanagh might have chosen 'know' instead of 'see' ('for without our knowing how ... ') for the verb *ver* in *que sin ver nosotros.*

107   It is possible that I read Teresa too critically, that I make demands on her prose that are unjustified, given the context and subject matter. However, I suspect that this is not the case, since glancing, seeing, gazing and not seeing are too significant in this and other passages to simply not matter (or, I think, to be interchangeable) in Teresa's analysis.

the lovers at each other is an *analogy* for the soul and God comprehending – that is, 'seeing', but not *literally* seeing. Put differently, looking is like not seeing. *Mirar de hito en hito*, moreover, has a further sense that is not acknowledged in either translator's rendering: to try every angle, every possibility, until one reaches one's goal (Basté). The intensity of the lovers' gaze in the Song (and lovers everywhere), the drive to find out every aspect until one is exhausted, is like, Teresa says, the kind of knowledge a soul has of God, without any visual experience of God at all.

At the risk of labouring the point, what exactly then is the nature of the relationship that Teresa is trying to explicate? Is it like the brief glance, that which does not require any touch or sign, but is, like a flash, complete in what it communicates? Or is it like the gaze of two lovers, the protracted stare that considers every angle until knowledge is exhausted? How, then, should the brief glance compare to the intense gaze? Is there a gradation of looking that is supposed to elucidate the soul's relation to God? Or, finally, is what Teresa is trying to explicate like the gaze of the *Song*'s lovers: exhaustive, but troubled, threatening to take over the other, and so overwhelming that the loved one must ask the gazer to stop?

Enticing as her mystery might be, my desire here is not to solve it definitively, even if I were able, but to ponder the eyes as they blink and shift focus, as they gaze intently, or perhaps do not see at all. Teresa is stumbling around the ineffable. She is trying to articulate what, if her broader works are any indication, she struggles to explain to herself: how the lover comes to know the beloved (how the soul comes to know God). For her, knowledge of a loved one in some of her visions happens in a flash, and in this way, the glance, without any other means of communication, is the best analogy. However, despite her indications to the contrary, a glance seems not quite enough, for there is an intensity, even an intensity that threatens to consume, in this communication that can only be understood in terms of the gaze. Yet, again, even the gaze is not entirely appropriate for Teresa's purposes, for it involves a mutuality (at least in terms of her understanding) that does not gibe with her understanding of God as the sole provider of the bridge between God and the seeking soul. In the end, it is not the work of the eye (or the soul) that matters, but what exceeds it or goes on despite it.

In all of this the eyes seem entirely necessary *and* entirely superfluous to knowledge of the other. They calculate and record the essence of the loved one, but in the end are incapable of rendering him or her in any kind of accurate way – in any way that matters, perhaps. What Teresa seeks seems only ultimately able to be granted by the one who is seen, or not seen; it appears to be a gift of the other, and one that renders the gazer in a state of complete dependence, at the mercy of the one whom she desires. Yet the desirer's compulsion is not to lower the eyes, but to look, to gaze intently, to try every angle that she can to see something that makes sense.

The desirer's role, therefore, seems to be integral to the process, not inconsequential to it. To translate this to human relationships, we might ask: if Teresa does not seek God, will she ever know God? By correlation, if the Song's lovers do not gaze, will their love have voice, take form, or be real? Furthermore, it must be observed that the object of this desire does not appear to be constant or unchanged in the process of the lover's gaze, despite Teresa's suggestions to the contrary. As Kavanagh, Rodriguez and Peers seem to indicate in their respective translations, there is mutuality in the seeing/not seeing that actually changes the other. We might therefore ask: does the beloved other indeed need the lover to gaze at him in order for him to exist?

'With One Glance of My I . . . '

These may appear to be random questions, drawn from a brief exploration of a mystic's musings on her subjective experiences of God. The questions, however, pertain to very central issues of agency, mutuality and desire, and, as it happens, they are questions that go very much to the heart of the body imagery in the Song of Songs. Moreover, though I do not pretend that they are Teresa's own, I venture that the questions do address issues of which she is quite aware. The sophistication of her analysis here and elsewhere suggests that it is precisely the Song's convolutions that draw her to use it to explore the difficult subject that she is trying to explicate. In addition, as Weber particularly has argued, it is likely that Teresa was working within a framework of a highly specialized and restricted discourse (a secret language perhaps). This had a particular audience in mind, and it was bordered by the specific requirements and constraints of the ecclesiastical community in which she was operating. Again, the Song is an apt resource for such formulations, given its own specialized discourse of dense imagery and hidden meanings.

The notion of a specialized discourse is an intriguing one. It is a matter with which Certeau engages in his study of Teresa, there in a configuration that is unique to his elaboration of *mystics*[108] and its particular languages and geographies. Teresa's systematization of her visions, as well as her elaborate structural metaphors of the soul's journey towards God (*The Interior Castle*) make her an ideal personage for Certeau in his discussion.[109] In them, she exemplifies, as did Bosch, an alternative space, where the ordinary rules of language are suspended, and where, as

108   As we saw in Ch. 2, the word is italicized in Smith's translation of Certeau (1992a) to best express the original term *la mystique*, used by the author to denote a 'science' of mysticism.

109   The language of *mystics* is, in Certeau's analysis, born of a specific historical time and place. It is a response to specific crises, such as war, economic recession and/or disadvantage due to progress and change (1986: 84). In bringing this into conversation, I am not suggesting that the Song overtly be considered *mystics*. I am more interested in its

Certeau says, the speaker has the right to exercise language otherwise. The nature of this speaking otherwise is one where the speaker is always the speaker-in-relation. Her writing is born 'in distress of expectation of a dialogue', meaning that she mourns the void between herself and her object of devotion, seeking a way to fill it by words and utterances. It is as if the speaking brings the other closer, makes the other real, in a world where the speaker knows the other is not – not ever – fully present.

I propose that it is no accident that the eyes are the analogy of choice for Teresa as she undertakes this speaking *other-ly*. Initially, one might perceive that there is a logical (and literal) connection between the lovers' gazing and the *visions* that Teresa wishes to explicate. Of course, this connection is even more pertinent when one considers that the language of love (and of the Song of Songs) is so often used by the mystical tradition; it is entirely understandable that Teresa would turn here.[110] The image is apt, too, because of the central feature that each action of looking/seeing plays in the relationships in question. Teresa makes it very clear that the mystical subject requires a particular relation to the vision (of Christ) in order to be constituted. The vision in effect creates (but does not necessarily complete) the connection that she seeks. In a like manner, the subjects of the Song have a specific and complex relation to *vision* – that is, the physical act of looking. In effect, the eyes form an important axis of the lovers' relationship: they help the lovers to experience each other.[111] By no accident, grotesque as they are, they also serve as the linchpin of the descriptions of the body in the Song.

Most significantly, the shifting nature of the eye images and their alignment with the grotesque make them extremely appropriate to Teresa's comments for an entirely different reason. In the multiplicity of the images and in the difficulty that seems to accompany the gaze, the eyes are a contested site. Their meaning always shifts; they are accepted and refused by the one at whom they look. In their contestability, the eyes illustrate well the battleground of which Certeau writes. They, too, are a place of siege, and as such they might reflect the mystical subject in distress. The struggle for meaning about which I have been writing, therefore, in essence mirrors the struggle of the subject-in-love, for she is

---

introduction into the mystical context by Teresa in her meditations, and in her inclusion of it in her explication of visions. What, picture, in effect, does reading these two contexts intertextually create?

110   See, for example, the work which is discussed in Astell 1990; Matter 1990; and Turner 1995.

111   It might be argued that there are other axes, since there are other senses mentioned in the Song, notably, smell, taste and touch. So much of what the lovers speak about, however, in addition to how each other's bodies look to them, involves the visual (how the world appears; whether they can see/find the other, etc.).

implicated in its midst as she tries to constitute her beloved other, who cannot be fully captured, but who always entices her to keep trying.[112]

As such, the subject-in-love (mystical or *Cantical*), is ideally understood as originating in absence or loss. Certeau begins his discussion of the institution of mystical speech with the following observation: 'The initial expression of the spiritual is nothing but the decision to leave' (1992a: 177). The spiritual subject, he explains, is born of an exile. 'He is formed by wanting *nothing* and being but the respondent of the pure signifier "God" or "Yahweh", whose acronym, since the burning bush, has been the act of burning all the signs: I have no other name than what makes you leave!' (1992a: 177). In the act of emptying him- or herself, the mystic has no mode but answering to the will of the other.

The absence to which Certeau refers, and which I perceive to be evident in the Song's subjects, is not a matter of the disappearing lover, but the lover who has replaced him- or herself with the other. This is not a matter of self-denial, or self-effacement (though many might argue this is part of the mystical personality); rather, it is the only solution to coping with the struggle over that which cannot be articulated. If we follow Certeau's analysis, the mystic is, on first examination, a kind of empty vessel. Seeking has taken such priority and is fraught with such difficulty that she must dispel all else in order to respond. In many ways, this appears a classic figuration of the mystic. There is, however, an important distinction that Certeau is making. It is not that the mystical subject disappears, to be replaced by God, but that the subject empties herself, so that another kind of subject might be constituted in her place. This is the subject-in-response, or, the subject who has made himself absent so that the other might be made known.

In making this link – this analogy – I do not mean explicitly to suggest that the beloved other in the Song is identical to God.[113] Certainly, if reading allegorically, one could come to this conclusion for the male lover, as has been the practice of allegorical reading of the Song for almost its entire history. The correlation is, however, not meant to be so direct. Rather, we might say that the beloved other resembles the divine as object of desire, in terms of the other's inaccessibility and in terms of the other's

112   I am using the feminine pronoun for the subject as a convention, since Teresa is female, and since it is the woman's voice we hear most in the Song. However, it is of course the man's voice that we hear most when the body is being described. Though it may appear that I am making a comment about power here in gendered terms, I am not: not yet. I will discuss the gender politics of this relationship in the next chapter.

113   Linafelt, though, has recently argued that the distance between divine and human subjects in the Song of Songs is not as great as readers might suppose. He approaches the matter from the other direction, suggesting briefly, via Bataille, that the divine might be as subject to risk and violence as his [sic] human counterpart (2002).

simultaneous calling of the lover and the other's failure to speak in a way that the lover can understand.

In the process of absenting the self, then, the mystic/lover has a need to 'found the place from which he or she speaks'. This means both creating the new subject – the 'I' – who will speak, but also, eventually, a space from whence to speak, 'an imaginary mode', a 'field for the development of discourse'. The 'I' momentarily takes the place of the other (inarticulable), and as a consequence, develops an equally substitutory locale from whence to speak. Certeau observes:

> A fiction of the world becomes the place in which a fiction of the speaking subject is produced – if by 'fiction' we understand that which is substituted (provisionally) and represents (contradictorily) the cosmos that served as a language for the speaking creator. This figuration of space is also, then, located at the threshold of mystic discourse. It opens, in an imaginary mode, a field for the development of this discourse. It makes a theater of operations possible. Thus it is the necessary fictitious space of the discourse. (1992a: 188)

For Certeau, the *morada* or dwelling of Teresa's *Interior Castle* is the fiction that represents the space required by the speaking subject. The castle, with its almost incomprehensible layerings of structure upon structure, can be known in its entirety only to Teresa (and, one assumes, God). And what does it articulate? It is a picture of the soul, which, though it may mean many things, chiefly refers to that which responds, in moaning or murmur, to the unknown (1992a: 189). It is the 'fictive place that makes possible the expression of a speaking that has no place of its own in which to make itself heard' (1992a: 189). It is a metaphor that occurs to her and speaks 'in place of' Teresa (1992a: 196). It is, as Certeau says, 'formed by being a response to that (God) which it does not know, in that it is a response to Unknownness: born of an Other and yet separated from that Other that would give it language' (1992a: 189). In sum, it is the soul in love: the respondent who speaks from her own experience of that which she cannot fully experience, or articulate.

Now, to bring the discussion back to the Song of Songs and its lovers, where is the corresponding substitutory locale, the *morada* in the world of the Song? Several opportunities arise for a fictional space from which the lovers might speak. Perhaps it is the natural world, with its pastures, its mountains, its lushness and fecundity. More particularly, it might be the mountains of spices, so attractive to both lovers, and both the place of meeting and, potentially, the site of separation. Alternatively, the mysterious mother's house, to which the man is invited, and under whose roof he would become closely entwined with the woman, is a contender. It also resembles Teresa's castle in the lure of its rooms and the promise of what might go on there[114] – though it is not, of course, as multilayered in its architecture and significance.

It seems, though, that the best candidate for the subjects' *morada* in the Song is not these places, but that which intersects with all of them; it is, quite unexpectedly, the body. It is from this physical site, so elaborately connected to the world around it, that the subject-in-love speaks. (The architectural body images make a particularly nice connection with Teresa's own castle.) But it is not the subjects' *own* bodies that allow them a voice: again, quite unexpectedly, the other's body is what allows the lover to speak, to articulate his or her desire, and hopefully, to seek its fulfilment. In practical terms, this means that the subject-in-love searches for the missing other by a roadmap that she or he creates out of the other's body. It is a complex, interlayered and grotesque patterning of parts that points some distance to the object of desire. As such, it implicates the figurer by bringing him or her into the midst of its convolutions and contradictions. The articulation of the other's body, in other words, takes the place of the other: speaking the body (through the grotesque) is the only way to make it present. As we have seen, however, it is not entirely successful at pinning down the beloved other, at capturing him or her so that desire is fulfilled. Indeed, this is the nature of desire.[115]

So, the eyes focus this act of creation. They are literally the vehicles by which the other might be atomized and constructed; they are the tool of choice in building the beloved into existence. As Wittig (whose *Lesbian Body* is brilliantly suffused with the visual) remarks:

> You gaze at m/e with your ten thousand eyes, you do so and it is *I*, *I* do not stir, m/y feet are completely embedded in the ground, *I* allow myself to be reached by your ten thousand glances or if you prefer by the single glances of your ten thousand eyes but it is not the same, such an immense gaze touches me everywhere ... (1975: 18)

Yet the eyes are also a cipher for the rest of the grotesque body. In their own shifting nature they invoke the changeability and transformations of the parts as they relate to the whole. Singular or swarming, they manage the malaise of the grotesque, the grating not-quite-rightness of their imposition into uncharted realms, a feather rubbing at the ocular surface. In their variability in the mouths of both lovers, they mark the inversions

---

114 I refer, generally, to some kind of intimate union. Teresa does not indicate an explicitly sexual union (and maybe the same is true for the Song's lovers – this is much debated in scholarship as we have seen), but as I noted above, the language of sexuality and eroticism is no stranger to mystical discourse.

115 With this specific connotation, it is possible after all to come a little closer to the position of Brenner and others who insist that the Song offers no *complete* image of the loved one. In the reading I have suggested, though, *complete* has more to do with the nature of the subject's relation to the other than it does to the quality of the image constructed.

that are so characteristic of the grotesque. And in their intricate relation with nature, they focus some of the themes that seem to accompany this type of figuration. So it is that we might call the eye a window not into the soul, but into its casing, the body.

In this way, a reading of the Song texts against the backdrop of mystical discourse is provocative for the Song and its lovers. However, one cannot get very far with these observations without being confronted with the question: why the grotesque? Why not speak the body another way? Furthermore, one notices almost immediately that there are significant differences between the ways that each lover figures the other. Therefore, the question arises as to whether the dynamics that I have been sketching for the lovers' relationship actually hold true for both, or whether they are better suited to one or the other. This is, indeed, part of a broader issue in the Song that concerns the differences in the ways that the bodies are figured (are both grotesque?) and the implications of that figuration. These matters have to do with the politics of gender in the Song. They also pertain to readerly responses to the book, and bring us back, full circle, to the place where I began this study. These matters, therefore, will be the subject of the next chapter, which deals with the implications of the grotesque and tries to gauge its effects on lovers and on readers.

Chapter 4

ON READING THE GROTESQUE (EROTICALLY)

There is not a great distance between the bodies of the lovers in the Song of Songs and the bodies of its readers. This chapter investigates the implications of reading the Song's imagery as grotesque, and in particular, it is about the relationship of lovers – those in the Song and those who love it. As we saw in the previous chapter, the identification of the grotesque body in the Song recasts troubling imagery in a new light, not to 'solve' its problematic nature, but to allow some of the features that are usually downplayed by readers to have an active role in the interpretive process. This recasting serves to elucidate the desires of the lovers which permeate the Song and make it electric with intercourse – verbal and sexual. The presence of the grotesque implicates readerly desires, too, and these appear to be as fraught with yearning and loss as those of the lovers.

There are three principal areas to explore. First, the investigation of Teresa of Avila's work at the end of the previous chapter prompts further investigation of the nature of the lovers' relationship. If, as I surmise, the subject-in-love locates in the other's body a place (a *morada*) from which to speak, it follows that the presence of the grotesque therein signals a specific type of foundation: it indicates, in other words, a particular kind of speaking. What, then, is the nature of this speaking? Why should the lovers speak through the grotesque, and what does it convey about their relationship? Second, since there are differences in how each lover articulates the other's body, Teresa also indirectly prompts questions about gender politics in the book.[1] Because the man speaks the body more than the woman, we must also ask about the status of the subject in love in terms of gender: is this, after all, a man's text, and not a woman's, as some feminist critics have argued?

And yet, the book's gender politics cannot be the *terminus ad quem* of

---

1 I use the term broadly to refer to how men and women are represented in the book, in terms of their voice, their bodies and their sexualities. The includes their treatment of each other, as well as their autonomy relative to each other and to the social standards that are indicated throughout the text (and indeed, throughout the biblical corpus), sexual and otherwise.

this study, for any assessment of gender implicates broader questions about the role of the reader in evaluating the status and liberty of the Song's players. Gender suggests, if the grotesque itself is to be taken as any indication, that it is the subject of some considerable mutability. The third area of exploration, therefore, draws my study back to the place where it began, namely, in pondering what reading the Song (as grotesque) means for readers. Principally, I want to explore the ambivalence that the peculiar marriage of the grotesque and the erotic generates. All this is in aid, ultimately, of discovering a clearer picture of the Song's treatment of the themes of love and desire. Far from depicting a simple and idealized world, these themes appear to be complexly layered and rich in dimension.

This complexity inevitably means that the lovers' relationship is open to considerable interpretation. That is, it is possible to view it from a number of different angles and consequently with a variety of implications. What follows, then, is not an effort to come to a specific conclusion about the relationship, but to touch on the range of possibilities for the lovers that the grotesque evokes. In addition, I also want to consider how the line between lovers and readers is blurred. Significantly, the embodied, gendered experiences of the book's lovers is one major area into which readers interpolate themselves as they experience the book. Thus, in this and other ways – which I'll suggest below – to have a discussion about the lovers' relationship is also to have a discussion about readers.

These are difficult tasks. Two important critics will be useful in this enquiry. The first, Roland Barthes, I have already considered in relation to his work on the Arcimboldo heads. In this chapter, his pursuit of an 'erotics of reading'[2] and his related metaphor of the textual body allow for a measurement of readerly relations with texts. Through his metaphor of the textual body, the text is personified and exhibits its own drives and desires. Influenced by his work, in this chapter I personify the Song and speak of the reading relationship as amatory. I examine several textual features, one of which is the grotesque imagery, as part of the Song's erotic technique or arsenal. Influenced by the whimsical and musing spirit that characterizes Barthes' works, however, I am not tempted to 'apply' Barthesian 'theory' or 'method' to the Song. Rather, in a less precise fashion, I play a little, that is, enquire how Barthes' pondering and instancing of amatory discourse might elucidate the process of reading the Song of Songs. Barthes helps to explain the attraction that readers seem to have to the Song, along with the difficulty that many have in reading this text and their compulsion to continue trying.

The second critic to enter the discussion, Julia Kristeva, will be familiar from Chapter 2 for her concept of the abject. The abject is an integral part

---

2   As far as I am aware, the phrase is Richard Howard's (Barthes 1990b: viii).

of Kristeva's thinking about the body and its figurations and borders, and though I touched on it in my definitions of the grotesque in the earlier chapter, it is the abject's impact on the matters of love and relationships that prompts my incorporation of it more fully into the conversation at this point. Also consequential are Kristeva's ruminations on love in her essay on the Song of Songs, which form part of a transhistorical and transcultural history written in *Tales of Love* (1987). Through Kristeva, I will investigate how it is that the grotesque and the erotic come to be so happily bedded in the Song.[3] Kristeva's work, too, returns my study to the matter of gender. Though it is not without its problems, we will see how Kristeva's reading opens up certain avenues for the Song: in Russo's terms, unlikely coalitions and prefigurative possibilities. I use her vision, therefore, as a springboard for considering the Song in conjunction with another story of bodies and love, that of a stranger to this ongoing conversation, Anna Swan. Anna's unique story is different enough to allow me to explore the interrelation of love and the grotesque from a new angle. Since that connection prompts important questions about autonomy and subjectivity, I consider it in light of one whose story can perhaps offer a fuller articulation of the perils and liberations of love for the grotesque subject.

Looking in at the Lattice: The Grotesque and the Lovers in the Song of Songs

It feels not a little voyeuristic to be plotting the rises and falls of the lovers' relationship in the Song. To be sure, they are fictional characters, but as Landy has noted, they are also universal or archetypal (1983: *passim*). One has a feeling, then, of not only looking in on one pair of lovers, but on lovers the world over. It may seem like a small point, but it indicates a larger matter: privacy. The lovers in the Song have precious little of it; they are not, on the face of it, expecting an audience. Their words and actions, therefore, are reserved for each other. However, to acknowledge a contradiction, the Song of Songs is, after all, quite obviously a text, and texts have readers. Whether or not the lovers are aware of our intrusions, and whether they welcome them or not, they naturally have an audience. This idyllic garden has flies perpetually on its walls, and evidently quite interested ones, too – this is, after all, erotic discourse.

---

3   In this conversation with Barthes and Kristeva, I will be speaking of readers and their responses to the text. It will be necessary, therefore, to invite a few back into the discussion, such as Goulder and Boer. In addition, the work entertains the autobiographical, in part, for being the one who has suggested a grotesque reading as an alternative to others, I must also acknowledge that my own interest and responses or affections towards the Song have a part to play in the discussion.

I mention this conflict of audience, this apparent contradiction between lovers as 'insiders' and readers as 'outsiders', because there is always the hesitation that to analyse the lovers' relationship would be somehow inappropriate – or impossible. Landy has said that old-fashioned character analysis is quite unproductive for the Song (1983: 61). This is true in at least one way: the lovers are not conventionally developed as characters here, nor is there much in the way of narrative action in the Song to assist in that development. However, perhaps to drop the adjective 'old-fashioned' is all that is needed to address Landy's objections. After all, these 'characters' still have somewhat recognizable personae, complete with habits, drives, successes and failures in love, and the like. Moreover, it may need to be pointed out that any readerly reconstruction of the lovers' world and the relationship at its centre is precisely that: a construction. Proper character analysis or no, readers make decisions about the qualities of these lovers, and these decisions both reflect and affect their views on love. It must also be acknowledged that to read with the grotesque is not – as should have become clear by this point in the study – a neutral stance to take. The picture that this reading strategy is going to create of the lovers must therefore explore similar features to those in my examination of the imagery: difference, disharmony and the like. This is not to say that the grotesque obviates any chance of love and harmony for the lovers, but what it does mean, I hope, is an opportunity to fill in or round out what that picture of love might be.

Beauty or the Beast?

The Song's discourse on beauty provides a winding avenue into an investigation of the descriptions and how they impact on the lovers' relationship. With a few exceptions, it is generally assumed that the lover's praise of the woman's beauty (1.15; 4.1, 7; 6.4; 7.2?) is genuine.[4] (The same might be concluded for the woman's feelings for the man, though she does not explicitly call him beautiful [cf. 5.16], and her description is not directly addressed to him.) Along with this, it is also usually assumed that this praise constitutes a legitimate expression of love.[5] The two assumptions in effect are bound together into an immutable view of the Song's lovers, from which few are willing to deviate. However, as I pointed out in my reading of the body images, the juxtaposition of the statements of

---

4   As noted previously, Waterman (1948) and Brenner (1993a) are the only scholars who have called this notion into question, Brenner only of the last description in Song 7.

5   Compare Bergant 2001: xiv–xv, 42–49; Bloch and Bloch 1995: 14–19; Exum 2005a: 17; Keel 1994: 25–37; Longman 2001: 12–14, 143–44; Murphy 1990: 158.

praise and the body descriptions make for a startling contrast, and they beg for the reader to re-evaluate their relation.[6]

Landy has skilfully shown that beauty in the Song is ambiguous (better yet, enigmatic),[7] and that ambiguity breeds ambivalence in lover and reader (1983: 137–42). His call to examine the statements about beauty critically is a crucial one for the Song (1983: 137); he does this by looking at four texts (1.5-6; 8.11-12; 8.8-10; 1.7-8). Landy writes of the 'powerful charge of repressed feeling' when one comes into contact with beauty, prompted by the 'wish to destroy it and the wish to preserve it' (1983: 142). His insights are perceptive, yet I wonder why the body descriptions that follow many of the attestations of beauty are not considered in his analysis, especially when commentators make strong connections between them, and seem so intent to preserve them.[8] Moreover, I wonder if it is not beauty that causes the unsettling in the lover,[9] but the body itself. These statements of beauty, therefore, surely signal to readers that the descriptions merit greater examination as texts which problematize the relation of the body to aesthetical evaluations of it. More globally, we might say that the relation of the statements to the descriptions calls into question how lovers choose to articulate their love.

If, then, the positive and verisimilitudinous relationship between the statements about beauty and the descriptions of the body may be problematized, what options are there for the lover's use of them? There seem to be two possibilities. The first is that the lover is being intentionally

---

6   As I suggested in the last chapter, it is a logical assumption for commentators to read the descriptions in a positive light, given their proximity to the statements about beauty. Yet, it is not entirely satisfactory. As I noted, the Song provides the only biblical instance of aesthetic evaluation juxtaposed with detailed bodily description. Moreover, the statements about beauty are not uniform: there is a somewhat disquieting progression from the general praise of 4.1, to the conflicted (?) praise of 4.7 and 6.4, and finally, the potential parodying of the ascription and the woman's beauty in the praise of her feet in sandals (7.2). These issues, when combined with descriptions that are so contended by commentators as to their significance, and which seem to unsettle readers to a great degree, mean at the very least that we should not consider the positive relation between praise and body image as a *fait accompli*.

7   Landy defines enigma as 'negative ambiguity' (1983: 140).

8   As a postscript, Landy does briefly consider 1.9, which it must be acknowledged is one of the more mystifying analogies the male lover makes (though not explicitly about the woman's body). His reading could benefit from some gender-critical analysis and frankly is not to my taste: 'The mare in battle is terrifying, partially because it is so attractive' (1983. 177). The interrogation of beauty and terror, when written particularly on the woman's body, is a matter which is not readily addressed in this work. However, his evaluation of the subservience of the mare is in concert with that of other readers, notably Pope. It also questions the ornamentation and decoration of the woman as ways to subdue her, which is interesting, given some of the directions in which a grotesque reading could take us.

9   Is it both or just one of the lovers who suffers thus? Landy's analysis seems quite androcentric here.

ironic or facetious in calling his partner beautiful; he is teasing her, or using some private language in his exchanges with her.[10] The second is that the intentions of his statements about her beauty are genuine, but that there is a disjunction – a cognitive dissonance, perhaps – in these and the grotesque descriptions that follow. These suggest that his attraction to her is more complicated than he might be aware. The descriptions betray his unconscious, which is threatened by the woman whom he loves.[11]

The woman is not allowed off the interpretive hook simply because her description of the man is somewhat different from the others in appearance and context. The options that I just described for the man also apply to her, though, as one might expect, there are some dissimilarities. The target audience in this instance has to be the other women, and not the man: as far as we know, he does not even hear this rendering of his body. In the first option, the woman would not be assisting the daughters in their search. She would be answering their ironic charge (Lys 1968: 218) with irony of her own, or sarcasm. The description could therefore be a competitive statement: her lover is well-built, phallically proficient, and rich to boot.[12] But if the images reveal unconscious fears and desires, the considerable emphasis on the phallic is suggestive. It might be an unconscious registering of her sexual desire in

10 Brenner 1993a. There are also some other possibilities along these lines, such as that he could be trying to arouse her, particularly in the mention of her sexual organs and sexuality. (See Freud [1960: 97–9] and his discussion of smut ['the intentional bringing into prominence of sexual facts and relations by speech'], at the root of which lies the unconscious [libidinal] desire to see the organs of another [the object of desire] exposed.) Or, he means to hurt her, and he can do so by picking up in his descriptions on the very features and issues that he knows make her uncomfortable or feel inadequate. This could culminate in physically displaying her before an audience (7.1-10), asking what the audience sees, and then, in the most detailed portrait available in the Song, subjecting her to a painstaking piece-by-piece ridicule.

11 On an unconscious level, could he be threatened by several aspects of her person? He might, for instance, find in her one who is dangerous, unpredictable, viraginous. He could also be threatened by her sexual aggressiveness, her autonomy. He might interrupt her seeking, her calling, and her perpetually active voice with 'poems' about her body that bear witness to his overwhelming discomfort that a woman should behave thus. At times, such fears might be admitted into his conscious mind, and he might express them: 'Turn your eyes away from me, for they alarm me' (6.5). Commentary is replete with examples of this perspective. It surfaces in particular in conjunction with texts such as Song 6.4, but is also evident in unexpected places, as in Keel's reading of Song 4.1, where he admits that the woman displays 'her own wild, almost demonic, lust for life' (1994: 142). Exum's commentary could also be added to this list, for the anxiety of the man about the woman seems to run as an interpretive thread throughout it (2005a: 21, 23, 160, etc.).

12 With extra encouragement in the form of expressed (hyperbolic) attraction and desire for his body, the lover might be persuaded to bound over the hills (2.8) back to his lovesick woman. Or, the description could be a heavy dose of fantasy, offered as if to tell the daughters to mind their own business. Their task is to convey her message, not to spend time enjoying her lover, either in actuality or in their imaginations.

the portrait of her lover. Or, as with his descriptions, the picture she paints might evidence some of her own fears and unease; she could be threatened by his remoteness, or even be reminded of an experience of physical assault that she suffered at the hands of others (5.7)?[13]

One could continue ruminating on the unconscious impulses of the lovers at length and in more depth (even more fantastically, as Boer's reading shows us; 1999).[14] The point of this brief speculation is to show that the grotesque bodies in the Song suggest a variety of implications for the lovers' relationship and consequently for the Song's presentation of love. What is more, these options are not necessarily consistent where the attitudes and emotional responses of the lovers are concerned. In light of this inconsistency, the grotesque body suggests a key issue for the lovers. Rather than existing in an idyllic place, where even brothers, foxes, vineyards and watchmen have no impact on love and happiness, it is certain that the lovers inhabit a world that has much more complicated textures, and which consequently requires further, and broader, exploration.[15]

His and Hers: Looking at Gender

The kind of speculation I engaged in above is limited in its usefulness. Given the porousness of the Song's imagery and the range of interpretive possibilities that it allows, it is conceivable that any one of the above scenarios could be taken as an interpretive key for the book, each

---

13   This is a bit clichéd, and I hesitate to voice it, but it bears mentioning because it is a possible reading of the scene. It should be pointed out that there is no direct evidence for sexual violence in the text, though the stripping of the mantle has been much discussed in scholarship (see, for example, Bergant 2001: 66; Bloch and Bloch 1995: 182; Exum 2005a: 197; Goulder 1986: 42; Longman 2001: 169; Murphy 1990: 165; Pope 1977: 527). It is therefore reasonable to consider the possibility of sexual violence if, in fact, the woman was stripped and exposed. If raped, however, the fear would doubtless not be articulated in the jubilant spirit in which the poem seems to be written. Besides, the fact that she concludes that all of him is desirable threatens this reading, and one is tempted more towards the possibility that she is aroused by her lover's body. At this point, we begin to get into a logical tangle that I am not convinced is really merited by this brief narrative moment in an otherwise poetic text, where surely what is being emphasized is violation and loss.

14   To this would need to be added the article by Burrus and Moore (2003) that so enthusiastically supports Boer's work (1999), but which does not, unfortunately, deal explicitly with the images.

15   I do not wish to suggest that I am unique in my undertaking of an investigation into these themes or in my recognition of their depth. As I have already mentioned, Landy's work has trodden these paths before, and very effectively, though undoubtedly in a different direction than what I propose here. To his, one could add more recent studies of the lovers' relationship, such as LaCoque's (1998), Walsh's (2000) and Carr's (2003), though Landy's remains, in my opinion, unparalleled in its insights and sophistication (notwithstanding my bias, that this kind of enquiry is most successfully launched via the Song's imagery).

contradicting or displacing the others.[16] That, in fact, is more to the point: I am much more interested in the range of implications that the grotesque seems to prompt than I am in arguing for a singular view of the lovers' relationship. It seems that it is actually that very range or indeterminacy that is the matter to be reckoned with where the lovers are concerned. What it leaves us with is an impression of a relationship that is not consistently one thing or another, but is somewhat variable in nature, always open to interpretation. That openness to interpretation is as true for readers as it is, I dare say, for the lovers themselves.

A considerable part of the variability that I have just described involves the fact that there are differences in the way that the lovers describe each other's bodies. These in turn are related to more global dissimilarities in gender roles as they appear to be presented in the Song.[17] A reading that might build on, for instance, a hypothesis about the anxiety of the man when faced with the woman's body particularly comes up against these matters. This means that interrogation of the way that the lovers relate (how they treat/view/talk about each other) needs to dialogue with particular (imagery-related), as well as global, issues of gender relations in the book. Such dialogue is needed, too, in the face of any hypothesizing about the potential rationale for, or implications of, grotesque figuration in the mouths of the lovers.

Many of the differences in the woman's and the man's descriptions were discussed in detail in the previous chapter, as one of the themes of grotesque figuration (inversion). The issues can be briefly restated as follows. The woman's body figures much more prominently than the man's, both because of the greater number of poems or descriptions about her, and because of the incidental references to her body, made either by her lover or herself. There is also the impression of her body being the subject of most of the action that is described in the text. In addition, readers have been right to notice the relatively static nature – some even say oddity – of the man's body compared with the woman's. Though both lovers use many of the same elements from nature and the world around

16   And this, perhaps, might be one reason why Landy has cautioned against character analysis. Walsh (2000) and Exum (2005a) provide two recent illustrations of my observation. Walsh's intensely positive interpretation of the lovers' relationship reads the imagery as support – it is gentle teasing. Exum's commentary, as noted, finds the man's descriptions to be evidence of his anxiety. In both cases, the reader finds herself wishing for further explanation (though in the case of the latter, such investigations would probably be beyond the scope of the commentary genre).

17   I refer to such matters as the relative freedom that the man seems to exhibit in coming and going, without censure; the woman's situation is quite different, especially as seen in 5.7. Other issues that she faces, for example, such as the anger of her brothers (1.6), or their attempts to speak for/control her (8.8) also possibly indicate typical social and cultural mores of the Song's setting.

them to describe each other, the finished picture of the man gives the impression that he is static and removed, whereas the woman is conceived much more dynamically. Finally, there seems to be in the woman's words a reformulation of the images that the man uses with respect to her body. This renders an alternative picture of him that is at once familiar to readers and lovers and unsettling in its alterations. When combined with the fact that the woman describes her lover in the third person, this picture initially creates an impression of distance, of a refusal to engage directly with her lover about his physical body. By contrast, he describes her to her face. She is always being looked at by her lover, and the majority of his words to her are comprised of descriptions of her body.[18]

As I observed in Chapter 1, difficulty with the disparity in the lovers' descriptions has troubled scholarship for some time. Before gender was even on the radar, Soulen made an offhand remark about the comparatively limited subject matter of the male body and the respective poetic imaginations of the poet and the poetess [*sic*] (1993: 216). Perhaps above all else, these remarks signalled to some subsequent readers that gender was indeed an important issue for scholarship on the Song's images. Soulen's reading has since been used by a few feminist scholars as a springboard, both to begin a gender-critical analysis of the images, and to elucidate how the ideological positioning of readers affects their impressions of them. But this is a fairly limited departure for feminist interests on the book, which have been most taken with the presence and predominance of the female voice in this text,[19] and have, on the whole, been enthusiastic and acclamatory.

As I pointed out above,[20] it is startling that the (problematic) figuration of the female body would not be globally at the forefront of feminist concerns. It is also surprising that feminist readers would not be more actively engaged in asking hard questions about the book, in terms of its politics of gender.[21] It is equally surprising that male readers (feminist or not) have not taken more of an interest in gender in the Song, to date. Might their interests also not be piqued by a book that appears to unsettle the predominant picture of gender relations in the Hebrew Bible? And yet,

---

18   She does, however, describe herself as well (e.g. 1.6; 8.10).

19   Two exceptions are Brenner (1993a) and Meyers (1993).

20   See also Black 2000a and 2000b.

21   Again, this is a fairly recent development for feminist critics. As Exum pointed out recently, the most rigorous critiques of gender relations in the Song (she refers to two) have so far come from men (1998: 228). For feminist critics, many of the readings have been (quite understandably) tempered by the affection that most readers seem to retain for the book. This does not mean that a feminist reader cannot be critical of the Song and appreciate it or enjoy it at the same time. The scholarship offers many fine examples of such instances of critical reading (Pardes 1992; Brenner 1993a, 1993b, 1993c, 1997a, 2005; Merkin 1994; Exum 1998, 2000, 2005a).

these questions perhaps polarize matters too much, for the text seems more to reveal gradations than it does absolutes. I am convinced that the key to understanding the lovers' relationship does not lie in successfully applying such labels as 'patriarchal' or 'gynocentric' to this text. Perhaps it is time, now, to move beyond these strategies – important as they have been for Song scholarship – and see if we cannot get to a position where we might ponder more closely the mechanics and implications of gender in the book.

Since they seem to be the two contentious issues in gender-related work on the Song, I suggest that an important strategy in understanding the lovers' relationship might be to explore the apparent disparity between the predominance of the female voice and the woman's experience as object of the gaze (or, to phrase it differently, the man's responsibility as operator of the gaze). The voice and the gaze[22] – issues that can be understood to have gender-critical implications in all literary texts – are of particular consequence here in the book, for they impact matters of autonomy and agency and seem to be positioned oppositionally. The concept of the gaze should be integral to any understanding of the body imagery, and for both lovers. Each is being itemized by the other, and each is being visually scrutinized by the other (positively, or negatively, depending on how one reads these texts). This scrutiny, furthermore, suggests a specific relation to power in the eyes of the beholder. Yet, the gaze here is inseparable from the voice, most obviously because the results of that visual perusal are verbalized, presented either to the other lover or to an audience. Now, as gender criticism has already shown, it is possible to read the Song by favouring or downplaying one or the other of these factors.[23] What is at stake here, thus, is not the discovery of a 'true' picture of gender relations in the book by some previously undiscovered means, but an analysis of what weight these issues are *given* in the evaluation of the lovers' relationship.

An initial appraisal of the body as I elaborated it in the previous chapter is a case in point. Aligned as it is with the grotesque, the figurations of the woman's body make for a disturbing and cogent reading

---

22   Whereas some readers have dealt with what might be called the politics of looking, it is only Exum in her 2005 commentary who has brought any explicitly feminist discussion of the gaze to the table. (Polaski uses the term in its gender-critical application, but his reading is of course not feminist.) I am using the term here as it has come to be used in gender criticism, informed as it is by psychoanalytical and feminist theory, particularly film theory.

23   I began this conversation in Ch. 1 with my discussion of the strategies of Meyers (1993) and Brenner (1993a). My observations there were that these two readers were still motivated by a version of the hermeneutic of compliment, and also that their readings were influenced by a desire to see mutuality in the text (though for neither does mutual mean identical). Though both write of the politics of looking, neither explicitly uses the discourse of the gaze that is being discussed at present.

against the liberty of the woman; they thereby offer a very specific picture of gender relations in the book. For, dependent as it is on the female body for its arsenal and its targets (and therefore clearly misogynistic in at least one way), the presence of the grotesque here reveals that the Song of Songs, like most other biblical texts, bears the stamp of its patriarchal origins. We might be tempted to read the descriptions of the woman as flattering, but really they ridicule, or worse, are repulsive, and as such they indicate something of the lover's unease about his love's body and her sexuality.

Moreover, the woman's grotesqueness is highlighted by the differences in the man's body. His closed and hardened form (his statuesque appearance) allows him to fit snugly into the classical side of Bakhtin's classical/grotesque framework. The elements that are used to build the man's body – and it does seem artfully constructed in comparison to hers – are not entirely unique to him, but they create a singular thematic unity that is not evident in the woman's body. He is made of costly items of luxury that are hardened, refined and meticulously crafted. Thus, his body is not as hybridized as the woman's, nor is it as volatile or as engaged in process as hers. The statuesque, highly decorative, classical nature of the man's physical form could therefore be said to emphasize the hybridized and peculiar nature of the woman's. Many see him as impressive, but remote, inactive apart from his facial features, of which there are few. In comparison, she is earthy, uncontrolled, volatile, always described. One could suggest that his closed, hardened body is so described so that he might highlight the grotesquerie of the woman's. Moreover, the woman in this case would be implicated in her own grotesque figuration, since it is she who describes her lover in a manner so opposed to the way he has configured her.

Contending the Gender Divide

Here, then, through reading material that has until now posed a problem for critics in a certain way, we encounter a way to answer the 'anomaly' (relative to Hebrew Bible norms) of the Song's protagonist. It might be that we have a text that *paradigmatically* reflects the patriarchal worldview and politics of the majority of the Hebrew scriptures. What is more, the text might actually be more dangerous than other, more overtly patriarchal, pieces, because it is deceptive.[24] And yet, as we might have come to expect with the Song of Songs by this point, the situation is somewhat more complicated than I have just described. If one contends

---

24   The idea that the text might actually be dangerous because it beguiles readers/hearers into thinking that it counters patriarchy has been suggested by Clines (1995). See below for further discussion.

the position of the voice or the gaze, an entirely different reading is possible. Several recent readers provide an opportunity to fill out the picture further.

Donald Polaski answers the charge of recent feminist criticism that the Song is rare in the Hebrew Bible because it is a 'place where women speak in an authentic voice, less trammeled by the conventions of patriarchal power' (1997: 64). Feminist critics have been able to assert this by arguing that the woman in the Song is the subject of the text, a reading supported by the presence of matriarchal themes and the predominance of the woman's voice in the book. In response, Polaski attempts, via Foucault, to analyse the woman's position as object of the male gaze from the perspective of the panopticon. His argument is that her subjectivity is constructed as a result of power relations; her subjectivity, in fact, is restricted to the disciplinary gaze, which she internalizes and from which she has no escape. He concludes that the woman is only 'empowered' in the Song in so far that she is complicit in its power/love game. The Song, therefore, may be more about 'a regime of discipline than the exercise of freedom' (1997: 81). Polaski declares his interest in this text to be primarily about what it does to readers, yet his reading does invite more global questions as to what place such a text might have in the Bible.

For his part, David Clines attempts to provide a rationale for the Song in the patriarchal reality of the canon.[25] He suggests that it is a beguiling book that was created by a (implied) male author because of the need of a (implied) male public for an erotic text. Moreover, its representation of gender equality or mutuality actually deceptively covers over the social reality of patriarchy in which it was written. The text, too, meets certain psychological needs of implied author and audience: it is a man's dream of a certain kind of woman: one who is autonomous, sexually assertive and who does nothing but sit around and wait for her lover to reappear. The text became a bestseller (a superlative Song of Songs) because this dream about a certain kind of woman, not available to Israelite men, appealed not only to the implied author, but to most of the population. Clines is also interested in taking these results to readers, to ask about the effects of reading such a Song in contemporary scholarship.

As I have been indicating, the grotesque figuration of the woman's body and the relative, classical nature of her lover's, as she sees it, might easily support – in fact, fill out – the perspective of these two readers. With the insights of a grotesque reading, the lover's dream[26] becomes one in which

---

25 Clines' chapter actually appeared before Polaski's; the latter takes up his questions, in fact, and reformulates them for his own reading. It is more constructive for me to discuss them in reverse order, however.

26 I am not convinced by Clines' construction of an implied author (who is the same as the lover, since this is supposed to be his fantasy). As Polaski has pointed out, Clines has

his woman not only allows her body to be presented and looked at in this way, but compounds her own oppression in her description of her lover, by marking it as more 'normal' than her own. In a like manner, the discipline of the gaze, as Polaski paints it, would result in reproductions of her body that indicate the woman's objectification and ridicule, and would likely internalize the fear that prompts her captors to imprison her. In Clines' dream and Polaski's prison, therefore, it would be no wonder that the man appears tall, statuesque, richly jewelled and unmovable.

It would seem, though, that the body troubles both Clines' and Polaski's readings. In his discussions of the imagery, Clines opposes the two types of descriptions as 'symbolic' (the woman's description of the man's) and 'physical' (the man's of the woman). In the process, while admitting that his observation cannot universally be upheld for the Song, he neglects to engage with the one major description (5.10-16) that undoes his argument. He says of it only, 'there is something odd about it [the man's body], and its significance remains a little elusive' (1995: 120). This image also is not given any weight in Polaski's reading, since it – as the author justifiably observes – is uttered in the third person. The man, he reasons, cannot be subject to the same oppressive gaze as the woman because he is not there to receive its resulting itemization of his body. Only he has the power of the gaze, and he directs it at her. He has 'almost complete, if not total access' to her body through the odd figurations he constructs (1997: 73).

In the Song, however, we cannot say that the female gaze is entirely absent, as these readings might lead us to believe. To be sure, it is differently constructed, but surely this is an important part of the picture. Nor can we say that the male body is built independently of the woman's gaze, and furthermore, that it is 'symbolic' but not 'physical'. The woman's gaze and the man's body as she creates it, then, prompt serious questions for Polaski and Clines. They challenge, for instance, Clines' idea that this text covers over the social realities of patriarchy.[27] They also beg the question as to why this figment of the author's imagination would be empowered to look – and construct – her lover in this fashion (why would men dream of a woman who looks at them in the same [?] way that they

difficulty keeping implied and actual social realities distinct; cf. Clines 1995: 94–5, Polaski: 1997: 67–8. For my purposes, it seems more straightforward to speak about the lovers in their poetic setting, as one reads it.

27   This prompts me to ask why such a text would become a popular purchase for those who are so privileged under its system (1995: 101). Certainly, I can see why *women* might wish to buy such a text, so that they might fantasize about a time and place where they have a voice and are free to direct their own actions where matters of love are concerned – but as Clines argues, there is no historical evidence for their literacy. On the other hand, there seems to be a lot of general historical evidence for men enjoying the privileges of patriarchal social structures where relationships are concerned, and doing what they can to maintain them.

look at women?).[28] Similarly, the woman's gaze and its resultant description as Polaski paints them make me wonder why she would mirror the voice of the disciplinary gaze, to target it not on herself, but on the other, the one who is presumably the owner of the gaze. How do these power relations play themselves out here through the images?

Both readers also neatly dispense with the voice, which might have further challenged the boundaries of their readings. Polaski, as I already noted, is providing a much-needed counter to feminist-critical readings that have emphasized the predominance of the woman's voice. Yet, in bracketing it entirely out of the picture, it lingers as an unspoken challenge to his construction of the woman's subjectivity. The possibilities of that challenge are grand, indeed. In his analysis of Foucault, Polaski acknowledges that feminist critics, such as Sandra Lee Bartky, have engaged with the philosopher's work, initially to elaborate it (e.g. the female subject who constantly polices herself; Polaski 1997: 70–71). He neglects, however, the fact that feminist critics have also been extremely vocal in their criticism of Foucault, specifically, that the conceptualization of women as docile bodies allows no room for the recognition of a female subject who is capable of resisting the effects of disciplinary practices.[29] In a similar manner, Clines, ventriloquizing the woman's voice into the mouth of the man, effectively diffuses the threat it poses to the reading of the text as a man's book for men. This threat is the woman's ability to resist the gaze, either through articulating the results of her own, or through bringing other matters to light that deflect the other's gaze from the body. I will return to this matter, for resistance is a critical issue where the politics of the gaze are concerned.

If gender might be contended by readers along the lines of voice and gaze, perhaps what is needed is a reading that might try to reconcile both, instead of privileging one over the other. Keenly aware of both the politics of looking and the power of the voice, Exum provides some redress to these two positions in her introduction to her commentary. For her, the predominance of the woman's voice is very much a part of this picture and not to be relegated to the sidelines. It indicates agency and conveys more to the reader about this figure through her thoughts and wishes than has

---

28   Clines' point that the implied author and the book's buyers wish for what they do not have is reductionistic, as he himself concedes (1995: 106 n. 23), and one finds oneself requiring more explanation. Is, for instance, the psychic byproduct of a dream about a woman who is more like a man than anything else (judging from Clines' analysis of Israelite culture) a way to accommodate an unconscious threat that femininity poses? Or, might men dream about masculine women as some kind of homoerotic fantasy?

29   See Jana Sawicki's critique of Foucault and others who have reproduced his ideas, such as Bartky and Bordo. See also Brown 1995; Sawicki 1988, 1996; and Hartstock 1990. Some feminist critics have turned to Foucault's later work to articulate a politics of resistance, but again, this is contentious.

been seen of any other biblical woman (2005a: 25). More than this, the voice indicates some of the differences between how the man and the woman love: he constructs his desire in pictures, through the gaze; she 'constructs the man primarily through the voice', through stories, quotation and construction of his speech (2005a: 14–15).

Exum also adds an important distinction about the gaze to this picture: the erotic look and voyeuristic gaze (2005a: 22–4). She admits that the distinction between the two – where one invites participation and the other objectifies – cannot be proved conclusively from the text; ultimately, it is left to the reader to judge (2005a: 24). However, she finds it a useful distinction to make because it elucidates her evaluation of the book as a mutual expression of love and desire. In her analysis, however, mutuality does not have to mean identical: the lovers describe each other differently according to their gender, to their experience and to social conventions. In her observations, Exum draws readers' attentions to matters such as the vulnerability of the lovers, or the power differentials that might be evident here, as vestiges of the culture in which this text was written.

Certainly, Exum's insights add considerable balance to the picture of gender relations in the text as it has been developed in work on the Song so far. For instance, she remedies what both Clines and Polaski argue because she creates a space for the woman's voice, which is so clearly prominent in the text, and so quickly dispatched by these other two readings. As a reader, though, I frequently feel rhetorically pushed into one of two opposing possibilities for either lover. The gaze could be erotic or voyeuristic (2005a: 22–4). His love is visual, hers verbal (2005a: 14). His imagery is animated, hers relational (2005a: 21). Her descriptions are textually motivated, while his are spontaneous outbursts (2005a: 21). These oppositions may certainly be the impression of the author and other readers. However, they work hard in the service of what Exum appears to want to find in the Song: mutuality. Each nicely balances the other, because this is a story of mutual desire. Once such a framework is applied to the Song's gender relations, though, I worry that we lose the chance to ponder difference and inconsistency in the book, thereby to illumine other aspects of its gender-contours. Readers in effect must choose between voyeurism and objectification on the one hand, and admiration and mutuality on the other.[30]

---

30 I draw the same conclusion of Landy's analysis, even though he brings the notion of ambiguity into the picture. (I have the repeated impression that it is ambiguity for the male lover in Landy's analysis, and not for both.) To be sure, it may seem as though reading with the grotesque forces the same choice in readers, especially since, in my efforts to explicate and identify the grotesque, I have only been painting this one side of the canvas. As I have been indicating, however, and hope to show more concretely towards the end of this chapter, the muddied middle (un-coincidentally where the grotesque is most at home) is where love seems most aptly explored and understood.

Might the relationship of the lovers not be all of this at once, though? That is to say, might lovers objectify as well as invite the other to be part of the looking? Might they intermittently hold power and be subject to it? I am not suggesting anything all that sinister here, just that variability is part of the lovers' experience, and that, probably, mutuality is too good to be true at every moment. Ultimately, in feminist readers' assertions about mutuality, I find a reluctance to draw this ambiguity into their arguments. The reluctance is obviously also part of androcentric (by which I mean from the male *lover's* perspective) readings such as Clines' and Polaski's, though there the balance is swung too heavily in the other direction.

The grotesque, in its own mutability, seems poised to fill out this dynamic. We have seen that the grotesque resists rigid and definite definitions. It is this feature, I suggest, that provides an important key for looking further at the implications of the body imagery for the Song's presentation of gender relations. It is true that the man's body is different, as Clines and Soulen before him observe. It is also true that the conditions of description are disparate, in terms of direct or indirect speech. The question is how that difference is to be interpreted. Do we, as I indicated above, allow the grotesque to feed into the male-(lover)-centred readings of commentators, pursuing the 'difference' of the woman over against her counterpart? Or, do we allow it the freedom to threaten that kind of reading to engender alternative and prefigurative possibilities?

There are, for instance, other features of the grotesque that rather destabilize (or else ignore) Bakhtin's grotesque/classical binarism and the scholarly, gender-biased practice of seeing the man's body as normative. Instead, they emphasize the feature of hybridization, which by its very nature is transgressive. Its efficacy in terms of the grotesque lies in its ability to 'produce new possibilities and strange instabilities in a given semiotic system. It therefore generates the possibility of shifting *the very terms of the system itself*, by erasing and interrogating the relationships which constitute it' (Stallybrass and White 1986: 58).[31] So the woman's body is a hybrid of various elements, much more so than the man's. Even in its comparatively limited hybridization, however, the man's body is able not only to subvert the classical/grotesque binarism (and the symbolic/physical binarism), but also its own 'normativeness' over against the peculiarity of the woman. The key to that subversion is situated in the division that lies within the man's body, that which exists between his face and the rest. These features interrupt the integrity of his closed, hardened, impermeable body. Moreover, their substances, myrrh (lips), spices

---

31   Emphasis original. They write, with respect to Bakhtin's work, that the second model (hybridization, or the 'inmixing of binary opposites') 'unsettles any fixed binaryism' (1986: 44), including, I would stress, the grotesque/classical binarism.

(cheeks) and milk (eyes), all provoke an engagement – literal and symbolic – with the woman's grotesque body.[32]

The point in all this is that the grotesqueness of the man's body can in fact be manipulated, with significant implications for gendered readings of the Song. Using Bakhtin's grotesque/classical binarism for both bodies, one could conclude that the man's is classical, non-grotesque, and this actually assists – in fact *makes* the reading I previously explicated. The hybridized nature of this body, in terms of the classical/grotesque binarism, however, challenges these preliminary conclusions. Additionally, it reopens the thorny issue of the status of the woman in the Song. If both bodies are grotesque, can we really say that her body is being objectified and, as a consequence, that the autonomy (sexual, verbal) that feminist critics have so enthusiastically identified is being challenged?

If we are willing to ask these questions, we must also ask if the grotesqueness of the female body can likewise be manipulated, or interpreted differently, to effect a different reading. It would seem that it can, for the heuristic of the grotesque body is not finished shifting. Against the apparent, problematic essentializing of woman as grotesque there operates a competing force: the alterity of the spectacle. According to Russo, though potentially tautologous and therefore misogynistic, the female grotesque can also open up a liminal space where women can transcend the political confines of the grotesque by embracing its concomitant notion of the spectacle. Such a move would not be a naïve hope that laughing at the joke somehow obscures that one is the brunt of it. Rather, 'making a spectacle of oneself', as Russo couches it, involves the use of the grotesque's weapons to effect one's own empowerment. It is to occupy the space between the status as (object of) the spectacle and as producer of it (1994: 165), where the former is used as a means to effect the latter. As I noted above, it is exactly this space that feminist readers insist must be accounted for in Foucault's ideas about power, subjectivity and the disciplinary gaze.

If such liberatory and spectacular avenues were to be pursued with respect to the woman in the Song, one strategy might be to emphasize the instances in which she describes herself, and the one text where she might be seen to be taking on the gaze directly (Song 7.1b). Here it is as if she invites the man/group of men to look, or even asks, 'Well, what are you looking at?!' ('How will you look at the Shulammite, in the dance of the

---

32 One could even go a step further and suggest that there is some mixing of gender happening in this sharing of imagery, some gender-bending of both bodies. See Landy on the androgyny of the lovers (1983: 73–112); and above, in the discussion of 5.10-16 in Ch. 3.

Mahănāyim?').[33] True, her lover describes her in the text that follows, but she effectively commands attention here and reclaims visual power from the onlookers by taking masterful control of what could be her undoing. Similarly, in the short texts where she describes her own body ('I am black and beautiful', 1.5; 'I am a rose of Sharon', 2.1; 'I am a wall and my breasts are like towers', 8.10), it could be the case that she takes the grotesque elements that will be or have been applied to her by her lover, and imposes them on herself, in effect challenging her lover's ownership of her body through his representation of it.[34] Is the man able to escape the confines of the grotesque by virtue of his own voice, too? One wonders. He never does describe himself.

Russo's projections indicate other possibilities for strategies, too. In her analysis of *Nights of the Circus*, she is interested not only in the words of Fevvers, and in what happens to her in the story, but also in the alliances that she makes, and in how she appears to be viewed by others from within the narrative world, as well as outside of it. Russo also cautions that women's production of themselves as spectacle is not a fail-safe way to create a successful and cohesive counterculture, but is merely an indication of the future, a 'prefigurative possibility' (1994: 221, n. 44). Russo's insights prompt me to ask whether such play could be undertaken with the Song. Could a reader enable the (man's) descriptions of the woman to be prefigurative; could he or she adopt a reading strategy that allows the woman to manoeuvre so that she becomes the agent of the spectacle? For instance: might the woman be read as *performing* the grotesque body as her lover describes it, to establish her own agency? Might agency about her body be evident in the paradoxes of her voice around the gaze ('do not look on me'/ 'what will you see as you gaze?'), and again in her reinterpretation of the man's descriptions as she applies them to him? Or, if readers were to take up suggestions that this was a woman-authored text, could they in turn perceive the man's descriptions as the thrown voice of the woman?[35]

---

33   As I noted previously, the speaker of this text is under dispute. In order to justify my reading, one would have to argue that she, and not her lover, speaks these words.

34   In order to read in this manner, one must give oneself permission to read the poems in a non-linear manner, as I have done previously (Black 2006). This is not of great consequence, especially given that many commentators view the book as a series of thematically related poems, rather than as a collection that develops a particular story or argument.

35   See Russo (1994: 175–6) on Fevver's voice. If my questions are to have any merit, they must also be translatable to matters of the man's body descriptions and his agency. They seem much more pertinent to the woman's situation, however, given: (1) the assumptions that readers have about the man's autonomy and power, a result of his social context; and (2) the tautologous potential of the female grotesque, as identified by Russo, which could cement the woman in the Song into an unstable and disempowered position.

To ask these kinds of questions is, to be sure, to enquire about who has authority in determining interpretive possibilities such as these, as much as it is to ask about what appears to be evident in the text. It is also to ask about relationships – the woman's and those of the readers of the book. The kinds of alliances that Russo identifies between Fevvers and Lizzie, these unexpected, transgenerational, non-biological 'mergings', are a potential source of empowerment and energy. Such political constellations might be possible, for example, between the woman in the Song and her female audience; or between her and her siblings.[36] They might also be possible, heretofore unthought-of alliances between certain readers and certain parts of the text.

Ultimately, what I am asking is whether or not the argument over autonomy, over predominance of voice, over aspects and potential problems with the gaze, is to be had essentially at the level of reading. In other words, are these not matters of interpretation that plague us, in the battle over the woman's sexual and social freedom – or, in the struggle to maintain the man's? As it was with the images, it does not seem to be the case that the text exhibits one view of gender roles consistently or universally. Rather, it seems to move about, sometimes shifting the very terms of the field itself. The same problems and potentialities exist for readers of the Song. Looking implicates the reader, who reads of the lovers' exploits and reflections on the beloved body, thus entering into their private world. Put differently, the reader is invited to participate in the lovers' gaze, and this has implications where the politics of reading are concerned. In fact, these implications are far-reaching, for not only are they mutable in terms of the different gender of the lovers, but they also shift to affect readers differently along the lines of their own genders.[37]

The Corpus *and the* Corps*: Barthes and the Song of Songs*

What is it about the Song – or its readers – that enables this interpretive movement around gender and the body? I take the variability in the lovers' relationship as a point from which to move into the rest of this chapter, and in a slightly different direction, spending some time on the

36   The answers to these questions, as well as the identification of some of these prefigurative possibilities, need to be deferred until issues involving the reading relationship have been discussed. The caution also must be expressed that they would need to be pursued with readerly dedication and integrity, as indeed Fontaine (2004) advises.

37   To my knowledge, the only work that has explored the implications of gender for the process of reading the Song is that of Brenner and van Dijk-Hemmes (1993), who propose a system of reading in their designation of texts as M or F. Given the variability of gender as exhibited from person to person (cultural conventions notwithstanding), I wonder whether these matters require further investigation.

readerly engagement with the Song. I suspect that the dynamism of the lovers' relationship is mirrored in the reader's experience with the text. Readers seem to find themselves both profoundly attracted to the book, but troubled by some of its features. This ambivalence, though, is not a detractor or a spoiler of relationships; on the contrary, it is essential for their existence and maintenance. Indeed, it causes us to look more closely into what the Song's presentation of love and its related discourse entails.

Readers who Love

It is hard to find a biblical critic who is negative or sceptical about the Song of Songs. As I noted in Chapter 1, there is an overwhelmingly positive attitude towards the Song in critical work; indeed, this can be traced to earlier interpreters as well, though the reasons for their exuberance are unexpectedly quite different from modern critics.[38] In the Song, readers find beauty and idyllic love. But their attraction seems to exceed an intellectual appreciation for what they read. Often, the comments made about the general nature of the Song are quite emotive and have a deeply personal aspect.

There are many versions of this story: some are to be found veiled seductively between the lines, but others display themselves boldly, especially as criticism of the Song becomes more autobiographical. Early in the Song's history of interpretation, Bernard of Clairvaux called the book 'not a melody that resounds abroad but the very music of the heart, not a trilling on the lips, but an inward pulsing of delight' (1971: 6–7). The Song is for Bernard an amorous source. Of Song 1.1, he writes, like an enamoured suitor:

> How delightful a ploy of speech, prompted to life by the kiss, with Scripture's own engaging countenance inspiring the reader and enticing him on, that he might find pleasure even in the laborious pursuit of what lies hidden with a fascinating theme to sweeten the fatigue of research. Surely this mode of beginning that is not a beginning, this novelty of diction in a book so old, cannot but increase the reader's attention. It must follow too that this work was composed, not by any human skill but by the artistry of the human Spirit, difficult to understand indeed but yet enticing one to investigate. (1971: 3–4)

---

38   It stands to reason that early interpreters who allegorized the Song in their particular contexts were motivated by different, more theological, concerns than many modern interpreters. This does not, however, exclude more recent critics from asking particular theological questions of the Song. Two recent allegories (Stadelman 1992; Robert and Tournay 1963) are exemplary; so are commentaries such as Krinetzki's (1980; in the Neuer Echter Bibel series) and Snaith's (1993); LaCoque's hermenuetical essay (1998) might also be cited here.

And, even earlier, could there be in the often quoted comment of Rabbi Akiba, that the Song is not to be sung out vulgarly in taverns, a hint of the man-as-lover, who was 'sympathetically sensitive to its erotic suggestion', as Landy (1983: 14) proposes?[39]

One need not go so far back for evidence of readers' feelings. Brenner writes of her 'emotive and intimate connection' with the book and identifies it as 'an important part of my formative years and still is a significant part of my daily existence. It belongs to my life experience, the emotive baggage that goes everywhere with me but becomes joyfully pronounced particularly when I am in Israel' (1997b: 570). Jack Sasson once remarked to me that he is fond of the Song partly because he used to read it as a child with his mother.[40] André LaCoque confesses, 'The more I entered into it myself, the more I became enthralled' (1998: ix). Exum remarks of writing her commentary that, in addition to being a resistant reader who investigates whether or not the Song challenges the biblical gender status quo, she wishes to be 'seduced by the Song of Songs, to enter into its idyllic world of eroticism' (1998: 248).

Honest remarks like these are not to be disparaged, even though those who might not share the connection that these readers seem to have with the book might find them wistful and idealistic. My interest in them is that sometimes they have a decidedly amorous, even erotic, quality about them. This was the case with Exum's wish, and it is especially so with LaCoque's (phallic?)[41] admission. One could, in fact, describe the reading relationship as amatory or erotic. It is even possible – if the anthropomorphism is allowable – to say that the Song is active in the relationship; it engages its readers *as a lover*. If any Hebrew Bible text does, the Song demands a little extra of the personal from its readers, not only because it touches on that which is personal – love, sex, desire – but because it has a unique way of drawing the reader in. As Exum rightly exclaimed, it is

39 'He who warbles the Song of Songs in a banquet-hall and makes it into a kind of love-song has no portion in the world to come' (*m. Yad.* 12.10). 'God forbid! No man in Israel ever contended regarding the *Song of Songs* [to say] that it does not render the hands unclean, [for all the ages of] the whole world are not worth the day whereon the *Song of Songs* was given to Israel, for all the *Hagiographa* is sacred, but the *Song of Songs* is the most sacred [of them all]' (*t. Sanh.* 3.5). It is intriguing just how many writers on the Song begin their work with a reference to Akiba's comments, even those who are unconcerned with the Song's allegorical history. See, for a few examples among many, Exum 1973; Falk 1982; Landy 1983; Pardes 1992; Soulen 1993. The appeal to this early Rabbi's words on the Song's greatness is curious. Why is Akiba invested with such authority by modern scholars? Is it only because his praise is superlative? Or, might other readers recognize the 'lover' in Akiba, and be somehow influenced by his obvious appreciation for and close personal connection with the Song?

40 I hope that Sasson will not mind my reproduction of part of our stimulating conversation about the Song, one November at an Society of Biblical Literature meeting.

41 *Pace* LaCoque: it is difficult to ignore the implications of his words, given the Song's subject matter.

entry into the Song's world that readers seek, not merely an understanding of its mystery. Moreover, readers respond in feeling and in writing, perhaps imposing upon the Song (and not simply the characters in it) the profile of an ideal relationship. In return, the *texte-amante* seems to bring out in its lovers their reluctance to tarnish it – and, better still, it encourages them to protect it and makes them blind to its faults. Discovering an idyllic world, readers seem loath to suggest that it may be flawed or spoiled in any way.

Barthes, the Body and the Text

In order to ponder this relationship more fully, I return to Roland Barthes, who in addition to his study of Arcimboldo's heads is also well known for wearing his heart on his page. Though I risk making the reading of this chapter much less *pleasurable* by diverting attention to Barthes' work at this point, I make this short digression in order to gather some theoretical tools for the journey, and to introduce Barthes' use of the corporeal metaphor. Eventually, it will be the place of the grotesque in this readerly relationship that I am aiming to interrogate, and once again, Barthes is useful for this elaboration. Two writings[42] are important in Barthes' œuvre for this subject, *The Pleasure of the Text* (1990b) and *A Lover's Discourse: Fragments* (1990a).[43] In addition, Barthes' metaphorical play with the body, made visible in the two terms, *corpus* and *corps*,[44] makes the important link between body and text that facilitates the consideration of the reading relationship as erotic.

Pleasure of the Text and *A Lover's Discourse*, both significant departures for Barthes in terms of subject matter and approach,[45] are

42   One runs into difficulties when discussing Barthes' writing. On the one hand, the term 'text' is highly specialized and should not be used of his material in the generic way I have been using it throughout this study. On the other, 'work' tends to be disparaging in Barthes' view: it is the classical, readerly (*lisible*) text, and not the text of *jouissance*. (For that matter, my use of the adjective 'readerly' to describe that which pertains to readers is also suspect in Barthes' analysis.) I will try to avoid 'work' and 'text' when referring to Barthes' writing, so as to avoid confusion with his theory on texts and works. 'Writing' (although also problematic for its potential confusion with the *scriptible* text) or 'work' in its abstract sense will have to suffice.

43   A third piece, his 'autobiography', *Roland Barthes* (1995), comes between these and will be mentioned where relevant. In Saint-Amand's opinion, this is the 'best sketch of a Barthesian erotics' (1996: 158), but in order to justify that observation, one would need to study the three pieces in more detail than is possible here.

44   Barthes only uses *corps* himself in *Pleasure of the Text*. The two terms appear in the title of Knight's article (1984: 831) and provide a good way of showing both the pun and the distinction being made.

45   In these books, one can detect a significant shift in Barthes' thinking, where writing and indeed reading is motivated almost solely by the pursuit of pleasure. The biographer Calvet (1994) divides Barthes' legacy into three phases. Whereas the first and second enquire

intimately concerned with the marginalization of amatory discourse, the latter the more so, because it seeks to recover the lost language of love by recreating it. In this re-creation, we find that Barthes is very much playing – with the subject, with us and with his writing (perhaps even with himself).[46] The writing is fragmentary and incomplete, and the books reveal, and subsequently invite, not an analytical systematization of their subject and themselves, but treatment in kind. They are designed to tease and show evidence of textual teasing. Moreover, they irresistibly brush up against each other, so that the fragments of *A Lover's Discourse* inevitably find their way into the mouths of all lovers, including the text which Barthes has embodied and personified. With even these brief observations, the applicability of such work to the Song of Songs – and readers' interactions with it – is clearly evident.

Pleasure of the Text might be called an enquiry into an erotics of reading, that is, into notions of reading and text that are based on the unstable opposition of texts of *plaisir* (pleasure) and texts of *jouissance* (bliss).[47] In what is now a much-quoted observation, Barthes contrasts these two types as follows:

> Text of pleasure: the text that contents, fills, grants euphoria; the text that comes from culture and does not break with it, is linked to a *comfortable* practice of reading. Text of bliss: the text that imposes a state of loss, the text that discomforts (perhaps to a point of a certain boredom), unsettles the reader's historical, cultural, psychological assumptions, the consistency of his tastes, values, memories, brings to a crisis his relation with language. (1990b: 14)

Here, Barthes appears to be roughly reformulating his earlier distinctions between readerly (*lisible*) and writerly (*scriptible*) texts. Only in the latter

---

into how texts are produced and the manner in which they are received and evaluated, the third, represented by the works just mentioned, is taken up with readerly pleasure and desire, among other things (1994: 206). This third phase is, as some have described it, without theory. In particular, it lacks his earlier semiological and Marxist interests (Calvet 1994: 223). It is not so much that Barthes was embarking on an intentionally a-theoretical project, but that he wished to emphasize writing for its own sake or in its own interest; he would therefore use his theoretical past when it suited him, without any concern to develop a theoretical system or method. It must be said that this evaluation of Barthes' third phase of writing is not universal. For instance, Barthes' work from 1968–73 has also been described as an 'impressive poststructural project' and his work in the *Pleasure of the Text* as his own private 'erotic variety of deconstruction' (Leitch 1983: 102).

46   The *double entendre* is not accidental. There is something distinctly auto-erotic about Barthes' work at times, both in terms of the texts on which he draws, and in terms of the enterprise that he encourages, which emphasizes the reader's pleasure.

47   'Bliss' is used by Richard Miller in his translation for *jouissance*, but the latter is preferable, since it is now well employed in academic discourse and conveys a broader range of meaning than the English.

can one experience *jouissance*, the true letting-go and loss of identity. It is, by contrast, in the classical text – the readerly one – that mere pleasure is experienced. But the opposition between the two text types is intentionally unstable. Barthes is avoiding creating a system of classification, and wants to encourage, instead, interaction that is affective and indeterminate.

> *Pleasure/Bliss*: terminologically, there is always a vacillation – I stumble, I err. In any case, there will always be a margin of indecision; the distinction will not be the source of absolute classifications, the paradigm will falter, the meaning will be precarious, revocable, reversible, the discourse incomplete. (1990b: 4)

The opposition, moreover, works partly because of the ambiguity of the term *plaisir*, which sometimes extends to *jouissance*, and sometimes is opposed to it (Barthes 1990b: 19).[48] The ultimate aim is not to decide whether a text is a text of *plaisir* or a text of *jouissance*, but, as Moriarty observes, to 'look at the form of the distinction' (1991: 151).

This brings us to Barthes' well-known metaphor of the text as body, or as part of a greater body, as in a body of literature (*corpus*, to use Knight's phrase). Quite distinct from the potential representation of the human body *in* the text (*corps*), then, Barthes envisions the text *as* body, that is, it is a figure with which readers might have a certain relation that is best described as erotic. For Barthes, this also includes the attributing of drives and desires to the text, which in turn prompt certain responses. As he explains:

> The *corpus*: what a splendid idea! Provided one was willing to read *the body* in the corpus: either because in the group of texts reserved for study (and which form the corpus) the pursuit is no longer of structure alone but of the figures of the utterance; or because one has a certain erotic relation with this group of texts (without which the corpus is merely a scientific *image-repertoire*). (Barthes 1995: 161)

Moreover, when Barthes writes of the eroticism of a text, he is not saying that its subject matter has to be erotic love, though it can be. In Barthes' view, a text, like the human form, has several bodies, one of which is erotic. He explains:

> Apparently, Arab scholars, when speaking of the text, use this admirable expression: *the certain body*. What body? We have several of them; the body of anatomists and physiologists, the one science sees or discusses: this is the text of grammarians, critics, commentators, philologists (the pheno-text). But we also have a body of bliss [*jouissance*] consisting solely of erotic relations, utterly distinct from

---

48 In its French original, the title of the book is ambiguous in another way as well: *Plaisir du texte* speaks both to the pleasure of reading (the pleasure to be found in the text), and the text's (personified) own pleasure (Gallop 1986: 20).

the first body: it is another contour, another nomination; thus with the text: it is no more than the open list of the fires of language ... Does the text have human form, is it a figure, an anagram of the body? Yes, but of our erotic body. The pleasure of the text is irreducible to physiological need.[49]

This erotic body, moreover, is erotic not because of certain 'erogenous zones', but because it is intermittent, showing itself like skin through gapes in a garment ('Is not the most erotic portion of the body *where the garment gapes?*'; Barthes 1990b: 9); the flash of skin, or the 'staging of appearance-as-disappearance' (Barthes 1990b: 10) is what seduces the reader. It is a fetish object, but in a typically Barthesian paradox, the fetish also desires the reader, through 'a whole disposition of invisible screens, selective baffles: vocabulary, references, readability, etc.' (Barthes 1990b: 27). Sexy sentences stand out/stand alone, and, like sexy bodies which invite the viewer to envision or imagine their erotic practice (Barthes 1995: 164) – not because of their beauty but because of the viewer's fantasy – they invite the reader to glimpse their eroticism through linguistic practice.[50]

For Barthes, these ruminations into the nature of text and reader did not quite go far enough. In *A Lover's Discourse: Fragments*, we see a subsequent attempt on his part to reproduce amatory discourse, in fits and starts. As I mentioned, the fragmentary nature of this writing allows for a teasing, a musing, and ultimately a resistance to totalizing or essentializing discourse about love. Barthes' own introduction is the best explication of what he intends here. His last sentence before the work begins reads, 'So it is a lover who speaks and who says' (1990a: 9). Barthes' intention? To bring to light what has been marginalized: 'The lover's discourse is today of *an extreme solitude*' (1990a: 1; original emphasis). What he offers are 'figures', posturings ('the body's gesture caught in action'; 1990a: 3), instances of amatory discourse. Readers will, he hopes, respond, 'That's so true! I recognize that scene of language!' (1990a: 4). Or, they might analyse further and see sketches or characters (Calvet 1994: 220), but they are never complete or definite. Barthes had difficulty deciding on the order

---

49   Barthes 1990b: 17. I find the translation of the last sentence to be limited, since the original conveys a more compelling comparison of the two bodies: 'Le plaisir du texte serait irréductible à son fonctionnement gramarien [phéno-textuel], comme le plaisir du corps est irréductible au besoin physiologique' (1973: 30).

50   Something could be made here of Barthes' sexual orientation, and the proposition in scholarship that this phase of his work (especially *A Lover's Discourse*) represents a homoerotic relationship. Critics do not agree, however, that Barthes' erotics of reading, particularly as evident in *A Lover's Discourse*, is explicitly queer (compare Schor 1987a; Heath 1983; Saint-Amand 1996). Barthes' work seems diffuse and sometimes asexual enough (in terms of genital sexuality) that it is suitable for a text like the Song of Songs, but it could also prod interesting homoerotic readings.

of the figures (Calvet 1994: 214), and though they are ordered alphabet-ically like the entries in *Pleasure of the Text* (and though he is deeply affected by the allure of the alphabet; Barthes 1995: 147), he insists that they are random. Barthes perceives of them as entries in a thesaurus, part of a reservoir where they are not linked by a particular logic or sense.

It goes without saying then, that at the root of both works, and Barthes' pursuit of pleasure throughout this phase of his writing, is the body. As he says, 'body' is a *mana*-word for him (Moriarty 1991: 186; Barthes 1995: 130), 'a word whose ardent, complex, ineffable, and somehow sacred signification gives the illusion that by this word one might answer for everything' (Barthes 1995: 129). Here, at the time of writing his autobiography, Barthes' *mana*-word 'blossoms, it flourishes' (Barthes 1995: 130). Of particular concern always for Barthes had been the sexual or erotic connotation of the body – the readerly body (his own especially).[51] In this phase of his work, Barthes' *mana* explodes everywhere. I write (and pun) ironically: Barthes' concept of the body is reputed to be non-phallic, non-genital, imprecise. As Saint-Amand notes, this imprecision has to do with the erasure of 'antimonies and binarisms that restrain sexual experience' (1996: 157). The result is a 'Neuter', a body unmarked by masculine/feminine and active/passive polarities. It is, moreover, sexualized, but the usual, genital locus for sexuality is replaced by a diffuse, non-centralized, but more sensual experience: 'The Barthesian sexual act is a patchwork of sensualities'. In confounding the significance of 'erotic gestures', we may see in Barthes the 'happy beginning of a reinvention of the body' (Saint-Amand 1996: 159). It could 'become an atopia … consist[ing] of sentences whose sexuality would not be phallocentric expressions of the violence between the sexes … and it would be quite unpreoccupied with conquering meaning, mastering it, reducing it to a system or a calculus. Such writing would be dedicated to foreplay and postponement rather than consummation' (O'Neill 1984: 196).

Barthes was able to explore this imprecise, differently sexed body through fragmentary reading and writing, a practice that, not coinciden-tally, also arose during this phase of his research. The fragmentation of writing has a direct correlation with Barthes' views on sexuality. Through it (and indeed *like* it, for the process is cross-fertilizing), the body can be

---

51 Barthes, however, was deeply closeted in his sexual orientation. His outing can in fact be attributed to the posthumous publication of a journal kept while he was visiting Morocco (*Incidents*. Paris: Seuil, 1987). The issue was always open to debate, but it was not until the appearance of the journal that it was confirmed in the scholarly world, and this gave rise to a re-interpretation of his earlier works. See Saint-Amand 1996; Schehr 1994.

conceived of as aleatory (Saint-Amand 1996: 159). Barthes' work becomes utopic[52] in a limited sense, intentionally incomplete, like musing.[53]

Fragmented, playful, erotic, but not explicitly sexual (in terms of genital sexuality), Barthes' writing seems a provocative background against which readerly relationships with the Song of Songs might be viewed. In Catherine Belsey's view, Barthes' style and content capture the discourse of desire well: 'It would be appropriate to write in a way that inhabits the terrain of desire without simply reproducing its self-effacing and ultimately evasive citationality' (1994: 18). Or, simply put, Barthes is able actually to exhibit the erotic instead of only talking about or around it. His usefulness for the Song is marked, for in capturing the erotic as he does, and in laying it against texts, he is able to emphasize not a theory of reading, but its affect.[54] In the same way that amatory discourse has been marginalized in Barthes' view, so too has discussion of the affect of the Song. And, as I have been arguing, an investigation into reading the Song

52   So says O'Neill: 'Barthes saw in the proliferation of literary language a utopian quest for an Adamic language that might name things prior to all divisions and conflicts' (1984: 191). Despite the fact that this utopic interest never really became politicized, and despite his 'apprenticeship to a transcendent structuralism', O'Neill thinks that this 'utopia of language remained a personal vision' throughout Barthes' life (1984: 191). It deepened in the third phase of his work to which I referred above (1984: 191). However, just how utopic his language might be is open to some debate. Feminist scholars have questioned the apparently 'feminist' or gender-egalitarian views of Barthes that some have located in *A Lover's Discourse*. See, among others, Gallop 1986, Kauffman 1995, Schor 1987a. It should also be noted that I just quoted O'Neill as identifying Barthes' sentences as atopic. I leave the deliberation over which it is to be, utopic or atopic, to him.

53   Again, to quote O'Neill:

Barthes' fragments are therefore deliberate play, promiscuous and excessive openings and foreclosuresf of literary desire drawn from nowhere, *hors-texte*, incomprehensible to the conventional commentator. He slipped through classifications, oppositions, and divisions of logic, drifting in language, ignoring alibis, the natural, the narrative as much as law, sex, and marriage … If Barthes' writings nevertheless collect, they do so as a personal encyclopedia of topics indulged for their own sake, as pleasurable incidents in a life compelled to find meaning. The futility in this compulsion to meaning is exonerated only through the author's surrender to the tide of words washing up their own meaning for him to surrender – like a child on the beach. (1984: 195–6)

54   Some clarification of terminology is important at this stage when writing of the effects of the text on readers and the 'affect' of reading. The first term, 'effect', refers to the results of a particular text and its reading on readers; these may be general and are, for the moment, possibly abstract. One could mention, for instance, the realization that the grotesque body elucidates the Song's gender politics. The second term, 'affect', pertains to the emotional or psychic impact of texts and readings upon readers. Its significance is specifically to foreground the participation of the reader in the reading process along these lines. Hence, it is possible to speak both of an 'effect' and an 'affect' of the text. I make the distinction because it is the latter with which Barthes is primarily concerned. Moreover, it is the latter with which I wish to continue my investigation of the implications of the grotesque body in the Song of

as grotesque necessitates some kind of treatment of what kinds of relationships readers have with the Song. Barthes' work shows promise for being able to assist in righting the balance.

The Pleasure of our Text

To speak of the Song as lover, then, is naturally, a decision about reading, a move to position the text as a speaking, feeling subject in order to identify and give voice to an 'other' party in the reading process. It is, in other words, a metaphor of reading – and Barthes would have to admit the same. The attribution of subjectivity gives the Song agency, and that agency functions heuristically to allow us to see how readers are implicated into a text with which they seem to have a unique connection.

With the benefit of Barthes' insights, then, 'lover' would not be a throwaway metaphor for the Song and for readers who engage with it. In Barthesian terms, we might say that the Song is embodied; it desires its readers; it has an erotic body that is an anagram of ours. We can see that the text is active in interacting with its readers. The Song's display of itself is intermittent, carried on through language that teases, baffles, attracts. It is, moreover, a jealous lover; it closely guards the enjoyment and liberties readers take in it. With its orchestration of various textual features, it prevents the easy assumption of various readerly pleasures, such as skipping through a text, or reading selectively. It commands constant attention, demands that readers always ask, 'What does this mean? What is happening here?'

The textual features in the Song's amatory arsenal are, I suggest, numerous. Three areas benefit from further enquiry. The first, the Song's imagery, we have already looked at in detail in the previous chapter. In what follows, I shall recast its obscurity and grotesquerie as amatory technique. Another technique, the Song's play with narrative or a 'plot' also bears investigation. These are intertwined with a third, the Song's erotic subject matter, which is displayed and concomitantly veiled through them. The techniques are effective because of their indeterminacy or fluidity. They enable the book to draw readers in and keep them interested; desire can be perpetuated because it is never satiated, in that readers are never fully satisfied by full and consistent knowledge of the text.[55] The Song's erotic content is the place where I will begin.

When we speak of the Song's eroticism, we encounter a duality. Taking a lead from Barthes' insights, I have called the Song an erotic text, and

---

Songs. The two issues I mentioned earlier, the problem of the body in erotic discourse and the difficulty that biblical scholars have had with the Song's images, are connected and can be investigated here, at the level of the affect of the text.

55 Arguably, this would be true of all texts of *jouissance* in Barthes' thinking, and not just the Song. It is, however, particularly evident here.

through a discussion of its erotic technique it will become clearer how I perceive this aspect of its nature is manifested. But the Song is also in part *about* erotic love. Thus we encounter a paradox: the Song is eroticized (in Barthesian terms) by way of its erotic content.

What does it mean to say that the Song is about erotic love? That it depicts two people in love with each other who express their desire for each other in lyrical, sometimes cryptic language, need not be disputed. But the Song's erotic content is not so obvious. It is, for instance, more difficult to assess whose desire (the man's or the woman's) is actually being revealed and how (what are the gender politics of the Song), and whether the Song hints more at sexual love than actually portrays it. In comparison to the Hebrew Bible's more regulated and efficient, 'and · he · knew · her · and · she · conceived' – sex undertaken (or inflicted) for procreative purposes – the Song's lyrics seem highly irregular, in Barthes' terms they are perverse, for they showcase sexual activity which is pursued or enacted for its own end.[56] More often than not, however, the 'good stuff' in the Song is obfuscated by cryptic imagery or is disappointingly *coitus interruptus*, so that what actually takes place remains clouded.

To speak of the Song's erotic content is to ask about readers as well as the book's lovers, to ask, erotic for whom? It is finally up to readers to decide whether the Song teases us with showing-of-the-ankles suggestion or clobbers us with full frontal. To some, references to sexual intercourse are obvious; so obvious, in fact, that they are added in where one might be hard pressed to find them – which in turn might lead other readers to speculate about interpreters' sexual interests, more than anything else. A small example from Goulder's commentary (1986) illustrates my point. Of Song 8.5, 'under the apple tree I awakened you' he writes:

> ... it could be that the place where she aroused him is an anatomical place as well as a place in a glade; and that it is thought of as an apple-tree by virtue of the two fruits hanging down above the 'trunk'; that there is a special force to 'under', because it is at the under end of this tree that the nerves are concentrated that make for such arousal ... (1986: 7–8)

Such a reading, still euphemistic in its own way, may prompt questions about the reader as much as it prompts us to think about the fluidity of the text. Goulder himself makes the point, too, that the Song 'can sail nearer the wind than this', meaning that it can be more overt in terms of its erotic content (1986: 8).

In my view, the text is purposely *fluid* in presenting its erotic material, that is to say, purposely suggestive. Moreover, its suggestiveness is what

---

56 Perversity is not a morally loaded term for Barthes in the way that it might conventionally be used.

makes it realistically and most effectively erotogenic. The speculations by commentators that seek to 'fix' and map out sexual events confirm this proposition. The key is in the speculation, not the definitive mapping, for, as Barthes observes, should the 'event' actually occur, there would be 'disappointment, deflation' (1990b: 58). That is, the all-too-available pattern in modern erotic literature of excitement/foreplay/consummation becomes dull and disappointing for those who read it (1990b: 58). Goulder's propensity to hammer the point home, and on texts that might not even warrant it, is a case in point. In asking, thus, 'have they done *it* yet?' or, 'did they do *it* here?' (a crude but accurate rendering of some commentators' interest in the lovers' consummation of their desire), readers of the Song participate in its strategy; they become willing objects of its amatory designs. They become enticed by the text. The Song's apparent ability to hold off from climaxing – we might call it its stamina – is a key to the success of its strategy. By teasing the reader (who, the Song might assume, reads it because he or she is interested in its contents), the Song keeps its lovers interested. As Barthes asks, 'Is not the most erotic portion of the body where the garment gapes?' (Barthes 1990b: 9).

Exploring the Song's Erotic Body

The Song's display and hiding of its erotic treasures can be more fully illustrated by looking at 5.1: 'I come to my garden, my sister my bride; I gather my myrrh with my spice, I eat my honeycomb with my honey, I drink my wine with my milk'. This text has been the (or one of the) frequently acknowledged consummation scene(s) for the lovers chiefly because it appears to be the man's positive response to an apparently direct invitation for sex from his partner:[57] 'Let my beloved come to his garden, and eat its choicest fruits (4.16)' (Bloch and Bloch 1995: 178; Fox 1985: 138–9; Goulder 1986: 39; Keel 1994: 184–5; Lavoie 1995: 145; Murphy 1990: 162; Pope 1977: 504–6; Rudolph 1962: 153). 'Come into' (בוא) here is understood in its sexual sense, and 'his garden' refers to the woman, so named by the man in 4.12 and 4.15. Verbs of eating and drinking, moreover, conjure up various consummatory proclivities (see Prov. 5.15, 19; Fox 1985: 139; Keel 1994: 185).

But is this scene as straightforward as commentators seem to think it is? In the first instance, the verbs of consumption in 5.1 are a series of four perfects, a tense which is usually translated to give a present, past or past perfect meaning, but which may also refer to that 'which is *represented* as accomplished, even though it [is] continued into the present time, or even

---

57 Other factors have also influenced the decision, such as the expectation in earlier commentaries that the couple, once married (Song 3), would have a wedding night (e.g. Budde 1898; Delitzsch 1877).

[is] actually in the future' (GKC 1910: § 47 n. 1, original italics).
Depending on their views of what is happening in the Song at this point,
then, commentators may play with the tenses and take advantage of their
relative fluidity, making the consummation either a past or a future event.
Pope lists some of the translations that have been employed to date: past,
present (implying either imminent – but not yet completed – action, or
future action), future perfect, and the *perfect confidentiae* (future action,
but so certain that it may be spoken of as having occurred; 1977: 504).

In the second instance, the greater context of texts such as this one may
also influence interpretation, as we saw with 4.16. Reading from that
point (as most do: see above), it seems likely that the lover's response
implies coitus. Quite a different state of affairs occurs with 5.2-8, however,
which is usually read as a separate and distinct scene from 5.1, thereby
removing any possible contradiction with the earlier text (Bloch and
Bloch, Fox, Goulder, Keel, Krinetzki [1981], Murphy, Rudolph; Pope is
an exception). But if 5.2 is read as following on from 5.1, we perceive that
the consummation has not been successful. For, according to 5.2-8, the
encounter in 5.1 seems to have failed; it results in the woman searching for
her lover who has abandoned her, and being beaten for her efforts. One
easily becomes embroiled in the logistics of the situation: have they just
consummated their love/marriage? If so, why is the meeting being
attempted all over again? Why is he knocking at her 'door' when he has
just entered her 'garden' (cf. Fox 1985: 144–6; Keel 1994: 192; Murphy
1990: 165, 170–71; Pope 1977: 517–19)? Does the scene imply that the
lovers have not yet come together, or that they must make another
attempt, or even that they are doomed never to be united?

In the case of 5.1, concern with the continuity of the Song's texts and
grammatical choices, such as decisions about verb tenses, indicate, among
other things, commentators' desires to make of the Song a story.[58] I see
readers' motivations to understand what is happening and indeed their
quest for coitus in the text as part of a novelistic drive that arises when
they are confronted with the Song of Songs. This drive is in response to
what may be called the second of the Song's amatory techniques, its play
with narrativity. Whereas we may say that readers of any text typically try
to 'make sense' of what they read, reading the Song is a unique enterprise
because of its unusual structure and content. I am not suggesting that
readers approach the book with the intention to render it into a narrative.
Rather, owing to the Song's meandering, lyrical style, its abrupt scene
changes and its ostensible plot in certain poems (Alter 1985: 187), readers

---

58   The separation of the Song into scenes also reflects this interpretive move, as with 5.1
and 5.2-8, just considered.

are compelled to try to unify what they read in order to make sense of it.[59] This compulsion to make sense of the text draws them in and keeps them interested. Certain questions plague them: Who are the characters in the Song? Is the book telling a story? Their story? How will it end? Moreover, the Song's physical structure adds to this confused picture in that readers must also ask how, physically, to go about reading the Song almost as soon as they start. Is the Song comprised of a series of poems? How, if at all, are they related? Once readers identify the Song's apparent intentions toward, or its baffling ignorance of, a tangible structure, they are better situated to make sense of its lyrical maze. Or so they figure.

When added to the Song's display of brief, veiled sexual encounters which, as I argued above, has also been stimulating the reader's drive, the quest for plot in effect becomes like a kind of coital quest itself. As with the Song's erotic subject matter, it is not the outcome that is the attraction (the completed and unified plot), rather its titillation, its promise. What better way to pursue the encounters of the lovers than to construct them into a narrative, where the excitement builds to a satisfying climax? At the centre of such drives is the question: What happens?

The Song entices us with the question, 'What happens?' as soon as the credits go by (1.1) with its opening shot of a man and a woman in love (1.2). But it is more than a static glimpse of the couple at work or at play. This first text, 'let him kiss me', is hardly an idle moment of wishful thinking. The statement has narrative currency, an urgency that jump-starts the story into motion. It implies that the presence of the one she seeks is imminent, so much so that we are not surprised when she addresses him in the next verse, or when she meets up with him in his chambers. Then, *what happens*, when, two verses later, we learn that the woman's siblings are angry with her: will they prevent the lovers from seeing each other again, in a sort of biblical Cinderella tale? The woman's first meeting with her lover in 1.4 was perhaps merely a tease. Sometimes, she calls and he is absent. Or she will send him away. Or maybe he will be the one looking for her. Sometimes they might meet each other. Sometimes obstacles prevent their uniting, be they watchmen (5.7), siblings (1.6), social mores and prohibitions (4.9, 10, 12; 5.1, 2; 8.1),[60] foxes (2.15), or the lovers' own whimsies (3.1; 5.6; 8.14). Then, even the last word in the book (8.14) is ambiguous: does ברח mean that the

---

59   The tradition of dramatic readings of the Song in commentaries can be seen as evidence of this. See Delitzsch 1877; Goulder 1986; Waterman 1948, among others.

60   See Brenner 1997: 100–1 on incest in the Song; also Pope 1977: 480–81; Murphy 1990: 160; and Keel 1994: 163, who, among many others, deny there is an incestuous component to the relationship. Compare Landy (1983: 97–100), who acknowledges that there might be, but affirms that it is a quasi-brother (not a real sibling) that the woman is looking for. Landy also draws attention to Cook who sees that all which is pleasurable, even that which may be forbidden, is available to the lovers (1968: 119).

woman is telling her lover to hurry to her (the mountains of spices), or to flee?[61] If it is the latter, the ending is most unsatisfactory for the diehard romantics among us. After all that chasing, seeking, finding and missed encounters, why would the book not end with the protagonist finally getting the kiss she looked for in 1.2, and more besides?

The two so-called dream sequences of 3.1-4 and 5.2-7 are a further and clearer example of the Song's narrative dynamism and inconsistency. As Alter observes, narrativity is often expected in the Hebrew Bible's parallelistic verse, but it is shortlived and incomplete. Here in the dream sequences, we see two unique pockets, 'whole poems in which all semblance of semantic equivalence between versets is put aside for the sake of narrative concatenation from verset to verset and from line to line' (Alter 1985: 187). The Song's usual figurative language is also suspended for the sake of the plot (Alter 1985: 188), but only briefly. And how do these two concentrated pockets of narrative fit together and function in the Song? The dream sequences mirror each other, encouraging readers to conflate them and create a plot of sorts that spans the space between, or perhaps affects the whole book. Such is the case, for instance with Goulder: the first dream sequence is pre-marriage; she invites him in and he leaves, but she finds him again. Later, they marry, and the second text represents what is perhaps a marital complacency: she is slow to get up and he leaves, so she must look for him (1986: 3). But any plot imposed on the two dream scenes will raise questions as much as it satisfies desires for coherence. Why the missing man in both texts? Why the woman's success at finding him in the first instance and her failure in the second? What is the reason for the violence? And on the Song continues, always prompting questions, always tantalizing readers with its 'story'.

Part of reading the Song, then, involves keeping track of the 'narrative' movement (or, imposing it), and, additionally, of who is speaking, who is searching, whose desire stimulates whatever action is occurring. Readerly desire persists, not merely to know what happens, or when it happens, but because what happens is accessible at constantly shifting intervals. In keeping track of its constant shifting, readers become personally involved

---

61   Most assume the former: Delitzsch 1877: 161–2; Fox 1985: 177; Keel 1994: 285; Murphy 1990: 200 (flee to her); Rudolph 1962: 186; Snaith 1993: 131. Pope does not commit himself either way (1977: 698–701). Some do insist that the verb means movement away, and in one case, away from the woman, so that he will not get caught (Bloch and Bloch 1995: 221). Fox points out that the verb ברח always means movement away from, so she is either telling her lover to depart from her, or, what is more likely, to leave his friends and come to her (1985: 177). There seems to be a nice ambiguity here, and perhaps Fox is right that the poet intends to leave the story *in medias res* (1985: 176). She asks him to flee (the same text as 2.17, where it is clearer that she wishes him absent until a given time), and the mountains could represent her, or they could not. Exum sees that the ambiguity is actually part of the meaning (2005a: 262–3).

in the Song, they feel the impetus to search and are devastated by missed encounters. The lover's quest for his or her beloved in effect becomes the reader's own.

If the reader decides that the Song tells a story, whatever its parameters, there is yet more that keeps the Song's lovers perplexed and interested. In terms of the book's amatory technique, we come here to the third factor, its use of imagery. In the last chapter, it was evident how puzzling or cryptic images exhibited various signs of the grotesque. That fluidity in image, like the Song's display of erotic material, and like its flirtation with narrative, is another site where readers are implicated into the Song's contours.

To return to a 'narrative' moment in the Song, the 'consummation' of 5.1, it is clear that a key role in the ambiguity or suggestiveness of the scene has to be the enticing and confounding nature of the images. In the first place, here, as elsewhere throughout the Song, readers are always confronted with the question, how do we know how the images are to be understood? Do we know that coming into a garden, plucking myrrh, eating honey and drinking wine with milk are to be taken as euphemisms for sex? In an obvious, literalizing alternative, if the identification of the garden and various foodstuffs with the woman's body is denied, a man simply walks into a garden and has a nice meal. If we allow that these elements do represent the woman's body (as we might, since he uses them to describe it in 4.10-15),[62] who is to say that eating, drinking or plucking (אָרָה) need indicate that coitus occurs here? Though they are verbs of consumption, might not the actions to which they refer still be relegated to foreplay, or some other private peculiarity between the lovers of which we are not aware? The images used in the lover's description, and indeed elsewhere in the Song, offer little help in deciding the matter. In 4.10, wine describes her דּוֹדִים, as it does his in 1.2. In 4.11, we see that honey and milk are under the woman's tongue. A long list of spices describes her 'groove' in 4.14. Do drinking, eating and plucking these various items correlate to particular parts of her anatomy or specific sexual activities? Moreover, what do their combinations in 5.1 signify? Is it important for the Song's erotic message that milk and wine are consumed together, for instance?

The 'dream scene' that follows 5.1, which I looked at earlier (5.2-8), is another, perhaps even more confusing example of the Song's weaving of erotic material, image and narrative. There, hands, bolts, doors and myrrh – all arguably parts or products of the lovers' bodies – give a suggestive but incomplete picture of what is happening.[63] Commentators debate the logistics of the scene, as we saw (Fox 1985: 144–6; Keel 1994: 192;

---

62   The woman, of course, also describes herself as a garden in 4.16b.
63   See Exum 1999 for a discussion of *double entendre* in this text.

Murphy 1990: 165, 170–71; Pope 1977: 517–19) and the significance of the imagery for their readings. Scenes like this one prompt important questions about imagery in relation to plot. In what manner or how far should one take the imagery as significant for the Song's presentation of the lovers' experiences? As I asked above, are the various natural and human-made features that are associated with the body to be taken as indicative of what those bodies are experiencing, or do they merely set an alluring scene whose specific details are to remain clouded from the reader's eyes forever?

Nowhere is this question more appropriate than in the case of the body images, which I examined in detail in the last chapter. As Alter observes, sometimes the lines between image and referent are so blurred that it is difficult to see where one begins and the other ends (1985: 193). Lovers and the natural world (or the urban world) are so effectively blended that they are assimilated into each other (see Alter 1985: 194). The temptation with the body images is not so much to make of them a plot as with the 'nuptial texts' I have been discussing above, but to fit them into the Song's context as love poetry. In other words, I too have been creating a narrative in effect – arguably a vague one – and that has been masquerading under the guise of 'love poetry'. How, I have been asking, does such figuration of the body fit into amatory discourse? What do these images mean for the body in love? And if these are grotesque, how does that affect the language of love? But, as I have been arguing, it is not only the lovers who are affected by these oddities. Reader-lovers are too. As Barthes' lover appropriately quips, 'Language is a skin: I rub my language against the other. It is as if I had ... fingers at the tip of my words' (1990a: 73).

This third measure of the Song-as-lover's-ploy to attract its readers, then, is the variance in clarity – or opacity – of the imagery. At times, the text is bold: 'Let him kiss me with the kisses of his mouth' (1.2); at others, it veils its meaning a little: 'With great delight I sat in his shadow and his fruit was sweet to my taste.' At its most enigmatic, the Song's imagery makes one ponder whether it is really expressive of desire at all, as in the four descriptions of the lovers' bodies. The variation of imagery in the Song flirts with innuendo and clarity and thus with readerly understanding. The Song's imagery is compelling, because it is sometimes clear, sometimes confusing, thereby displaying its erotic content openly and concurrently secreting it away.

The Right of Reply

One last issue remains in the investigation of the readers' erotic relationships with the Song, and that is their right of reply. If, as Barthes has observed, language is a skin, that skin prompts a response:

'Every contact, for the lover, raises the question of an answer; the skin is asked to reply' (1990a: 67).

The Song may be a jealous lover, ensuring that it constantly has the attentions of its readers, but it is not unjust. It does seem to allow the right of reply. The intermingling of erotic content, words, images and narrative play allows for the participation of readers, as we have seen. There is yet more, however, in that the Song maybe offers more than readers will take on, or it allows some of its overtures to be resisted. I want to turn here in a slightly different direction, therefore, and return to the Song's erotic content. If the Song is by no means clear about sex as we have seen, even when commentators think it is at its most blatant, the reverse must also be acknowledged: sometimes, the Song may actually suggest what commentators might not wish to acknowledge.

This feature of Song scholarship was the impetus behind Goulder's focus in his commentary (1986: 8), but even he, for example, has limits as to what he will and will not write about. A fairly uncontroversial or unremarkable text (in terms of sexual content), 2.3 and its counterpart in 8.5, illustrates my point. In 2.3, the woman compares her lover to an apple tree, 'As an apple tree among the trees of the wood, so is my love among young men. With great delight I sat in his shadow, and his fruit was sweet to my taste.' In Chapter 1, we saw how Goulder, in the introduction to his commentary (1986: 7), provocatively identified the tree in 8.5 with the lover's genitalia. After that reading, I expected to find a rather explicit explanation of 2.3 in the commentary that follows. Perhaps Goulder might have commented on the lover's priapic prowess (a tree among trees?), and maybe have explicated – or at least alluded to – the 'oral arts' of the woman who sits in the lover's shadow and who finds his fruits sweet to her taste. Instead, however, Goulder's reading of the apple tree's significance in 2.3 is so veiled that it is almost missed: 'the apple forms a suggestive pair to the lily ['singled out for its deep calyx'; 1986: 18], with its fruit often borne in pairs along a rising spur' (1986: 19). The connection is made not between the tree and the mouth, as the text intimates, but the tree and the lily of the previous verse (2.2). Moreover, a comment in the following paragraph seems to contradict Goulder's earlier, quietly uttered suggestion as to the phallic significance of the tree here in 2.3: 'The sweetness of the fruit to her palate suggests that they now kiss' (1986: 19). This, he decides, is what occurs because of the wider context of the verse (2.4-6 and 1.2).[64]

Goulder's reading is not unique. Something prevents him, and other commentators, from being tempted by the apples in 2.3 and 8.5 (compare

---

64 Pope also writes of kissing and intercourse (the reference in 8.5 is cited to support his reading) (1977: 371–2); Murphy the 'delights of love' (1990: 136); Fox of kisses, and also the egalitarian nature of the relationship: here she is in his protection (shade), in 1.3, he was in

Murphy 1990: 132, 136; Fox 1985: 107; Keel 1994: 82, among others). It is not, moreover, the case that only a few ambiguous references might be skirted in Song scholarship, such as these ones in 2.3 and 8.5 and, for example, in 7.10. The Song abounds with references to eating and drinking and is a catalogue of comestibles (see Lavoie 1995).[65] Though Goulder and others have been quite willing to venture into discussing sexuality in the Song, at times somewhat explicitly (even when it involves female genitalia),[66] there remains a definite barrier at the point of what might be considered 'appropriate' discourse about what is taken to be discussable (conventional?) sexual activity.

There are, however, other places to occupy on this spectrum of readerly sensibility. Of these, Boer's pornographic rendering of the Song is a good example. Boer's porn-essay raises the question, how much is too much? A reader is uncomfortably forced to play the voyeur in his reading, and my issue is not so much that he or she must question how comfortable he or she is with reading about explicit sex (pornographic sex being still another issue), but whether the Song has not been taken advantage of quite unfairly. That is, in Boer's reading, the pleasure of the text becomes, as Barthes has referred to it, like the spectator who leaps on stage to hasten the stripper's unveiling (1990b: 11), only I am not so sure, as Barthes stipulates, that the order of the ritual has been respected here. So, it is perhaps the seductive side of the Song that Boer resists. His reading, I think, in effect denies the text its erotic freedom by rushing through foreplay, stripping and *fucking* it before it has had the chance to show a little skin.[67]

---

hers (1985: 108); Keel, the 'tenderness and erotic attention of the lover' (1994: 82); Lavoie that he is '*l'aphrodisiaque*', the lover who, 'loin d'assouvir la faim de sa bien-aimée, lui creuse l'appétit' (1995: 133).

65   A detailed enquiry into its sexual content will eventually have to take these on board and consider them as part of an erotic vocabulary. Boer (1999) is the only exception of which I am aware. Even Lavoie, who promises a discussion of '*tendresse canibalique*' does not take the step.

66   Interestingly, commentators, primarily male to date, seem to be significantly more comfortable with discussing female genitalia in (explicit) detail than male. If the penis is referred to, it will often be called the 'phallus' (e.g. Pope 1977: 517), or treated euphemistically, as in Goulder's discussion of the apple tree, see above, and the 'tusk' of ivory (5.14; 1986: 6). This does not mean that the female genitalia is not also referred to euphemistically – Pope will sometimes use euphemisms ('evermoist receptacle' is one of the most creative; 1977: 617), in addition to the regular, anatomical terms (vagina, vulva). Compare, however, Goulder's and Eslinger's detailed anatomical descriptions of the woman's sexual organ (Goulder 1986: 38; Eslinger 1981: 276–7), which seem to have not the literary text as their context, but the gynaecologist's office.

67   *Pace* Boer: taken to this logical extent, my image becomes one of violation, I realize. The violence may or may not have been anticipated by Boer in his retelling of the Song, but I go there because I feel that his reading does invite the analogy.

It is obvious that I, too, as a reader have 'sensibilities' of my own about the Song's erotic material which make me critical or uncomfortable with how other readers have read it; all readers do. I also have my own ideas about what the Song is and is not trying to say in terms of its erotic content. Thus the manner in which or the degree to which readers *want* to read the erotic content of the Song is also a significant feature of the amatory relationship between Song and reader. The fact that the Song can support readings as varied as Bernard's[68] and Boer's indicates not only that its imagery is opaque and can be read in a variety of ways – that, as a lover, it is quite versatile – but also that there are restrictions (a kind of censorship?) in terms of what can be discussed around the eroticism of the Song. This is extremely significant for its success as a lover.[69]

Boer's work urges the question of whether it is necessary to break through certain barriers (in his case, to 'cross over' into 'pornography') before one can actually discuss what might be seen as the full erotic range of the Song.[70] And in doing so, will it be necessary to take the kind of risks of marginalizing oneself from 'polite' and acceptable academic discourse in our discipline that Boer does?[71] Further, are these the only risks of such a reading? Indeed, reading the Song in any way seems risky: to read it is to replay the book. Readers interpolate themselves into the text's contours as they become personally involved in them, as they are compelled to ask, what happens? Or, what does this mean? But their interpolation is hardly objective; rather, it is deeply personal, affective (*What does this mean for me?*). They might identify with the lovers in the Song, but they also become lovers of it themselves and are subject to the desires and whimsy of the text, which teases them by playing at display and hiding. Moreover, they respond with their own demands and restrictions, resulting in constant dialogue and negotiation between the two. So it is that both lovers (text and reader) may say:

> *I am caught in this contradiction: on the one hand, I believe I know the other better than anyone and triumphantly assert my knowledge to the other (I 'know you – I'm the only one who really knows you'); and on the*

68 Allegorical readings of the Song would provide a fruitful field of enquiry for this topic. In one of his sermons, Bernard of Clairvaux makes a reference to the garden in 5.1 as representative of one of the stages of scriptural history: 'The man who thirsts for God eagerly studies and meditates on the inspired word, knowing that there he is certain to find the one for whom he thirsts. Let the garden, then, represent the plain, unadorned, historical sense of Scripture' (Bernard of Clairvaux 1983: 28 [Serm. 23.2]).

69 See Boer's comments on the relationship between censorship and pornography (1999: 53–4).

70 See also Burrus and Moore's (2003) important discussion in this light.

71 Boer is not uncomfortable with this position (see 1999). Of course, one might also ask – as he doubtless does – if the risk of marginalization from mainstream academic discourse is not such a bad thing.

> *other hand, I am often struck by the obvious fact that the other is*
> *impenetrable, intractable, not to be found; ... Who is the other? I wear*
> *myself out, I shall never know.* (Barthes 1990a: 134; emphases added)

Indeed, to risk replaying the book is to encounter the contours of intimate relationship. In Landy's words, 'we find ourselves spoken there' (1983: 7).

Desire and the Grotesque: Reading the Song of Songs with Kristeva (and Teresa)

Teresa of Avila may have appreciated Barthes' words, above. One gets the impression from reading her that she finds herself in the same contradiction: she does truly come to know the object of her devotion the more ardently she searches; yet this knowledge is never complete. It is always troubled by the distance that remains between the lover who seeks the other. As she has written, 'If the love You have for me, / my God, is like the one I have for You, / tell me, what is holding me back? / Or You, what is keeping You?' (Vogt 1996: 15).

Carole Slade is convinced that the nun knew of this contradiction and explored it especially in her writing on the Song, most notably in her *Meditaciones sobre los Cantares*.[72] In fact, Slade believes that particular text to be a text of *jouissance*, one in which 'the reader experiences the mystical paradox of the loss that produces gain' (1986: 33). Moreover, this is a deeply personal text for Teresa, not just because of the subject matter, but also because of its approach. As Slade observes, 'in Barthes' hermeneutics of bliss, private meaning precedes and undermines collective meaning' (1986: 33). This indicates that Teresa's subjective experience – her cultural, historical, religious, social *and erotic* experience – is essential for making the bridge needed between herself and her lover. The subjective, though, is dangerous to Teresa's confessors, not only because it is female subjectivity that is being expressed here, but because it is also potentially heretical in its de-emphasizing of works over personal faith.[73] One wonders, in fact, if the expression of the personal is also highly suspect because it is affective, not rational. As do other mystics, therefore,

72   Teresa wrote a quasi-exegetical text on the Song of Songs between 1566 and 1577 (Boucher 1999: 1). She was ordered to burn it by one of her confessors in 1580 'since it seemed ... very unorthodox and dangerous for a woman to write about the *Song of Songs*. He was moved by his pious concern that, as St Paul says, women should be silent in God's church' (Boucher 1999: 2, quoting Fr Gracián). Burn it, she obediently did. The text only discusses five verses of the Song (1.1; 1.2; 2.3; 2.4; 2.5). Teresa makes incidental references to the Song in other writings, as in the *Vida*.

73   The controversy over the heresy of illuminism was particularly at issue here. See Slade 1986; Boucher 1999; and Weber 1990 for more information.

Teresa employs certain strategies to cover herself, such as throwing her voice by posing as the Virgin Mary or the Samaritan woman.[74]

This improvisation – or, one might say, vamping[75] – by Teresa is characteristic of the mystical experience. It is suggestive of some of the strategies engaged in order to cope with the vicissitudes of the mystical life, forever on the margins of church authority, forever subject to its censure (with very real consequences for its transgression). The ability to shift the self also prefigures the attempt to locate the identity of the other (as we saw with Certeau), so that the subject-in-love can make the other real. Vamping also suggests, however, a visual quality: a looked-at-ness of the subject who must design or comport herself legitimately so that the expression of her love is palatable to those who hear it. And yet, the singularity of the lonely heart that might be implied here is missing. Barthes writes, quoting Angelus Silesius, that 'the eye by which I see God is the same eye by which he sees me' (Barthes 1990b: 29; Slade 1986: 33). In this quotation, Slade observes a mutuality[76] here, a transformative *blending* of the lover with the object of her search, not unlike the loss-and-replacement of the other by the mystical subject that Certeau describes.

How unsurprising that the eye surfaces again; this eye that 'perforates the pictorial sky and judges us';[77] this eye that glances *and* gazes, but does not see; this eye that forms the axis of the lovers' visual relationship in the Song; this eye that alarms but entices. Indeed, Teresa and her lover *speak out of their eyes*. As we saw, though, they move away from the literal confines of the gaze and the word to a merging, a knowledge of each other that is at the heart of the erotic.[78] Fusion of this nature requires a special (secret) language; it also requires avenues for its displacement, or failure, so that in deferral, the subject keeps seeking/speaking. This is the 'speaking otherly' of which I wrote earlier: for the lovers in the Song, it is the grotesque rendering of the body wherein the subject-in-love finds a place from which to speak.

74   Other such strategies were discussed in Ch. 3. See Slade 1986 and Boucher 1999 for more discussion.

75   I am using the word in its archaic sense, to indicate improvisation on the stage or in music. The Blessed Virgin Mary and the Samaritan woman are probably Scripture's two least likely vamps in the sexual sense.

76   In this instance, she is writing of the blending of the lover and the beloved, but she may also be implying a gender mutuality, since this is the spirit in which she begins her article (1986).

77   Certeau (1992a: 54) observed this of the Bosch paintings, in an effort to show the incorporation of the viewer into the midst of the art.

78   I am making a leap here, from Slade's observations on the *Meditaciones* to Teresa's other writing on the Song as part of the *Vida*, discussed at the end of Ch. 3. My interpretive assumption of Teresa's texts (and Slade's reading) is that there is a commonality of *jouissance* that pervades her writing on the Song, wherever it appears. Given the repetition of themes in Teresa's use/treatment of the book, this is a reasonable assumption to make.

Kristeva on Love

It remains to explore further how it is that the grotesque comes to be bedded with the erotic with apparent ease, and indeed, how both seem to thrive so well in each other's company. We might also ask what this situation tells us about the context of amatory discourse in which it occurs, especially as it is manifested in the Song. Here, we come full circle to the questions I asked at the beginning of this book. To ask them is in the final analysis to ask about love and desire, the central themes of the Song. It is also, however, to return to the matter of subjectivity, most notably, that of the subject-in-love.

In order to interrogate these issues, I shall draw, in a fairly general way, on Kristeva's systematization of love.[79] Kristeva essentially takes up Barthes' interests in what happens at the 'edge of language', which he explores in part in his work in *Pleasure of the Text*. Lechte explains that unreadable or opaque texts (those which defy understanding, for the pleasure of the text is ultimately the pleasure of understanding) are 'unreservedly texts of *jouissance*', and it is these with which Kristeva is concerned in her exploration of the arts, particularly her writing on the avante-garde (Lechte 1990: 67). The latter is for Kristeva an ideal site of enquiry for exploring the semiotic realm; this in turn is the ideal locus for the language of love.

In order to explore Kristeva's work on love, it is useful to return briefly to her understanding of the abject, discussed in Chapter 2. As we saw, the abject is an essential part of Kristeva's conceptualization of the semiotic, a rough (but not identical) correspondent to the Lacanian Imaginary, the pre-symbolic (pre-Oedipal) state. In the semiotic realm, we find the child in undifferentiated union with the mother. There is yet no sense of individuality or identity, but this ideal state can never remain because the child will eventually develop consciousness and realize it is a separate being from its mother. Chaotic drives (which comprise the *chora* in Kristeva's system) orient the child towards separation from the mother and entry into the realm of the symbolic. The abject is that which marks the rejection of the mother, that which has to be discarded or rejected in order for the separation so necessary to the creation of the subject to occur. It is not a final banishment of the rejected elements, but one which constantly threatens the cohesion of the subject, even once the subject is fully formed. So, what is abjected always remains to be abjected, since

---

79   Kristeva's work is not as broad a theoretical jump from Barthes' as it might first appear. Certainly, the important contribution of Barthes to the field of semiotics was influential in Kristeva's earlier work; in John Lechte's view, he is her 'Parisian Mother' (1990: 66). In Barthes' later 'theorizing' of amatory discourse, however, there are also important correspondences which make Kristeva's work on love quite a suitable way to follow my work with Barthes and his erotics of reading. See also Kristeva 1997 for more on Barthes.

reminders of this primary process constantly penetrate the symbolic in three areas: food, waste and sex (Kristeva 1982: 2–3).

In this analysis, that which is abjected has a counterpart in the 'sublime ideal'. The latter is an image which the child creates as a substitute for the mother who is lost. As subjectivity is not fully formed, this image of an 'other' is at the same time an image of the self. In this way, the idealized other (that is, the idealized self) also marks the point of primary narcissism. But rather than seeing narcissism as pathological, Kristeva's view of it is intensely positive. Narcissism is the first step towards the ability to love others. It is, in a manner of speaking, a trial run at love. It is not the narcissism that ultimately effects love, though: a narcissistic person would not be capable of healthy love. Rather, it is the conceptualization of a third element, an Other, that sets the amatory system going. This Other makes it possible for the subject to recognize someone who is like herself; in other words, not the mother, and not the ideal set up in place of her, but an Other who has traversed the same ground on the road to subjectivity. But love never forgets its origins: the idealized other never fully replaces the mother. One pole always leads back to the other as neither is fully satisfactory. Instead of constantly oscillating between these two poles, however, love actually unifies them. It allows them to be held together in a state of tension. We might, in fact, say that the tension is necessary for love to exist. And, as Kristeva quips, love is imperative for the life of the subject: 'If it is not in love, it is dead' (1987: 15).

The Song of Songs plays an important part in the development of Kristeva's history of love (1987: 83–100). First and foremost, she identifies the Song as love poetry, and, as such, sees that it reflects the conflicted nature of love that she seeks to explicate. In the Song, Kristeva observes a 'compositional disorder' that consists of structured and unstructured elements and a polyvalence of meaning. Despite this, however, a clear amatory message emerges (1987: 92). Kristeva also locates opposing themes of presence and absence, order and disorder, and incarnation and ecstasy. As part of amatory discourse, these opposites are able to be maintained in tension without the need for resolution – 'a basic separation that nevertheless unites' (1987: 95). What readers experience in the Song is a poem whose terms remain fundamentally opposed, in which meaning is left undecided, though the greater text is unified through the binding effects of love. Consequently, this text remains open and capable of constant renewal.

Love and a Little Madness: Kristeva and the Song of Songs
It follows from Kristeva's analysis that amatory discourse (love poetry), if it is at all revelatory of love (and Kristeva argues it is), would exhibit the

tension between abjection and desire that Kristeva has elucidated. That is, when two people express desire for each other, or when readers exhibit desires for the Song (and vice versa), one would expect the conflict to be present. In short: we might say that love is by necessity conflicted, and by extension, so is its discourse. In terms of the Song, what might this mean? I suggest that it provides a way to complete the enquiry into reading that Song that I began above. It also sheds more light on the Song's specific manifestation of its central theme of desire, depicted through the relationship of the two lovers in the book. These we might see as sites of conflict which must remain as such – in text and commentary – if the Song is to relate its 'love story' effectively.

This book has not, except in passing, asked the question, do the lovers love each other? As I noted, such feelings are usually taken for granted about them, as indeed it is usually taken for granted that the Song is love poetry (what else could it be?). The difficulty has been how to fit the (grotesque) descriptions of the body into the language of love, for they seem to reveal that for the lovers, the other's body prompts a range of contradictory possibilities, among them that it unsettles, provokes laughter or instils fear. Of course, the view that this is a problem for love poetry could merely be motivated by a naïve and idealistic view of love that has specific ideas about what might be appropriate representation of the body in amatory discourse. Perhaps, but it seems that this would be a very limited way of viewing the situation. Kristeva's perception of love fills out the picture better, so that we might see that the body as problem is actually critical for the maintenance of love.

The grotesque does not complicate the lovers' desires for each other, though it may appear to, nor does it negate them. It is, by contrast, a necessary and natural part of their survival. Love is a conflictual site, where in the first instance, the lover must encounter the conflict of his or her own self, that which exists between what is abjected and what is desired. In imposing the signs of the abject on each other's bodies, the lovers replay the psychic drama of identity formation. In other words, in seeing the abject on the other, the lover replays love's origins, abjecting what must be thrown away and desiring that which cannot be attained, and in the process, constantly reaffirming the place in this process for a third party, that which has been created solely for the Other. It should, moreover, come as no surprise that that which is to be abjected by the lovers in the Song is written on the body, for, as in Kristeva's conceptualization, the three loci of abjection are somatic and material: food, waste, sex. Additionally, the separation that abjection facilitates is a material one: mother and child are wrenched apart. Such replay of the creation of the subject, it should be noted, will have specific effects on the lovers. In order for the abject to work, it must repulse, or evince enough strength of feeling so that that which needs to be pushed away can be. So, in terms of the lovers' erotic relationship, the presence and subsequent denial of the abjected on the other's body manifests a certain ambivalence in the lovers that continually reminds them of love's origins (and its newly created room for the Other), yet also of love's imperfectability, since what is really desired can never be.

In terms of the greater context of the Song of Songs text and the body imagery in it, it is possible to draw some further conclusions. With the benefit of Kristeva's work, we can say that in order to ensure the effectiveness of love poetry, the grotesque and the erotic (of which desire is the central part) both ensure that the other thrives: the grotesque cannot exist without the urge to make it otherwise (the grotesque body cannot exist without the lover's longing to see perfection and the ideal) and desire would expire if not continually threatened by its corruption (the lovers' desires would be effaced if allowed to be consummated and completed). The grotesquerie of the body keeps desire in the Song alive: it contains the endless complications and foreclosures of desire that ensure that the Song of Songs works as a text of *jouissance*.

It is also possible to turn these insights onto the readers. Above, I spent a considerable space looking into the nature of the relationship between the Song, as embodied text, and the lovers. This was an effort to find some way of speaking about what I perceive to be a unique relationship between this one biblical text and its long string of lovers (interpreters). At the textual level, I located several features – in keeping with my metaphor, I described them as amatory techniques – which it seemed worked to entangle readers (Kristeva's conceptualization of the Song as compositionally disordered would fit well into this analysis). Again, in keeping with the metaphor, it seemed that these kept readers interested, made them become involved in the text's intricacies, yet also made them keep their distance. Though I have been arguing in this book that it is the body imagery in the Song which might be viewed as grotesque, I also made the suggestion that these textual features, by virtue of their ability to manipulate the reader, might also, after a fashion, be seen as grotesque.

Textual grotesquerie functions in much the same way as the grotesquerie imposed on the lovers' bodies. The grotesque interrupts and threatens the amatory relation between readers and text, but is also vital in the continuance of it. Readers are startled and frustrated by the Song's incongruities. The Song's structure and lyric/narrative mix repel readers, disallowing the ultimate readerly pleasure – making sense of or understanding the text. Semantic play and abnormalities frustrate the process too, especially the academic enterprise: interpreters are subject to distraction from their erotic encounters when they must pause and turn to commentators or dictionary editors for an explanation. Even the Song's sexual content, a sure thing for lighting one's fires, is reduced to a dull flicker by the Song's refusal to be clear about what happens to whom and when. Yet, as we saw above, the Song is not entirely opaque, for who would be interested in it if it did not tease? The textual features I mentioned above are also compelling enough to keep readers interested and to secure their involvement. Plot, imagery and sexual content require readerly involvement for their existence. The grotesque fulfils its dual role of repulsion and attraction quite adeptly here in the Song too, seen nowhere more clearly than with the Song's major grotesque feature, the body imagery. It could be argued, then, that the ultimate site in the Song for fostering readerly inquisitiveness and participation is that occupied by the body. This same energy that the Song secures from its readers suggests, however, that there is more to their interests than a curiosity as to the meaning of the pictures. The grotesquerie of the body must be covered up, interpreted away, because it is ultimately threatening; it repels.

Ultimately, the force and effectiveness of the grotesque body imagery in the Song has to be attributed to the fact that it involves intensely intimate issues for readers. The presence of this intimacy is caused by the body (not the textual corpus, but the human form) which is displayed as the object of sexual desire. This is the same canvas on which all readers, at some time or another, are displayed for their lovers and on which their lovers view them. In this way, too, then, the reader–text relationship can be seen to replay the psychic drama that I described above with respect to the lovers in the Song. I suggest that the dual role played by the grotesque when readers encounter the Song, that is, its compelling nature and its repulsive aspects, are mirrors of the earliest desires in the constitution of readers as subjects.

The Song's body, as Kristeva's work elucidates, is a site of psychic fascination as it contains both the signs of order (the symbolic) and the seeds of the ideal/abject relation (visible in the semiotic). It is the reader's own *morada*, the grounds wherein readers find a place to speak their own subjectivity as lovers. As an 'unreserved text of jouissance' (Lechte 1990: 67), moreover, the Song is especially an ideal locus for interrogating the revolutionary power of the semiotic. Yet, we cannot assert that it is victorious in its revolution. Kristeva's system, notably her triumphing of the semiotic, has been the subject of considerable discussion and dispute.[80] That critical response cautions that we should at the very least be willing to see the semiotic as an intermediate locus, a place of potential, rather than posit it as a real (and effective) opposite of the oppressive power of the symbolic. Indeed, the latter is always needed to constitute the former, to allow it 'its own ludic space' (Russo 1994: 37). Let us, therefore, say this

---

80   See especially Russo's discussion and her reconciliation of the problem (1994: 37–8, 53–73).

of the Song: reading it is bittersweet. It is a disquieting, unsettling, experience and at the same time entry into a peaceable kingdom.

Shall I Compare Thee to a Gargantua? Or a Pantagruel?

I am reluctant to end the discussion here. If lovers negotiate the disquieting and the peaceable, and if, furthermore, this negotiation is necessary to their love, what more can be said of the individual in the midst of love, in terms of agency and, with a nod to Teresa, her or his ability to bridge the gap between the self and the object of devotion? As we saw above, it is particularly the woman's experience in the book that seems to be the target of such questions.[81] Gender issues, it seems, do not 'go away' just because one can establish their mutability and openness to interpretation or readerly manipulation.[82] I begin to suspect, however, that they point to larger matters, as I indicated earlier, such as what bearing the evaluation of gender has on the subjectivity of the lovers – and readers.

Exum's comments notwithstanding (2005a: 25), I find myself wishing we knew more of this woman. How does she fare when she hears her lover's poems? What does she mean in her retort to the daughters of Jerusalem? Do we know for certain that she is able to view herself in her own frame, instead of in another's? How does she cope with the indeterminacy of 'promiscuous and excessive openings and foreclosures of (literary) desire'?[83]

Whereas the text may not address these matters conclusively enough to satisfy all readers, I venture that they might be explored intertextually, in the story of Anna Swan. Anna was a Nova Scotian giant, who measured almost eight feet at her full height, and who lived much of her life as a transplanted Canadian in the United States, working for P.T. Barnum. Anna is an historical personage, but Susan Swan (a distant relative?)[84] has recast her story in fictional form in her novel *The Biggest Modern Woman*

---

81 A particular issue that the woman faces, for example, is that though the man is ever present in his descriptions, he has a curious habit of being ever-absent when he is being sought. The same seems to be true for Teresa, who claims that God is ultimately responsible for making the link between them. That both seekers are women has not escaped my notice; I will return to this below.

82 To be sure, these questions also reflect my own interests. For me as a reader, it is the woman's position that I keep returning to, probably in part because of my own gender, but also because of sheer stubbornness. As I noted above, it is not the man's autonomy as a lover that is usually questioned by readers of the Song, but the woman's.

83 O'Neill 1984: 195; parentheses added.

84 Swan says that the connections are difficult to make, from both families' perspectives, but that there are some clues to indicate some degree of relationship (2001: preface).

of the World.[85] Far distant literary cousins – Anna and the woman in the Song – it might be that both giants have something to say to each other of life, gender and love.

Two aspects of the novel interest me in this light. One is the exchange that takes place between Anna and her fiancé, Kentucky giant Captain Martin van Buren Bates, during a performance orchestrated by Barnum. (The couple seems destined to depict much of their courtship and eventual marriage on stage.) The performance is a hymeneal, and it is co-written by Anna and Martin. The other aspect of interest is the spieling undertaken by Anna as part of her employment. This is set within the broader narrative of her life, in which Swan plays with history and fantasy as a means of problematizing the genre of life writing and exploring female subjectivity.[86]

Spieling is the stuff of circus life. Anna entertains the crowds with several versions of her life, often elaborating or altering the scripts as she goes along. In so doing, she distinguishes herself as more than just an object to be looked at: she is actually a creator of the story in which she so prominently figures, sometimes to the consternation of Ingalls, who manages the performances. Nevertheless, her true 'story' is kept under wraps to a certain extent: the audience is never sure exactly what is historically verifiable and what is not. This, to be sure, is part of the attraction, since it blends reality with the fantastic and it plays on viewers' stereotypes and fears. Anna's person, then, is split in a variety of ways for her audience and for readers. It is confounded by the spieling, which is itself embedded in Swan's *mélange* of fact and magical realism. Who, indeed, is the real Anna?[87]

There is also the matter of how Anna is viewed by others in the story, especially those who should know her intimately, such as her lover or her fiancé/spouse. In fact, Swan's book ends intriguingly: after Anna's final words that bear witness to how hard it is to get the measure of the woman, the remaining major characters pen short statements or reflections about

---

85   Swan says that she is guided by the major details of Anna's life, but allows these facts to be 'in the service of the marvelous' (2001: preface). (Note: For clarity, when referring to the author, 'Swan' will be used; the character in Swan's book will be called by her first name.)

86   See especially Heffernan 1992.

87   A rather nice illustration of this dynamic exists in *real life*, where two museums about Anna's life compete in a small town in rural Nova Scotia, Tatamagouche. One is managed by a relative of Swan's, and is purported to have authentic family memorabilia. The other, housed in the town's cultural centre (and the recipient of some government funding), appears to be much more commercialized. It has authentic artifacts of the giant's life, but was represented to me as being 'much more Disney' in its approach. Indeed, a perusal of the centre's website has a virtual museum that visitors can tour, as well as games that can be played (http://www.sunrisetrail.ca/places/Fraser.htm). I gathered from an associate of the former with whom I spoke that there was some 'competition' between the two museums over who might be best representing Anna.

the figure. So it is that Swan is able to render problematic the ability for any one person to really know another, even if that other happens to be in love with her.

A case in point is Martin's tribute to his fiancée during 'Shipboard Romance (from the Route Book of Hiriam Percival Ingalls). The tribute is extensive and it exhibits his unique philosophy, which is reproduced in full in his pamphlet, *Species Development, or a Tract towards Continual Anatomical Wonders*. Based loosely on Darwin's *Origin of the Species*, Martin's tract argues for the fulfilment of the human species as a race of giants, the 'Americanus'. 'Discovering' Anna on board a ship, he begins to court her. Later, he has the ship's doctor examine her (while he watches through a peephole) to confirm her ability to be the vehicle to bear this race. Moreover, his treatise is overwritten with the themes of manifest destiny; Anna will not only bring humankind to fruition (with his help), but, representing Canada, will bring America to its mastery of the continent. He exclaims:

> I will speak my will to Anna
> that she will lie down
> and tip south her giant womb
> all by herself
> she is the giantess next door
> her name shall be
> my all American girl
> ...
>
> Your eyes are like the future
> gazing down on me.
> Your head is the far North
> your neck – the long wolf's throat to the sea
> the Near North is your shoulder
> draped with trade staples and immigrants
> who will learn to boast
> of your bitter winds and thousands
> of unproductive acres
> your breasts are cod canneries
> a continental refuge
> for America's old head
> your belly is a topped up
> basin
> fenced in by fir
> and river valleys ... (Swan 2001: 180–82)

The description of Anna's body, of course, is startlingly similar to the descriptions in the Song.[88] Here in the novel, though, Anna has immediate right of reply:

> What? Bury my polar cap
> in your southern
> past and thaw my icy
> tongue in your adolescent
> fountains!
>
> I do not want to spring up
> chewing April strawberries
> and June melons but who needs
> to be scourged by your bulk?
>
> I'll pull the continent
> about me to stop you
> from making more of yourself –
> The Wisconsin could freeze
> your grasping hand up my skirts
> before you respect my rights
> (let alone learn to acknowledge them).
>
> I'll be damned, Martin
> if I'll be crammed
> on the seat of your imperial fantasy,
> The world knows
> we have an eternal engagement –
> but I'm not a giantess
> who gets laid
> for one or two silly visions.
> Such is the heart of your fresh-water virgin,
> Sons of America. (Swan 2001: 183)

Christopher Gittings argues that '[t]he hymeneal that Anna co-writes as a counter-discourse to American imperialism is a self-reflexive system of meaning which she creates in an attempt to take control of, and order her fragmented life by subverting the metanarrative of manifest destiny: in short, it is a metafiction' (1994: 87). I would add that Anna's fragmentary life, evident in her displacement from home and family and the degree of peripatetic existence imposed upon her as a performer, is augmented by the fracture of her body by grotesque themes and images. Martin is a chief proponent of these. They are, however, also evident in the more

---

88 Steenman-Marcusse has also noticed the parallel (2002: 185). Interestingly, she calls Martin's version a parody of the Song of Songs, seemingly basing her evaluation not on the similarity of ways the bodies are figured, but on the role of the land in the poems.

fantastical details of Anna's life supplied by Swan, such as the rain shower that falls on passersby when Anna's waters break, or the fact that at another time, the onset of menstruation is influential enough to bring the entire female population of Seville to the same point.

This movement in the book between the fictional and the purportedly historical, and the (sometimes fractured) bodily figurations of the giants as compared with the 'normals', is key to the establishment and maintenance of Anna's subjectivity. So, too, is the variability of the narrative that Swan constructs, along with its framing against metanarratives such as manifest destiny. It is not, however, at the edge of either spectrum (fiction/history or giant/normal) or in the narrow confines of 'historical truth' that Anna is able to discover or assert herself. It is at times in the small spaces between them. Even so, her final words are ones of some resignation and despair: 'I was born to be measured and I do not fit in anywhere' (Swan 2001: 332). In the midst of this life, however, Anna does manage to find love, together with some degree of sexual satisfaction.[89] She also becomes wealthy and ends her career by being in a position to determine her own fate. Compared to where she started, these are giant steps indeed.

I do not argue that there is an exact replication of the lovers' story in the Song here in *The Biggest Modern Woman of the World*. Yet, I am provoked by the strategies that Anna employs to create and maintain a sense of her self. What is more to the point, hers is a self in the process of seeking, and finding, love. These strategies involve Anna's narrative journey, as well as the layerings of story and history that concurrently hide and display her. They are also performative: Anna dresses the part; she acts in skits; and, like Teresa, she throws her voice. If the Song of Songs is to be read at all as the story of the subject-in-love, might we not perceive a similar undertaking here for her in its poetic contours? In the midst of the lovers' dialogue, the seeking and (not) finding, the negotiation of the interference of outsiders, and the lover's voice that asserts itself on her body, she *is*. How is she? She is something of the performer, the woman who dares, symbolically, to launch herself into the air, to cast about for her lover, to display her body for his – and our – inspection. She is the subject who entertains 'provisional, even uncomfortable coalitions of bodies' (Russo 1994: 179), even coalitions *on* the body, in order to reject the possibility that every body might be kept in its place (Russo 1994: 179). She is the subject who speaks volumes – in another's words. She is the subject who risks an encounter with the other, so that she might live.

As Russo, Miles and others have indicated, however, these risks are

---

89   Ironically, despite his grand aims for peopling the future race of Americans, Martin's 'small nub of purple' is not up to the task (Swan 2001: 209). Anna's determination to teach him how to pleasure her, and eventually to seek sexual intimacy elsewhere, mark her at various points on her journey towards creating a sexual identity for herself.

mortal. Until now, the only negative moment some critics have identified in the Song[90] is the reference to death in 8.6.[91] Even here, the meaning inferred by critics is usually a positive one: despite physical death, love persists. But if the Song accurately depicts the love 'story' of two people whose passion for each other implicates them fully and threatens to consume them, there must also be the possibility of yet another kind of death, visible, to be sure, in the *petites morts* of sexual love, but more broadly understood as death of the self as it struggles to configure itself in relation to the other.[92] Desire, in other words, involves tensions and inconsistencies – darker moments, times of doubt, loss of drive, the quest for possession, envy, perhaps even repulsion, if only fleeting. It could be that the grotesque figuring of the object of desire (for both lovers) is a signal of just such an aspect of their relationship. It could also be that the experience of the grotesque in relation to one's own body – heard, accepted, performed – signals those risks, yet also opens up vast possibilities. What is more, one needs these tensions and inconsistencies in order fully to live: 'if it is not in love, it is dead' (Kristeva 1987: 15).

In a way, then, Teresa, Anna and the woman in the Song teach us that gender is not the issue. Or, perhaps to state this more accurately, we might say that they teach us that the contention over gender politics in the Song cannot be allowed to remain *the* issue, in part because it may never be settled to the satisfaction of any one reader, and in another, because the contention seems to point to other matters. Unequivocally, I do not mean by this observation that in the Song gender does not matter. It does. Gender issues cannot be overcome or ignored: for instance, the fact that the man dominates in his descriptions of the woman is inescapable. My question is more concerned with what about it matters. What is troubled by gender-issues? Is it the woman's liberty; the man's social and cultural autonomy; the reader's sensibilities; the feminist reader's demands? In short: is it our expectations as readers? Undoubtedly it is. But it is also more than this. In both lovers, we are able to see the shifting, voluble self as it encounters the other's gaze, as it founds in the other a place to speak, as it worries over the other's distance. This self – male or female, lover or other – offers reflections on various parts of the process of becoming the subject who loves. Gender differences, however we come to interpret

90   As I noted in my discussion of 5.10-16 in Ch. 3, the beating and stripping of the woman in 5.7 is frequently excused or ignored. See Ch. 3, n. 77 for bibliography. Fontaine's (2004) recent musings on how to read this text are also important here.

91   To call death a 'negative moment' is, of course, an oversimplification. See Landy's adept analysis of the love/death opposition (interrelation) (1983: 113–33). Linafelt's discussion of this text is also insightful (2002).

92   Is the other also at risk? Undoubtedly. See discussion of Certeau and Barthes, esp. in Ch. 3. Also see Linafelt's provocative suggestion that the deity might also be at risk in eros (2002).

them, seem a tool to that effect. The woman's place in the toolbox is both problematized by and a crucial component of that dynamic. Radically, the subject-in-love must become the woman in the Song. She (or he) must be a spectacle by her (or his) own choosing; she (or he) must be turned into an autonomous, engaged subject, in order to love and live.

CONCLUSION

This book has been following a lengthy path. It began with my curiosity about the strangeness of the body images in the Song of Songs. It followed them through some of the history of their interpretation to discover that they have been, and continue to be, difficult for many interpreters. In an attempt to explore the problem, I focused in on what seemed to be a quiet admission in many of these works, that the images appear grotesque. I tried the grotesque out as a heuristic for reading the imagery, not to serve as an exclusive or final meaning for them, but as an experiment. What happens, I asked, when the viewer's lens is focused slightly differently, or manipulated in an alternative direction? The question had implications not just for how the images could be interpreted, but for the Song's broader context of a relationship between two people.

Those implications were the subject of my final chapter. There, I brought together several ideas about the relationship of the lovers, the impact of the grotesque in their midst, and the nature of readers' involvement with the Song. All of these represent the ultimate directions of a grotesque reading, which is to try to understand, via the imagery, what might be learned about the Song's language of love. As it turns out, it also prompted me to ask about love *for* the book, because interaction with the imagery and with the relationship of the lovers strongly and deeply implicates the reader. Since that chapter in effect sought to begin the process of identifying implications for my reading, here I will briefly continue that path and also point to some future directions for approaches of this type. More importantly, there remains some 'unfinished business' over the matter of the subjectivity of readings of this nature.

'Am I ... are we ... Falling in Love (with the Song of Songs)?'

One could never tell another how to love. Kristeva's system of love, if it is intended to be prescriptive at all, is that way only as a psychoanalytic cure, an indicator of a right relation between analyst and analysand (1987:

372–83). Does it prescribe a right way to read the Song? In the sense that a right reading indicates the existence of a single, correct interpretation, the answer must be no. Does it suggest itself as a model for 'real relationships', that is, those outside the analytical relationship? Again, no: at least, the author makes no initial claims to this effect.[1] Kristeva's model, however, along with Barthes' insights, does indicate something of an innovation for reading the Song, and their combination might be taken as a prescription for a reading that is liberatory and at the same time that allows love its complexity, danger and allure – for the Song's world and the reader's. Moreover, with Barthes, we might have a deeper understanding of what goes on between reader and text that makes the images such a stumbling-block in the first place. Then, Kristeva provides a key that both accounts for the lovers' apparently conflicted treatment of each other, and for the ambivalence that the readerly relationship seems to present. Kristeva motions towards the grotesque and embraces it, and reading with her, readers of the Song may do the same; yet they may still ponder, and experience, love.

If Kristeva's prescription is written for the analytical relationship, though, does that mean that it is still useful in a reading relationship such as mine?[2] Since how a person loves is unique to him or her, it stands to reason that Kristeva's model would have to be tailored to the individual under analysis. Yet, the vision offered in 'Holy Madness' is a singular one, and it is marked, not unexpectedly, by a particular ideological perspective. That perspective is heterosexist and monological in its acceptance of the monotheistic hierarchy that is integral to the tradition(s) served by the Song. Kristeva's interpretation is perhaps unsurprising, given the Song's subject matter and its long history of allegorical interpretation, yet it casts a shadow on her euphoric celebration of the woman in the Song as 'sovereign before her loved one' (1987: 99). It also casts aspersions on the usefulness of the Song for every and all types of lovers. As I indicated in the last chapter, I do value the insight that Kristeva brings to my study. These complications, though, prompt me to ask whether Teresa of Avila's authorizations of her own 'private meaning' (Slade 1986: 33) as authentic renderings of the Song are crucial here. Indeed, what more might be said of the role of the subjective in determining the Song's message? It seems to me that this is an especially pertinent question if that subject is a critical reader, arguing for insertion of the grotesque into the book's midst.

---

1 Of course, the collections of these 'tales' into one study, framed as it is against the backdrop of the psychoanalytical relationship, clearly imply that Kristeva hopes her work will have relevance not only to the analytical relationship, but beyond it. The message in this history of love is that the issues she identifies are to a degree disparate from case to case, yet still universal.

2 Is, for instance, my reading symptomatic of a wrong relation? Does it need to be fixing in the terms that Kristeva prescribes?

So, Three Women Walk into a Bar, Right? ...

There's a sixteenth-century mystic and lover – of God; there's Anna Swan, celebrated Nova Scotian giant and circus-performer; and there's a biblical scholar. (Actually, she came by herself, but got swept up with the others because of those swinging doors that they sometimes put in bars.)

It may seem an odd diversion at this stage, but I have been wondering what some of my reading companions in this book might say to each other if they ever met. The source of my wondering is the realization that personal interest and ... well ... *personality* have a significant amount of influence in what biblical scholars choose to read, and how they go about that reading. Clearly, too, these matters impact the final results of one's engagement with the text and are open to the responses and reactions of other readers. In fact, two of the very first readers of this manuscript once remarked to me, as they were commenting on my remarks about other readers, that my own grotesque interpretation might have a thing or two to say about me, too. By this they meant, I assume, that by displaying an interest in the grotesque, and in reading for the themes that it allows, I was divulging something that was inherently personal, and able to be critiqued for being just as 'revealing' as the other readers' reflections on which I had been commenting. In other words, my reading might open me up to the same objections that I was making about previous work on the Song, only they would occupy another space in the spectrum.

I have been thinking about that observation a great deal. At first, they were more irrational, 'Oh-hell-what-have-I-written???' kinds of thoughts, but these have been tempered by more sedate musings over the years about subjective involvement in reading and writing on biblical texts. Indeed, how is the self represented in readings of the Bible, and what should be made of other readers' interpretations of that self? To engage with these matters now is, in a way, a bastardization of what cultural critics of the Bible – of the Sugirtharajah, Segovia kind – advocate. That is, it is not an acknowledgement of my social or cultural location before I read, but a retrospective glance once I've been there.

It is necessary that the glance be retrospective, because it was important first to see how reading the imagery – especially with the grotesque – incorporates the reader in its midst. My claim all along has been that one's recognition of and reaction to the grotesque is inherently subjective. What, therefore, should be said of my own subject (if anything) at this stage of the reading? Though the temptation to try to control the responses of other readers is a strong one – to assure them that resistant readers of the Song are honest readers too, for instance – in many ways the judgement of what a particular interpretation might convey is not up to its author. In other words, to add a series of subjective statements here might just add another layer of interpretive text to negotiate for other readers, rather than providing any clear recipe for the conveyance of meaning. However, these matters also raise a more important one at this juncture, which is how does one begin to write about a topic that clearly intersects with the personal, in a way that acknowledges that intersection, but at the same time remains critically focused and rigorous?

Autobiographical theory wrestles with such questions and it has been used to some good effect in biblical studies. There is no need to delve fully into that theoretical body here, but a few summary statements facilitate my ruminations on the subjective. Originally developed to cope with the genre of autobiography, the theory has morphed to be used in conjunction with a variety of texts because it problematizes the construction of the writing/reading subject and the indeterminacy of life-history. It also provides some vocabulary and method for the interpolation of the self (selves?) into the text(s) under scrutiny. In the discipline of biblical studies, autobiographical writing has provided one way of dealing with scholars' reluctance to acknowledge the role of the subjective in their study of the Bible; it has also helped to break down some hegemonic reading practices that insist on a 'right' and historically accurate interpretation of a given biblical text. For now, the discipline as a collective still seems to be feeling its way into this space.[3] So far, there has been quite a range of use of the personal voice (from the inclusion of biographical details, to the fictions of the self, to ghostwriting the stories of others).[4]

Provocative in particular is Brenner's recent reading of the Shulammite in her collection entitled, *I Am. . ..: Biblical Women Tell their Own Stories*. It is an exploration of the use of personal voice in the field by scholars of the Bible, especially by extending it to serve as a means of elaborating the unwritten lives of women in the Hebrew texts. (In this way, Brenner plays with her own identity as it comes into contact with or takes on that of some of the women she examines.) Biblicists have debated the usefulness of the critical autobiographical 'I' in the study of the Bible, and this mode of reading is not everyone's cup of tea, especially with the bold confessions and self-revelations that come with it. I don't propose to review those issues here. I mention Brenner specifically, however, because she experiments with the matter of the fictionalizing of the autobiographical subject – something that we have seen before with reference to the story of Anna Swan – and in her book, boldly tries it out on the woman in the Song. Brenner's book, and especially the chapter on the Song, wrestles with how

---

3   See the excellent responses of Runions and Aichele in Black (ed.) 2006, for example, as indications of the successes and failings of this type of approach.

4   A full bibliography is available in my introduction to a volume of autobiographical/ cultural-critical readings of the Bible (Black [ed.] 2006). See also my own article therein (Black 2006), which specifically deals with the Song of Songs.

we come to tell such important stories when there is little historical frame
of reference for them.

A suggestion for a solution comes from outside the canon, perhaps.
Noting the oddity that Anna Swan is much less known in history than her
male counterpart, Angus McAskill, Conny Steenman-Marcusse avers that
readers need to help to construct her story by supplying those of other
female giants to fill in the picture and better understand her. The problem
is, there aren't any; hence Swan's solution to involve fiction in the process,
especially to push the limits of history. And so, if we are to supply other
stories to fill out that of the potentially historical, but mostly fictional,
woman in the Song, whose stories would we choose? The woman of
Shunem? The Queen of Sheba?[5] Or, given the woman's untraceability, our
own stories? Consequently, I find myself asking: Anna/ 'the Shulammite' /
the grotesque reader of the Song of Songs – whose story is this, now?

*'Do you come here often?' Anna asked. Lately she'd been feeling braver
about making the first move in these kinds of social situations. It wasn't
exactly that she wanted to 'pick up' (such a crude, crude world these days),
just that she was tired of waiting to be approached with curious questions,
the inevitable result of being the elephant in the room (almost literally). The
woman with the wimple and sandals didn't seem as though she'd be the type
to point and laugh, but Anna has thought that about others before. She has
also thought that seven-foot giants should be equipped to be good lovers –
but that's another story. The other woman, the one with the dark hair and
glasses, didn't give out such clear indications of how she might respond.*

*Both answered evasively. Wimple muttered something about looking for a
lost friend, but really she seemed to be drinking herself, rather heavily, into
forgetting something; Glasses (sunglasses, by the way) tried to capitalize on
that answer, but lamely finished with an excuse about 'research'. She was on
her third glass too, Anna noticed. Clearly the conversation wasn't going
anywhere.*

*Wimple tried next. 'I wish people wouldn't be so fucking – sorry, bloody –
demonstrative in public places', she said looking askance at the couple at the
next table. 'They are making such a disgusting spectacle of themselves.
Don't you find that uncomfortable?' Anna coloured and looked at her shoes
(she loved the curve of the heel). She was getting kind of hot under the
collar, actually. She didn't say anything. Glasses thought about it and tried
to offer some perspective about contemporary gender roles. Silence.*

*Feeling awkward, Glasses felt embarrassed into trying to salvage the
moment somehow. 'How does my ass look in this?' she asked, standing up
and turning around to give her companions a better view. 'I can never get an*

---

5   These are two suggestions for the identity of the mysterious 'Shulammite' in the Song
(see Pope 1977: 596–601 for a detailed discussion and Black 2006 for the précis).

honest answer out of my partner!' What followed was an animated discussion
– it was as if the women had come alive. *The ins and outs of the conversation*
need not be reproduced here, but suffice it to say that Glasses took home
some constructive criticism about cuts of skirts, some new-found appreci-
ation of her own curves, and a remarkably intimate knowledge of the variety
in women's behinds.

In fact the women hit it off so well that they began to meet on a weekly
basis to have a drink and a laugh. Wimple moved on to other relationships
(it turns out that she'd been trying to get out of a bad one); Anna opened a
plus-size lingerie and sexy-fun shop; and Glasses, well ... she took off her
glasses and started wearing jeans again.

The frustrating thing about autobiography is that it is remarkably
imprecise. Those who have used it in biblical studies have bravely revealed
parts of themselves as a means of getting behind the self who hides behind
the Book.[6] Their intentions, indeed, are excellent. The finished product,
though, causes me to wonder about its efficacy, since everything that is
revealed is carefully chosen and arranged; and everything that remains
concealed – well, readers hope to keep the curtain drawn on all that. Time
and time again, readers who read these constructions get it wrong when
they respond. (But historically wrong, or literarily wrong?!) Moreover,
readers are left wondering about the usefulness of these *partial* selves in
criticism of the Bible. And yet, still the best part of these readings – for me
as a reader, anyway – has got to be the *artifice* of them all. Those who are
very, very good at it are also very proficient at constructing personae with
witty or ornate turns of phrase, with tantalizing titbits of history, and with
a few good *goujons* of fictional meat.

So, an autobiographical reading of the Song might not be the best way
for me to elaborate my own subjectivity in order to render a true account,
but it still might be a way to foreground the matter of subjectivity in the
interpretive process. Certainly, it would be one way of formalizing or
containing the role of the personal in the Song, which is so vital to
understanding how we as readers come to deal with this text, in our times
and in others. If the self is going to leak out anyway, one might as well
direct the flow to useful means. *And yet, I don't want to.* I am not thick-
skinned or weathered enough to do so, nor do I suppose that these titbits
would be constructive as far as reading the Song goes.[7]

---

6   I think this phrase may be Stephen Moore's, but I cannot determine from where.

7   Previously, I was too hard on Brenner in my discussion of her chapter on the
Shulammite in her book *I AM* (Black 2006: 180). I criticized her for not actually *telling* the
woman's story, but she had probably realized something in her writing that I had not at the
time when I wrote. This story cannot be written fully, not without complete and total self-

P.S.: I Love You!

As a reader who has undertaken to identify the grotesque body in the Song of Songs, though, I must at least do this: I must state a specific hermeneutic of my own. I must say that I do not share the 'hermeneutic of compliment' that I identified in the majority of readings of the Song (Ch. 1), but neither do I espouse its opposite, a 'hermeneutic of ridicule' or a 'hermeneutic of repulsion', or the like. Instead, I hope that my reading advocates an approach to the text which embraces, in fact foregrounds, difference and incongruity in it, while at the same time, allowing for the presence of beauty and idyllicism. It is hoped that these can be held together in tension so that more of the Song's complicated textures may be elucidated. It is a resistant reading, to be sure, but it is not antagonistic. It is a reading that, like all others, tries to make sense of what one finds. It foregrounds the process of reading and the ambiguities therein, but it does not claim victory in that battle. Why do it, then? Well, should I not?

*   *   *

Oh, and one more thing: Deeply, yes, I love the Song of Songs.

I love the razor-cut of its jaw; I love the tartness of its bite. I love the warping of its curves; I love the fancy of its whims. I love the darkness of its eyes; I love the denting in its skin. I love the strangeness of its gaze; I love the splatter of its voice.

I love, I love, I love ... I-el-oh-vee-ee. I.

But does it love me too? 'I wear myself out; I'll never know.'[8]

---

eviseration-by-page on the one hand, or without the problems and pitfalls of writing the subjective on the other. And again, it cannot be written fully because it is everystory, and how does one write that in any way that might convince anyone besides oneself?

8   Barthes 1990a: 134.

BIBLIOGRAPHY

Adams, James Luther and Wilson Yates (eds)
  1997   *The Grotesque in Art and Literature: Theological Reflections* (Grand Rapids, MI: Eerdmans).
Aherne, Jeremy
  1995   *Michel de Certeau: Interpretation and its Other* (Stanford, CA: Stanford University Press).
Ahlgren, Gillian
  1996   *Teresa of Avila and the Politics of Sanctity* (Ithaca, NY, and London: Cornell University Press).
Alden, Robert L.
  1988   'Song of Songs 8.12a: Who Said it?' *JETS* 31: 271–8.
Alter, Robert
  1985   *The Art of Biblical Poetry* (New York: Basic Books).
  2002   'The Song of Songs: An Ode to Intimacy', *Bible Review* 18: 24–32, 52.
Andiñach, Pablo R.
  1991   'Critica de Salomon en el Cantar de los Cantares', *RevistB* 53: 129–56.
Angénieux, J.
  1965   'Structure du Cantique des Cantiques', *ETL* 41: 96–142.
  1966   'Les trois Portraits du Cantique des Cantiques', *ETL* 42: 582–96.
  1968   'Le Cantique des Cantiques en huit chants à refrains alternants', *ETL* 44: 87–140.
Astell, Ann W.
  1990   *The Song of Songs in the Middle Age* (Ithaca, NY: Cornell University Press).
Babcock, Barbara A. (ed.)
  1978   *The Reversible World: Symbolic Inversion in Art and Society* (Ithaca, NY, and London: Cornell University Press).
Bach, Alice
  1997   *Women, Seduction, and Betrayal in Biblical Narrative* (Cambridge: Cambridge University Press).

Bach, Alice (ed.)
1996 *Biblical Glamour and Hollywood Glitz* (Semeia, 74; Atlanta, GA: Scholars Press).
Bakhtin, Mikhail M.
1981a 'Discourse in the Novel', in Holquist 1981: 259–422.
1981b 'Forms of Time and the Chronotope in the Novel', in Holquist 1981: 84–258.
1984a *Problems of Dostoevsky's Poetics* (ed. and trans. Caryl Emerson; Minneapolis, MN: University of Minnesota Press).
1984b *Rabelais and his World* (trans. Hélène Iswolsky; Bloomington, IN: Indiana University Press).
Bal, Mieke
1988 *Death and Dissymmetry: The Politics of Coherence in the Book of Judges* (Chicago, IL: University of Chicago Press).
1991 *Reading 'Rembrandt': Beyond the Word–Image Opposition* (Cambridge: Cambridge University Press).
Balakian, Anna
1971 *André Breton* (New York: Oxford University Press).
Baldass, Ludwig von
1960 *Hieronymus Bosch* (London: Thames Hudson).
Barasch, Frances K.
1971 *The Grotesque: A Study in Meanings* (The Hague: Mouton).
Barbiero, Gianni
1995 'Die Liebe der Töchter Jerusalems: Hld 3,10b MT im Kontext von 3, 6–11', *BZ* 39: 96–104.
Barthes, Roland
1973 *Le Plaisir du texte* (Paris: du Seuil).
1980 *Arcimboldo* (Milan: F.M. Ricci).
1990a *A Lover's Discourse: Fragments* (trans. Richard Howard; London: Penguin).
1990b *The Pleasure of the Text* (trans. Richard Miller; Oxford: Basil Blackwell).
1995 *Roland Barthes* (trans. Richard Howard; London: Macmillan).
Bartky, Sandra Lee
1988 'Foucault, Femininity and the Modernization of Patriarchal Power', in I. Diamond and L. Quinby (eds), *Feminism and Foucault: Reflections on Resistance* (Boston, MA: Northeastern University Press): 61–86.
Bax, D.
1979 *Hieronymus Bosch: His Picture-writing Deciphered* (trans. M.A. Bax-Botha; Rotterdam: A.A. Balkerma).

Beal, Timothy K.
1994 'The System and the Speaking Subject in the Hebrew Bible: Reading for Divine Abjection', *BibInt* 2: 171–89.
Bekkenkamp, Jonneke and Fokkelien van Dijk-Hemmes
1993 'The Canon of the Old Testament and Women's Cultural Traditions', in Brenner 1993: 67–85.
Belsey, Catherine
1994 *Desire: Love Stories in Western Culture* (Oxford: Basil Blackwell).
Bergant, Dianne
1994 ' "My Beloved is Mine and I am His" (Song 2.16): The Song of Songs and Honor and Shame', *Semeia* 68: 23–40.
1998 *Song of Songs: The Love Poetry of Scripture* (Spiritual Commentaries; Hyde Park, NY: New City Press).
2001 *The Song of Songs* (Berit Olam; Collegeville, MN: Liturgical Press)
Bernard of Clairvaux
1971 *On the Song of Songs, I: Sermons 1–20* (trans. Kilian Walsh; Cistercian Fathers Series, 4; Kalamazoo, MI: Cistercian Publications).
1983 *On the Song of Songs, II: Sermons 21–46* (trans. Kilian Walsh; Cistercian Fathers Series, 7; Kalamazoo, MI: Cistercian Publications).
Bernat, David
2004 'Biblical *wasfs* beyond the Song of Songs', *JSOT* 28: 327–49.
Berrong, Richard M.
1986 *Rabelais and Bakhtin: Popular Culture in* Gargantua *and* Pantagruel (Lincoln, NB: University of Nebraska Press).
Biale, David
1997 *Eros and the Jews: From Biblical Israel to Contemporary America* (Berkeley, CA: University of California Press).
Black, Fiona C.
1999 'What is my Beloved? On Erotic Reading and the Song of Songs', in Black, Boer and Runions 1999: 35–52.
2000a 'Beauty or the Beast? The Grotesque Body in the Song of Songs', *BibInt* 8: 302–23.
2000b 'Unlikely Bedfellows: Feminist and Allegorical Readings of Song 7.1-8', in Brenner and Fontaine 2000: 104–29.
2001 'Nocturnal Egressions: Exploring Some Margins of the Song of Songs', in A.K.M. Adam (ed.), *Postmodern Interpretations of the Bible* (St Louis, MN: Chalice Press): 93–104.
2006 'Writing Lies: Autobiography, Textuality, and the Song of Songs', in Black (ed.) 2006: 161–83.

Black, Fiona C. (ed.)
2006   *The Recycled Bible: Autobiography, Culture, and the Space Between* (Semeia Studies, 51; Atlanta, GA: SBL Press).

Black, Fiona C., Roland Boer and Erin Runions (eds)
1999   *The Labour of Reading: Desire, Alienation and Biblical Interpretation* (Semeia Studies, 36; Atlanta, GA: Scholars Press).

Blackman, Philip
1964   *Mishnayoth* (Vol. VI; New York: Judaica Press).

Bloch, Ariel and Chana Bloch
1995   *The Song of Songs: A New Translation with an Introduction and Commentary* (Berkeley, CA: University of California Press).

Bloom, Harold
1988   *Modern Critical Interpretations of the Song of Songs* (New York: Chelsea House).

Boer, Roland
1999   'Night Sprinkle(s): Pornography and the Song of Songs', in *Knockin' on Heaven's Door: The Bible and Popular Culture* (London: Routledge): 53–70.
2000   'The Second Coming: Repetition and Insatiable Desire in the Song of Songs', *BibInt* 8: 276–301.

Boucher, Teresa
1999   'Craving Credibility: Teresa of Avila's Shifting Discourse in Meditaciones sobre los Cantares', http://tell.fll.urdue.edu/ RLA-Archive/1999/Spanish/BOUCHER.HTM, accessed 11 November 2005.

Boyarin, Daniel
1991   'Literary Fat Rabbis: On the Historical Origins of the Grotesque Body', *Journal of the History of Sexuality* 1: 551–84.
1992   'The Great Fat Massacre: Sex, Death, and the Grotesque Body in the Talmud', in Eilberg-Schwartz 1992: 69–100.
1993   *Carnal Israel: Reading Sex in Talmudic Culture* (Berkeley, CA: University of California Press).
1997   *Unheroic Conduct: The Rise of Heterosexuality and the Invention of the Jewish Man* (Contraversions, 8; Berkeley, CA: University of California Press).

Brenner, Athalya
1983   'Aromatics and Perfumes in the Song of Songs', *JSOT* 25: 71–85.
1989   *The Song of Songs* (OTG; Sheffield: JSOT Press).
1990   'On the Semantic Field of Humour, Laughter and the Comic in the Old Testament', in Radday and Brenner 1990: 38–58.

1992 'A Note on *Bat-Rabbîm* (Song of Songs VII 5)', *VT* 42: 113–15.

1993a '"Come Back, Come Back the Shulammite" (Song of Songs 7.1-10): A Parody of the *wasf* Genre', in Brenner 1993: 234–57.

1993b 'To See is to Assume: Whose Love is Celebrated in the Song of Songs?' *BibInt* 1: 265–84.

1993c 'On Feminist Criticism of the Song of Songs', in Brenner (ed.) 1993: 28–37.

1993d 'Women Poets and Authors', in Brenner (ed.) 1993: 86–97.

1994 'Who's Afraid of Feminist Criticism? Who's Afraid of Biblical Humour? The Case of the Obtuse Foreign Ruler in the Hebrew Bible', *JSOT* 63: 38–55.

1997a *The Intercourse of Knowledge: On Gendering Desire and 'Sexuality' in the Hebrew Bible* (*BibInt* Series, 26; Leiden: E.J. Brill).

1997b '"My" Song of Songs', in Athalya Brenner and Carole Fontaine (eds), *A Feminist Companion to Reading the Bible* (Sheffield: Sheffield Academic Press): 567–79.

2003 'Gazing Back at the Shulammite, yet Again', *BibInt* 9: 295–300.

2005 *I Am …: Biblical Women Tell their Own Stories* (Philadelphia, PA: Fortress Press).

Brenner, Athalya (ed.)

1993 *A Feminist Companion to the Song of Songs* (Sheffield: JSOT Press).

Brenner, Athalya and Fokkelien van Dijk-Hemmes

1993 *On Gendering Texts: Female and Male Voices in the Hebrew Bible* (*BibInt* Series, 1; Leiden: E.J. Brill).

Brenner, Athalya and Carole Fontaine (eds)

2000 *The Feminist Companion to the Song of Songs* (Sheffield: Sheffield Academic Press, 2nd edn).

Brenner, Athalya and Yehuda T. Radday

1990 'Between Intentionality and Reception: Acknowledgement and Application (A Preview)', in Radday and Brenner 1990: 13–20.

Breton, André

1969 *Selected Poems* (trans. Kenneth White; London: Cape).

Brown, Francis, S.R. Driver and Charles A. Briggs

1979 *The New Brown–Driver–Briggs–Gesenius Hebrew and English Lexicon* (Peabody, MA: Hendrickson).

Brown, Wendy

1995 'Postmodern Exposures, Feminist Hesitations', in *States of*

                    Injury: Power and Freedom in Late Modernity (Princeton,
                    NJ: Princeton University Press): 30–51.
Bruneau, Marie-Florine
    1992   'Psychoanalysis and its Abject: What Lurks behind the Fear
                    of the "Mother" ', *Studies in Psychoanalysis* 1: 24–38.
Budde, Karl
    1898   'Das Hohelied', in Karl Marti (ed.), *Kürzer Hand-
                    Commentar zum Alten Testament* (Tübingen: J.C.B. Mohr
                    [Paul Siebeck]): 1–48.
Burns, Stuart L.
    1972   'Freaks in a Circus Tent: Flannery O'Connor's Christ-
                    Haunted Characters', *Flannery O'Connor Bulletin* 1: 3–23.
Burrus, Virginia and Stephen D. Moore
    2003   'Unsafe Sex: Feminism, Pornography, and the Song of
                    Songs', *BibInt* 11: 24–52.
Burwick, Frederick
    1987   *The Haunted Eye: Perception and the Grotesque in English
                    and German Romanticism* (Reihe Siegen, 70; Heidelberg:
                    Carl Winter Universitätsverlag).
Buzy, Denis
    1940   'La Composition littéraire du Cantique des Cantiques', *RB*
                    49: 169–94.
Bynum, Caroline
    1995   'Why All the Fuss about the Body? A Medievalist's
                    Perspective', *Critical Enquiry* 22: 1–33.
Calvet, Louis-Jean
    1994   *Roland Barthes: A Biography* (trans. Sarah Wykes;
                    Cambridge: Polity Press).
Camp, Claudia
    1985   *Wisdom and the Feminine in the Book of Proverbs* (Sheffield:
                    Almond Press).
    1994   'Metaphor in Feminist Biblical Interpretation: Theoretical
                    Perspectives', *Semeia* 61: 3–36.
    2000   *Wise, Strange and Holy: The Strange Woman and the
                    Making of the Bible* (JSOTSup, 320; GCT 9; Sheffield:
                    Sheffield Academic Press).
Carr, David McLean
    2003   *The Erotic Word: Sexuality, Spirituality, and the Bible* (New
                    York: Oxford University Press).
Carr, G. Lloyd
    1979   'Is the Song of Songs a "Sacred Marriage" Drama?', *JETS*
                    22: 103–14.
Carter, Angela
    1994   *Nights at the Circus* (London: Vintage Books).

1995   *Shadow Dance* (London: Virago).

1996   *Burning your Boats: Collected Short Stories* (London: Vintage Books).

Caws, Mary Ann

1970   *The Poetry of Dada and Surrealism* (Princeton, NJ: Princeton University Press).

1971   *André Breton* (Twayne's World Author Series, 117; New York: Twayne).

Certeau, Michel de

1986   'Mystic Speech', in *Heterologies: Discourse on the Other* (trans. Brian Massumi; Minneapolis, MN: University of Minnesota Press): 80–100.

1992a   *The Mystic Fable. Volume One: The Sixteenth and Seventeenth Centuries* (trans. Michael B. Smith; Chicago, IL: University of Chicago Press).

1992b   'Mystics', *Diacritics* 22.2: 11–25.

Charry, Ellen

1987   'Female Sexuality as an Image of Empowerment: Two Models', *St Luke's Journal of Theology* 30: 201–18.

Churchill, Laurie J.

1988   'Discourses of Desire: On Ovid's *Amores* and Barthes' *Fragments d'un discours amoureux*', *Classical Modern Literature: A Quarterly* 8: 301–7.

Clark, John R.

1991   *The Modern Satiric Grotesque and its Traditions* (Lexington, KY: University Press of Kentucky).

Clark, Katerina and Michael Holquist

1984   'Rabelais and his World', in *Mikhail Bakhtin* (Cambridge, MA: Harvard University Press): 295–320.

Clark, Sandra

1985   '*Hic Mulier, Haec Vir*, and the Controversy over Masculine Women', *Studies in Philology* 82: 157–83.

Clayborough, Arthur

1965   *The Grotesque in English Literature* (Oxford: Clarendon Press).

Clines, David J.A.

1995   'Why is there a Song of Songs and What Does it Do to you if you Read it?', in *Interested Parties: The Ideology of Writers and Readers of the Hebrew Bible* (JSOTSup, 205; GCT, 1; Sheffield: Sheffield Academic Press): 94–121.

Clines, David J.A. (ed.)

1993–   *Dictionary of Classical Hebrew* (6 vols; Sheffield: Sheffield Academic Press; Sheffield: Sheffield Phoenix Press).

Cohen, Jeremy
   1986   'Scholarship and Intolerance in the Medieval Academy: The
            Study   and   Evaluation   of   Judaism   in   European
            Christendom', *American Historical Review* 91: 592–613.
Coleman, Dorothy Gabe
   1971   *Rabelais: A Critical Study in Prose Fiction* (Cambridge:
            Cambridge University Press).
Cook, Albert
   1968   *The Root of the Thing: A Study of Job and the Song of Songs*
            (Bloomington, IN: Indiana University Press).
Corey, Susan
   1997   'The Religious Dimensions of the Grotesque in Literature:
            Toni Morrison's *Beloved*', in Adams and Yates 1997: 227–
            42.
Craigie, Peter C.
   1971   'The Poetry of Ugarit and Israel', *TynBul* 22: 3–31.
Crim, K.,
   1971   ' "Your Neck is like the Tower of David" (the meaning of a
            simile in Song of Solomon 4.4)', *Bible Translator* 22: 70–74.
   1983   'Love Lyrics from the Bible: A Translation and Literary
            Study of the Song of Songs', *Bible Translator* 34: 341–42.
Dacos, Nicole
   1969   *La Découverte de la Domus Aurea et la formation des
            grotesques à la Renaissance* (Leiden: E.J. Brill).
Davidson, Bernice F.
   1985   *Raphael's Bible: A Study of the Vatican Logge* (Philadelphia,
            PA: Pennsylvania State University Press).
Davidson, Richard M.
   1989   'Theory of Sexuality in the Song of Songs: Return to Eden',
            Andrews University Seminary Studies 27: 1–19.
Delitzsch, Franz
   1877   *Commentary on the Song of Songs and Ecclesiastes* (trans.
            M.G. Easton; Edinburgh: T. & T. Clark).
Di-Renzo, Anthony
   1993   *American Gargoyles: Flannery O'Connor and the Medieval
            Grotesque* (Carbondale, IL: Southern Illinois University
            Press).
Dijk-Hemmes, Fokkelien van
   1993   'The Imagination of Power and the Power of Imagination:
            An Intertextual Analysis of Two Biblical Love Songs: The
            Song of Songs and Hosea 2', in Brenner 1993: 156–70.
Dillenberger, John
   1999   *Images and Relics: Theological Perceptions and Visual*

Images in Sixteenth-Century Europe (Oxford: Oxford University Press).

Dirksen, P.B.
1989   'Song of Songs III 6–7', *VT* 39: 219–24.
Dobbs-Allsopp, F.W.
2005   'The Delight of Beauty and Song of Songs 4.1-7', *Int* 59: 260–77.
Dorsey, David A.
1990   'Literary Structuring in the Song of Songs', *JSOT* 46: 81–96.
Douglas, Mary
1966   *Purity and Danger: An Analysis of the Concept of Pollution and Taboo* (London: Routledge Kegan Paul).
1999   'The Compassionate God and his Animal Creation: Rereading Leviticus', paper presented to the Catholic Biblical Association of Great Britain Annual Meeting, Newman College, Birmingham, 17 April.
Dove, Mary
2000   'Literal Senses in the Song of Songs', in Philip D.W. Krey and Lesley Smith (eds), *Nicholas of Lyra: The Senses of Scripture* (Leiden: E.J. Brill): 129–46.
2001   'Merely a Love Poem? Common Sense, Suspicion and the Song of Songs', in Frances Devlin-Glass and Lyn McCredden (eds), *Feminist Poetics of the Sacred: Creative Suspicions* (Oxford: Oxford University Press): 151–64.
Eagleton, Terry
1981   *Walter Benjamin, or, Towards a Revolutionary Criticism* (London: Verso).
Edwards, Mark U., Jr
1983   *Luther's Last Battles: Politics and Polemics, 1531–46* (Ithaca, NY: Cornell University Press).
Eilberg-Schwartz, Howard
1992   'The Problem of the Body for the People of the Book', in Eilberg-Schwartz 1992: 17–46.
Eilberg-Schwartz, Howard (ed.)
1992   *People of the Body: Jews and Judaism from an Embodied Perspective* (Albany, NY: SUNY Press).
Elliott, M. Timothea
1989   *The Literary Unity of the Canticle* (Europäische Hochschulschriften, 371; Frankfurt a.M.: Peter Lang).
Elliott, Mark W.
1994   'Ethics and Aesthetics in the Song of Songs', *TynBul* 45: 137–52.
Emmerson, Grace
1994   'The Song of Songs: Mystification, Ambiguity and

Humour', in P. Joyce, D. Orton and S. Porter (eds), *Crossing the Boundaries: Essays in Biblical Interpretation in Honour of Michael D. Goulder* (Leiden: E.J. Brill): 97–111.

Eschelbach, Michael
2004 'Song of Songs: Increasing Appreciation of and Restraint in Matters of Love', *Andrews University Seminary Studies* 42: 305–24.

Eslinger, Lyle
1981 'The Case of an Immodest Lady Wrestler in Deuteronomy XXV 11–12', *VT* 31: 269–81.

Exum, J. Cheryl
1973 'A Literary and Structural Analysis of the Song of Songs', *ZAW* 85: 47–79.
1993 *Fragmented Women: Feminist (Sub)Versions of Biblical Narratives* (Philadelphia, PA: Trinity Press International; Sheffield: Sheffield Academic Press).
1996 *Plotted, Shot, and Painted: Cultural Representations of Biblical Women* (JSOTSup, 215; GCT, 3; Sheffield: Sheffield Academic Press).
1998 'Developing Strategies of Feminist Criticism, and Developing Strategies for Commentating the Song of Songs', in David J.A. Clines and Stephen D. Moore (eds), *Auguries: The Jubilee Volume of the Sheffield Department of Biblical* (JSOTSup, 269; Sheffield: Sheffield Academic Press): 206–49.
1999a 'In the Eye of the Beholder: Wishing, Dreaming and *Double Entendre* in the Song of Songs', in Black, Boer and Runions 1999: 71–86.
1999b 'How does the Song of Songs Mean? On Reading the Poetry of Desire', *SEÅ* 64: 47–63.
2000 'Ten Things Every Feminist Should Know about the Song of Songs', in Brenner and Fontaine 2000: 24–35.
2003a 'Seeing Solomon's Palanquin (Song of Songs 3.6-11)', *BibInt* 11: 301–16.
2003b '"The Voice of My Lover": Double Voice and Poetic Illusion in Song of Songs 2.8-3.5', in J. Cheryl Exum and H. G. Williamson (eds), *Reading from Right to Left: Essays in Honour of David J.A. Clines* (JSOTSup, 373; Sheffield: Sheffield Academic Press): 146–57.
2005a *Song of Songs* (OTL; Philadelphia, PA: Westminster John Knox Press).
2005b 'The Poetic Genius of the Song of Songs', in A.C. Hagedorn (ed.), *Perspectives on the Song of Songs/Perspektiven der Hoheliedauslegung* (Berlin: deGruyter): 78–95.

2005c   'The Little Sister and Solomon's Vineyard: Song of Songs 8.8-12 as a Lovers' Dialogue', in Ronald Troxel, Kelvin Freibel and Dennis Magary (eds), *Seeking out the Wisdom of the Ancients: Essays Offered to Honour Michael V. Fox on the Occasion of his Sixty-fifth Birthday* (Winona Lake, MN: Eisenbrauns): 269–82.

2005d   ' "Seeing" the Song of Songs: Some Artistic Visions of the Bible's Love Lyrics', in John Barton, J. Cheryl Exum and Manfred Oeming (eds), *Das Alte Testament und die Kunst* (Berlin: LIT Verlag): 91–127.

Falk, Marcia

1982   *Love Lyrics from the Bible: A Translation and Literary Study of the Song of Songs* (Sheffield: Almond Press).

1993   'The *wasf*', in Brenner (ed.) 1993: 225–33.

Ferguson, Margaret W., Maureen Quilligan and Nancy J. Vickers (eds)

1986   *Rewriting the Renaissance: The Discourses of Sexual Difference in Early Modern Europe* (Chicago, IL: University of Chicago Press).

Feuillet, André

1961   'La Formule d'appartenance mutuelle (II, 16) et les interprétations divergentes du Cantique des Cantiques', *RB* 68: 5–38.

1971   ' "S'asseoir à l'Ombre" de l'époux (Os., XIV 8a et Cant., II, 3)', *RB* 78: 391–405.

Fisch, Harold

1988   'Song of Songs: The Allegorical Imperative', in *Poetry with a Purpose* (Bloomington, IN: Indiana University Press): 80–103, 187–9.

Fitzmyer, Joseph

1966   *The Genesis Apocryphon of Qumran Cave 1: A Commentary* (BibOr, 18; Rome: Pontifical Biblical Institute).

Fontaine, Claire R.

2004   'Watching out for the Watchmen (Song 5.7): How I Hold myself Accountable', in Charles Cosgrove (ed.), *The Meanings we Choose* (London: T&T Clark): 102–21.

Foucault, Michel

1990   *The History of Sexuality.* Vol. 1: *An Introduction* (trans. Robert Hurley; New York: Vintage Books).

Fox, Michael V.

1983a   'Love, Passion, and Perception in Israelite and Egyptian Love Poetry', *JBL* 102: 219–28.

1983b   'Scholia to Canticles (i 4b, ii 4, i 4ba , iv 3, v 8, vi 12)', *VT* 33: 199–206.

1985   *The Song of Songs and the Ancient Egyptian Love Songs*
        (Madison, WI: University of Wisconsin Press).

Freccero, Carla
1986   'The Other and the Same: The Image of the Hermaphrodite
        in Rabelais', in Ferguson, Quilligan and Vickers 1986: 145–
        58.

Freud, Sigmund
1925   'The "Uncanny"', in *Collected Papers*, Vol. 4. *Papers on
        Metapsychology. Papers on Applied Psychoanalysis.*
        (London: Hogarth Press): 368–407.
1960   *The Standard Edition of the Complete Psychological Works
        of Sigmund Freud.* Vol. 8. *Jokes and their Relation to the
        Unconscious* (London: Hogarth Press).

Frohlich, Mary
1993   *The Intersubjectivity of the Mystic: A Study of Teresa of
        Avila's* Interior Castle (Atlanta, GA: American Academy of
        Religion).

Fuchs, Esther
1985   'The Literary Characterization of Mothers and Sexual
        Politics in the Hebrew Bible', in Adela Yarbro Collins
        (ed.), *Feminist Perspectives on Biblical Scholarship* (Chico,
        CA: Scholars Press): 117–36.

Gallop, Jane
1986   'Feminist Criticism and the Pleasure of the Text', *North
        Dakota Quarterly* 54: 119–34.

Garrett, D.
1993   *The New American Commentary: An Exegetical and
        Theological Exposition of Holy Scripture. Proverbs,
        Ecclesiastes, Song of Songs* (Nashville, TN: Broadman
        Press).

Gelles, Benjamin
1981   *Peshat and Derash in the Exegesis of Rashi* (Etudes sur le
        judaïsme médiévale, 9; Leiden: E.J. Brill).

Gentry, Marshall Bruce
1986   *Flannery O'Connor's Religion of the Grotesque* (Jackson, MI:
        University Press of Mississippi).

Gerleman, Gillis
1962   'Die Bildsprache des Hohenliedes und die altägyptische
        Kunst', *Annual of the Swedish Theological Institute* 1: 24–30.
1965   *Ruth · Das Hohelied* (BKAT, 18; Neukirchen-Vluyn:
        Neukirchener).

Gibson, J.C.L.
1977   *Canaanite Myths and Legends* (Edinburgh: T&T Clark).

Gibson, Walter S.
1973   *Hieronymus Bosch* (The World of Art Library; London: Thames Hudson).
1977   *Bruegel* (The World of Art Library; London: Thames Hudson).

Gittings, Christopher
1994   'A Collision of Discourse: Postmodernisms and Post-Colonialisms in *The Biggest Modern Woman of the World*', *Journal of Commonwealth Literature* 29: 81–91.

Goitein, S.
1965   'Ayumma Kannidgalot (Song of Songs VI. 10): "Splendid like the Brilliant Stars" ', *JSS* 10: 220–21.
1993   'The Song of Songs: A Female Composition', in Brenner (ed.) 1993: 58–66.

Good, Edwin M.
1970   'Ezekiel's Ship: Some Extended Metaphors in the Old Testament', *Semitics* 1: 79–103.

Gordis, Robert
1969   'The Root DGL in the Song of Songs', *JBL* 88: 203–4.
1974   *The Song of Songs and Lamentations: A Study, Modern Translation and Commentary* (New York: KTAV).

Görg, Manfred
1987   'Eine Salbenezeichnung in HL 1,3', *BN* 38/39: 36–8.
1994   ' "Kanäle" oder "Zweige" in Hld 4,13?', *BN* 72: 20–23.

Goshen-Gottstein, M.H.
1959   'Philologische Miszellen zu den Qumrantexten', *RenQ* 2: 43–51.

Gottwald, Norman K.
1976   'The Song of Songs', in George Arthur Buttrick (ed.), *Interpreter's Dictionary of the Bible* (Vol. 4; Nashville, TN: Abingdon): 420–26.

Goulder, Michael D.
1986   *The Song of Fourteen Songs* (JSOTSup, 36; Sheffield: JSOT Press).

Green, Deirdre
1989   *Gold in the Crucible: Teresa of Avila and the Western Mystical Tradition* (Shaftesbury: Longmead Books).

Greenblatt, Stephen J. (ed.)
1981   *Allegory and Representation: Selected Papers from the English Institute 1979–80* (Baltimore, MD: Johns Hopkins University Press).

Greenspahn, Frederick E.
1984   *Hapax Legomena in Biblical Hebrew: A Study of the Phenomenon and its Treatment since Antiquity with Special*

Reference to Verbal Forms (SBLDS, 74; Chico, CA: Scholars Press).

Greenstein, Edward L.
    1984   'Medieval Bible Commentaries', in B. Holtz (ed.), *Back to the Sources: Reading the Classic Jewish Texts* (New York: Summit Books): 213–31.

Grober, S.F.
    1984   'The Hospitable Lotus: A Cluster of Metaphors. An Enquiry into the Problem of Textual Unity in the Song of Songs', *Semitics* 9: 86–112.

Grossberg, Daniel
    1981a   'Sexual Desire: Abstract and Concrete', *HS* 22: 59–60.
    1981b   'Canticles 3.10 in the Light of a Homeric Analogue and Biblical Poetics', *BTB* 11: 74–76.
    1994   'Two Kinds of Sexual Relationships in the Hebrew Bible', *HS* 35: 7–25.
    2005   'Nature, Humanity, and Love in the Song of Songs', *Int* 59: 229–44.

Grosz, Elizabeth
    1987   'Language and the Limits of the Body: Kristeva and Abjection', in E. Grosz, T. Threadgold, D. Kelly *et al.* (eds), *Future Fall: Excursions into Postmodernity* (Sydney: Power Institute Publications): 106–17.
    1989   'Julia Kristeva: Abjection, Motherhood and Love', in *Sexual Subversions: Three French Feminists* (Sydney: Allen Unwin): 70–99.
    1990   *Jacques Lacan: A Feminist Introduction* (London and New York: Routledge).

Hailperin, Herman
    1963   *Rashi and the Christian Scholars* (Pittsburgh, PA: University of Pittsburgh Press).

Harpham, Geoffrey Galt
    1982   *On the Grotesque: Strategies on Contradiction in Art and Literature* (Princeton, NJ: Princeton University Press).

Hartsock, Nancy
    1990   'Foucault on Power: A Theory for Women?', in L. Nicholson (ed.), *Feminism/Postmodernism* (London and New York: Routledge): 157–75.

Haverluck, Bob
    2002   'Song of Love, Song of Revolt: Re-reading the Song of Songs', *Arts: The Arts in Religious and Theological Studies* 14: 14–20.

Heath, Stephen
    1974   *Vertige du déplacement: Lecture de Barthes* (Paris: Fayard).

1983   'Barthes on Love', *SubStance* 37/38: 100–106.
Heffernan, Teresa
1992   'Tracing the Travesty: Constructing the Female Subject in Susan Swan's *The Biggest Modern Woman of the World*, *Canadian Literature* 133: 24–37.
Hermann, Wolfram
1963   'Gedanken   zur   Geschichte   des   altorientalischen Beschreibungsliedes', *ZAW* 75: 176–96.
Hill, Leslie
1988   'Barthes' Body', *Paragraph* 11: 107–26.
Hines, Melissa
1977   'Grotesque Conversions and Critical Piety', *Flannery O'Connor Bulletin* 6: 17–35.
Hirschkop, Ken and David Shepherd (eds)
1989   *Bakhtin and Cultural Theory* (Manchester: Manchester University Press).
Holladay, William L.
1988   *A Concise Hebrew and Aramaic Lexicon of the Old Testament* (Grand Rapids, MI: Eerdmans; Leiden: E.J. Brill).
Holquist, Michael
1981   'The Politics of Representation', in Greenblatt 1981: 163–83.
Holquist, Michael (ed.)
1981   *The Dialogic Imagination* (trans. Caryl Emerson and Michael Holquist; Austin, TX: University of Texas).
Horine, Steven C.
2001   *Interpretive Images in the Song of Songs: From Wedding Chariots to Bridal Chambers* (New York: Peter Lang).
Horst, Friedrich
1961   'Die Formen des althebräischen Liebesliedes', in *Gottes Recht: Gesamelte Studien zum Recht in alten Testament* (TBü, 12; Munich: Chr. Kaiser): 176–87.
Hunter, Jannie
2000   'The Song of Protest: Reassessing the Song of Songs', *JSOT* 90: 109–24.
Hwang, Andrew
2003   'The New Structure of the Song of Songs and its Implications for Interpretation', *WThJ* 65: 97–111.
Jefferson, Ann
1989   'Bodymatters: Self and Other in Bakhtin, Sartre and Barthes', in Hirschkop and Shepherd 1989: 152–77.
Jones, Ann Rosalind
1984   'Julia Kristeva on Femininity: The Limits of a Semiotic Politics', *Feminist Review* 18: 56–73.

Kahane, Claire Katz
  1979   'Comic Vibrations and Self-construction in Grotesque
            Literature', *Literature and Psychology* 29: 114–19.
Kauffman, Linda S.
  1995   'Dangerous Liaisons: The Reproduction of Woman in
            Roland Barthes and Jacques Derrida', in Richard Harvey
            Brown (ed.), *Postmodern Representations: Truth, Power and
            Mimesis in the Human Sciences and Public Culture* (Urbana,
            IL: University of Chicago Press): 168–96.
Kaufmann, Thomas DaCosta
  1987   'The Allegories and their Meaning', in Pontus Hulten (ed.),
            *The Arcimboldo Effect: Transformations of the Face from the
            16th to the 20th Century* (New York: Abbeville Press).
Kautzsch, E (ed.)
  1910   *Gensenius' Hebrew Grammar* (rev. and trans. A.E. Cowley;
            Oxford: Oxford University Press).
Kayser, Wolfgang
  1963   *The Grotesque in Art and Literature* (trans. Ulrich Weisstein;
            Bloomington, IN: Indiana University Press).
Keefe, Alice A.
  1995   'The Female Body, the Body Politic and the Land: A
            Sociopolitical Reading of Hosea 1–2', in Athalya Brenner
            (ed.), *The Feminist Companion to the Latter Prophets*
            (Sheffield: Sheffield Academic Press): 70–100.
Keel, Othmar
  1984   *Deine Blicke sind Tauben: Zur Metaphorik des Hohen Liedes*
            (SBS, 114/115; Stuttgart: Katholisches Bibelwerk).
  1994   *The Song of Songs* (trans. Frederick J. Gaiser; Minneapolis,
            MN: Fortress Press).
Knight, Diana
  1984   'Roland Barthes: The *Corpus* and the *Corps*', *Poetics Today*
            4: 831–7.
Koehler, Ludwig, Walter Baumgartner, and J.J. Stamm
  1994–99 *Hebrew and Aramaic Lexicon of the Old Testament* (trans.
            and ed. M.E.J. Richardson; 4 vols; Leiden: E.J. Brill).
Kriegeskorte, Werner
  1993   *Giuseppe Arcimboldo* (Cologne: Benedikt Taschen).
Krinetzki, Günter (= Leo)
  1980   *Hoheslied* (NEchB; Würzburg: Echter).
  1981   *Kommentar zum Hohenlied: Bildsprache und theologische
            Botschaft* (Frankfurt a.M.: Peter Lang).
Kristeva, Julia
  1981   'The Maternal Body', *m/f* 5/6: 158–63.

1982   *Powers of Horror: An Essay on Abjection* (trans. Leon S. Roudiez; New York: Columbia University Press).

1987   *Tales of Love* (trans. L. Roudiez; New York: Columbia University Press).

1997   'Barthes: l'intraitable amoureux', in *La Révolte intime: Pouvoirs et limites de la psychanalyse II (discours direct)* (Paris: Fayard): 211–24.

Kuryluk, Ewa
1987   *Salome and Judas in the Cave of Sex. The Grotesque: Origins, Iconography, Techniques* (Evanston, IL: Northwestern University Press).

LaCocque, André
1998   *Romance she Wrote: A Hermeneutical Essay on the Song of Songs* (Harrisburg, PA: Trinity Press International).

Landsberger, Franz
1954   'Poetic Units within the Song of Songs', *JBL* 73: 203–16.

Landy, Francis
1979   'The Song of Songs and the Garden of Eden', *JBL* 98: 513–28.

1983   *Paradoxes of Paradise: Identity and Difference in the Song of Songs* (Sheffield: Almond Press).

1990   'Humour as a Tool for Biblical Exegesis', in Radday and Brenner 1990: 99–115.

1993   'Mishneh Torah: A Response', in Brenner (ed.) 1993: 260–65.

Laqueur, Thomas
1987   'Orgasm, Generation, and the Politics of Reproductive Biology', in Catherine Gallagher and Thomas Laqueur (eds), *The Making of the Modern Body: Sexuality and Society in the Nineteenth Century* (Berkeley, CA: University of California Press): 1–41.

1990   *Making Sex: Body and Gender from the Greeks to Freud* (Cambridge, MA: Harvard University Press).

Lavoie, Jean-Jacques
1995   'Festin érotique et tendresse cannibalique dans le Cantique des Cantiques', *SR* 24: 131–46.

Lechte, John
1990   *Julia Kristeva* (London: Routledge).

Lecoutex, Claude
1993   *Les Monstres dans la pensée médiévale Européenne* (Cultures et civilisations mediévales, 10; Paris: Presses de l'Université de Paris-Sorbonne).

Leitch, Vincent
    1983   *Deconstructive   Criticism: An   Advanced   Introduction*
              (London: Hutchinson).
Linafelt, Tod
    2002   'Biblical Love Poetry (. . . and God)', *JAAR* 70: 323–45.
    2005   'The Arithmetic of Eros', *Int* 59: 244–58.
Loewe, Raphael
    1966   'Apologetic Motifs in the Targum to the Song of Songs', in
              Alexander Altmann (ed.), *Biblical Motifs: Origins and
              Transformations* (Studies and Texts, 3; Cambridge, MA:
              Harvard University Press): 159–98.
Long, Gary Alan
    1996   'A Lover, Cities, and Heavenly Bodies: Co-text and the
              Translation of Two Similes in Canticles (6.4c; 6.10d)', *JBL*
              115: 703–9.
Longman, Tremper III
    2001   *Song of Songs* (NICOT; Grand Rapids, MI: Eerdmans).
Lord, M.G.
    1994   *Forever Barbie: The Unauthorized Biography of a Real Doll*
              (New York: Avon Books).
Louth, Andrew
    1992   *Eros and Mysticism: Early Christian Interpretation of the
              Song of Songs* (Guild Lecture, 241; Guild of Pastoral
              Psychology).
Lubac, Henri de
    1988   *Medieval Exegesis.* Vol. 1: *The Four Senses of Scripture*
              (trans. Mark Sebanc; Grand Rapids, MI: Eerdmans;
              Edinburgh: T&T Clark).
Luzarraga, Jesus
    2002   'El Cilantro en 4QCant[b] 4,16b', *Estudios biblicos* 60: 107–
              23.
Lys, Daniel
    1968   *Le plus beau Chant de la création: Commentaire du Cantique
              des Cantiques* (Paris: Cerf).
MacCannell, Juliet Flower
    1986   'Kristeva's Horror', *Semiotica* 62: 325–55.
Macky, Peter
    1990   *The Centrality of Metaphors to Biblical Thought* (Lewiston,
              NY: Edwin Mellon Press).
Matter, E. Ann
    1990   *The Voice of my Beloved: The Song of Songs in Western
              Medieval Christianity* (Philadelphia, PA: University of
              Pennsylvania Press).

Mazor, Yair
    1990   'The Song of Songs or the Story of Stories? "The Song of Songs": Between Genre and Unity', *SJOT* 1: 1–29.

Meek, Theophile James
    1924   'Babylonian Parallels to the Song of Songs', *JBL* 43: 245–52.

Merkin, Daphne
    1994   'The Woman in the Balcony: On Rereading the Song of Songs', in C. Büchman and C. Spiegel (eds), *Out of the Garden: Women Writers on the Bible* (New York: Fawcett Columbine): 238–51, 342.

Merrill, Eugene
    1978   'Rashi, Nicholas de Lyra and Christian Exegesis', *WThJ* 38: 66–79.

Meyers, Carol
    1988   *Discovering Eve: Ancient Israelite Women in Context* (Oxford: Oxford University Press).
    1991   '"To Her Mother's House": Considering a Counterpart to the Israelite *Bet 'ab*', in David Jobling, Peggy L. Day and Gerald T. Sheppard (eds), *The Bible and the Politics of Exegesis* (Cleveland, OH: Pilgrim Press): 39–51.
    1993   'Gender Imagery in the Song of Songs', in Brenner (ed.) 1993: 197–212.

Miles, Margaret
    1991   *Carnal Knowing: Female Nakedness and Religious Meaning in the Christian West* (New York: Vintage Books).

Miller, Patricia Cox
    1986   'Pleasure of the Text, Text of Pleasure: Eros and Language in Origen's *Commentary on the Song of Songs*', *JAAR* 54: 241–53.
    1988   'Poetic Words, Abysmal Words: Reflections on Origen's Hermeneutics', in C. Kannengesse and William Petersen (eds), *Origen of Alexandria: His World and his Legacy* (Notre Dame, IN: University of Notre Dame Press): 165–78.

Moi, Toril
    1985   *Sexual/Textual Politics: Feminist Literary Theory* (London: Methuen).

Moore, Stephen D.
    2001   *God's Beauty Parlour and other Queer Spaces in and around the Bible* (Stanford, CA: Stanford University Press).

Morel, Phillippe
    1997   *Les Grotesques: Les Figures de l'imaginaire dans la peinture italienne de la fin de la Renaissance* (Paris: Flammarion).

Moriarty, Michael
1991   *Roland Barthes* (Cambridge: Polity Press).
Morson, Gary Saul and Caryl Emerson
1990   *Mikhail Bakhtin: Creation of a Prosaics* (Stanford, CA: Stanford University Press).
Moye, Jerry
1990   'Song of Songs: Back to Allegory? Some Hermeneutical Considerations', *AsiaJT* 4: 120–25.
Muller, Gilbert H.
1972   *Nightmares and Visions: Flannery O'Connor and the Catholic Grotesque* (Athens, GA: University of Georgia Press).
Müller, Hans-Peter
1984   *Vergleich und Metapher im Hohenlied* (OBO, 56; Göttingen: Vandenhoek & Ruprecht).
Munro, Jill M.
1995   *Spikenard and Saffron: A Study in the Poetic Language in the Song of Songs* (JSOTSup, 203; Sheffield: Sheffield Academic Press).
Murphy, Roland
1973   'Form-Critical Studies of the Song of Songs', *Int* 27: 413–22.
1979   'The Unity of the Song of Songs', *VT* 29: 436–43.
1981a   'Patristic and Medieval Exegesis – Help or Hindrance?', *CBQ* 43: 505–16.
1981b   *Wisdom Literature: Job, Proverbs, Ruth, Canticles, Ecclesiastes, and Esther* (FOTL, 13; Grand Rapids, MI: Eerdmans).
1985   'The Song of Songs: Critical Biblical Scholarship vis-à-vis Exegetical Traditions', in James T. Butler, Edgar W. Conrad and Ben C. Ollenburger (eds), *Understanding the Word: Essays in Honour of Bernhard W. Anderson* (JSOTSup, 37; Sheffield: Sheffield Academic Press): 63–69.
1986   'History of Exegesis as a Hermeneutical Tool: The Song of Songs', *BTB* 16: 87–91.
1987   'Dance and Death in the Song of Songs', in John H. Marks and Robert M. Good (eds), *Love and Death in the Ancient Near East: Essays in Honour of Marvin H. Pope* (Guildford, CT: Four Quarters): 117–19.
1990   *The Song of Songs* (Hermeneia; Minneapolis, MN: Fortress Press).
Neusner, Jacob (trans.)
1981   *The Tosefta Translated from the Hebrew. Fourth Division* (New York: KTAV).
Niccacci, Alviero
1990   *The Syntax of the Verb in Classical Hebrew Prose* (trans.

Wilfred G.E. Watson; JSOTSup, 86; Sheffield: Sheffield Academic Press).

Oboussier, Claire
　　1994　'Barthes and Femininity: A Synaesthetic Writing', *Nottingham French Studies* 33: 78–93.
　　1995　'Synaesthesia in Cixous and Barthes', in Diana Knight (ed.), *Women and Representation* (London: WIF): 115–31.

O'Connor, Flannery
　　1990　*The Complete Stories* (London and Boston: Faber & Faber).

Ogawa, Yasuhiro
　　1997　'Grinning Death's-Head: *Hamlet* and the Vision of the Grotesque', in Adams and Yates 1997: 193–226.

Oliver, Kelly
　　1993　*Reading Kristeva: Unraveling the Double-bind* (Bloomington, IN: Indiana University Press).

O'Neill, John
　　1984　'Breaking the Signs: Roland Barthes and the Literary Body', in John Fekete (ed.), *The Structural Allegory: Reconstructing Encounters with the New French Thought* (Manchester: Manchester University Press): 182–200.

Origen
　　1957　*The Song of Songs: Commentary and Homilies* (trans. and ann. R.P. Lawson; Ancient Christian Writers, 26; Westminster, MD: Newman Press; London: Longmans, Green).

Palmer, Pantina
　　1987　'From Coded Mannequin to Bird Woman: Angela Carter's Magic Flight', in Sue Roe (ed.), *Women Reading Women's Writing* (New York: St Martin's Press): 179–205.

Pardes, Ilana
　　1992　*Countertraditions in the Bible: A Feminist Approach* (Cambridge, MA: Harvard University Press).

Payne, Michael
　　1993　*Reading Theory: An Introduction to Lacan, Derrida, and Kristeva* (Cambridge, MA: Blackwell).

Paz, Octavio
　　1996　*The Double Flame: Love and Eroticism* (trans. Helen Lane; New York: Harvest Books).

Perez-Romero, Antonio
　　1996　*Subversion and Liberation in the Writings of St Teresa of Avila* (Amsterdam: Rodophi).

Phipps, William E.
　　1974　'The Plight of the Song of Songs', *JAAR* 42: 82–100.

Piras, Antonio
1994   'At ille declinaverat atque transierat (Cant 5,2–8)', *ZAW* 106: 487–90.
Polaski, Donald C.
1997   'What Will Ye See in the Shulammite? Women, Power and Panopticism in the Song of Songs', *BibInt* 5: 64–81.
Pope, Marvin H.
1977   *Song of Songs* (AB, 7C; New York: Doubleday).
1988   'Metastases in Canonical Shapes of the Super Song', in G. M. Tucker, D.L. Petersen and R.R. Wilson (eds), *Canon, Theology, and Old Testament Interpretation* (Philadelphia, PA: Fortress Press): 312–28.
Rabin, Chaim
1973/4 'The Song of Songs and Tamil Poetry', *SR* 3: 205–19.
Radday, Yehuda T.
1990   'On Missing the Humour in the Bible: An Introduction', in Radday and Brenner 1990: 21–37.
Radday, Yehuda T. and Athalya Brenner (eds)
1990   *On Humour and the Comic in the Hebrew Bible* (Sheffield: Almond Press).
Raymond, Marcel
1970   *From Baudelaire to Surrealism* (London: Methuen).
Renan, Ernest
1995   *Le Cantique des Cantiques* (Paris: Arléa).
Robert, André and Jacques-Raymond Tournay
1963   *Le Cantique des Cantiques: Traduction et commentaire* (Paris: J. Gabalda).
Robertson, Duncan
1987   'The Experience of Reading: Bernard of Clairvaux *Sermons on the Song of Songs, I*', *Religion and Literature* 19: 1–20.
Rosen, Elisheva
1990   'Innovation and its Reception: The Grotesque in Aesthetic Thought', *SubStance* 62/63: 125–35.
Roth, Norman
1982   'Seeing the Bible through a Poet's Eyes: Some Difficult Words Interpreted by Moses Ibn Ezra', *HS* 23: 111–14.
Rouselle, Aline
1988   *Porneia: On Desire and the Body in Antiquity* (trans. Felicia Pheasant; Oxford: Basil Blackwell).
Rowley, Harold H.
1952   'The Interpretation of the Song of Songs', in *The Servant of the Lord and Other Essays* (London: Lutterworth Press): 189–234.

Rozelaar, Marc
    1988   'An Unrecognized Part of the Human Anatomy', *Judaism*
            37: 97–101.
Rudolph, Wilhelm
    1962   *Das Buch Ruth · Das Hohe Lied · Die Klagelieder* (Gütersloh:
            Gerd Mohn).
Ruskin, John
    1904a   'Of the True Ideal: – Thirdly, Grotesque', in E.T. Cook and
            A. Wedderburn (eds), *Modern Painters*, Vol. 3 (The Works
            of John Ruskin, 5; London: George Allen): 130–48.
    1904b   'Grotesque Renaissance', in E.T. Cook and A. Wedderburn
            (eds), *The Stones of Venice*, Vol. 3 (The Works of John
            Ruskin, 11; London: George Allen): 135–95.
Russo, Mary
    1994   *The Female Grotesque: Risk, Excess and Modernity* (New
            York: Routledge).
Sachs, Arieh
    1969   *The English Grotesque: An Anthology from Langland to
            Joyce* (Jerusalem: Israel Universities Press).
Sadgrove, Michael
    1978   'The Song of Songs as Wisdom Literature', *StudBib* 1: 245–
            48.
Saint-Amand, Pierre
    1996   'The Secretive Body: Roland Barthes' Gay Erotics', *Yale
            French Studies* 90: 153–71.
Sandmel, Samuel
    1972   *The Enjoyment of Scripture: The Law, the Prophets, and the
            Writings* (New York: Oxford University Press).
Sasson, Victor
    1989   'King Solomon and the Dark Lady in the Song of Songs',
            VT 39: 407–14.
Sawicki, Jana
    1988   'Feminism and the Power of Discourse', in J. Arac (ed.),
            *After Foucault: Humanistic Knowledge, Postmodern
            Challenges* (New Brunswick, NJ, and London: Rutgers
            University Press): 161–78.
    1996   'Feminism, Foucault and "Subjects" of Power and
            Freedom', in Susan Hekman (ed.), *Feminist Interpretations
            of Michel Foucault* (Philadelphia, PA: University of
            Pennsylvania Press): 159–78.
Schehr, Lawrence R.
    1994   'Roland Barthes' Semierotics', *Canadian Review of
            Comparative Literature* 21: 107–26.

Schor, Naomi
    1987a   'Dreaming Dissymmetry: Barthes, Foucault, and Sexual
             Difference', in Alice Jardine and Paul Smith (eds), *Men in
             Feminism* (New York: Methuen): 98–110, 272–6.
    1987b   *Reading in Detail: Aesthetics and the Feminine* (New York
             and London: Methuen).
Schwartz, Avraham and Yisroel Schwartz (trans.)
    1983   *The Megilloth and Rashi's Commentary with Linear
             Translation* (New York: Hebrew Linear Classics).
Screech, M.A.
    1979   *Rabelais* (London: Duckworth).
Segal, M.H.
    1962   'Song of Songs', *VT* 12: 470–90.
Shaktini, Namascar
    2005   'The Critical Mind and the Lesbian Body', in Namascar
             Shaktini (ed.), *On Monique Wittig: Theoretical, Political and
             Literary Essays* (Urbana, IL: University of Illinois Press):
             150–59.
Shea, William H.
    1980   'The Chiastic Structure of the Song of Songs', *ZAW* 92:
             378–95.
Showalter, Elaine
    1987   *The Female Malady: Women, Madness and English Culture,
             1830–1980* (London: Virago).
Silverman, Kaja
    1988   *The Acoustic Mirror: The Female Voice in Psychoanalysis
             and Cinema* (Bloomington, IN: Indiana University Press).
Simon, M. (trans.)
    1939   *Midrash on the Song of Songs* (London: Soncino Press).
Slade, Carole
    1986   'Saint Teresa's *Meditaciones sobre los Cantares*: The
             Hermeneutics of Humility and Enjoyment', *Religion and
             Literature* 18: 27–44.
    1995   *St Teresa of Avila: Author of a Heroic Life* (Berkeley, CA:
             University of California Press).
Smith, Paul Julian
    1986   'Barthes, Góngora, and Non-Sense', *PMLA* 101: 86–94.
Snaith, John G.
    1993   *The New Century Bible Commentary on the Song of Songs*
             (Grand Rapids, MI: Eerdmans).
Soulen, Richard
    1993   'The *wasfs* of the Song of Songs and Hermeneutic', in
             Brenner (ed.) 1993: 214–24.

Stadelman, Luis
 1992 *Love and Politics: A New Commentary on the Song of Songs* (New York: Paulist Press).
Stallybrass, Peter
 1986 'Patriarchal Territories: The Body Enclosed', in Ferguson, Quilligan and Vickers 1986: 123–42.
Stallybrass, Peter and Allon White
 1986 *The Politics and Poetics of Transgression* (Ithaca, NY: Cornell University Press).
Stanton, Domna C.
 1986 'Difference on Trial: A Critique of the Maternal Metaphor in Cixous, Irigaray, and Kristeva', in Nancy K. Miller (ed.), *The Poetics of Gender* (New York: Columbia University Press): 157–82.
Stechow, Wolfgang
 1997 'Hieronymus Bosch: The Grotesque and We', in Adams and Yates 1997: 113–24.
Steenman-Marcusse, Conny
 2002 'The Rhetoric of Autobiography in Susan Swan's *The Biggest Modern Woman of the World*', in Conny Steenman-Marcusse (ed.), *The Rhetoric of Canadian Writing* (Amsterdam: Rodopi): 179–88.
Stone, Jennifer
 1983 'The Horrors of Power: A Critique of Kristeva', in Francis Barker *et al.* (eds), *The Politics of Theory: Proceedings of the Essex Conference on the Sociology of Literature, July 1982* (Colchester: University of Essex Press): 38–48.
Swan, Susan
 2001 *The Biggest Modern Woman of the World* (Toronto: Key Porter Books).
Teresa of Avila (St) (Teresa de Jésus)
 1960 *Libro de la Vida* (ed. and trans. E. Allison Peers; http://www.catholicfirst.com/thefaith/catholicclassics/stteresa/life/teresaofavila.cfm, accessed July 2006).
 1970 *Obras completas* (Estudio Preliminar y notas explicativas por Luis Santullan; Madrid: Aguilar).
 1976–85 *The Collected Works of St Teresa of Avila, Vols 1–3* (ed. and trans. Kieran Kavanagh and Otilio Rodriguez; Washington, DC: ICS Publications).
Thompson, Philip
 1972 *The Grotesque* (The Critical Idiom; London: Methuen).
Tournay, Jacques-Raymond
 1980 'The Song of Songs and its Concluding Section', *Immanuel* 10: 5–14.

1982   *Quand Dieu parle aux hommes le langage d'amour: Études sur le Cantique des Cantiques* (Cahiers de la Revue Biblique, 21; Paris: J. Gabalda).

Trible, Phyllis
1973   'Depatriarchalizing in Biblical Interpretation', *JAAR* 41: 30–48.
1978   *God and the Rhetoric of Sexuality* (London: SCM Press).

Turner, Denys
1995   *Eros and Allegory: Medieval Exegesis of the Song of Songs* (Cistercian Studies Series, 156; Kalamazoo, MI: Cistercian Publications).
1998   'Metaphor or Allegory? Erotic Love in Bernard of Clairvaux's Sermons on the Song of Songs', paper presented to the Catholic Biblical Association of Great Britain Annual Meeting, Newman College, 10 April.

Vitruvius
1960   *The Ten Books on Architecture* (trans. Morris Hicky Morgan; New York: Dover Publications).

Viviers, Hendrick
2002   'The Rhetoricity of "the Body" in the Song of Songs', in Stanley E. Porter and Dennis L. Stamps (eds), *Rhetorical Criticism and the Bible* (Sheffield: Sheffield Academic Press): 237–54.

Vogt, Eric
1996   *The Complete Poetry of Teresa of Avila: A Bilingual Edition* (New Orleans, KY: University Press of the South).

Waldberg, Patrick
1997   *Surrealism* (World of Art; London: Thames Hudson).

Waldman, Nahum M.
1970   'A Note on Canticles 4^9', *JBL* 89: 215–17.

Walsh, Carey Ellen
2000   *Exquisite Desire: Religion, the Erotic, and the Song of Songs* (Philadelphia, PA: Fortress Press).

Waterman, Leroy
1925   'The Role of Solomon in the Song of Songs', *JBL* 44: 171–87.
1948   *The Song of Songs Translated and Interpreted as a Dramatic Poem* (Ann Arbor, MI: University of Michigan Press).

Watson, Wilfred G.E.
1995a   *Classical Hebrew Poetry: A Guide to its Techniques* (JSOTSup, 26; Sheffield: Sheffield Academic Press).
1995b   'Some Ancient Near Eastern Parallels to the Song of Songs', in Jon Davies, Graham Harvey and Wilfred G.E. Watson (eds), *Words Remembered, Texts Renewed: Essays in Honour*

   of John F.A. Sawyer (JSOTSup, 195; Sheffield: Sheffield
   Academic Press): 253–71.

Weber, Alison
 1990 *Teresa of Avila and the Rhetoric of Femininity* (Princeton,
   NJ: Princeton University Press).

Webster, Edwin C.
 1982 'Pattern in the Song of Songs', *JSOT* 22: 73–93.

Weems, Renita
 1992 'Song of Songs', in Carol A. Newsom and Sharon Ringe
   (eds), *The Women's Bible Commentary* (London: SPCK;
   Louisville, KY: Westminster/John Knox Press): 156–60.
 1995 *Battered Love: Marriage, Sex, and Violence in the Hebrew
   Prophets* (OBT; Minneapolis, MN: Fortress Press).

Welsford, Enid
 1966 *The Fool: His Social and Literary History* (Gloucester, MA:
   Peter Smith).

Wetzstein, J.G.
 1873 'Die syrische Dreschtafel', *Zeitschrift für Ethnologie* 5: 270–
   302.

Whedbee, William J.
 1993 'Paradox and Parody in the Song of Solomon: Towards a
   Comic Reading of the Most Sublime Song', in Brenner (ed.)
   1993: 266–78.

White, John Bradley
 1978 *A Study of the Language in the Song of Songs and Ancient
   Egyptian Poetry* (SBLDS, 38; Missoula, MT: Scholars
   Press).

Wills, Clair
 1989 'Upsetting the Public: Carnival, Hysteria and Women's
   Texts', in Hirschkop and Shepherd 1989: 130–51.

Winandy, Jacques
 1965 'La Litière de Salomon (CT. III 9–10)', *VT* 15: 103–10.

Winterson, Jeanette
 1996 *Written on the Body* (London: Vintage Books).
 2000 Interview by Eleanor Wachtel, *Writers and Company*,
   Canadian Broadcasting Corporation, 11 February.

Wittig, Monique
 1973 *Le Corps lesbien* (Paris: Editions de Minuit).
 1975 *The Lesbian Body* (trans. David Le Vay; Boston, MA:
   Beacon Press).
 2005 'Some Remarks on the Lesbian Body', in Namascar
   Shaktini (ed.), *On Monique Wittig: Theoretical, Political
   and Literary Essays* (Urbana, IL: University of Illinois
   Press): 44–8.

Wright, Elizabeth (ed.)
   1992   *Feminism and Psychoanalysis: A Critical Dictionary* (Oxford: Basil Blackwell).

Würthwein, Ernst
   1969   'Das Hohelied', in Otto Eissfeldt (ed.), *Die Funf Megilloth* (HAT, 18; Tübingen: J.C.B Mohr [Paul Siebeck]): 25–71.

Yasif, Eli
   1992   'The Body Never Lies: The Body in Medieval Jewish Folk Narratives', in Eilberg-Schwartz 1992: 203–21.

Yates, Wilson
   1997   'An Introduction to the Grotesque: Theoretical and Theological Considerations', in Adams and Yates 1997: 1–68.

Index of Biblical Passages

Index of Names